LUCAN PERSPECTIVE *on* PAUL

Narrative and Theological Exposition of Paul in the Acts of the Apostles

JANUSZ KUCICKI

WestBow Press books may be ordered through booksellers or by contacting:

WestBow Press
A Division of Thomas Nelson & Zondervan
1663 Liberty Drive
Bloomington, IN 47403
www.westbowpress.com
844-714-3454

ISBN: 978-1-6642-6727-5 (sc)
ISBN: 978-1-6642-6728-2 (hc)
ISBN: 978-1-6642-6726-8 (e)

Library of Congress Control Number: 2022909565

Print information available on the last page.

WestBow Press rev. date: 06/06/2022

CONTENTS

To my mother, Wiesława Kucicka,

and her sisters,

Grażyna Jędrzejak
Ewa Jankowska
Joanna Cyżyk

PREFACE

It is close to impossible to find something original to say about Paul of Tarsus, as the existence of so many studies concerning him is ample proof that the apostle to Gentiles was, is, and probably will continue to be the most intriguing personality in the New Testament, ranking almost with Jesus of Nazareth. Paul first attracted my attention in his letter to the Romans. At the beginning of my conscious stumbling along the path of the Christian faith, this letter presented a challenge that occupied me for several years as I attempted to understand the theology of this supreme example of perfection. Later, when unpleasant circumstances called my attention to issues regarding life, death, and life after death, the letters to the Thessalonians captivated me with Paul's teaching about the Second Coming of the Lord. The letter to Philemon came next in what would be a series of explorations into Paul's writings. Finally, I realized that the powerful message of each of Paul's letters has its source in the needs of others (whether individuals or communities) to which he gives appropriate assistance that is always based on his faith and real-life experience. His experience became a direct reason for my interest in Paul's life, which was another journey in my exploring the New Testament that naturally led me to the writings of Luke—his Gospel and his Acts of the Apostles.

Before I started to study Acts, I was convinced that I knew Paul from his letters, which tell us much about his character, life, and thought. However, Paul's self-presentation, without exception, strongly depended on particular situations, which allow us to see some elements of his character from particular angles but not necessarily to get a full and coherent picture of who Paul was. Fortunately, Paul is not merely the person who contributed the most to the canon of the New Testament, but he also became the central character in the second part of the Acts of the Apostles. There, rather than giving a strict historical account of Paul's life, Luke presents his perspective on Paul. Naturally, Paul knew himself better than Luke did, but Luke could see and evaluate Paul in more holistic terms than probably even Paul himself could. Luke's specific perspective on Paul is the topic of this book, in which the focus is on the way in which Luke chose to present Paul's life. I hope that this approach will allow readers to recognize Luke's unique skill as a writer and his deep understanding of Paul and the purpose of his life.

Preparation for writing a book and the process of writing itself is always a time of new adventure, with a considerable degree of new discovery but also with inevitable struggle and uncertainty. The excitement of exploring a new topic does not lessen the work involved or excuse one from mundane daily work and duties. Developing a random idea into a full-scale study takes time and requires determination on the part of the writer, as well as the constant support of friends. In this last, I found myself fortunate in the support I received from Nanzan University and the Japan Province of the SVD, which I gratefully acknowledge. I also owe special thanks to Professor Walter Dunphy and Associate Professor Jakub Rajčáni, who contributed much to ensuring that the book took shape.

There are many more friends and supporters who should be mentioned and thanked. I single out, in particular, Z. Smith, R. Strzyżewski, E. Ziebura, P. Filadelfi, and N. Nishida. Finally, a special word of gratitude goes to all the members of my family.

LIST OF ABBREVIATIONS

1. The Bible

The Old Testament

Amos	Amos
Bar.	Baruch
1–2 Chron.	1–2 Chronicles
Dan.	Daniel
Deut.	Deuteronomy
Est.	Esther
Exod.	Exodus
Ezek.	Ezekiel
Ezra	Ezra
Gen.	Genesis
Hab.	Habakkuk
Hag.	Haggai
Hosea	Hosea
Isa.	Isaiah
Jer.	Jeremiah
Job	Job
Joel	Joel
Jon.	Jonah
Josh.	Joshua
Jth.	Judith
Judg.	Judges
1–2 Kings	1–2 Kings
Lam.	Lamentations
Lev.	Leviticus
1–2 Macc.	1–2 Maccabees
Mal.	Malachi
Mic.	Micah
Nahum	Nahum
Neh.	Nehemiah
Num.	Numbers
Obad.	Obadiah
Prov.	Proverbs
Ps.	Psalms
Qoh.	Qoheleth
Ruth	Ruth
1–2 Sam.	1–2 Samuel
Song of Sol.	Song of Songs
Tob.	Tobit
Ws.	Wisdom
Zech.	Zechariah
Zeph.	Zephaniah

The New Testament

Acts	Acts	Luke	Luke
Col.	Colossians	Mark	Mark
1–2 Cor.	1–2 Corinthians	Matt.	Matthew
Eph.	Ephesians	1–2 Pet.	1–2 Peter
Gal.	Galatians	Phil.	Philippians
Heb.	Hebrews	Philem.	Philemon
James	James	Rev.	Revelation
John	John	Rom.	Romans
1–3 John	1–3 John	1–2 Thess.	1–2 Thessalonians
Jude	Jude	1–2 Tim.	1–2 Timothy
		Titus	Titus

2. Dictionaries, Commentaries, Series, Journals

AB	Anchor Bible
BA	Biblical Archaoelogist
ABD	The Anchor Bible Dictionary
ACr	Analecta Cracowiensia
AnBib	Analecta Biblica
ASNU	Acta Seminarii Neotestamentici Upsaliensis
AThANT	Abhandlungen zur Theologie des Alten und Neuen Testaments
BDB	The Brown-Driver-Briggs Hebrew and English Lexicon
Bib	Biblica
BKUL	Biblioteka KUL
BibR	Biblical Research
BibTh	Biblical Theology
BSac	Bibliotheca Sacra
BU	Biblische Untersuchungen
CBQ	Catholic Biblical Quarterly
ConcTr	Concilium Tridentinum

CT	Collectanea Theologica
DB	Dictionary of the Bible
DDD	Dictionary of Deities and Demons in the Bible
DNTB	Dictionary of New Testament Background
DPL	Dictionary of Paul and His Letters
EBC	Expositor's Bible Commentary
EtB	Etudes Bibliques
EDNT	Exegetical Dictionary of the New Testament
EDSS	Encyclopedia of the Dead Sea Scrolls
EJ	Encyclopedia Judaica
EKK	Evangelisch-Katholischer Kommentar zum Neuen Testament
EstB	Estudios Biblicos
ETL	Ephemerides Theologicae Lovanienses
EvQ	The Evangelical Quarterly
EWNT	Exegetisches Wörterbuch zum Neuen Testament
ExT	The Expository Times
GELS	A Greek-English Lexicon of the Septuaginta
HBD	Harper's Bible Dictionary
HTR	The Harvard Theological Review
ICC	International Critical Commentary
IDB	Interpreter's Dictionary of Bible
InThSt	Indian Theological Studies
JBL	Journal of Biblical Literature
JQR	The Jewish Quarterly Review
JSJ	Journal for the Study of Judaism in the Persian, Hellenistic, and Roman Periods
JSNT	Journal for the Study of the New Testament
JSNTSS	Journal for the Study of the New Testament, Supplement Series
JSS	Journal of Semitic Studies
JTS	Journal of the Theological Studies
LCL	Loeb Classical Library

LEH	A Greek-English Lexicon of the Septuaginta
Liddell-Scott	A Greek-English Lexicon of the New Testament
LPSt	Library of Pauline Studies
MC	Mount Carmel
MoffatNTC	The Moffat New Testament Commentary I-XVII
NBibD	New Bible Dictionary
NedThT	Nederlands Theologisch Tijdschrift
NICNT	The New International Commentary on the New Testament
NIVAC	NIV Application Commentary
NIGTC	The New International Greek Testament Commentary
NovT	Novum Testamentum
NTA	Neutestamentlische Abhandlungen
NTS	New Testament Studies
PFES	Publications of the Finnish Exegetical Society
Pr	Pravnik
PRSt	Perspectives in Religious Studies
RB	Revue Biblique
RHPR	Revue d'histoire et de philosophie religieuses
RoBl	Rivista Biblica
RQ	Revue de Qumran
RScRel	Recherches des science religieuse
SANT	Studien zum Alten und Neuen Testament
SBLMS	Society of Biblical Literature. Monograph Series
SBLDS	Society of Biblical Literature. Dissertation Series
SBT	Studies of Biblical Theology
SCM	Student Christian Movement
SEA	Svensk Exegetisk Årsbok
SEv	Studia Evangelica
SHBC	Smyth & Helwys Bible Commentary
SJT	Scottish Journal of Theology
SNTS	Society for New Testament Studies

ST	Studia Theologica
StEv	Studia Evangelica
StThSt	Stellenbosch Theological Studies
STV	Studia Theologica Varsaviensia
SUNT	Studien zur Umwelt des Neuen Testaments
SWJT	Southwestern Journal of Theology
TCGNT	A Textual Commentary on the Greek New Testament
TDNT	Theological Dictionary of the New Testament
THNT	Theology of the New Testament
ThSt	Theologische Studien
ThZ	Theologische Zeitschrift
TynBul	Tyndale Bulletin
TZTh	Tübinger Zeitschrift für Theologie
VT	Vetus Testamentum
WBC	Word Biblical Commentary
WUNT	Wissenschaftliche Untersuchungen zum Neuen Testament
ZNW	Zeitschrift für die neutestamentlische Wissenschaft und die Kunde der älteren Kirche
ZSTh	Zeitschrift für systematische Theologie
ZThK	Zeitschrift für Theologie und Kirche
ZWTh	Zeitschrift für wissenschaftlische Theologie

3. Classical Writings

Ant.	*Antiquitates Iudaicae*, Flavius Josephus
Bell.	*De bello Iudaico*, Flavius Josephus

INTRODUCTION

1. The Reason for Studying Luke's Perspective on Paul

Paul is one of few persons who not only contributed to the New Testament canon (the letters) but also became a "hero" of another writer (Luke), who also contributed to the canon. Considering the importance of Paul's theological contributions and Luke's considerable interest in Paul's missionary activities, it must be accepted that the New Testament provides sufficient material for studying the person of Saul, also called Paul. This does not mean, however, that all information regarding Paul is provided. The quantity and variety of the available material results in many different studies that approach the person of Paul from almost every possible angle, which results in many perspectives on Paul that are dependent on the method, axiomatic statement, purpose of study, scientific or religious attitude, comprehension, or the use of the sources by a challenger. In some cases, studies use the primary sources and secondary sources in a complementary way, which leads to the creation of a kind of picture named "Saint Paul." However, in some cases the studies use the sources in a comparative way, which brings drastically different evaluations and presentations of Paul.[1]

---

[1] For a very comprehensive and extremely balanced exposition of many different views, approaches, and perspectives on Paul, indispensable and obligatory is the work of M. Zetterholm, *Approaches to Paul*, where the most essential studies regarding Paul from the last two hundred years are presented. M. Zetterholm, *Approaches to Paul: A Student's Guide to Recent Scholarship* (Minneapolis: Fortress Press, 2009).

Although no one should complain about the abundance of research, sometimes too much can also be a problem. Concerning the study on Paul, the problem relates to the fact that each of the studies on Paul is, to a sufficient degree, dependent on the personal preferences of the author. An example of the problem is the existence of many extremely important studies that make it possible to look at Paul from many different perspectives but that do not necessarily help in the creation of the most adequate presentation of Paul.

As a result, each generation of scholars produces its own picture, painting, statue, or perspective on Paul, but surprisingly, none of them stands the test of time. This somewhat confusing statement led us to the question about the possibility of the existence of a truly thorough perspective on Paul, to which we found not even one positive answer. Although it is a rather unhelpful outcome, it nonetheless redirects our focus to the oldest presentation on Paul found in the Acts of the Apostles, where Luke presents his perspective on Paul, composed from information concerning historical events blended with considerably developed literary techniques. Based on written and oral sources, as well as his own personal experiences, Luke makes his own opinions about Paul, which are exposed in Acts.

We assume that what is written about Paul in Acts is a result of Luke's private perspective on Paul (the first methodical assumption), which he uses to create a coherent "portrait" or "statue" of Paul (the second methodical assumption). The attempt to prove and expose these two assumptions is the main aim of this study. In order to achieve this, we divided it into three chapters, where the first chapter will concern the "Saul period," the second chapter will analyze the "Paul period," and the third chapter will gather all the results of the analysis provided in chapters 1 and 2 in order to expose the Lucan approach to the presentation of Paul. Concerning the presentation of Saul's period, which is narrated by Luke in a very comprehensive manner, with numerous summaries instead of detailed accounts, some appendixes will be attached at the end of the book. The appendixes will contain particular issues regarding Saul's period, which were the subject of our studies and articles in the past and now will be partly used in order to approach the facts from Saul's life from a wider perspective. Not only will accounts from Acts be considered but also relevant information from Paul's letters, which will complement the limited narrative of Acts. These appendixes, however, are not necessary for the purpose of the study, and their inclusion is done in order to provide for students and beginners in Bible studies a more detailed background for the Acts account of Saul's period. In analyzing the texts of Acts that regard Saul/Paul, we will use mostly narrative criticism and literary criticism, with occasional use of an exegetical method.

2. "The New Perspective on Paul" in Light of Luke's Perspective on Paul

A very vivid and very inspiring discussion about Paul, commonly known as "the new perspective on Paul," has two distinct issues that create the core of the whole research movement. The first distinction concerns the underlining of Paul's "Jewishness," which comes directly from challenging a traditional understanding of Paul as a Christian at the expense of his Jewish roots. In his process, how important of a role the church's traditional simplification—*Peter, the apostle to Jews, and Paul, the apostle to Gentiles,* which greatly reduces the complex issue surrounding this somewhat doubtful axiomatic statement—plays is another problem. However, this does not directly concern our study.

Peter was not an apostle only to Jews, as Acts 10–11 undoubtfully shows, nor was Paul only an apostle to Gentiles, which is attested by every single one of Luke's accounts of Paul's missionary activities. Peter suffered some losses in his mission work with Palestinian Jews and had some success with Gentiles; Paul's mission work with Jews and Gentiles was also part failure and part success. The claim that Peter can be called the apostle to the Jews is based on his contribution toward shaping the first Judeo-Christian communities and their structure and doctrinal identity. The claim that Paul can be called the apostle to the Gentiles is based on his successful transmission of a strictly Judaic religious heritage into the Hellenistic world in a way that could be accepted, even by those who were not yet familiar with a monotheistic religion. Probably for this reason, the new perspective on Paul is focused almost entirely on Paul's letters, which, in the majority of cases, recorded this transmission.

The strong focus on Paul's letters is the second very important distinct quality of the new perspective on Paul. The prioritization of Paul's letters by the new perspective neglects (to some degree) the Acts of the Apostles because it is the secondary source.[2] It may be seen as a small mistake, especially if we consider the important observation of Crossan and Reed:

> The New Testament content and sequence has literally and figuratively framed Paul by locating those seven authentic Pauline Letters after Luke's Acts of the Apostles, which corrects Paul's story before we read him, and among or before those inauthentic letters, which correct Paul's theology after we have read him.[3]

The most important concerns in this observation relate to the function of Acts as the preparatory writing that, in large part, presents to the readers of the New Testament the story about Paul (introduces Paul) before they are faced with his own writings.[4] Paul's writings are not philosophical or abstract theories put into words that have little to

---

[2] Concerning different opinions about the relationship between Luke's Acts and Paul's letters; cf. A.J. Bale, *Genre and Narrative Coherence in the Acts of the Apostles* (London: T&T Clark, 2015), 27–31. Personally, the outcome of Pervo's research is very convincing to us (e.g., Acts 13:39 exposes the same theological conviction found in the famous Romans 3:21–23). R. I. Pervo, *Dating Acts: Between the Evangelists and the Apologists* (Santa Rosa: Polebridge, 2006), 149–199.

[3] J. D. Crossan, J. L. Reed, *In Search of Paul* (New York: Harper San Francisco, 2004), 106.

[4] It seems reasonable, if one considers today's custom of putting a short biographical note on the cover of a book.

do with reality; on the contrary, his writings come from his personal experience, times spent engaged in mission activities, the needs of particular communities, and problems that had to be solved. That means that his writing is very closely related to his life, including his background, because something can't come from nothing.

The Acts of the Apostles is not historical in a scientific way, as much as we would like to see it today, but it is Luke's story about two of the most influential (from his position) men who considerably shaped the movement called Christianity. The highly personalized character of the story does not automatically make it "unhistorical"; rather, it is a history seen and told from a personal perspective, according to a personal approach and designed for a personal purpose. In the case of Acts, unfortunately, it is the only story about Paul that was created or managed to survive, which makes it the only history available to us. Despite all scientific doubts regarding Acts, Luke's writing was and still is an extremely important source for understanding the man who contributed the most (directly or indirectly) to the canon of the New Testament. Luke is the first person (known to us) who recognized the importance of Paul's life and his mission activities, as well as Paul's innovative interpretation of the entire Jewish tradition (that can be compared only with Copernicus's statement) that resulted in a totally new concept of the relationship between humans and God, where the center of the relationship is Jesus of Nazareth, the resurrected Messiah for both Jews and Gentiles. Although Luke did not save Paul for us because Paul produced many writings on his own, he did give us a very important look at Paul (which possibly was shared not only by him) that balanced the rejection of Paul as the Jewish teacher (in very general terms) with his indispensable contribution to transferring the Jewish concept of God into the Hellenistic religions' systems.

Without the Acts of the Apostles, we would have to create a picture of Paul based on his writings, which is quite a challenging task, if one considers, for example, the differences in Paul's attitude as it is found in the letter to the Galatians and the letter to the Philippians. If the letters of Paul (in general) gave us some accounts about Paul's attitude and thoughts in particular situations, then Luke's Acts supplies this particular perspective (present also in Acts) with a deeper evaluation of Paul by a second witness, who is also interested in understanding and interpreting the events in which he was involved or at least heard about. Luke definitely wants to present to the reader "his Paul," who does not necessarily have to be unlike the historical Paul.

3. Luke's Literary Exposition of Paul

The story of Acts covers the period of about thirty years after Jesus's death and Resurrection, and because no other valuable records about the first twenty years after Jesus's death exist today, the retrospective account of Acts related to this period is of crucial importance. Though not so popular from the beginning, Acts became the basic source for knowledge about the beginning of the Christian Church in later periods, when oral kerygma of the apostles and their successors' tradition turned into the theological doctrine and the faith credo of the Christian community. It automatically gave Acts the status of historical writing, the history of the primitive Christian Church, the one only included in the New Testament. For centuries, literary and doctrinal interpretations have brought severe criticism on Acts as "history," in the sense that this term is understood in the science age. This criticism has turned into long, ongoing debates that produce many fascinating studies, which, at the beginning of the twenty-first century, tend to recognize Acts as writing based on historical events but created according to the literary and theological preferences of the author.[5] This kind of consensus is in accord with the prologue of Luke's Gospel:

> Ἐπειδήπερ πολλοὶ ἐπεχείρησαν ἀνατάξασθαι διήγησιν
> περὶ τῶν πεπληροφορημένων ἐν ἡμῖν πραγμάτων,

[5] Several aspects of the debate are presented in a very holistic way by Keener in his monumental commentary on Acts: C. S. Keener, *Acts, An Exegetical Commentary*, vol. 1 (Grand Rapids: Baker Academic, 2012), 51–382.

καθὼς παρέδοσαν ἡμῖν οἱ ἀπ' ἀρχῆς αὐτόπται καὶ ὑπηρέται γενόμενοι τοῦ λόγου, ἔδοξεν κἀμοὶ παρηκολουθηκότι ἄνωθεν πᾶσιν ἀκριβῶς καθεξῆς σοι γράψαι, κράτιστε Θεόφιλε, ἵνα ἐπιγνῷς περὶ ὧν κατηχήθης λόγων τὴν ἀσφάλειαν. (Luke 1:1–4)

Many have undertaken to draw up an account of the things that have been fulfilled among us, just as they were handed down to us by those who from the first were eyewitnesses and servants of the word. With this in mind, since I myself have carefully investigated everything from the beginning, I too decided to write an orderly account for you, most excellent Theophilus, so that you may know the certainty of the things you have been taught. (Luke 1:1–4 NIV)

This text includes many pieces of important information. Starting with verse 1, we learn that Luke was not the first person who attempted to write down an account about Jesus the Messiah because there were others who, probably successfully, had undertaken this task, which indirectly relates to the Gospels that were written earlier and which became the source for Luke's work.[6] We also recognize that his work is a monography that should serve as the testimony concerning the events of Jesus (Luke 1:2). This testimony is based on oral tradition (kerygma) and written tradition (at least other Gospels) transferred to the author by the eyewitnesses and servants of Jesus (the Word), which gives Luke's work credibility.[7] Luke 1:3 shows that Luke joined this group of "many, who have undertaken the effort" and became one of them but in his own way ("With this in mind, since I myself

[6] Most probably, this statement is restricted only to the Gospel, and it does not concern the Acts of the Apostles; namely, the history of the first-generation Christian movement.

[7] This statement also concerns only the Gospel of Luke and does not concern Acts. This verse obviously refers to the twelve apostles but is not necessarily limited only to them.

have carefully investigated everything from the beginning"—Luke 1:3 NIV), which in some cases will complement previous works (e.g., the infant narrative), as well as extend the testimony about parts (the early history of the messianic movement) that had not yet been written by anyone before him.

All this is Luke's attempt to testify the truth of the teaching Theophilus has heard (Luke 1:4). The short interpretation of the prologue to Luke's Gospel shows that he wrote about historical facts, not just to prevent the facts from being forgotten (like the other Gospels that were written) but also to give them the power of convincing arguments. Considering the prologue of Acts, which refers of the Gospel of Luke, it is possible to assume that what Luke said about the manner and purpose of his attempt in the prologue of the Gospel is valid also in regard to Acts, but with the exception to the uniqueness of Acts. In both cases (the Gospel and Acts), Luke says the story in order to give testimony that will lead the reader to the faith; in the case of the Gospel, he is following others, but in the case of Acts, he is the one who paves the way.

In order to present a coherent and orderly story to readers, Luke has to put a thirty-year period of history—with many heroes, events, and places—into the limited space of a volume, which is a task that requires discipline and results in the use of various sources, as well as great literary skills to condense the stories to a reasonable size without omitting the most important facts. Luke's Acts is a masterpiece of literature, exposing the great skills of the author. It starts with a simple but accurate structure (Acts 1:8), which makes the writing an "orderly account" (Luke 1:3). This is followed by the use of many literary devices, such as narratives, speeches, dialogues, prayers, etc., which make the story vivid and interesting to read on the one hand, and allows the author to expose desired theological thoughts and ideas on the other.[8] It ends with Luke's exceptional

---

[8] For example, we can look at one of the speeches in Acts (especially the topic speeches) in order to see how Luke develops one theological idea within three "topical speeches." Probably the best example will be one of the speeches in the narrative regarding the three mission journeys of Paul, where each of them

skills to create changeable, emotional, and dramatic shifts of action, which gives the narrative real excitement in some cases; for example, in the narrative regarding the attempted assassination of Paul (Acts 23:12–35). All these show that, for Luke, historical facts and accuracy are important, and the literary exposition of narrative topics are also of crucial value for him. Everything on these literary aspects that relates to Acts in general also fully refers to the particular narrative regarding Luke's presentation of Saul/Paul.

Luke's presentation of Paul in Acts is concentrated on Paul's period rather than on Saul's period, where the latter is indispensable background that exposes the contrast between it and the former. Saul's period (Acts 7:58–8:3; 9:1) starts Luke's narrative regarding Paul in a manner that leaves the reader with an unsatisfied feeling because it's very schematic and short nature provides us with a kind of summary that gives information with a barely developed narrative. We were informed of what Saul was doing but without closer specification regarding his reasons, emotions, or thoughts, which makes the primary introduction of Saul one that exposes him as a dangerous, enigmatic persecutor. However, all information that was omitted in the initial introduction of Saul will be supplied in the following narrative by information provided by Paul in his apologetic speeches, which mostly are related to the period of Paul's imprisonment. Luke puts more effort into the presentation of Saul in the narrative regarding his conversion (Acts 9:1–31), where the whole process of Saul's conversion is presented with many details in order

---

(despite the fact that the span of journey was at least two years and during this time many speeches were delivered) contains only one topical speech, which serves as an exemplary speech for the particular journey. The speech at Pisidian in Antioch is an example of the speeches that Paul delivered to an audience with a Jewish background (Acts 13:16–41), which is in accordance to the narrative purpose that focuses on Paul's mission to Diaspora Jews. The speech at Areopagus (Acts 17:22–31) is an example of Paul's speeches to a Gentile audience, which is placed in the narrative of his second mission journey, mostly exposing the Gentile environment. The speech at Miletus (Acts 20:18–35) is an example of Paul's speeches addressed to a Christian audience, which is placed in the narrative concerning the successful mission in Ephesus.

to convince the reader that the persecutor Saul became a follower of Jesus.

For this reason, short narratives about his mission activities in Damascus, as well as his visit to Jerusalem and his unsuccessful mission to former co-persecutors are included. At the end of the narrative regarding Saul, Luke sends the converted Saul back to his hometown, with an additional summary suggesting that his disappearance from Judea served everyone (Acts 9:31). After narrating the process of Saul's conversion, Luke excludes him from his narrative for a while in order to separate this period from the second period of Saul's life, which concerns the learning of Christian life at the feet of Barnabas. The narrative regarding Saul's period in Syrian Antioch seems to serve two functions: it ends the period of Saul, and it smoothly transfers it into the period of Paul. Antioch was the school of effective mission work for Paul, where he learned from the extraordinarily skilled teacher Barnabas, who served as a kind of steppingstone for a still-looking-for-his-own-way Saul.

4. The Hardest Egg

The last issue we would like to discus in this introduction concerns the recognition of Lucan writings as the finished or unfinished undertaking. The canon of the New Testament contains two works of Luke; namely, the Gospel according to Luke and the Acts of the Apostles. These were designed by the author as two parts of one project, where the Gospel concerns the story of Jesus, and Acts details the stories of Peter and Paul, who are axiomatically exposed as the most influential witnesses who, to a considerable degree, have shaped the future of the messianic movement. Concerning Acts, Luke narrowed the perspective by focusing the narrative almost exclusively to the west, neglecting almost entirely the other directions the movement had been spread. This attitude was naturally forced by the recipient of Luke's works (Theophilus, if he was the individual, or the Christian community in Rome, if the name in Luke 1:3 is taken collectively), who has his own particular interest in acknowledging the Christian movement from its beginning in Palestine to its presence at the heart of the Roman Empire.

We know from Paul's letter to the Romans that the community in Rome was not established by Paul, and at the time Paul reached Rome as a prisoner, he was welcomed by the "brothers" of the community in Rome (Acts 28:15). Luke, however, wrote nothing about the beginning of Christian communities in Rome, and instead, he ends his story with Paul's reaching Rome and making an initial meeting with the authority of the Jewish community in the city. Such an ending of Acts, even with a short and very general summary (Acts 28:30–31), leaves the reader in a considerable degree of confusion. Is that all that Luke intended? When Luke was creating his two volumes, the Jerusalem Temple was already gone, and the Christian community in Rome was still recovering after the very severe persecution under Nero.

In this context, the reason for ending Acts with a narrative regarding Paul's reaching Rome must be exposed, at least on the hypothetical level. The story of Jesus and his disciples (the Gospel) is followed by the story of the transferring of the messianic movement into the primitive stage of the Christian communities, where the main focus is put on Peter and Paul. The story of the second hero in Acts occupied more than half of the second volume of Luke's works, which does not necessarily mean that it is the main aim of the story. Looking at the end of the Gospel (Luke 24:50–52) and the beginning of Acts (Acts 1:3–11), it easily can be detected that the author connected these two volumes with the same topic (Jesus between his Resurrection and his ascension to heaven) that is exposed twice but each time in different way.[9] Similarly, the summary (Acts 28:30–31) that ends the Acts of the Apostles possibly suggests that the brief information regarding Paul's two-year stay in Rome and his teaching to those who

[9] The narrative at the end of the Gospel is considerably shorter than the narrative at the beginning of the Acts of the Apostles.

came to him would be elaborated in the following volume, which would be the third part of the Lucan writings.[10] Although it is only a supposition, considering the fact that in Acts, Luke frequently uses a *triptych pattern* (triptych arrangement of the topical speeches—the three trials, the three mission journeys), it is likely that he thought in the same way when he started working on his *opus magnum.*

Pushing this hypothesis a little further, if a third volume was intended or was written but got lost, what was or would be its topic? We should expect that the new volume would start with a narrative regarding Paul's teaching activity among the Roman Gentiles, as Acts 28:28 suggests, but it would hardly be entirely devoted to this topic. Probably, we would learn more about his waiting for the trial and the trial itself, as well as Paul's life after he was found innocent of all accusations. Less possible is the hypothesis that Luke would have concentrated on Paul's mission activities outside Rome, if we consider Luke's attitude toward progressing the narrative in a linear way, rather than going back to an already explored theme. That leaves us with two possible topics: the first would concern Paul's mission to Spain, and the second would concern a narrative regarding the Christian community in Rome, which possibly would include the period of Nero's persecution and possibly Paul's death. This divagation seems to open the doors for a kind of suspense theory rather than an academic discourse, but the excuse for that approach is in regard to the question of whether or not Acts really ends as desired by Luke in his presentation of Paul.

---

[10] Concerning the reason for such an end of Acts, Walaskay includes five proposals:

1. Luke died before he could finish his work.
2. The original ending, which reported Paul's martyrdom, has been removed.
3. Luke intended to write a third volume to Theophilus.
4. Luke ceased writing because he knew no more.
5. Luke chose not to continue his narrative, even though he knew Paul's fate.

P. W. Walaskay, *And So We Came to Rome. The Political Perspective of St Paul* (Cambridge: Cambridge University Press 1983), 18–19, and 70 for notes.

Phrased another way, is Luke's perspective of Paul in Acts complete or not? If the answer to this question is affirmative, we expect from this study confirmation that Luke, in his own and sufficiently coherent way, had created the one finished picture of Paul. If the answer is negative, this study should expose that although the presentation of Paul is, to a considerable degree, coherently elaborated by Luke, it does not create the finished picture of Paul, leaving the presentation of Paul on the level of many detailed expositions, which are still far from completion. However, there is another possibility that assumes Luke's deliberative attitude to leave the portrait of Paul unfinished in order to not create of Paul as a kind of idol for his readers but instead to leave his presentation on the level of a useful example. This possibility is more likely in two-set Lucan writings (the present state of the Lucan writings). However, considering Luke's general tendency in the exposition of each topic present in the Gospel or Acts, where systematic and progressive elaboration leads to a logical conclusion or end, it is reasonable to expect the continuity of Acts in order to grasp the true purpose of the Lucan literary enterprise.

1

SAUL, ACCORDING TO LUKE'S NARRATIVE

Luke, in Acts, uses two names for the same person, which is hardly a coincidence. Rather, it is characteristic of Luke—a way to indicate his literary approach to the presentation of the person Paul. In the very first mention, Luke uses the name Saul in Acts 7:58 without any indication of the name Paul. The name Paul doesn't appear until Acts 13:9—"Then Saul, who was also called Paul" (NIV)—after which it is used constantly by Luke until the end of Acts, except in Paul's speeches regarding his past. This distinction naturally frames Luke's presentation of Paul into a gatefold, with the left side designed for Saul and the right one for Paul. Both sides are complementary and necessary for a full exposition of Paul's phenomenon. Although each side is made in a different manner and for different reasons, each has the same purpose. These different techniques are reflected in Luke's literary approach and are caused by the drastic differences between the period of Saul and the period of Paul. Luke wrote little (and in a very schematic manner) about Saul, but at the same time, he gave a sufficient enough account to create a general picture of Saul's transformation from the former persecutor into the well-prepared witness, ready to fulfil the task that was appointed to him.

1. The Young Man Called Saul (Acts 7:58; 8:1, 3)

> Καὶ ἐκβαλόντες ἔξω τῆς πόλεως ἐλιθοβόλουν. καὶ οἱ μάρτυρες ἀπέθεντο τὰ ἱμάτια αὐτῶν παρὰ τοὺς πόδας νεανίου καλουμένου Σαύλου [dragged him out of the city and began to stone him. Meanwhile, the witnesses laid their coats at the feet of a young man named Saul]. (Acts 7:58 NIV)

> Σαῦλος δὲ ἦν συνευδοκῶν τῇ ἀναιρέσει αὐτοῦ. [And Saul approved of their killing him.] (Acts 8:1 NIV)

> Σαῦλος δὲ ἐλυμαίνετο τὴν ἐκκλησίαν κατὰ τοὺς οἴκους εἰσπορευόμενος, σύρων τε ἄνδρας καὶ γυναῖκας παρεδίδου εἰς φυλακήν. [But Saul began to destroy the church. Going from house to house, he dragged off both men and women and put them in prison.] (Acts 8:3 NIV)

At the end of Acts 13:1, Luke introduces a new agent who will become the main hero till Acts 28:31. He does this in three steps, each of which exposes a gradual schematic and holistic characteristic of the person.

From the first account in Acts 7:58, we learn three bits of information about the person: his name, his approximate age, and his social relationship. The person was called Saul, which was also the name of the first king of the Israel kingdom.[11] Through Luke's

[11] The first appearance of the name Saul (שָׁאוּל meaning *asked for* or *prayed for*) in the Bible refers to the son of Kish from the tribe of Benjamin, who was the first king of Israel from 1047 to 1001 BC (1 Sam. 9:1–2; 10:21; 14:5; Acts 13:21). Saul of Tarsus, also from the Benjamin tribe, was named after the greatest hero of the tribe's history. The accounts regarding King Saul's reign are negatively assessed by the author of 1 Samuel. This was probably caused by the Judea tribe perspective on the Israelites' history, rather than simple facts concerning the king, especially when compared to King David of the Judea tribe. King Saul remained one of the greatest figures in the history of Israel. Considering that the united kingdom

use of the term *νεανίας*,[12] we can determine that Saul was a young man, approximately twenty-five years of age. Luke only exposes Saul's relation to οἱ μάρτυρες (witnesses) who put their clothes under Saul's watch when they were involved in Stephen's stoning.[13] Closer identification of these witnesses makes it possible to determine a social group related to Saul to some extent. Twice, Luke refers to people who accuse Stephen (Acts 6:11, 13). They are identified as "those who belonged to the synagogue of the Freedmen (as it was called), Cyrenian, Alexandrians, and others of those from Cilicia and Asia" (Acts 6:9), proving that the group standing against Stephen consisted of people from different synagogues in Jerusalem.[14] Among

---

of the twelve tribes survived no more than 110 years, the strong tribal identity should be recognized as an integral part of the Diaspora Jews' constant struggle for surviving on political and religious levels. For more information concerning King Saul, see 1 Samuel 9–13. For a historical presentation of King Saul, see S. S. Brooks, "Saul and Saul's Family," in *Dictionary of the Old Testament. Historical Books*, eds. B. T. Arnold and H. G. M. Williamson, 880–884.

[12] In his book *De opificio mundi*, Philo, following the division of human life presented by Hippocrates, divided the human life into the periods. They are as follows: *παιδίον* (*paidion*), a child seven years of age; *παῖς* (*pais*), a child between eight and fourteen; *μειράκιον* (*meirakion*), a young lad from fifteen to twenty-two; *νεανίσκος* (*neaniskos*), a young man from twenty-three to twenty-eight; *ἀνήρ* (*aner*), an adult man between twenty-nine and forty-nine; *πρεσβύτης* (*presbytes*), an elderly man from fifty to fifty-six; and *γέρων* (*geron*), an old man above fifty-seven. In his book *De cherubim*, however, Philo uses a different terminology. Instead of μειράκιον, he uses the term *πρότογενειος*, and instead of the term ἀνήρ, he uses the term *τελείως ἀνήρ*. Philo uses the term νεανίσκος to refer to a young man in the period between twenty-three and twenty-eight years of age and the term πρεσβύτης to refer to the old man in the period between fifty and fifty-six.

[13] E. J. Schnabel, *Exegetical Commentary on the New Testament. Acts* (Michigan: Zondervan, 2012), 391–392.

[14] Several opinions were presented concerning the number of the synagogues in Jerusalem. Jews who took part in the stoning of Stephen could belong to two synagogues (the synagogue of freedman and the synagogue of Diaspora Jews); four synagogues (the synagogue of freedman, the synagogue of Alexandrian, the synagogue of Cyrenians, and the synagogue of those from Cilicia and Asia); or five synagogues (the synagogue of freedman, the synagogue of Alexandrian, the synagogue of Cyrenians, the synagogue of Cilicians, and the synagogue of people from Asia).

the listed synagogues, Luke mentions the synagogue of people from Cilicia, which was Saul's homeland (Acts 22:3). This strongly suggests that Saul was related to this synagogue and identified himself with Diaspora Jews from Cilicia.[15] As a member of the Cilician synagogue, Saul was probably involved in discourse with Stephen, since he attended Stephen's trial before Sanhedrin and followed the crowd to a place of stoning. But Saul did not take active participation in carrying out the death penalty. In the first appearance of Saul, Luke exposes him in a passive manner, almost neutrally.

In Acts 8:1, Luke reveals a new aspect about Saul, changing his quasi-neutral account in Acts 7:58. Luke straightaway informs readers that "Saul approved of their killing him" (Acts 8:1 NIV), which is a direct exposition of Saul's responsibility for *τῇ ἀναιρέσει αὐτοῦ* (killing him), which is the term referring to legal or quasi-legal procedures of putting someone to death. His responsibility is exposed by the term *συνευδοκέω* (I, consenting together with others), which shows that, although he did not take active participation in stoning, he wills it to be done. In light of this statement, the information from Acts 7:58 about "the witnesses laid their coats at the feet of a young man named Saul" (NIV) loses its neutral meaning. Instead, it informs readers that Saul could be seen as some kind of leader for those who took active roles in killing Stephen or at least for those of the Cilician synagogue.[16] After acknowledging the information provided by Acts 8:1, readers can no longer think of Saul as a person accidentally involved in Stephen's case.

In Acts 8:3, Luke makes a full-scale presentation of Saul, which is reduced to only one aspect: his attitude toward those who recognized Jesus as the Messiah. Verse 3 is the last stage of the initial presentation

---

[15] Acts 9:1–2 identifies *οἱ μάρτυρες* as the Sanhedrin; however, in Luke's narrative regarding the stoning of Stephen, the Sanhedrin does not act as the witness but as the judging body (Acts 7:1). Jews from Jerusalem's synagogues insisted on the action against Stephen, which consequently made his case a matter of the trial before the Sanhedrin (Acts 6:11–12).

[16] L. T. Johnson, *The Acts of the Apostles* (Collegeville: The Liturgical Press, 1992), 141.

of Saul. After we are informed that Saul was a passive presence at the stoning of Stephen (Acts 7:58) and that he agreed with the impulsive decision of the crowd (Acts 8:1), we now learn that he was actively involved in ravaging the messianic community in Jerusalem (Σαῦλος δὲ ἐλυμαίνετο τὴν ἐκκλησίαν). Luke used this final description to expose Saul.[17]

The second part of verse 3 (κατὰ τοὺς οἴκους εἰσπορευόμενος, σύρων τε ἄνδρας καὶ γυναῖκας παρεδίδου εἰς φυλακήν) exposes the way Saul did his work.[18] The key information regards Saul as the persecutor, ravaging the community. The first phrase, "Saul ravages" (Σαῦλος ἐλυμαίνετο), is the term that indicates possible mistreatment, torture, military devastation, or outrage, and the use of the imperfect form of the verb exposes that this action continued for long time, but at the moment of writing the Acts, his activities no longer influenced the present.[19] Finally, in his initial introduction of Saul, Luke reveals the true and brutal face of the "young man" (Acts 7:58) who agreed with the stoning of Stephen (Acts 8:1). Saul, as presented by Luke, is the persecutor; he was him already in Acts 7:58 and in Acts 8:1. It was not the case that Stephen's issue forced Saul to become the persecutor; rather, he was already an opponent to the Way at Luke's first mention of him.[20] Luke had chosen a firm but gentle way to gradually present Saul's evil.

---

[17] Luke will present more information concerning Saul in a direct narrative concerning his first years after conversion (Acts 9:1–31; 11:19–30; 12:24–13:12) and in retrospective summaries concerning the early stage of Paul's life, found in his apologetic speeches (Acts 22:1–21; 26:1–23).

[18] Acts 8:3 sums up Saul's attitude, ending the first introduction of a narrative regarding Saul that will find its conclusion in Acts 9:1, where the final evaluation of Saul's actions is presented.

[19] C. S. Keener, *Acts. An Exegetical Commentary*, vol. 2 (Grand Rapids: Baker Academic, 2013), 1484.

[20] Acts 8:2 should be placed before Acts 8:1b because it creates the natural end for the narrative concerning Stephen's death. Placing the information regarding Stephen's burial (Acts 8:2) between two items of information concerning Saul (Acts 8:1.3) suggests that the persecution of the Jesus's followers in Jerusalem, in which Saul took a significant part, started instantly after Stephen's death; cf. C. S. Keener, *Acts. An Exegetical Commentary* vol. 2, 1467.

Luke determined the subject of Saul's persecution, writing "But Saul began to destroy the church" (Acts 8:3 NIV), where the term τὴν ἐκκλησίαν refers to the Jerusalem community of those who believe in Jesus as the Messiah.[21] It means that Saul was not concentrated on destroying the structure or system of the community; he simply headed to eliminate those who believed that Jesus of Nazareth was the Messiah.[22] He directly acted against people, since destroying people would bring the end the community itself. In order to expose this idea indirectly, Luke adds specification regarding the way in which Saul realized his plan. He indicates that Saul entered private property, arrested men and women, and put them in prison. This one short sentence contains lots of hidden information that exposes the scale and nature of Saul's activity. Information concerning the private houses shows that Saul possessed a special prerogative to enter private properties, which usually were not disturbed without permission of local authorities. An arrest at home was viewed as more severe than an arrest in a public place.[23] Information concerning the arrest of men and women shows cruelty and an uncompromised aim of Saul's activity, since women were less often arrested than men. Keener is of the opinion that Luke's mention of the women serves to show their courage and faithfulness, which is in accord with Luke's general views on women's positions in the primitive Christian movement. In our opinion, it serves to expose the scale of Saul's ravaging, but it also may be taken as a parable, which indicates that the entire family

---

[21] The term comes from Greek secular language, where it refers to the casual meeting. Here, it refers to a group of people with the same religious convictions, gathered together; cf. J. Schmidt, ἐκκλησία, in *TDNT* vol. III (Grand Rapids: Eerdmans, 1995), 513–517. We should be aware that Luke uses the term in a different way from the meaning the term takes in modern times, as referring to the institutionalized religious system; cf. J. Schmidt, ἐκκλησία, 504–505.

[22] Zetterholm is of the opinion that there was also a political reason for Saul's hostility. M. Zetterholm, *Approaches to Paul. A Student's Guide to Recent Scholarship* (Minneapolis: Fortress Press, 2009), 16–17.

[23] C. S. Keener, *Acts. An Exegetical Commentary,* vol. 2, 1482–1483.

(including children) were put in prison.[24] Information concerning the imprisonment of those who believed in Jesus as the Messiah suggests that they were sent to the prison for the trial or after the trial. At this moment, it is impossible to determine which of these two possibilities is more accurate but Acts 9:1 probably will help us to clarify the problem. Luke, indirectly in verse 4, informs us that Saul's activity, although it caused the exodus of the Messianic Jews from Jerusalem, did not destroy the community, which may indicate only a partial success of Saul's attempt.[25]

Conclusion

Concerning the persecution of the messianic movement in Jerusalem, Luke exclusively concentrates on one person, Saul, who, although he is not presented as kind of lone wolf, is shown as representative figure of a much broader systematic opposition to the new sect. Luke's approach is connected to the role that Saul will play in the following narrative of Acts, and for this reason, the extreme contrast between two different parts of the same life serves the theological purpose of the author. Luke did an extremely negative introductory presentation of Saul in a schematic and euphemistic way, without highlighting his responsibility, which easily might be recognized by those who can read between lines. Behind a simple indication, in a general manner, of Saul's actions, there was the very harsh reality for Jesus's followers, which Luke does not ignore, despite the

---

[24] This information strongly suggests that Saul's attitude was an attempt to exterminate the followers of Jesus.

[25] Luke wrote nothing directly about Saul's persecution of the twelve but Acts 9:26 suggests that the disciples were afraid of Saul. This may also include the apostles, but they are not mentioned in a direct or an indirect manner as the subject of Saul's persecution (Acts 8:1). The fact that Luke exposes the persecution of the twelve by the Sanhedrin (Acts 5:12–42) does not mean automatically that they were also persecuted by Saul. Saul's action against the twelve is possible but not attested. However, Acts 9:26 will be a better fit to the narrative context if Saul's action against the twelve has occurred in the past.

way in which he exposed it (a short and laconic mention). However, Luke consciously focuses on the unintentionally positive side of the persecution; namely, spreading the kerygma to neighboring regions (Acts 8:4–40), which prepares the ground for a narrative regarding Saul's conversion and the beginning of spreading the kerygma to the end of the world.

2. The Young Man on His Quest (Acts 9:1–19)

In Acts 9:1–19, Luke presents one of the most critical events in Saul's life, which is connected with his quest to Damascus. Saul is still actively and zealously involved in destroying the messianic movement within Judaism, and his commitment to this task is described as, "Saul was still breathing out murderous threats against the Lord's disciples" (Acts 9:1 NIV).

In this way, Luke not only picks up the track of the narrative in Acts 8:3 and turns the narrative topic to the person of Saul, but he also exposes the final consequences of Saul's actions. Saul was a real threat to Messianic Jews, which is indicated in Acts 26:10–11 in more detail, where some of his practices left no doubt about his extremely harsh and determined attitude toward the community in Jerusalem.[26] The narratives of Acts 8:1–3 and Acts 9:1 show that the persecution of Jesus's believers was organized and systematic, and it strongly motivated the character ideologically, which took the shape of an ongoing policy with a precisely defined aim.[27] Saul was a part of this terror machine, and Luke makes him a representative face for all that happened in Jerusalem.[28]

---

[26] We are of the opinion that the three accounts concerning the Damascus event are complementary, where each of them brings some new perspective or evaluation of the event. For a different opinion, cf. E. P. Sanders, *Paul. The Apostle's Life, Letters, and Thought* (Minneapolis: Fortress Press, 2015), 98.

[27] E. J. Schnabel, *Exegetical Commentary on the New Testament,* Acts, 440–443.

[28] Luke's particular focus on Saul's attitude as the persecutor does not necessarily means that Saul was the only persecutor acting against the Way or that he was the

It is not clear if Saul finished his work or if he interrupted his activities in Jerusalem in order to extend them to the neighboring regions. Most probably, his decision was caused by his consciousness of the fact presented in Acts 8:4, where Luke informs about the believers, who fled to safer places. According to Luke, Saul chose Damascus, where the Jewish population was dwelling and spreading their beliefs.[29] The Jewish community had to be considerably large enough to possess the synagogue, and those who believed in Jesus as the Messiah were still part of the synagogue. For this reason, Saul asked the high priest for kind of recommendation letter that makes possible cooperation of Jewish local authorities with young zealous Jew, who most probably rather in the name of his own convictions then on the order of the Sanhedrin was searching for everyone who believed in Jesus as the Messiah, in order to bring them to Jerusalem.[30] In this way, Luke shows that the Temple's authority at least approved Saul's action and was eager to help him continue the work among the Diaspora Jews. Problematic is that if Saul could arrest the believers in Damascus and bring them to Jerusalem, in time, then, Damascus would be under the rule of Nabatean's king Aretas IV Philopatris.[31] Punishments in synagogues were generally acceptable (Acts 26:11),

---

worst among other persecutors. Saul is just an example of many like him who acted evilly against the followers of Jesus. He was chosen by Luke, however, because of an extraordinary case—namely, his conversion—which must be understood as the exception or as very rare if similar causes took place. In Luke's narrative, Saul's conversion is presented as a miracle, where his inconceivable evil deeds could be overcome by divine intervention only.

[29] The fact of conversion to Judaism in Damascus is attested by Josephus (cf. Josephus, *Bell*, 2.559–61; *Bell*, 7.368). He informs about persecution of the Jewish community in Damascus. According to Acts 9:31, Jesus's believers escaped to the regions of Judea and Samaria, but Lucan Saul did not search for them in these places. It is possible that Luke consciously omitted this period of Saul's persecution activities due his narrative strategy (only the most crucial events for the presentation of Saul/Paul are recorded), rather than that Saul neglected his persecution actions in these places.

[30] C. S. Keener, *Acts. An Exegetical Commentary*, vol. 2, 1619–1620.

[31] This name of the king is mentioned only in Paul's letter (2 Cor. 11:31), but not in the narrative of Acts. Rather less possible during the Roman period is a kind

and Saul practiced it during the persecution, but the extradition of inhabitants or even fugitives must be taken as only Saul's wish or as Luke's expression, showing the degree of Saul's commitment.[32]

In Acts 9:1–2, Luke exposes Saul's disposition at a moment when his life suddenly and diametrically changed direction, and for this reason, it should be understood as necessary background for the narrative regarding Saul's conversion, in order to underline its unnatural character.[33] Acts 9:3–6 regards an event that changed Saul by breaking his strong conviction, serving as a fundament for his hostility toward Jesus's disciples.[34] It was an unexpected and

of extradition (extradition of fugitives) that is mentioned in 1 Macc. 15:16–21; cf. H. Conzelmann, *Acts of the Apostles* (Philadelphia: Fortress Press, 1987), 71.

[32] Concerning a purpose of Saul's mission in Damascus that headed toward putting Jesus's followers on trial in Jerusalem, it is possible to treat Saul as the Temple authorities' agent. However, it seems unlikely that Saul just acted according to instructions of the Sanhedrin. Lucan narrative suggests that persecution in Jerusalem was initiated and preceded by Saul and the group of zealous Jews related to the synagogues of Diaspora Jews in Jerusalem.

[33] The term *conversion* is here used in the sense of changing the conviction (from a person not believing in Jesus to person believing in Jesus), and it is not use in the sense of changing the religion (from Judaism to Christianity). The event at Damascus and Paul's conversion are discussed in broader perspective in appendix 1 at the end of the book.

[34] The New Testament does not provide information regarding a date of Saul's conversion. It forces us to deduce the date of his conversion based on indirect information provided by a primary source (Gal. 1:18), concerning Saul's first visit to Jerusalem. Paul paid a visit to the elders in Jerusalem three years after his conversion. It is very useful information concerning relative chronology; concerning the absolute chronology however, the information needs to be set as a precise date or historically confirmed event. Concerning the historically confirmed event that can place information of Acts 1:18 on the level of absolute chronology, Paul, in 2 Corinthians 11:32–33, says that a reason for his leaving Damascus was that King Aretas ordered his arrest. It is possibly external sources that determined that King Aretas IV ruled the territory of Moab and Edom from 9 BC to AD 38–39. He lost the favor of Caesar Tiberius (AD 14–37) due to a military conflict with Herod Antipas, the king of Judea and a personal friend of Caesar. It can be assumed that until the death of Caesar Tiberius (AD 37), King Aretas could barely rule the territory of Damascus, which was a part of Syria, a province of the Roman Empire. However, it became possible during the reign of the next

sudden event that occurred just before he reached Damascus. The manner in which Luke narrates an epiphany exposes the power of the revelator and the weakness of the receiver.[35] In verse 3, Luke writes about "a light from heaven flashed around him" (Acts 9:3 NIV) that shows God's power overwhelming Saul. The light put him down to the ground, which is normally a position of a weaker or defeated one.[36] This interpretation is supported by a question addressed to Saul, where the revelator reveals Saul as his oppressor (v. 4). The revelator knows Saul's name but not vice versa, which cause Saul's question regarding the revelator's nature (v. 5).[37] The revelator exposing his name (Jesus) for the second time indicates Saul's crime against him (v. 5). Saul, who persecuted Jesus's believers

---

Caesar, Caligula (AD 37–41), who had a debt of gratitude toward King Aretas, as in AD 18–19, when he was in conflict with the king of Syria, he received military help from the father of King Aretas IV. If this is a case, the reign of King Aretas IV over Damascus from AD 37 to 38–39 (beginning of his reign and the death of King Aretas) could be possible without any conflict with the empire. In this way, it is possible to determine the period (AD 37–39) when the action against Saul was undertaken, but without the possibility of pointing accurately to a precise year, which opens the possibility of many assumptions based on particular interpretations of valuable sources. We assume that King Aretas IV acted against Saul at the beginning of his reign in Damascus, rather than at the end of his reign (to earn the favor of the Jewish community in Damascus, the king grounded their request). For this reason, the most possible date of Saul's escape from Damascus should be taken as AD 37. In this case, Saul's conversion had taken place a little more than three years before he escaped from Damascus. Finally, it allows us to determine the probable year of Saul's conversion as AD 34.

[35] Concerning a motive of *light* as the element of biblical theophany, cf. L. T. Johnson, *The Acts of the Apostles*, 162–163.

[36] Luke's narrative concerning the event at Damascus is placed in context of struggling between two opposite powers (human power and divine power), where the losing one is Saul. It gives the event a military rather than a worshipping nature. A different interpretation presents Schnabel, who interprets the information of Saul put down to the ground as the typical reaction of a human being during an encounter with heavenly power and takes it as the most common pattern in the Bible. E. J. Schnabel, *Acts. Exegetical Commentary on the New Testament*, 443–444.

[37] The question concerning the name of the revelator may suggest a kind of reference to the epiphany on Mount Sinai.

is found guilty of persecuting Jesus himself.[38] According to Luke's narrative, Saul makes no forward self-defense, which may suggest his subordination to Jesus and recognition of his wrongdoing. In verse 6, Luke presents Saul as the person subordinated to Jesus, who makes a direct order with an enigmatic addition concerning forward plans. It indirectly indicates that Saul, from the agent who opposed the movement claiming that Jesus of Nazareth is the resurrected Messiah, turned into a follower of Jesus, the one who was subordinated to the will of Jesus. For this reason, calling the event at Damascus the *conversion of Saul* seems justified.[39]

Acts 9:7–9 shows Saul's condition after the epiphany.[40] The physical effect of the epiphany was that Saul's blindness continued for three days. Although Johnson interprets this blindness in the category of punishment, the following narrative suggests that the aim of the revelation was to change Saul but not to punish him.[41] Rather it is an external sign that exposes Saul's weakness—instead of entering the gate of Damascus in his healthy posture with strong self-confidence, Saul enters it as a blind man with an obvious need for assistance.[42] The revelation has its internal effect, which is exposed by the mention of Saul's fast.[43] It is not that Saul could not eat and drink; rather, it is that he chose abstention from food. This action was connected with his conversion (changing his way of thinking concerning Jesus of Nazareth), which seems to be attested by Acts 9:11, where Luke mentions Saul's praying, as well as it is connected

---

38 The narrative indirectly exposes the statement that the persecution of Jesus's followers is the persecution of Jesus Himself. This statement reminds that Paul's teaching regards the church as the body of Christ, and for this reason, it takes a theological meaning, rather than literary.

39 Concerning the problem of Saul's conversion, cf. appendix 1 at the end of the book.

40 Dunn presents many different aspects of Saul's conversion.

41 L. T. Johnson, *The Acts of the Apostles*, 163. Acts 9:16 indicates the cost of being a witness to the resurrected Messiah, rather than some kind of necessary hardship that is a kind of consequence, caused by a choice that has been made.

42 H. Conzelmann, *Acts of the Apostles*, 72.

43 J. A. Fitzmyer, *The Acts of the Apostles* (New Haven & London: Yale University Press, 1998), 426.

with the narrative concerning Saul's healing and baptism (Acts 9:10–19). It strongly suggests that the revelation caused Saul's shock (external and internal), as his firm conviction about the wrongness of proclaiming Jesus as the resurrected Messiah has been undermined by his own experience, and the way to conversion went by temporary physical disability. Despite the possibilities of various interpretations of the narrative, Acts 9:7–9 undisputable is the fact that Luke presents Saul as broken man, quite disoriented, as the world he has known has just come to end for him.

In Acts 9:10–16, Luke presents the reason, way, and aim of Jesus's revelation to Saul. The main agents of this account are Jesus and Ananias, but Saul is only a subject of a discussion between them. The protagonist is Jesus, who is about to force one of his believers to act according to the Lord's will, even if, initially, Ananias has little interest in undertaking the action. In extensive dialogue between them, Luke includes some very detailed information regarding Saul, where some of it takes a biographical character but other parts of it are more of a personal nature. As to the personal information, Saul was staying in the house of a certain Judas, living on Straight Street, who possibly was the owner of the house that provided accommodation for Jewish travelers.[44] Barrett supposes the he was one of Jesus's followers, but it is rather more possible that he was just the owner with whom Saul possibly had made arrangements.[45] This information shows that in Damascus there existed a large community of Jews with a well-developed socioeconomic system, which Saul could use for the purpose of his quest, and a kind of Jewish hotel would be an excellent place for gathering necessary information. The second piece of information regards Saul's biography, and it concerns the fact that Saul comes from Tarsus, the Greek city in the region of Cilicia (Acts 9:11); that information is exposed by Luke for the very first time in Acts. This information makes Saul to be

---

[44] Regarding historicity of the information, cf. E. J. Schnabel, *Acts. Exegetical Commentary on the New Testament*, 446.

[45] C. K. Barrett, *The Acts of the Apostles*, vol. 1 (Edinburg: T&T Clark, 1994), 453.

a Diaspora Jew.[46] The third personal piece of information concerns the image of Saul that was spread among Jews living in the Diaspora (Acts 9:13–14), which agrees with the information provided in Acts 8:1–3 and Acts 9:1–2.[47] Other information of a personal nature is the mention of Saul's praying (Acts 9:11), which indicates that he was a pious Jew, who observed the most basic regulation of the Law and tradition. The information concerns Saul's vision, with regard to his encounter with Ananias before it occurred, should be counted as little bit peculiar (Acts 9:12).[48] The placing of this information in the middle of narrative, where Jesus and Ananias are the focus, probably serves as another of Luke's layers, which shows that Jesus "works on" Ananias, in order that his relationship with Saul could be possible.[49] Other information concerns Saul's fate, as it was planned by Jesus. Saul does not choose Jesus; it is Jesus who chose Saul, and the reason for his choosing was to become a "chosen instrument," which will be used to achieve the aim determined by Jesus.[50] The aim is described as "to proclaim my name to the Gentiles and their kings and to the people of Israel" (Acts 9:15 NIV), who determine Saul's status as the witness rather than the missionary, since each of these

---

[46] In an introductory narrative regarding Saul, Luke wrote little about Saul's Jewish background. Instead, in the narrative concerning Paul's mission journeys and his imprisonment, Paul speaks much more about Saul and his Jewishness (in the speeches of Paul). It is a Lucan narrative concept used to give the presentation of Saul/Paul a more retrospective and contextual character than just simply an editorial character.

[47] Here, Luke exposes that Jews community in Damascus had possessed knowledge about Saul and his antagonistic attitude toward the Way.

[48] Luke, in his narrative, uses a well-known biblical pattern, where prayer is connected with vision (Luke 1:10; 3:21; 9:28; Acts 10:2–4; 22:7).

[49] The narrative serves to expose the fact that Saul's conversion (including the involvement of Ananias) is exclusively Jesus's plan. Luke does not give credit to Saul, in the sense of his active and indispensable contribution to all events leading to his conversion.

[50] Hanges, in his books, looks on Paul as "the founder" who is compared to the founders of the Greek cults, but he recognizes the important rule of prophetic tradition that influenced Paul's understanding of his calling. J.C. Hanges, *Paul, Founder of Churches* (Tubingen: Mohr Siebeck, 2012), 16–17.

three steps will be realized due to particular circumstances in which he will find himself and be forced to give witness.[51] Saul's witness will be connected with suffering and persecution, which can be interpreted as kind of punishment for antagonism toward the church (less preferred) or an indication of the cost for giving witness to Jesus, the resurrected Messiah (more preferred).[52] The second possibility indirectly indicates that at this stage of development, the messianic movement, proclaiming Jesus as the Messiah, was tantamount to exposing himself to various forms of persecution.

Acts 9:17–19 ends the section concerning Saul's conversion (Acts 9:1–19), which starts with the presentation of Saul as still actively involved in the persecution of Jesus's followers and ends with narrative indicating that he became a follower of the messianic movement. The person chosen by Jesus to activate Saul was Ananias, who, after a prolonged argument with the Lord, was finally convinced to accept the task to incorporate the former persecutor and now still blind and broken young man, into the community of Jesus, the resurrected Messiah.[53] Luke's narrative recorded Saul's incorporation into the messianic movement in a short and schematic way, where Ananias called Saul by his name, laid his hand on Saul, and recognized him as a brother, which altogether must be interpreted as signs of accepting Saul among the Jesus's followers in Damascus. It makes Ananias act as the leader of the believers' community in this city, which does not automatically mean that he actually was the leader. Saul, who was blinded by Jesus, now is informed by Ananias that his healing is the will of Jesus, who also fills him with the Holy Spirit (Acts 9:17).[54]

---

[51] Paul's witness to the king and the people of Jerusalem (Acts 27) during the time of his imprisonment should be recognized as fulfilment of this narrative's indication (Acts 9:15) that takes the form of Jesus's direct speech.

[52] E. J. Schnabel, *Acts. Exegetical Commentary on the New Testament*, 449.

[53] H. Conzelmann, *Acts of the Apostles*, 73.

[54] Johnson, in the information concerning Saul's sight restoration (v. 18), in context of following the narrative (Acts 9:19–25) concerning Saul's activities in Damascus, interprets figuratively and refers it to Saul's recognition of Jesus as the resurrected Messiah. L. T. Johnson, *The Acts of the Apostles*, 165. However, Saul subordinated himself to Jesus as his Lord at the very beginning of his conversion,

According to the will of Jesus, Saul was healed by the hands of Ananias, and then, by the same hands, he was baptized (Acts 9:18). It is not clear if the laying hands on Saul is connected with his healing or with his being filled with the Holy Spirit or with both events (as the syntax suggests). However, Luke's narrative clearly indicates that both events are strictly Jesus's orders, executed by Ananias. For this reason, the issue of Saul's baptism probably also is related to Ananias, who possibly provided it in the River Barada that runs through Damascus.[55] The baptism ends the whole process of Saul's conversion, which starts with Jesus's revelation and ends with the incorporation of Saul into the messianic community in Damascus. It is attested by unnecessary (from a narrative point) information that Saul, after healing and baptism, again starts to accept food that helps him to rebuild his strength. Actually, it means that Saul returned to the normal state of existence (its physical aspect).[56]

Conclusion

Luke arranged the narrative concerning Saul's conversion in two sections; the first one concerns putting down the persecutor Saul (Acts 9:1–9), and second one concerns incorporation of the former persecutor Saul into the community of Jesus's believers in Damascus (Acts 9:10–19). Considering the first section (Acts 9:1–9), the next structure can be detected. Verses 1–3 introduce the main agent, who is Saul (this subsection we mark as A). Verses 4–6 regard the encounter of the main agent Saul with Jesus (this subsection we mark

---

which was dialogue with the resurrected Jesus (Acts 9:4–6). It is worthy to note that Acts 9:19–25 contains two items of information regarding Saul's kerygma spread in Damascus, where the first concerns Jesus as the Son of God (Acts 9:20), and the second concerns Jesus as the Messiah (Acts 9:22). In both cases, the statements are based on Saul's experience.

[55] Keener specifies the most probable location of Paul's baptism as the River Barada that runs east-west through Damascus, not so far from Straight Street. C. S. Keener, *Acts. An Exegetical Commentary,* vol. 2, 1667.

[56] L. T. Johnson, *The Acts of the Apostles*, 165.

as B). Verses 7–9 concern the result of the encounter between Saul and Jesus (this subsection we mark as C). Considering the second section (Acts 9:10–19), the next structure can be detected. Verse 10 introduces the main agent of the section, who is Ananias (this subsection we mark as A^1). Verses 11–16 concern the encounter of the main agent Ananias with Jesus (this subsection we mark as B^1). Verses 17–19 regard the results of the encounter between Ananias and Jesus (this subsection we mark as C^1). Parallelism in the construction of each of the sections is striking. It indicates also that the main agent of the first section is Saul, but the main agent of the second section is Ananias. It may be interpreted as the way in which Luke indicates an important rule of Ananias in the finalization of Saul's conversion process. The breaking of the young and determined persecutor of the messianic communities was a task that simple believers or even the apostles could not possible do, and for this reason, Saul had to be defeated by Jesus himself, which indicates that Saul lost not to the kerygma proclaimed by the messianic Jews but to Jesus himself, who, although in public but still in a very exclusive epiphany, revealed himself to the persecutor as the resurrected Messiah in heavenly glory. However, the task of incorporating the broken former persecutor Saul into the community of Jesus's believers in Damascus was something that could be done by the power of the believers, who are represented in Luke's narrative by Ananias. His fear and prejudice had to be defeated by Jesus before he would be ready to obey the will of the Lord and to interact with Saul. In Luke's narrative, both agents (Saul in the first section and Ananias in the second section) changed their positions, and in both cases, it was due to divine intervention.

It is unlikely that this construction of the narrative is just the redaction of the sources; rather, it is a skillfully crafted hidden message for the reader: that in process of cultivating Saul to make of him a witness to Jesus, the resurrected Messiah, Jesus used the help of those who believed in him. Striking is fact that, as in the case of Saul's conversion, similar patterns will be used in the case of Saul's acceptance into the Jerusalem community and then in the case of Saul's mission activation by Barnaba in Syrian Antioch.

3. The Beginning of the New Life (Acts 9:19–31)

In Acts 9:19–31, Luke presents Saul's life after his conversion. The powerful experience during Jesus's epiphany, amplified by physical weakness and probable spiritual-intellectual confusion, was for Saul the experience that incited a new and unexpected way that he would explore for the rest of his life, but it also was an event that drastically changed his life, not only regarding his worldview or his conviction but also in strictly an existential sense, since he had to leave all that he had been hard working for and start to work hard again from the beginning in the new reality.

3.1. In Damascus (Acts 9:19–25)

The first natural consequence of Saul's metamorphosis was departure from the society of the Diaspora synagogue in Jerusalem and joining the community of the messianic Jews in Damascus (Acts 9:19).[57] Luke writes that Saul stayed with disciples in Damascus for several days, which may indicate that Saul left Damascus for some period and then returned to the city or that he departed from the house of some of Jesus's followers and started to live on his own.[58] According to Luke's narrative, the second possibility should be preferred, since an entire section of Acts 9:19–25 concerns Damascus, and Saul's moving to his own place may have been caused by the character of his mission in Damascus, which possible could have been dangerous for Jesus's followers in this city.[59] It may explain the use of the term *immediately* regarding Saul's activities in the Damascus synagogues,

---

[57] After his conversion, Saul was not accepted by Hellenists in Jerusalem (Jews speaking Greek, the formal friends of Saul), which is attested by short information regarding their attempt to exterminate Saul (Acts 9:29).

[58] The first possibility is in accordance with information provided by Galatians 1:17 and 2 Corinthians 11:32. Comparing the Luke narrative with Paul's letters, Luke does not mention Saul's trip to the Nabateans region. cf. C. S. Keener, *Acts. An Exegetical Commentary,* vol. 2, 1668–1671.

[59] Differences between Acts and Paul's letters regarding the narrative of Saul's activities in Damascus caused discussion concerning the historical credibility of

which creates the impression that immediately after Saul started to live on his own, he also started to proclaim the kerygma in the synagogue.[60] As the most representative key term for Saul's kerygma, Luke choses the phrase *Son of God*, which is the most important title in Pauline theology, but it is not really preferred by Luke in Acts; he more gladly uses the term *Christ*.[61] For this reason, we suppose that there is another purpose for using the term than Luke's appeal to Pauline Christology. Since the statement that Jesus is the Son of God was a blasphemy for every Jew who did not accept Jesus as the Messiah, we should not be amazed by their reaction.[62] According to Luke's narrative, the Jewish community was aware of Saul's activities in Jerusalem and his purpose for coming to Damascus (Acts 9:21). Concerning Saul's work in Jerusalem, they were of the opinion that he made havoc of the Jerusalem community, which is exposed by using the participle aorist πορθεῖν (Acts 9:13).[63] Then, concerning Saul's arrival in Damascus, they were of the opinion that he wanted to arrest Jesus's believers and take them to the chief priest in Jerusalem

---

Acts. The discussion of this problem is presented in appendix 2 at the end of the book.

[60] Saul was proclaiming the kerygma that "Jesus is the Son of God" in the synagogues of Damascus (Acts 9:20), which, for Jews, was a blasphemy endangered by penalty. For this reason, Jews' hostility toward Saul was based on rational reasons that made sufficient explanation for their action.

[61] Lucan Saul/Paul uses the term *Son of God* in Acts 9:20; 13:33; 20:28. cf. B. M. Metzger, *A Textual Commentary on the Greek New Testament* (Stuttgart: Deutsche Bibelgesellschaft, 2002), 427.

[62] The term *Son of God* itself was not treated as blasphemy in the Old Testament writings and in Judaism of the second Temple period. However, Saul applies the term to Jesus, explicitly exposing his exclusivity as the only Son of God, supported by indirect claimed equality between Jesus and God (Acts 7:56), which was an interpretation that could not be accepted by devout Jews. C. S. Keener, *Acts. An Exegetical Commentary,* vol. 2, 1671–1672.

[63] Menoud, based on Galatians 1:13–23, thinks that the term is used in a moral sense (only Saul's teaching against those who accepted Jesus as the Messiah), with no reference to physical persecution. Ph. H. Menoud, *Jesus Christ and the Faith* (Pittsburgh: Pickwick, 1978), 47–60. His opinion, however, is undermined by Acts 8:1, where physical destruction is clearly indicated.

(Acts 9:14). We might wonder why Luke twice presents the same information with some differences in the details but not the main message.[64] In our opinion, it is not due to Luke's distractions, but it is a consciously chosen way to present Saul by using a supplementary approach to presentation of the information. The account of Acts 9:13–14 and Acts 9:21 are not different; they are supplementary.[65] For Damascus Jews, the fact that Saul did not conduct himself in a way they expected (Acts 9:21) was not the only problem concerning the relationship between them, as he also taught that Jesus is the Messiah in way that very much disturbed the community.

Luke writes that Saul is proving that Jesus is the Messiah, which indicates that he is presenting convincing and logical arguments, and his action was going on for considerable time.[66] In Acts 9:20, Luke writes that Saul proclaimed Jesus as the Son of God; in Acts 9:22, he writes that Saul kept confusing the Jews by proving that Jesus is the Christ (Messiah). Proving that someone is the Son of God is a rather difficult issue, even when using the scripture; proving that someone is the Messiah by using the scripture is a much easier tusk. Consider Acts 9:19–25; there is not a naturally clear reason why the Jews in Damascus were about to kill Saul, for that was presented in Acts 9:20 or in Acts 9:22 or maybe in both of them. The narrative context preferred is Acts 9:22 (Saul's proclaiming Jesus as the Christ), which is sufficient reason for the Jews' decision (Acts 9:23), if we

---

[64] There are some differences between Ananias's evaluation of Saul (Acts 9:13–14) and the Damascus Jews' evaluation of Saul (Acts 9:21). When Lucan Ananias speaks about "much harm Saul has done to Jesus' followers in Jerusalem," Damascus Jews speak about Saul causing "such havoc in Jerusalem." Definitely, there is a different level of evaluation of Saul's actions. Also, when Ananias speaks about Saul going to Damascus with authority from the high priest to arrest the believers (Acts 9:14), Lucan Damascus Jews speak about Saul who comes to the city to arrest the believers and to take them to the high priests in Jerusalem. Here, the difference concerns the rule the high priest played in the Saul's activities.

[65] Ananias's evaluation of Saul and the Damascus Jews' evaluation of Saul are complementary, and they have one common element: that Saul, after his conversion, challenged their common expectations.

[66] E. J. Schnabel, *Acts. Exegetical Commentary on the New Testament*, 451–452.

consider that for a long time, Saul successfully argued this matter.[67] Short and schematic is the manner in which Luke informs about a Jewish plot against Saul, in the same way he informs that Saul acknowledges the Jews' plan (Acts 9:24) and the manner in which Saul escaped from Damascus (Acts 9:25). In both cases, Luke is not interested in providing more information than is necessary for a coherent account. However, it is still possible to make suppositions concerning the event.

First, in Damascus, Saul met some supporters (those who informed him about the plot) and some opponents (those who wished him to die). Second, both groups were determined in their actions. The opponents made a great effort (watching the gates of the city) to catch and exterminate Saul, and the supporters (here, called *his disciples*) took a great risk in helping Saul. Third, the timing and manner of the escape suggest great despair in Saul and those who helped him.[68] All this information, in an indirect way, exposes that Saul's activities in the city made considerable impact on the Jewish community in Damascus.[69] The positive information considers the fact that Saul has his own disciples, who come from Jews, who, due to Saul's teaching, came to believe in Jesus as the Messiah. The negative information considers the opponents, who would like to see him dead due to his activities and teaching (converting Jews; proclaiming that Jesus is Son of God and that Jesus is the Messiah).

---

[67] Striking is the fact that only in Acts 9:20 does Luke, in a direct and clean manner, use the term *Son of God.*

[68] Lucan narrative concerning Saul's activities in Damascus makes room for doubt regarding his mission's success in the city. J. A. Harrill, *Paul the Apostle. His Life and Legacy in Their Roman Context* (Cambridge: Cambridge University Press, 2012), 38–39.

[69] Saul's presence and activities in Damascus definitely made a great impact on the Jewish community in the city—in a negative way on the Jews who did not accept Jesus as the Son of God or as the Messiah, and in a positive way on Jews who accepted Saul's kerygma and became disciples. However, the latter is doubtful, considering a lack of forward mention in Acts about the disciples from Damascus. Does the term disciples refer to Saul's disciples, or to Jesus's disciples who ran away from Jerusalem?

Conclusion

Although Saul spent three years in Damascus, a time span comparable to each of Paul's mission journeys, Luke wrote no more than seven verses—that is just the size of an introduction compared to the narrative of the mission journeys. Since Luke spent a considerably long time with Paul, he has enough information to write a more elaborated narrative regarding this stage of Saul/Paul's life, and if he did not do that, he must have done it for a particular reason. Acts 9:19–20 strongly suggests that Luke consciously omitted something (most probably, Saul's visit to Arabia) in order to create the monothematic narrative (the primary motive) or to underline Saul's independence in activities during the period spent in Damascus (the secondary motive).[70] Luke presented Saul almost as only one persecutor of the community in Jerusalem; now he is presenting Saul as the only one of Jesus's disciple who, actively and without any compromises, proclaimed Jesus as the Son of God and convincingly argued that he is the Messiah.[71] In Jerusalem, Saul persecuted people for believing in Jesus, but in Damascus (among Diaspora Jews), he proclaims Jesus, the Christ. He did things in Damascus that he himself never thought he could possibly do. And what he was doing in Damascus was totally different from his earlier plans. Luke's narrative clearly heads for approving Saul's conversion, and for that, he mentions a three-year period of Saul's mission activities, which finally led to attempting his termination. Lucan Saul changes the side, but he still stays a zealous and determined young man, so confident in his mind

---

[70] Concerning the comparative approach regarding Saul in Damascus, between the accounts of Acts and accounts found in Paul's letters; cf. appendix 2 at the end of the book.

[71] Despite the laconic character of Lucan narrative (Acts 9:19–25), it is self-explanatory that the narrative creates Saul, the new convert, as the hero of the following narrative.

and actions, going on his own, taking risks and trying to avoid the consequences of his actions.[72]

Luke obviously connects Saul in Damascus with Saul in Jerusalem, rather than with Paul, the missionary to Gentiles, in order to expose a radical change of thought regarding the messianic movement and following it.[73] For this reason, Saul's successes in Damascus (mentioned in Acts 9:25) were presented in a rather laconic manner and, in context, exposed a struggle and serious problems, rather than systematic and fruitful mission activities. In this way, Luke probably wants to show that the Saul's conversion was just the beginning of a much longer and complex process of growing to the position of the apostle to Gentiles, rather than an immediate transformation of Saul into the Paul, like those found in fairy tale stories.

3.2. In Jerusalem (Acts 9:26–29)

According to Luke's narrative (Acts 9:26–29), after Saul's escape from Damascus, he went directly to Jerusalem with a clear intention of joining the disciples.[74] Since Luke provides no information on Saul's decision, we can only assume that, for some reason, Jerusalem was the better option for Saul than a direct return to Tarsus. But knowing Luke, there probably is some reason why he places this short account regarding Saul's visit to Jerusalem. Acts 9:26 suggests Saul's conviction that he will be accepted by the disciples in Jerusalem, most probably because from his perspective (as well as from the perspective of the reader) three years of zealous activities in Damascus and proclaiming Jesus as the Messiah was enough to prove himself as

[72] Here, there is some kind of irony in Lucan narrative. Saul's activities forced many believers of Jesus in Jerusalem to run away to Damascus; now, in order to save his own life, Saul has to run away from Damascus to Jerusalem.

[73] Often, the narrative regarding Saul's activities in Damascus is analyzed from the perspective of Paul's mission activities, which, in our opinion, is the approach that neglected Luke's narrative strategy in the presentation of Saul/Paul.

[74] Concerning the comparative approach to narratives found in Acts and in Paul's letters; cf. appendix 3 at the end of the book.

a true convert. However, the disciples in Jerusalem still remembered Saul, the great persecutor, and were not eager to believe in the news was true.[75] In this way, Luke shows the situation in which Saul found himself after the conversion, as a believer of Jesus—on one hand, he was not accepted by Jesus's believers due to his past persecutor's evil fame, and on the other hand, as Jesus's believer, involved in spreading the messianic movement in Damascus, he could not seek help from his "old friends" in Jerusalem. Acts 9:27 suggests that this problem continued for some days, until he met Barnabas, one of the most important men in his life after the conversion. Barnabas himself was a convert from Cyprus, a Levite well known among Jerusalem's disciples and the apostles, as well to the readers of Luke's story, as he presented Barnabas earlier in his narrative (Acts 4:36–37).[76] Luke informs that Barnabas was the first disciple of the Jerusalem community who accepted Saul, and then he finally introduces him to the apostles. Luke honestly exposes that Barnabas had to convince the apostles about Saul's conversion by telling the story regarding his conversion (meeting and dialogue with Jesus) and his activities in Damascus as the witness to the resurrected Messiah. The fact that Barnabas was Saul's warranty (first but not the last time, according to Luke's narrative) exposes Saul's very weak position among the disciples in Jerusalem, although he was accepted and permitted to

[75] Tabor insists that the relationship between Saul/Paul and the apostles in Jerusalem permanently had a sporadic character. J. D. Tabor, *Paul and Jesus. How the Apostle Transformed Christianity* (New York: Simon & Schuster Paperbacks, 2012), 18.

[76] The introduction of Barnabas in Acts shows Luke's literary skill. Before he connected the fate of Saul with Barnabas (the mission in Antioch), he introduced him in a sightly accidental manner in Acts 4:36, then he mentions him again in the narrative regarding Saul's visit to Jerusalem (Acts 9:27), and finally exposes him as the main hero of his narrative in Acts 11:22–30.

It is problematic to agree with the opinion of Conzelmann, who thinks that Luke "concluded from the letter cooperation of Barnabas and Paul that Barnabas was the intermediator," because this statement neglects the fact that in Luke's narrative, Barnabas is the hero connected with the Jerusalem and Antioch communities (Barnabas's layer) and not just supernumerary in Saul's presentation. H. Conzelmann, *Acts of the Apostles*, 75.

proclaim the name of Jesus (Acts 9:28). The words "and moved about freely in Jerusalem" (Acts 9:28 NIV) may suggest his considerable freedom in proclaiming Jesus as the Messiah; namely he could work with disciples or work on his own.[77] The next verse (Acts 9:29) shows that Saul used this freedom in a particular way to approach the Hellenists (Jews from the Diaspora who spoke Greek) with his message about Jesus the Messiah. It is very possible that the place where Saul approached the Hellenists was the same synagogue that Luke mentions at the beginning of narrative regarding Stephen (Acts 6:9). If it is, Luke makes another hyperbole, placing Saul's after his conversion as the witness of Jesus the Messiah, in the same place where Stephen proclaimed the same message, which led him to death, which was proved also by Saul, who was about to persecute the community of Jesus's followers (Acts 8:1). The results of his activities were similar to those of Stephen; namely, the Hellenists did not accept his kerygma and took action that could lead to his death (Acts 9:29). There is no information concerning the time span of Saul's activities or the way the disciples learned about the Hellenists' intention. Similar to the event in Damascus, the disciples helped him to get out of trouble by sending him by the sea to his hometown, Tarsus (Acts 9:30).

Conclusion

Luke's account regarding Saul's first visit to Jerusalem after his conversion concentrates on two relations: the first regards Saul's relationship with the community of Jesus's believers, and the second concerns his relationship with Jews (not Jesus's believers) in Jerusalem. Both of them still will be the subject of Luke's narrative in next parts of the Acts, which will culminate in Acts 21:17–23:35. For this reason, from a literary approach, Acts 9:26–30 serves as preparation, which heads to introduce these two, the most critical relationships of Saul's life. Concerning the relationship with the

[77] E. J. Schnabel, *Acts. Exegetical Commentary on the New Testament*, 457.

disciples in Jerusalem, the narrative ends the section regarding Saul's persecution activities in Jerusalem with his surprising acceptance by the apostles and the disciples after his conversion. The indication of some initial tension between Saul and the Jerusalem community may be taken as a kind of generalized characterization of the relationship (especially between Saul/Paul and the apostles), which is detectable in the narrative concerning the so-called Jerusalem Council (Acts 15:4–35), and in a direct manner, it is exposed in the narrative of Paul's visit to James (Acts 21:17–26).[78] Much more certain is the purpose for the presentation of Saul's relationship with Diaspora Jews in Jerusalem, since the track made in Acts 9:28–30 will be picked up by Luke in the narrative starting from Acts 21:27, where Paul's trouble was caused again by Diaspora Jews.

3.3. Saul in Tarsus (Acts 9:30)

Concerning Saul's stay in Tarsus, according to Luke's account, we can say with strong confidence that it starts a few weeks after he was forced to leave Jerusalem (Acts 9:30), and it ends when Barnabas invited him to work together at Syrian Antioch (Acts 11:25). Luke puts more interest in this stage of Saul's life, despite its length (at least several years).[79] After excluding the possibility that Luke possessed no knowledge about this period, only two explanations can be proposed. The first one is that Saul, during all these years, did not take any mission initiative, and his life was devoted to simple existence occupied by manual work. The second one is that Saul undertook several mission initiatives among Diaspora Jews dwelling in the Cilicia region, probably with considerable success (or without considerable success), which Luke decided to omit due to his narrative

[78] Paul's presence in Jerusalem was "very inconvenient" for the members of Jerusalem community, and his way of proclaiming the kerygma was found "controversial," as Acts 15:5 and Acts 21:20–25 will explicitly expose it.

[79] Concerning so-called unknown years of Saul, more information, including the records from Paul's letters, is provided in appendix 4 at the end of the book.

concept, strongly influenced by his theological approach and his perspective on Saul/Paul.

According to Luke's theological axiom, Saul/Paul is designated to become the apostle to Gentiles, and because of that, all other commitments that do not fit this narrative purpose were probably reduced or ignored. Both proposals are strictly speculative, but the second seems more plausible, if we consider Galatians 1:21–22. Unfortunately, Luke himself does not give any information that can be used as an argument. The kind of summary (Acts 9:31) that ends the first major part of Saul's history (Acts 6:8–9:31), related to the history of the first generation of Jesus's believers, suggests the author's intention to evaluate the period of Saul's active presence in Jerusalem, which, based on Luke's narrative, was marked by serious problems for the communities.[80] It applies both to his activities as the persecutor and his proclaiming of the resurrected Messiah.

The first activities put direct danger on the communities, and the second activities put indirect danger on the community, since Saul's bold proclaiming of the kerygma might meet strong opposition toward him or at least antipathy toward the whole movement. Luke probably wants to indicate the message that Saul's presence in Jerusalem, from the very beginning (and it stays in this way to the end), was problematic for Jesus's communities in Judea. This is the Luke's first attempt to present that Saul's missions among Palestinian Jews did not end with successes.[81]

The summary (Acts 9:31) may suggest that Luke evaluates Saul's return to Tarsus as the end of the persecution in Judea and neighboring regions. If that is the case, Saul would take exclusive responsibility for the persecution, and his departure from Judea would be the reason for the peace. Luke's narrative is narrowed to the case of Saul, but the author gives the strong impression (Acts 9:1–2) that Saul was just one of the participants taking an active role in solving the problem of the messianic movement. Probably, in Acts 9:1–2, Luke treats

---

[80] H. Conzelmann, *Acts of the Apostles*, 75.

[81] L. T. Johnson, *The Acts of the Apostles*, 175.

Saul's example (personal) as a general statement, which regards all persecutors and all persecuted communities (universal), about whom and which Luke made no direct records.[82]

4. Reactivation of Saul (Acts 11:25–30; 12:25)

In Luke's narrative, Saul, as the person connected to Jerusalem's society, disappeared in Acts 9:30 in order to appear again in Acts 11:25 in a totally different context. From a historical perspective, several years (approximately seven) had passed, and from a narrative perspective, Luke progressed his story concerning the mission in Samaria, with the most important point regarding the acceptance of Gentiles who believed in Jesus among the communities of the messianic Jews (Acts 11:17–18). Saul appears in Luke's narrative in a totally different socioreligious context, where he is suddenly part of the community consisting of Gentiles and Jews (Acts 19–21) that exists in the Greek-Roman city of Antioch.[83] The background for Saul's appearing is a dynamic development of a Christian community (Acts 11:25–26) in the city that was noted by the community in Jerusalem, which sent Barnabas to Antioch with the mandate of an emissary (Acts 11:22), who most likely had to evaluate the new situation that was created when Jewish Christians accepted among themselves Gentile Christians (Acts 11:19–21).[84] The evaluation

[82] The basic message of Acts 9:31 is that the persecution, which started after Stephen's stoning, came to an end. Placing the summary (Acts 9:31) next after information of Saul's comeback to Tarsus (Acts 9:30) may not be accidental, although it is deductive.

[83] More detailed information regarding the background of Barnabas and Saul's activities in Syrian Antioch are presented in appendix 5 at the end of the book; cf. A. Drimbe, *The Church of Antioch and the Eucharistic Traditions (ca. 35–130CE)* (Tübingen: Mohr Siebeck, 2020).

[84] According to his narrative strategy, Luke's giving the background information concerning the community in Antioch makes some important statements. First, Stephen's death and the starting of the persecution caused great emigration of Jesus's believers from Judea to many places (Luke mentions only Phoenicia, Cyprus, and Antioch), which launched a new stage in the realization of Jesus's

was positive, and it encouraged Barnabas to undertake the mission activities (Acts 11:24) in the city, which was a challenge that soon requested a coworker capable of fulfilling the mission requirements in Antioch. Lucan Barnabas, instead of looking in Jerusalem for someone, went directly to Tarsus, searching for Saul. After finding him, they came back to Antioch to work together for one year (Acts 11:25–25). During that year, Barnabas and Saul were teaching (Acts 11:26) and were elected by the Antioch community as the delegates by whom the support for the Jerusalem community was sent.[85] In this laconic narrative, Luke makes Barnabas to be the main agent, to whom Saul is subordinated in his actions. It is Barnabas who wants to cooperate with Saul. He made an effort and went to Tarsus, searching for Saul. He brought Saul to Antioch, and he worked with Saul for one year. Definitely, it is Barnabas who chose Saul and not vice versa. It is possible to say that Saul was trained by Barnabas to grow up to the stature of an effective missionary. In fact, it is the very first account in Acts where Saul's effort does not end with disaster or problems. It is also the first time that Luke directly indicates that Saul made a mission with another brother in the faith. Acts 11:30 shows that Barnabas and Saul created the duo, not only working in Antioch but also being recognized by the community as trustworthy, to whom financial issues can be entrusted to the brothers from Jerusalem. It

---

mission order (Acts 1:8). Deduction allows us to assume that the number of Jews who believed in Jesus as the Messiah decreased in Jerusalem. Second, they initially proclaimed the message about Jesus only to Jews (Acts 11:19). Third, there were Diaspora Jews who first started to proclaim Jesus as the Messiah to Gentiles in Antioch, which was information that exposed the progressive faction in the Antioch community. All this information is necessary to prepare directly for Acts 13:1–3 and indirectly for Acts 15:1–2.

[85] Luke stays that in Antioch, for the first time, Jesus's believers, the members of the messianic movement, were called Christians, a name most likely given to them by Gentiles, in our opinion, in order to make the distinction between Jews associated with Gentiles and Jews not associated with Gentiles. If that is the case, the term *Christian* in this context should mean "the messianic Jews." It is not clear if this statement has a direct connection with information regarding Barnabas and Saul's activities. A. Drimbe, *The Church of Antioch and the Eucharistic Traditions (ca. 35–130CE)*, 52–57.

is natural that Barnabas was sent as the delegate, as he was officially sent by the Jerusalem church as the member of this community, but choosing Saul is less convincing, if we consider his past, his experience in Jerusalem after the conversion, and his no-longer-than-one-year experience as a member of the Antioch community.[86] Saul was sent to Jerusalem because he was working with Barnabas, a supposition that may be supported by a fact that Luke placed Saul's name after Barnabas's name. Another reason for sending the Barnabas and Saul duo to Jerusalem together is of a narrative nature, as in Acts 12:25, Luke mentions that on the way back to Antioch, Barnabas also took his nephew John, called Mark, the same who would take part in the mission journey of Barnabas and Saul and who, in the end, became the reason for the split of this mission team.

Conclusion

In the narrative regarding Saul's one-year presence in the Antioch community (Acts 11:25–30), Luke prepared the ground for the narrative of his mission journey as a member of the Antioch community (Acts 13:4–14:28).[87] These two accounts are connected by Acts 12:25, regarding Saul and Barnabas's return to Antioch after completing the task in Jerusalem. The account is of crucial importance in Luke's presentation of Saul because it exposes a way in which Saul, the former persecutor who, after his conversion, rather unsuccessfully attempted to make his stand in Damascus and Jerusalem, finally

[86] Surprisingly Moore sees this action of the Jerusalem Church as a kind of "colonization." E.C. Moore, *Claiming Places*, Tübingen: Mohr Siebeck, 2020, 131–134.

[87] Johnson points to a fact that narrative concerning Barnabas and Saul visit to Jerusalem, may serve in Luke's narrative as the way of exposing fellowship of Antioch community with mother church in Jerusalem, on the one hand, and Saul and Barnabas rule as the agents of the community, on the other hand. L.T. Johnson, *The Acts of the Apostles*, 209. In our opinion, the narrative indicates also unbreakable relation of Barnabas and Saul with the Jerusalem community, which is an aspect of special importance for Saul/Paul presentation in Acts.

makes his breakthrough. Luke's narrative honestly exposes that it happened with little cooperation from Saul, and almost all credit goes to Barnabas, the same "man of consolation" who helped him in Jerusalem (Acts 9:27). Although Saul is presented here as a coworker, Luke suggests that Barnabas was the mentor for Saul, who, beside him, gradually was growing to the status of a man fully prepared to fulfill the task for which he was chosen.

5. The Mission of Antioch's Community on Cyprus (Acts 13:1–28)

Luke's narrative concerning Saul's cooperation with Barnabas in Antioch exposes considerable changes in the way Saul approaches the mission activities, which is indicated by the fruitfulness of the work and a lack of records regarding a problematic situation during the work. The year in Tarsus likely made an immense impact on Saul's understanding and comprehending his previous experiences, which contributed greatly to his personal development. However, Luke writes nothing directly about this aspect of Saul's life in Antioch, which means that he wants the reader to connect Saul's metamorphosis with his work in Antioch. The general impression of the narrative regarding Saul's activities after his conversion is that he did not fit well as the new man (the convert) in the old world (Palestinian Judaism). The relationship of the brothers in faith was stigmatized by the past, and relationships with former friends turned into open hostility. Saul, the convert, did not find a place for himself in Palestinian Judaism. A different impression comes after reading Luke's account of Saul's presence in Antioch, which may indicate the author suggests that the context of Diaspora Judaism better serves the task for which Saul was chosen (Acts 9:15–16). The narrative regarding the so-called first mission journey (Acts 13:1–14:28) seems to confirm this supposition, if we consider Acts 13:9–13, in which Luke links Saul with Paul, which is one of the most important points for recognition of his specific perspective on Paul.

5.1. The End of Saul (Acts 13:1–12)

Acts 13:1–3, which is a kind of introduction to the narrative regarding the so-called first mission journey of Paul, explains the reason for undertaking mission activities by the Antioch community. Acts 13:1 indicates that in the Antioch community, there existed a group of prophets (Acts 11:27) and teachers (Acts 11:26), here named by Luke in manner probably suggesting a hidden message for the reader. Barnabas is mentioned as the first and Saul is mentioned as the last, which may suggest their positions in this charismatic group (in particular) or in the Antioch community (in general), if we consider Acts 11:22 and Acts 11:25–26.[88] However, the positions of Barnabas and Saul in this listing may also create brackets, including those who were prophets and teachers.[89] In this case, Barnabas and Saul are the teachers sent for proclaiming the kerygma outside Antioch. This action was inspirited by the Holy Spirit, (which in a Lucan theological concept exposes divine intervention), who communicated by the prophets (Acts 13:2).[90] Luke does not clarify if the event was a matter within the group of prophets and teachers of Antioch community or if it involved the entire community of Antioch. Is the acting agent in Acts 13:2 the same as the acting agent in Acts 13:3? The Lucan narrative suggests that the acting agent is the same, and it is a group of prophets. However, the accounts of Acts 6:2–6; 14:27–28; 15:4–30 rather suggests the entire community. If we accept a suggestion of Schnabel, that the leaders of the Antioch community were prophets and teachers, it is possible to say the church in Antioch acted according to the leaders or that the leaders acted on behalf of the entire community.[91] Despite some lack of clarity of the narrative,

---

[88] W. S. Kurz, *Acts of the Apostles* (Grand Rapids: Baker Academic, 2103), 202–203.

[89] The one common element concerning all who are listed in Acts 13:1 is the fact that they were not Antiochian. E. J. Schnabel, *Acts. Exegetical Commentary on the New Testament*, 554.

[90] R. N. Longenecker, "Acts," in *The Expositor's Bible Commentary. Luke-Acts*, eds. T. Longman III & D. E. Garland (Grand Rapids: Zondervan, 2007), 910–911.

[91] E. J. Schnabel, *Acts. Exegetical Commentary on the New Testament*, 553.

Luke, in this prelude to the following narrative, shows the mission of Barnabas and Saul as initiated by God and as authorized by the leaders of the local community.[92]

After presenting the necessary background for the narrative concerning the mission activities of Barnabas and Saul in Cyprus, Luke offers a very selective account of this mission.[93] All lack of clarity in Acts 13:2–3 is solved by information provided in verse 4, where the Holy Spirit is directly named as the sender of Barnabas and Saul in Cyprus.[94] Although it is obviously Luke's theological interpretation (according to his general theological axiom), it directly shows that all things connected to the mission journey are of divine origin, even if they are strongly connected to sociopolitical context.

Cyprus was Barnabas's homeland (Acts 4:36–37); even if he departed from it and for a considerable time lived in Jerusalem and then in Antioch, he still preferred to undertake mission activities in an environment already known to him. Luke, in the narrative concerning the mission in Cyprus, mentions by name only two places: the first, Salamis, and the last, Paphos, which are two cities situated on the east coast of the island (Salamis) and on the southwest coast of the Cyprus (Paphos).[95] Most of the author's attention is given to the mission in Paphos (Acts 13:6–12), and the mission in Salamis has only a short summary (verse 5), which indicates mission activities in Jewish synagogues, where they proclaimed the kerygma

---

[92] Lightfoot contends that there were three orders in the community of the first generation of Christians, where the first were the apostles (the group not present in Antioch, according to Luke's account), the second were prophets, and the third were teachers. J. B. Lightfoot, *The Act of the Apostles*, eds. B. Witherington II & T.D. Still (Downers Grove: IVP Academia, 2014), 168.

[93] A. Nobbs, "Cyprus," in *The Book of Acts in Its First-Century Setting, Volume 2, Graeco-Roman Setting*, eds. D. W. J. Gill and C. Gempf (Grand Rapids: The Paternoster Press, 1994), 280–289.

[94] Luke, in his narrative, indirectly suggests that John was not an official member of the mission duo sent to Cyprus (Acts 13:2–3), but he was chosen by Barnabas and Saul as their helper (Acts 13:5). H. Conzelmann, *Acts of the Apostles*, 99.

[95] Cyprus, from the east coast to the west coast, measures about 220 kilometers.

with some help from John.[96] Luke does not inform about the length of their activities in Salamis or about the results.[97] In fact, it seems that this part of the mission was of less interest to Luke. From verse 6, the narrative concerns the mission in Paphos, where the mission group found themselves almost instantly, after laconic information that they walked the distance (about 220 kilometers) but without any information about their activities in cities they visited along the way. Until this part of narrative, neither Barnabas nor Saul was mentioned by name, which suggests that Luke presents their relationship within the mission group in a neutral manner.

In Paphos, they met a Jewish magician, the false prophet Bar-Jesus (Elymas), who introduced them to the proconsul Sergius Paulus (verse 7).[98] Although the good will of the proconsul cannot be doubted (verses 7–8), Bar-Jesus's good will, as a reason for introducing Barnabas and Saul to the proconsul, can be doubted when we consider the magician's reaction to the positive interaction of Paulus Sergius to the kerygma proclaimed by Saul.[99] This made

[96] The mention of John is another layer created by Luke (John Mark's layer), which serves the particular narrative's purpose (the conflict between Paul and Barnabas). Mark was mention for the first time in Acts 12:25 as the nephew of John, living in Jerusalem, whom Barnabas and Saul took with them on their return to Antioch. The second time he is mentioned during the mission in Cyprus (Acts 13:5) as the helper of Barnabas and Saul. He will be mentioned again in Acts 13:13 and Acts 15:36–41. L.T. Johnson, *The Acts of the Apostles*, 222.

[97] Considering that Luke used a plural "synagogues" and that they encounter the Jews of the city during the Sabbath, it may be assumed that they stayed in the city a considerably long time (some weeks).

[98] Most probably, the proconsul learned about Barnabas and Saul (note that Mark is not mentioned), the two Jewish teachers, from the false prophet. Verses 7–8 suggest that Sergius Paulus's encounter with two Jewish teachers was positive (to hear the Word of God) rather than negative (interrogation based on some suspicious). E. J. Schnabel, *Acts. Exegetical Commentary on the New Testament*, 558.

[99] Kurz interprets verse 8 as the first of Paul's proclaiming the kerygma to a Gentile (Sergius Paulus). W. S. Kurz, *Acts of the Apostles*, 206–207. However, Luke's narrative (Acts 13:7–8, 12) suggests that the proconsul may be a God-fearer. If so, Paul proclaimed the kerygma to the Gentile who, to some extent (association with the Jewish magician; interest in meeting the Jewish teachers), was associated with Judaism.

Bar-Jesus, the influential man, as an enemy of Saul (Acts 13:10–11). Luke still uses the name *Saul*, but here, for the first time, he indicates that he was also called Paul, which was his cognomen (the third name or nickname) that he possessed but was not used in Luke's narrative until now.[100] Usually, scholars who mention the cognomen here use the argument that Saul's encounter with the proconsul is the beginning of his mission to the Gentiles, but here, two names are used by Luke, where the second one (Paul) seems to be additionally mentioned, probably in preparation for the next stage of his narrative, where this name (Paul) will be used exclusively from now on. In our opinion, Acts 13:8 is the place in Luke's narrative where Luke finished the narrative concerning Saul, the young convert who struggled to make his stand in the new reality; now, he is about to give the account of Paul, the prepared missionary who is ready to face new challenges. It is really a demarcation line. Until now, Luke never recorded the words of Saul after his conversion; he informed about the facts of teaching and arguing, but no record was made. Acts 13:10–11 is, in fact, the only example of Saul's arguing against those who opposed the kerygma. This arguing is bold, offensive, uncompromised, challenging (v. 10), and supported by the punishing miracle (v. 11). Does Luke, in this way, at the end of the narrative part concerning Saul, give readers a reason for Saul's problems in proclaiming the kerygma immediately after his conversion (Damascus, Jerusalem)?[101] It seem so for us, as after Acts 13:13, Lucan Paul speaks a lot with great power and wisdom that leads to desirable effects for him (the speech at Miletus—Acts 20:18–35).

5.2. The Birth of Paul (Acts 13:13–14:28)

From Acts 13:13, Luke starts a totally new narrative; although it continues the account concerning the so-called first mission journey,

---

[100] C. S. Keener, *Acts. An Exegetical Commentary*, vol. 2, 2018–2022.

[101] Bar-Jesus, the false Jewish prophet, is presented by Luke as the opponent of the kerygma proclaimed by Saul and Barnabas.

it gives a new Lucan perspective on Paul.[102] In verse 13, Luke includes four indicators of his new approach to the presentation of the apostles to Gentiles. First, Luke exclusively uses the name *Paul* from now on (instead of the name he preferred—Saul—in Acts 7:56–13:12). Second, in his narrative, he starts to place Paul before Barnabas (until the split of the mission team, with the exception of Acts 15:12), which is a meaningful change, exposing the author's priority. Third, he changes the place of the narrative from Cyprus to the regions of Pamphylia and Pisidia, which usually indicate a new part of the narrative. Fourth, he changes the mission group by indicating that John ended the mission work and returned to Jerusalem, which means that Paul left with Barnabas.[103]

After establishing a new layer of his narrative, Luke, with little interest in Paul and Barnabas's work in Perge, rushed the narrative of the mission to its apogee, which is the mission activities in Pisidian Antioch, where Luke placed the speech of Paul (not Barnabas) that is the quintessence of Paul's proclaiming the kerygma to Jews in Diasporas.[104] Verse 14 indicates also Paul's modus operandi, which is identical to that used in Cyprus; namely, enter the synagogue and interpret the scripture in way the proves that Jesus is the Messiah.[105] Most of the narrative regarding the mission in Pisidian Antioch (twenty-seven of thirty-eight total verses) takes the shape of Paul's

---

[102] More detailed sociohistorical background of Paul's first mission journey is presented in appendix 6 at the end of the book.

[103] The information concerning John takes a preparatory function, since it will testify Paul's decision, made during the conflict with Barnabas (Acts 15:37–38).

[104] This is the only speech of Lucan Paul addressed to the Diaspora Jews during his entire mission career, which Luke recorded, despite much information of Paul's teaching activities addressed to Jews living outside Palestine. For this reason, this speech should be taken as the speech representing the way Paul proclaimed the kerygma to Diaspora Jews, rather than an accurate stenographic record of the speech that was given at Pisidian Antioch. Concerning the details of the speech, see E. C. Moore, *Claiming Places*, 178–210.

[105] A primary target of Paul and Barnabas's mission activities was Diaspora Jews, which expose, in general, the modus operandi, not only this mission journey but also all Paul's journeys recorded by Luke.

speech (Acts 13:16–41, 46–47), which indicates that it is of crucial importance for this narrative.[106] The first part of the speech (Acts 13:16–22) presents Paul as a Jew who recalls the history of his nation from the beginning until the time of the second king of the Jews, David.[107] The purpose of recalling this historical account is an indication of God's promise given to King David concerning fulfilling God's will. For authorization of his words, Lucan Paul used the scripture quotation (Psalm 89:21 mixed with 1 Samuel 13:14).

The next step in Paul's speech is the presentation of the statement that Jesus, who is descending from King David, is the Savior of Israel by whom God fulfilled his promise (Acts 13:23). The second part of the speech (Acts 13:23–41) is an argument for this statement. The first argument concerns John the Baptist's testimony about Jesus (Acts 13:24–25), which takes powerful meaning, if John's reputation among Jews (also those in Diasporas—Acts 18:25) is considered.[108] The second argument concerns Paul and Barnabas as those who were sent to proclaim the salvation (in Jesus) to Jews and those who fear God (v. 26). In order to authorize his claim, Paul mentions that Jerusalem (the authorities and the people) rejected Jesus and put him to death (Acts 13:27–29). The third argument regards fact that Jesus, rejected by people, was resurrected by God, and he appeared to his disciples, who now are his witness (Acts 13:30–31). Among them are also Paul and Barnabas, who proclaim realization of the good news promised by God to the ancestors. The fourth argument, the good news, concerns Jesus's Resurrection (Acts 13:32–37), forgiveness of sins, and justification by the faith (Acts 13:38–41), which altogether makes Jesus the salvation for Israel.[109] This first

---

[106] The analysis of the speech is presented in appendix 7 at the end of the book.

[107] cf. D. G. Peterson, *The Acts of the Apostles* (Grand Rapids: Eerdmans, 2009), 387–388.

[108] W. Neil, *The Acts of the Apostles* (London: Oliphants, 1973), 158–159.

[109] F. F. Bruce, *The Book of the Acts* (Grand Rapids: Eerdmans, 1988), 260–261. Concerning the issue of Jesus's Resurrection in Paul's speech, see B. D. Crowe, *The Hope of Israel. The Resurrection of Christ in the Acts of the Apostles* (Grand Rapids: Baker Academic, 2020), 49–65.

part of the speech strongly exposes Paul as Jesus's witness to people connected to Judaism. For this reason, Lucan Paul strongly accents continuity between his teaching and the promises of old times, in order to show the good news about salvation in the name of Jesus as the fulfillment of Judaism's heritage.[110] This fulfillment is, to some extensive, challenging for Jews (Acts 13:27, 40–41).

This speech was warmly welcomed, as Paul and Barnabas were invited for the next Sabbath, and Gentiles who converted to Judaism and many Jews showed some signs of deep interest.[111] Until verse 43, Luke presents Paul's mission in Antioch as successful. However, the last part of the narrative (Acts 13:44–52) concerning the mission in this city (which includes the second part of the speech) exposes a negative attitude toward Paul and Barnabas, who in the next week were speaking to a large crowd gathered in a synagogue. The narrative suggests the presence of not only Jews, God-fearers, and proselytes but also Gentiles (v. 44). Luke suggests that Paul was speaking the same or very similar sermon (no record of this sermon), but this time, Jews (the only explicitly mentioned group) openly opposed Paul's kerygma (v. 45). Paul and Barnabas's reaction to this was to declare a change of the target of the mission, since those who naturally were the first in line to hear the good news rejected it, and because of that, the good news would be addressed to Gentiles (vv. 46–47).[112] This declaration was warmly welcomed by Gentiles (v. 48). On one hand, it brought a positive result to the mission work in this region, but on the other hand, it caused strong and consolidated opposition, with considerable power that influenced the establishment of the city to launch persecution that forced Paul and Barnabas to leave Antioch (Acts 13:50).[113]

---

[110] Wright recognizes this speech as "missional hermeneutic." N. T. Wright, "Paul and Missional Hermeneutics," in *The Apostle Paul and the Christian life*, eds. S. McKnight and J. B. Modica (Grand Rapids: Baker Academic, 2016), 179–192.

[111] E. J. Schnabel, *Acts. Exegetical Commentary on the New Testament*, 586.

[112] W. S. Kurz, *Acts of the Apostles*, 218–219.

[113] Most probably, between Paul's second visit to the synagogue (Acts 13:44) and the Jews' plot against Paul (Acts 13:50–51), there was a considerably long time,

In this short narrative, Luke indicates several important generalized statements that characterize Paul's mission to Diaspora Jews. First, although Paul's modus operandi gives Jews preference as the first to listen and answer to the kerygma, they rejected the kerygma (in general but not in particular) proclaimed by Paul, just like the Jerusalem authorities rejected Jesus. Second, the mission to the Gentiles, which is a direct consequence of Jewish rejection of the kerygma (negative aspect) and a positive answer from the Gentiles to the message (positive aspect), is here presented as successful (in very general terms).[114] Third, a strong opposition always acts directly against the person of Paul (not only by opposing his teaching). Fourth, the Jewish teacher addressing the Gentiles was not tolerated by the local Jewish establishment. These elements found in the narrative concerning the mission in Antioch (particular characteristics) also can be found in the following narratives regarding the relationship between Paul and the Diaspora Jews.

After Paul and Barnabas left Antioch in Pisidia, they headed for Iconium, another city in the region with a large Jewish Diaspora community that possessed the synagogue.[115] According to Luke (Acts 14:1) not only was Paul's modus operandi identical in Antioch (activity in the synagogue) but also the results (Jews and Gentiles started to believe in Jesus as the Messiah—Acts 14:1.3). Similar is the problem regarding opposition to Paul (Acts 14:2, 4), as well as the reason for ending the work and fleeing to the Lyconia region (Acts 14:5–7). The narrative of the mission in Iconium supports the thesis

---

which is the supposition that seems to be supported by Acts 13:48–49; cf. A. Van Ryn, *Acts of the Apostles. The Unfinished Work of Christ* (Palala Press, reprint of Loizeaux Brothers from 1961), 111–112.

[114] Holladay rightly says that Paul, before the speech at Pisidian Antioch, was teaching the Gentiles in Syrian Antioch. C. R. Holladay, *Acts. A Commentary* (Louisville, Kentucky: Westminster John Knox Press, 2016), 82. However, Luke does not record that, probably not because of lack of information to recreate the speech but rather to his distinction between the period of Saul and the period of Paul, where all good credits are given to the second period.

[115] Concerning the last part of the first mission journey, see appendix 8 at the end of the book.

that Luke's narrative concerning Paul's mission at Antioch should be taken as the general characteristic of the mission to the Diaspora Jews.

Luke puts much more attention to the narrative of the mission in Lystra, which is of crucial importance for two reasons: the first concerns the author's narrative concept (expanding of the mission to strictly a Gentile context), and the second is the presentation of the first of two reasons that make the mission to Gentiles difficult.[116] Although the mission in Lystra is not the first case of Paul's mission to Gentiles, it is the first case (in Luke's narrative) where Gentiles are not coexisting with a community of Diaspora Jews. Luke informs about Paul and Barnabas's mission in this city (Acts 14:7. 9. 20) without mentioning the existence of the synagogue and the considerably large Jewish community, although the existence of some individual Jews in this city is confirmed by Acts 16:1. In fact, Luke's narrative begins directly with the miracle performed by Paul (Acts 14:8–10), to which the crowd responded by grounding Paul and Barnabas with divine dignity and sacrifices (Zeus and Hermes—Acts 14:11–13).[117] Paul and Barnabas harshly opposed this, attempting, in the speech, to proclaim the only one God to the local Gentiles (Acts 14:14–18).[118] The attempt ended successfully (the offering in names of Paul and Barnabas was not done), but Luke mentions any positive results of the mission in this place.[119] Contrary, Luke writes that Paul's opponents, the Jews from Antioch and Iconium, came to the city, raised the local community against Paul, and led them to stone him (Acts 14:19).

This narrative contains several characteristics of Paul's mission to the Gentiles. First, the miracle, which in Judaism is a sign of

---

[116] The exposition of the second reason that makes the mission to Gentiles very difficult will be done in the narrative regarding Paul's mission in Athena, during his second mission journey.

[117] cf. C. S. Keener, *Acts. An Exegetical Commentary,* vol. 2, 2148–2149.

[118] A part of Paul's short speech will be partly used again by Lucan Paul in the speech at Areopagus, during his mission in Athena. J. A. Fitzmyer, *The Acts of the Apostles*, 532.

[119] R. A. Erric and G. M. Lamsa, *Aramaic Light on the Acts of the Apostles* (Smyrna, Georgia: The Noohra Foundation, 2007), 123–126.

God's intervention, was, in the Gentiles' religious system, a sign of divine origin.[120] In this way, Luke exposes the first great difficulty in proclaiming the kerygma, based on a monotheistic religion system to those who never had been exposed to such a system. Second, in this case, before Paul starts teaching about Jesus the Messiah, he had to teach about the only one God. This indirectly indicates the necessity of understanding the Judaic tradition in order to accept the realization of God's promises in Jesus. Third, from the very beginning of his activities, Paul had a strong and determined group of Jews opposing his teaching, not only within Jewish context but also in strict Gentile context. Fourth, there is the very first time in Luke's narrative when Paul (note a contrast to Saul) does not manage to escape from danger but faces the bitterness of persecution.

Paul and Barnabas left for Derbe, where they undertook mission work (Acts 14:20–21), but Luke leaves the reader with the laconic summary that they had won many disciples in this city.[121] Again, Luke is not interested in giving an accurate account of this period, most probably due to his narrative strategy, which prefers only these events that the most contribute to presentation of characteristic for each period of Paul's mission activities and consequently to the presentation of Luke's perspective on Paul. As Luke already presented a general characteristic of Paul's mission among Diaspora Jews, the account of the Derbe period is not necessary.

Luke treats the narrative regarding Paul and Barnabas's way back home (Acts 14:21–28) in the same manner. This narrative contains a short description of their service for already established communities, where two important points are made.[122] First, they encourage the believers to persevere in the faith during the time of persecution (Acts 14:22). The second concerns the building of the structure of

---

[120] Strelan shows several miracles known to Greek literature that were connected with divine origin of the healer. R. Strelan, *Studies in the Acts of the Apostles* (Eugene: Pickwick Publisher, 2020), 113–114.

[121] See C. S. Keener, *Acts. An Exegetical Commentary,* vol. 2, 2176–2177.

[122] W. Neil, *The Acts of the Apostles*, 158–159.

local communities by establishing the elders (Acts 14:23).[123] This is the first summary of Paul's concerns for the communities that was established, which will find its full exposure in Paul's speech to the elders at Miletus (Acts 20:17–35). Because Barnabas and Paul were sent by the Antioch church, after their return to Antioch, they gave a positive report that was well received by the community (Acts 14:27–28).

Conclusion

Luke's narrative regarding the mission of the Antioch community (called the first mission journey of Paul) presents Saul/Paul as one of two members of the local community established for mission work among Diaspora Jews. Until the mission exclusively concerned the Diaspora Jews, Luke still used the name Saul (mission on Cyprus), but as soon as Saul and Barnabas encountered the Gentiles, Luke started to use the name Paul.

In the narrative concerning the mission outside Cyprus, Luke establishes Paul as the main hero (dominant protagonist), who still follows the modus operandi of the mission work but it forced, more and more, into encounters with Gentiles, due to the rejection of his kerygma by Diaspora Jews, who made a great effort to prevent his mission activities among Diaspora Jews. Doing this, Luke suggests that Paul's mission to the Gentiles (although in accordance with Jesus's words to Ananias, about which Saul still does not know, according to Luke's narrative) was not caused by his deliberate decision, based on knowledge about Jesus's designation for him; it was a chain of natural events that happened in specific socioreligious contexts, which slowly but consequently involved him in working with Gentiles, rather than with Diaspora Jews. After Luke exposed

---

[123] The information regarding establishing of the elders of the local communities is interpreted by Conzelmann as influenced by church structure, characteristic of post-Pauline times, rather than a real stat of things during the first mission journey. H. Conzelmann, *Acts of the Apostles*, 112.

that Saul, after his conversion, did not find himself well in the context of Palestinian Judaism, he showed that the mission to the Diaspora Jews was not warmly welcomed by them. For Luke, all this is a way in which Jesus actualizes his plan toward Saul, the narrative layer that will be presented in full account concerning the second mission journey.

6. Paul in the Middle of the Conflict (Acts 15:1–35)

The account concerning the so-called Jerusalem Council is the last one where Paul acts based on the mandate of the Antioch community (Acts 15:3). The problem that led to the council in Jerusalem started in the Antioch community but was initiated by the believers from the Jerusalem community, who, on their own authority (Acts 15:24), attempted to impose the Jewish Gentile community's in Antioch the necessity for circumcision of Gentile Christians, bases on theological argument (salvation; Acts 15:2).[124] After Luke, in Acts 10–11, approaches the problem of acceptance of Gentiles among Jewish Christians with a clearly indicated solution, raising the problem again, there seems to be unnecessary repetition.[125] However,

---

[124] Donaldson thinks that some Jews accepted the possibility that righteous Gentiles could be saved even without conversion to Judaism. T. L. Donaldson, *Paul and the Gentiles. Remapping the Apostle's Convictional World* (Minneapolis: Fortress Press, 1997).

[125] It is worthy to indicate that in Luke's Acts, Peter plays a considerably important role in process of incorporating Gentiles within Jewish Christian communities. This process began with Peter's very first speech at Pentecost, which is given in Jerusalem to Jews from many different counties but also to proselytes (Gentiles who accepted Judaism), showing that Peter's kerygma is addressed not exclusively to Jews but also to those Gentiles who accepted Judaism or who expressed interest in Judaism, and that should be recognized as the first step in approaching Gentiles in a direct way by the Christian movement. Padilla insists that the speech is addressed strictly to Jews, but he recognizes the possibility of the prefiguring interpretation of the speech, also referred to as salvation of Gentiles. O. Padilla, *The Acts of the Apostles. Interpretation, History and Theology* (Downers Grove: IVP Academic, 2016), 161.

the problem here concerns the two connected communities, where one (Jerusalem) is dominated and the second is subordinated. In this context, unauthorized members of the Jerusalem community represented the believers who strongly related salvation in Jesus exclusively within a Judaism event, which created the grounds for their strong conviction that Gentile Christian conversion to Judaism was necessary in order to be saved.[126]

Surprisingly, Luke does not present the opinion of their opponents—namely, Paul and Barnabas, which can be deduced, since they were opposed to the opinion of the brothers from Jerusalem, but details and a way of argumentation stay mysterious.[127] Instead, the author indicates that the issue became a topic of strong and unsolved controversies, where the only possible solution to the problem was to subordinate to the decision of the apostles and the elders of Jerusalem communities (Acts 15:2). Luke, shortly but precisely, exposes the problem between Christians with a Palestinian Judaism background and Christians with a Diaspora Judaism background, concerning the way of salvation for Gentiles.[128] Paul and Barnabas (although not exclusively) are again representing the Antioch community (Acts 11:30; 12:25; 13:1–3; 15:2), this time regarding a very crucial point that could change the fate of the mission to the Gentiles and the *par excellence* fate of the messianic movement itself. The reason for Paul and Barnabas's opposition to claiming the believers from Jerusalem, as well as their appointment as the representatives of the Antioch community before the apostles, was their mission experiences, probably among many other reasons.[129] At least, Luke's narrative

[126] In a negative way, they thought that outside Judaism, there was not salvation for Gentiles, despite their faith in Jesus as the Messiah.

[127] Connecting the issue of circumcision with theological theme of salvation may suggest Luke's knowledge of Paul's letters. See D. B. Capes, R. Reeves, and E. R. Richards, *Rediscovering Paul. An Introduction to His World, Letters, and Theology* (Downers Grove: InterVarsity Press, 2017), 65.

[128] Luke hardly indicates the more complex problem, which is of crucial importance for Paul, as his letter attests it (Rom.; Gal.).

[129] Luke hardly mentions the opposition to Paul and Barnabas in Jerusalem (Acts 15:5) and their testimony regarding the mission among the Gentiles (Acts 15:12).

structure strongly suggests it, since the author named only the members of the Antioch community team for the mission in Cyprus, and at the same time, he hardly mentions others who accompanied them (Acts 15:2).

Luke narrative regarding the council is mostly built on three speeches (Acts 15:7–11, Peter's speech; Acts 15:13–21, James's speech; and Acts 15:23–29, the decree of the Jerusalem Council), with little narrative section.[130] Paul and Barnabas gave no speeches (recorded by Luke in Acts) during the council, but they gave a testimony about their positive mission experiences with Gentiles (Acts 15:12). It is not accidental that Luke placed this information between the speeches of Peter and James.[131] When Peter puts an end to the controversy regarding salvation (Acts 15:11) and James puts an end to the discussion regarding the necessity of circumcision (Acts 15:19), Paul and Barnabas give a report of the actual state of things, with a strong accent put on "signs and wonders" (Acts 13:11; 14:3. 8–10), which are arguments that God's power works among Gentiles.[132] The report gives these two speeches (both arguing on an academic level) the force of critical argument, which is attested by mission experiences.[133] In the entire narrative (Acts 15:1–35), Paul and Barnabas are mentioned six times—four times as "Paul and Barnabas" (used in the narrative that is Luke's perspective-

---

S. G. Wilson, *The Gentiles and the Gentile Mission in Luke-Acts* (Cambridge: Cambridge University Press, 1973), 185.

130 The narrative regarding the Jerusalem Council (Acts 15:4–29) is mostly built on the three speeches, and for this reason, Paul and Barnabas's testimony (Acts 15:12) is marginalized. However, if the speeches are omitted, the testimony would be the center of the remanded narrative.

131 Peter, in his speech, puts considerable attention on the gift of the Holy Spirit as the sign of the faith, and James, in his speech, attests to the accuracy of Peter's experience with the teaching of the scripture. J. C. O'Neil, "The Connection between Baptism and the Gift of the Spirit in Acts," *JSNT* 63 (1996), 93–94.

132 E. J. Schnabel, *Acts. Exegetical Commentary on the New Testament*, 636–637; D. Marguerat, *The First Christian History. Writing the Acts of the Apostles* (Cambridge: Cambridge University Press, 2002), 84.

133 J. A. Fitzmyer, *The Acts of the Apostles*, 549.

oriented; Acts 15:2, 22, 35) and two times as "Barnabas and Paul" (used in the narrative that is the Jerusalem Council-oriented; Acts 15:12, 25).[134] Of very special importance is verse 25, which is a part of the decree, where Barnabas and Paul are mentioned as "our dear friends" (Acts 15:25 NIV), which is the phrase that recognized the mission authority of Barnabas and Paul. It is placed in the official documents of "the mother community," addressed directly to the Antioch community (particular aspect), but indirectly serving as kind of an official teaching concerning Gentiles (general aspect; Acts 16:4), given with the strongest of possible recommendations.

Conclusion

Luke's narrative clearly indicates Paul's involvement and his importance in events that led to the council in Jerusalem (Acts 15:1–4). Paul, together with Barnabas, is presented as the main opponent and the leader in discussion with Jews from Jerusalem, who did not seek the compromise for saving the peace in the community but who stood for the truth they believed in, even if it led to open conflict that could not be easy solved. Less clear is Luke's presentation of Paul's involvement during the council. First, according to Luke, Paul delivers no speech during the council, even though he was the one who strongly opposed the circumcision of Gentiles and imposing the Mosaic Law upon them. Second, his appearance is limited to an account of his experiences regarding the mission among Gentiles, which would support the statement made by Peter.[135] However, even in this case, he does not act as individual (Barnabas and Paul). Third, in the narrative concerning the council (Acts 15:5–29), Luke mentions Paul's name twice but always after Barnabas's name (Acts 15:12, 25).

[134] In narrative regarding the Jerusalem Council, the name of Barnabas is again mentioned before the name of Paul. This Lucan approach may indicate Barnabas's position in the Jerusalem community. See C. S. Keener, *Acts. An Exegetical Commentary,* vol. 3, 2240.

[135] Possibly Paul and Barnabas were actively involved in the discussion mentioned in Acts 15:7. However, Luke, for some reason, does not mention it.

Since Acts 13:13 Luke usually placed Paul's name before Barnabas's name.[136] Fourth, none of Paul's thoughts concerning circumcision or the Law is presented in the narrative of Acts 15, 5–29 in the way that Paul presents them in his letters. All these show that Luke presents only two general items of information concerning Paul's involvement on the council. The first one concerns his presence at the council, which, most probably, was attested by the Antioch sources, and the second concerns his small contribution to the council and even less to the final decree of the council. Certainly, Luke does not present Paul as one of the main heroes of his narrative concerning the council. We can point out a possible reason for Luke's approach to this issue. First, he concisely emphasized the rule of Peter and James in order to give the decree a kind of authoritative legacy, which Paul uses during his mission journey (Acts 16:4). In this way, Luke makes Paul and his mission activities beneficent of the decree.[137] Second, Luke, in Acts, constantly indicates some difficulties in the relationship between Paul and the community in Jerusalem, to which the narrative regarding council seems to be no exception (Acts 9:26–30; 21:17–26). Third, in the team of Paul and Barnabas, Paul was less preferable because of Barnabas's relationship with the Jerusalem church and the apostles (Acts 4:36; 11:22–24). However, even Barnabas is not much exposed in Luke's narrative in Acts 15. Concerning Acts 15 in regard to presentation of Paul, Luke wrote less than a minimum about him, which makes the evaluation of Paul's contribution to the council more dependent on the general evaluation of Paul, based on the whole narrative of Acts 13–28 and his own letters, than on Acts 15 itself. The decree mentions Paul, together with Barnabas and two official delegates of the Jerusalem Council (Judas and Silas), as one of four to whom the delivery of the decree to Antioch, Syria, and Cilicia was entrusted. Until now, all that was only the internal matter of the Antioch community with regard to Paul, since the council was recognized by the authorities of the Jerusalem community. That

[136] C. S. Keener, *Acts. An Exegetical Commentary*, vol. 3, 2240.

[137] T. R. Schreiner, *Acts and Paul's Letters* (Grand Rapids: Baker Academic, 2019), 29–32.

concerned his teaching and mission prerogative.[138] This indirect information takes significant meaning in context of the following narrative of Acts, where Paul, after conflict with Barnabas, starts his independent mission activities, which, in the end, earns him the name of apostle to the Gentiles. The kerygma proclaimed by Paul and his apostolic authority in the end was recognized by authorities of the Jerusalem community. According to Luke's somehow laconic narrative, it occurred during the Jerusalem Council.

We share an opinion that it was the main aim of Luke's narrative concerning Paul's involvement in the council.[139] According to Luke, Paul did not contribute much to the final decree of the council, but the council, in the decree, indirectly recognized Paul (together with Barnabas) and his teaching, which gave Paul the greatest beneficence of the council, if we consider the following narrative of Acts.

7. Paul in Conflict with His Mentor (Acts 15:36–41)

After returning to Antioch, Paul and Barnabas worked together in Antioch for a considerable period, as did many other brothers in the faith (Acts 15:35–36). In Acts 15:36, Luke informs that Paul proposed to Barnabas to undertake another journey to places they had visited.[140] The official reason for that was Paul's caring for established communities, which, according to Luke's narrative (Acts 13:1–14:28), would apply to places in Pisidia, Pamphylia, and Lycaonia, as there was information of converts and communities in these places.[141] This interpretation excludes Cyprus, as in Acts 13:1–12, there is not even

[138] Concerning Paul's teaching and his prerogative, the account of Acts 15:25 (the secondary source) agrees with that account of Galatians 2:6–9 (the primary source).

[139] The decree did not definitively put an end to the controversy within Christian communities regarding the subjects, but it undoubtedly sufficiently calmed down the temporary situation in the Antioch community.

[140] According to Lucan narrative, the proposal was Paul's private initiative, which has no connection with the mission strategy of the Antioch community.

[141] This is the second time that Luke indicates Paul's ongoing responsible attitude toward the communities he established.

a single mention of establishing a community during the mission in the region. Even more, in verse 36, Luke informs that Barnabas was willed to undertake the journey (deduced meaning of v. 36) and he wanted to take John (called Mark) with them (direct meaning of v. 36). Paul did not agree to Barnabas's proposal, and Luke gives the reason for his refusal, which is that Mark left them in Pamphylia and did not work with them in the regions mentioned above (v. 38). In this way, Luke very strongly suggests that Paul thought about visiting Pisidia, Pamphylia, and Lycaonia, rather than about Cyprus. They did not find a compromise in the polarized differences of opinion, which naturally led to only acceptable solution for both sides: separation and working independently (v. 39).[142] That means the end of the Barnabas and Paul team and Paul's departure from his mentor, but it does not mean enmity between the master (Barnabas) and his apprentice (Saul) who had grown to stature of independent missionary (Paul).[143]

In verse 40, Luke presents the results of this split, which turn out not to be a disaster (the end of the mission activities) but a beginning of two mission groups, where Barnabas and Mark worked in Cyprus, and Paul and his new coworker, Silas, went on the road, first to the regions of Pamphylia and Pisidia.[144] This very general indication of Paul's mission aim corresponds well with Luke's narrative concerning so-called the second mission journey, which shows Paul as the man searching for new places to proclaim kerygma, rather than a man going in an already determined direction (Acts 16:6–10).[145] Indicating the general direction of Paul's mission (northwest), Luke named Syria and Cilicia as regions where the Christian communities existed, which partly may indicate the mission activities of the Antioch

[142] Analyses regarding Acts 15:36–41 are presented in appendix 9 at the end of the book.

[143] Paul does not depart from the Antioch community, and his ongoing relationship with the community in Antioch is attested in Acts 18:22–23.

[144] Acts 15:40 shows only general information without specified direction.

[145] Paul's mission attitude during the second mission journey (searching for the place to proclaim the kerygma) is totally different from the mission attitude during the third mission, during which the activities in one region are preferred. However, the differences in attitudes can be only the issue of Luke's narrative strategy.

community (Syria) and partly Saul's supposed activities during his so-called "unknown years in Tarsus" (Cilicia).

Conclusion

The short but very informative narration (Acts 15:36–41) ends the part of Acts that regards Paul's times in Antioch, where he, at Barnabas's feet, grew to be a man fully prepared for a mission. In order to show his quality, he must depart from his mentor—it is usually only a matter of time before a pupil starts to contest his teacher. On the other hand, this narrative prepares a new environment for the next progressive step in Luke's presentation of Paul. Considering these two purposes of Luke's narrative, we should focus less on the conflict itself, as Mark will work with Paul later again (Phil. 24; Col. 4:10; cf. 2 Tim. 4:11), and Paul positively evaluates the work of Barnabas (1 Cor. 9:6).

2

PAUL, ACCORDING TO LUKE'S NARRATIVE

In the narrative of Acts concerning the activities of the Antioch community, Luke, for the most part, presents it as a time of transformation of Saul, the former persecutor, into Paul, the witness of Jesus, the resurrected Messiah. The main focus is on his gradual separation from Palestinian Judaism and, at the same time, his development in becoming a missionary to the Diaspora Jews, which is presented in a chain of events leading to the realization of Jesus's plan for Saul (Acts 9:15–16), which will be actualized when his mission also embraces the Gentiles. Luke's narrative, after preparing the necessary background—the encounter with Gentiles in Pisidia; the decree of the Jerusalem Council; the separation from Barnabas—when presenting the account regarding Paul's activities as the apostle to the Gentiles, is schematic and generalized, with strong theological influence on the interpretation of the facts during this most intense and troubled period of Paul's life.

1. Searching for Direction (Acts 16:1–18:22)

1.1. In Lycaonia (Acts 16:1–5)

After separating from Barnabas, Paul, together with Silas, launched his own mission to places in Lycaonia where the Christian communities had been established during the last stage of the first mission journey (Acts 16:1–5).[146] Concerning the return visit to Derbe and Lystra, Luke omitted all reference to mission activity, reducing the account to the circumstances surrounding the acceptance of Timothy from Lystra as Paul's second coworker (Acts 16:1–3).[147] Before Timothy joined Paul and Silas, he was circumcised by Paul, since his father was Greek, and his mother was Jewish Christian, but Timothy had not been circumcised.[148] In the narrative concerning the Jerusalem Council, Luke presents the apostles' conviction that circumcision is not a requirement for Gentiles to be saved or to join the Christian movement, but now he gives the practical (not dogmatic) reason for Paul's action (Acts 15:3).[149] In this way, Luke shows Paul's pragmatic attitude toward a very sensitive issue. In a dogmatic context relating to the salvation of the Gentiles, Paul did not accept that circumcision was necessary, but in this particular socioreligious context, in which Timothy was the uncircumcised son of a Jewish mother, Paul did not object to the circumcision.[150]

Luke summarizes this part of the second mission journey of Paul with two general statements that apply to the whole mission activity of Paul in this region: the first (Acts 16:4) regards the conditions for acceptance of Gentile Christians among the Jewish Christians, as decreed by the Jerusalem Council; the second concerns the positive

[146] Silas is mentioned as the official delegate of the Jerusalem community, sent together with Judas, called Barabbas, to Antioch, in order to confirm the decision made by the council and described in the decree (Acts 15:22, 27). Luke presents Silas and Judas as prophets who undertook some activities in Antioch (Acts 15:32) before they returned to Jerusalem (Acts 15:33). Although Luke writes nothing about Silas's return to Antioch, this must have occurred, since Acts 15:40 presupposes Silas's presence in the city. H. Conzelmann, *Acts of the Apostles*, 72–73.

[147] W. Neil, *The Acts of the Apostles*, 177.

[148] L. T. Johnson, *The Acts of the Apostles*, 283–284.

[149] Concerning the question of Paul's attitude toward circumcision, see appendix 1 at the end of the book.

[150] On Paul's attitude toward circumcision in a dogmatic context, see also appendix 2 at the end of the book.

evaluation of their work among the already established communities. This takes the shape of a general summary that is typical in Acts 16:5.

1.2. In Asia Minor (Acts 16:6–10)

The narrative concerning the second stage of this mission journey is another example of Luke's approach to the presentation of facts regarding Paul and his mission. In five verses (Acts 16:6–10), Luke presents Paul and his companions' attempt at mission activity in the northwest part of modern Turkey. This must have taken at least a few months. After visiting Lycaonia and probably Pisidia, the three missionaries headed for the region of Phrygia and Galatia in order to proclaim the kerygma (v. 6). However, Luke writes that the Holy Spirit himself prevented them from doing that, a statement that would be very surprising, were we to take it literally. Even more surprising is the assertion that the Spirit of Jesus prevented the missionaries also from proclaiming the kerygma in the region of Mysia and Bithynia (v. 7).[151] In fact, they were prohibited from proclaiming the Word in the whole northwestern part of present-day Turkey. However, if we consider that Luke, in verses 6 and 7, uses the phrase "Paul and his companions traveled throughout" (Acts 16:6 NIV), which is also used in Acts 8:4 and Acts 13:6 in direct connection with proclaiming the kerygma, we can suppose that in Acts 16:6–7, this word also indicates the mission activity and not merely their passing though the regions. In this case, Acts 16:6–7 points to a lack of results in the mission work, rather than a lack of any attempt to proclaim the kerygma.[152]

Luke's message is that the mission team, without any significant success, went through the northwest regions and finally reached the

[151] The phrases "the Holy Spirit" (v. 6) and "Spirit of Jesus" (v. 7) are synonyms in referring to the Holy Spirit. The alternative version used in verse 7 makes a link to Acts 9:15–16, where Jesus's control over the actions of Saul/Paul is indicated. D. G. Peterson, *The Acts of the Apostles*, 454–455.

[152] How far it reflects the reality and to what extent this account is influenced by Luke's narrative concept (according to which mission in Asia Minor is almost exclusively reserved to the narrative regarding the third mission journey) is impossible to determine.

harbor city of Troas (v. 8).[153] Luke's narrative rushes to tell the story about the missions in Macedonia and Achaia, which, according to his testimony, is the result of Paul's vision in Troas, which forced him to enter Europe, since he took it as a sign from God (vv. 10–11).[154] This account has one more turning point, in that the narration changes from using the third-person-plural pronoun to using the first-person plural (Acts 16:10). From here on, this will be the case whenever Luke accompanies Paul.[155] Luke's narrative on these occasions becomes more detailed, more personal, and more emotionally involved.

Conclusion

The accounts concerning Paul's mission in the region of Lycaonia (Acts 16:1–5) and in Asia Minor (Acts 16:6–10) contain two important messages addressed to the reader regarding Paul's presentation by Luke. The first (Acts 16:4) concerns the authorization of Paul's mission and his teaching that was given in the decree of the Jerusalem Council. At the same time, it shows that Paul was of the same mind as the apostles and the Jerusalem church regarding the question of Gentile Christians. The second concerns the fact that Paul's mission from the beginning is guided by the Holy Spirit (Acts 16:6–7); that means that it is under the control of divine power, rather than being

[153] In the narrative concerning the beginning of the third mission journey, Luke mentions that Paul, on the way to Ephesus (Acts 19:1), visited the regions of Galatia and Phrygia, strengthening all the disciples. The fact that Luke speaks about disciples rather than about communities or churches (as in Acts 16:5) may support the interpretation we offer; cf. B. Witherington III, *The Acts of the Apostles*, 477–478.

[154] D. G. Peterson, *The Acts of the Apostles*, 456–457.

[155] Acts contains four so-called "we" sections: Acts 16:10–17; Acts 20:5–15; Acts 21:1–18; Acts 27:1–28:16. It is striking that all of them are connected to narratives regarding Paul's voyages by sea (Acts 20:5–12; 21:7–18). For more information regarding the "we" section, cf. B. Witherington III, *The Acts of the Apostles*, 480–486. The "we" sections indicate that the author of Acts was together with Paul and his companions during the sea voyages, which seems to support the conviction (based on church tradition) that Luke was a ship's doctor.

merely part of Paul's clear mission strategy. These two points are fundamental in understanding Paul's activity among the Gentiles, as it is recorded by Luke.

1.3. In Philippi (Acts 16:11–40)

Before Luke recounts Paul's imprisonment in Philippi, which is the central aim of the account of the mission there, he first offers some necessary background concerning the city and Paul's encounter with the local community of Jews. Philippi was a Roman colony (*Colonia Augusta Iulia Philippensis*), the leading city (but not the main city) of the province of Macedonia, lying on the *Via Egnatia* (Acts 16:12), which derived its prestige from being in a strategic position to control the gold mines nearby.[156] The inhabitants were mainly veteran soldiers and Romans. It is probable that some Jews lived in the city, but their number was not large enough to afford them a synagogue. They gathered for the Sabbath prayers outside the city near the River Gangites, two kilometers from the city.[157] This knowledge, together with Luke's information about the women whom Paul met at the place of prayer (Acts 16:13) and the accusation against Paul (Acts 16:20–21), allows us to suppose that the Jewish minority did not enjoy a good reputation among the citizens. Although Paul was following his usual modus operandi, any other mission activity addressed to Jews (with the exception of his talking with women) is not mentioned.

Luke focuses on the conversion of Lydia, a God-fearer, a merchant dealing in purple cloth from the city of Thyatira, which was famous as a center for the industry of purple dye. She was probably a woman with a high social standing and enjoyed importance in the local community, as is attested by two hints given by Luke. First, Luke mentions her by name and not by her cognomen—in Greco-Roman

---

[156] C. S. Keener, *Acts. An Exegetical Commentary,* vol. 3, 2380–2383; E. J. Schnabel, *Exegetical Commentary on the New Testament, Acts*, 678–679.

[157] Conzelmann found this information to be strange. H. Conzelmann, *Acts of the Apostles*, 130.

society, only well-known women were addressed by name in public.[158] Second, Lydia was involved in the purple-cloth trade (Acts 16:14) and may even have managed her own business. If that is so, it would mean she had family links with the imperial household, since the purple-cloth trade was an imperial monopoly. It is hardly possible that she was a patrician; more likely, she was a freedwoman in the service of the emperor.[159] Consequently, she was a woman of status also in the Philippi community, as Philippi honored Thyatira's purple dyers as citizens of the city.[160] According to Luke, she became not only the first in the city to become a convert to believe in Jesus but also the first whose entire household became a Christian community (Acts 16:14–15).[161] As a result, her house became the headquarters for Paul and his companions during the mission in Philippi (Acts 16:15, 40).

In this narrative, two points are of crucial importance. First, the first convert in Philippi is a Gentile woman, a God-fearer, who has learned Judaism's concept of monotheism (Acts 16:14). Second, her conversion caused the conversion of her entire household (Acts 16:15).[162] After this necessary introduction (Acts 16:11–15), Luke's narrative advances to the main theme of the account regarding the mission in Philippi, which concerns Paul's imprisonment. The reason for Paul's troubles in Philippi was an exorcism of a maidservant who was considered to have a gift of divination, and this was used by her owners for profit (Acts 16, 16).[163] Paul's exorcism was provoked by her behavior, as she declared, "These men are servants of the Most

158 B. Witherington III, *The Acts of the Apostles*, 491–492.

159 cf. C. S. Keener, *Acts. An Exegetical Commentary*, vol. 3, 2394.

160 C. S. Keener, *Acts. An Exegetical Commentary*, vol. 3, 2396.

161 Surprisingly, her name is not mention in Paul's letter to the Philippians. H. Conzelmann, *Acts of the Apostles*, 130.

162 This is a pattern that will be used again in the narrative concerning conversion of the jailer (Acts 16:29–34).

163 Although the owners present the accusation against Paul and Silas in strictly political terms, their real purpose was to receive compensation from Paul and Silas for their loss. C. S. Keener, *Acts. An Exegetical Commentary*, vol. 3, 2468. It is the first case in Acts where the negative impact of Paul's activity on economic elements of society is shown.

High God, who are telling you the way to be saved" (Acts 16:17 NIV), a message that deeply annoyed Paul due to the ambivalent meaning of the prophecy (Acts 16:18).[164] Although the prophecy might be acceptable to Jews and even Christians, in a non-Jewish context, such as the society of Philippi, the Roman colony, the citizens understood in a way that reflected their polytheistic thought. When she referred to the *Most High God*, most people thought this was a reference to Zeus or some other gods but certainly not to the only God, as understood by Jews. When she mentioned *the way to be saved*, they understood this to refer to any of a number ways of salvation but certainly not about salvation in the name of Jesus.

This unwanted introduction by the servant worked against Paul's mission. After the exorcism, when she lost her power to prophesy, her owners seized Paul and Silas and dragged them into the agora (the gathering place), where they accused Paul of a political crime (Acts 16:19–20).[165] The accusation was of committing the serious offense of disturbing the peace in the city. The way in which the accusation was made shows a mixture of anti-Judaism and local populist patriotism (Acts 16:20–21).[166] Since the conversion of Roman citizens to Judaism was a punishable act, according to Cicero,[167] Paul's mission activity in the city could be considered to be Jewish agitation, which offended the socioreligious status quo of Philippi. In this context, Luke's information that Paul and Silas were beaten (Acts 16:22–23) without any trial takes a special significance, since it shows that anti-Jewish prejudice was part of the reason for the crowd's harsh action, but it also shows another problem in proclaiming the kerygma to Gentiles; namely, the Gentiles' ignorance

[164] The maidservant served as a fortune teller (Acts 16:16–17). She was possessed by πνεῦμα πύθωνα—the Python Spirit, (Apollo, the Pythian deity; Acts 16:16). Her paranormal skills would interfere with the kerygma proclaimed by Paul and his coworkers due to different semantic content of similar terms used by both sides.

[165] Note that the same pattern (socioeconomical reason for persecution) will be used by Luke in the narrative concerning the disturbance in Ephesus at the end of Paul's third mission journey (Acts 19:21–40).

[166] Note the specifically anti-Jewish argument.

[167] H. Conzelmann, *Acts of the Apostles*, 132.

regarding Judaism that makes them incapable of distinguishing between the many different ways within Judaism. The whole event ends with Paul and Silas being imprisoned (Acts 16:23–24), but at the same time, this is the beginning of the next stage of the narrative regarding another mission success for Paul in this city (Acts 16:25–34).

Luke's narrative suggests that on the first night that Paul and Silas spent in prison, an earthquake occurred, which led to several events that are narrated in a very vivid way and for a precisely determined purpose. The first information concerns the attitude of Paul and his companion. Although they had been severely beaten, they prayed and sang hymns, something that attracted the attention of the other prisoners, as the condition of the two hardly justified an attitude of gratitude (Acts 16:25). In this way, Luke puts Paul at the center of everyone's attention, making him the main character of the narrative. Paul's prayer was unrelated to the earthquake, which was, according to Luke, a natural event that destroyed the prison and probably many other buildings in the city, although we are not informed about destruction in the city.[168] The earthquake caused not only the destruction of the prison, but it also loosened the chains of all the prisoners, who, surprisingly, did not take advantage of the situation (Acts 16:27–28).[169] The jailer naturally expected the

[168] In Hellenistic religion, earthquakes were considered to be divine signs. L.T. Johnson, *The Acts of the Apostles*, 300. Luke tries to avoid the connection between the earthquake and theophany by keeping the narrative on the natural and rational level, which is a very different approach from that in his narrative concerning Peter's imprisonment (Acts 12:1–19). Here, in Paul's case, divine assistance is exercised by nature.

[169] The chains could have been loosened when the walls of the prison were destroyed, and the lack of any attempt by the prisoners to run away could be explained by the shock caused by the earthquake or by the fact that they were in the dark innermost part of the prison (Acts 14:24, 29). E. J. Schnabel, *Exegetical Commentary on the New Testament, Acts*, 689. In Acts 16:26, Luke writes that the chains of all the prisoners were broken, but he does not directly indicate that this also applied to Paul and Silas, whose legs were fettered in the stocks. Luke writes in Acts 16:24 that the legs of Paul and Silas were put in stocks (πόδας ἠσφαλίσατο αὐτῶν εἰς τὸ ξύλον); then, in Acts 16:26, he writes that the chains were unfastened (τὰ δεσμὰ ἀνέθη), which may suggest that the reason for the imprisonment of Paul

prisoners to escape, and under the pressure of the situation, he was ready to take responsibility for failing his duties and intended to commit suicide (Acts 16:27).[170] Paul's words saved his life (Acts 16:8), which is the issue that starts the process leading to the jailer's conversion.

At this point Luke's narrative narrows and concentrates exclusively on the conversion of the jailer's household by Paul (Acts 16:29–34). The first reaction comes from the jailer: "The jailer called for lights, rushed in and fell trembling before Paul and Silas" (Acts 16:29 NIV). The reason for the jailer's trembling is clear, but the fact that he fell down before the Jewish teachers requires some explanation. Luke, however, gives no explanation, nor can it be deduced from the context, leaving us to speculate on the significance of this. Paul does not oppose the jailer's action, and the jailer says nothing to him (Acts 16:29). The jailer, who, moments earlier, was ready to take his own life because he thought that the prisoners had escaped, now takes two of them outside the prison, where Paul showed him the way by which he can be saved (Acts 16:30–31).[171]

Paul also proclaimed the kerygma to him and his household (Acts 16:32), which led them to become Christians (Acts 16:33). The jailer, for his part, provided for them in his own house; he washed their wounds, and he gave them food (Acts 16:33–34). According to Luke's narrative, all this happened for one night. The narrative of Acts 16:25–34 seems to be a summary of a much longer story, taken from different sources, which Luke used to create another general

---

and Silas differed from that of the other prisoners, who were only put in chains. This may help to explain the decision of the praetors, as given in Acts 16:35.

170 Luke does not give any reason for the prisoners' lack of reaction, but he describes the jailer's conduct as honest. As a Roman soldier who failed in his duty, he wanted to commit suicide (Acts 16:27). The jailer was convinced that he had failed in his duty, which meant that as a soldier in charge of the prisoners, he was expected to kill them to prevent their escape. For a similar case, see the narrative in Acts 27:42–43.

171 Although the jailer's question is ambiguous, Lucan Paul makes it clear that the jailer's question has a soteriological implication (compare Acts 2:37). J. F. Fitzmyer, *The Acts of the Apostles*, 589.

statement concerning Paul's mission to the Gentiles. This statement concerns two interacting events: the first concerns the imprisonment of Paul and Silas, which is presented in a strictly Gentile context, in which no Jews are involved; the second relates to the fact that during this imprisonment, Paul brought to the faith the entire family of a Gentile (who was probably also a Roman veteran).

The first event will have its continuation in the following narrative (Acts 16:35–40); in fact, the second event (Acts 16:25–34) seems to interrupt the general description of the imprisonment of Paul and Silas in Philippi (Acts 16:16–24, 35–40) by adding particulars concerning the conversion of the jailer (Acts 16:25–34).[172] For this reason, the Acts 16:25–34 must have some special function in Luke's narrative. Considering that half of the narrative concerning Paul is focused on his imprisonment (Acts 21:27–28:31) and ends with Paul still in prison, we can suppose that Acts 16:25–34 serves as an indicator of Paul's mission activity during his imprisonment. This supposition is supported by the narrative itself concerning his imprisonment (Acts 21–28), but in particular by the contents of the speeches that are considerably multiplied in this part of Acts.[173] The first general conclusion about the narrative concerning Paul's imprisonment in Philippi is that even during his imprisonment, he successfully proclaimed the kerygma. The second conclusion concerns the fact that for the first time, the topic of Paul's imprisonment is contained in the narrative layer of Luke's perspective on Paul.

The third part of the narrative concerning Paul's imprisonment in Philippi concerns his release from prison (Acts 16:35–40). The day after the arrest, the town magistrates decided to release Paul and Silas (v. 35), which indirectly indicates that the arrest had a

---

[172] J. B. Green, *Luke as Narrative Theologian* (Tübingen: Mohr Siebeck, 2020).

[173] This part of the narrative (Acts 21:27–28:31) contains the following speeches: during the imprisonment in Jerusalem (Acts 22:3–21; 23:1, 6; 23:26–30), during the imprisonment in Caesarea at the time of the procurator Felix (Acts 24:2–8; 24:10–21; 24:22), during the imprisonment at the time of the procurator Festus (Acts 25:8–11; 25:13, 21; 25:24–27; 26:2–29), during the voyage to Rome (Acts 27:10; 27:24; 27:33–34), and finally, in Rome (Acts 28:17–20; 28:21–22; 28:25–28).

strictly preventive character and the magistrates did not accept the claim of the slave girl's owners.[174] Paul and Silas heard the news of their release from the jailer (probably the same man who would be converted), instructed by a messenger sent by the magistrates (v. 36).[175] It stated that before morning, they had to be returned to the prison. Rather surprisingly, although Paul did not complain about the decision itself, he strongly opposed the manner in which the magistrates attempted to resolve the issue. After concluding that they did not recognize the accusation of the slave girl's owners—this making the punishment received by Paul to be unjust—Paul appealed to Roman law (v. 37), based on the fact that both Paul and Silas possessed Roman citizenship.[176]

In general, without a trial and official sentence, the beating of a

---

[174] We can only guess at the reason for the magistrates' decision, and scholars offer different explanations. For example, when Witherington III points to weakness of the *meritum* to make the case a subject for trial (B. Witherington III, *The Acts of the Apostles*, 499), Keener points to a practical aspect; namely, that the prison was damaged by the earthquake, and the authorities were forced to release those in prison for less serious crimes (C. S. Keener, *Acts. An Exegetical Commentary*, vol. 3, 2515).

[175] The jailer used a greeting characteristic among Jews and Christian—*go in peace*. C. S. Keener, *Acts. An Exegetical Commentary*, vol. 3, 2516.

[176] According to the narrative, this is the first time that Paul used the argument of his possessing Roman citizenship. H. Conzelmann, *Acts of the Apostles*, 133. Acts 16:37–38 suggests that not only Paul but also Silas was able to claim Roman citizenship, which is shown by the use of the first-person plural of the verb. However, Silas's Roman citizenship is not attested in other references in the New Testament. J. A. Fitzmyer, *The Acts of the Apostles*, 590. Keener, in his commentary, presents a very accurate analysis of the topic of Paul's Roman citizenship (C. S. Keener, *Acts. An Exegetical Commentary*, vol. 3, 2517–2527). Paul used this argument also in Acts 16:16–40; 22:24-39; 23:27; 25:10–12. There were three possibilities for Diaspora Jews to obtain Roman citizenship: service in the Roman army; liberation from slavery; and as a reward for special service to the Roman Empire. Although Roman citizenship was not automatically associated with special privileges, possession of it had practical benefits, due to some restrictions concerning the treatment of Roman citizens by the local Roman administration (*lex Julia de vi publica*). It is worthy of note that Paul, in his letters, does not mention that he possessed Roman citizenship.

Roman citizen was not allowed, but it was tolerated in the case of non-Roman citizens. Paul and Silas were treated as Jews, which, in the context of Acts 13 and Acts 16:20–21, suggests a less tolerant attitude and even prejudice toward Jews and Judaism. Paul asked for satisfaction from the magistrates themselves, which was granted to him and Silas (Acts 16:37–39). After meeting Paul's claim, however, the magistrates asked them to leave the city, which, in fact, put an end to their mission there. It is probable that their leaving the city was part of the order presented in verse 36 (but it was not directly expressed), but now it is made to be an urgent matter.[177] It may indicate that Paul's mission activity in the city was a great inconvenience for the authorities, due to the fact that it was done by Jewish missionaries with Roman citizenship in a city that was a Roman colony. In the summary, Luke records that Paul and Silas met Lydia and the brothers (v. 40), which comes here as a surprise because, with the exception of the household of the jailer, there is no other mention of "brothers" in the narrative.

Conclusion

The narrative of the mission in Philippi is dominated by one topic; namely, Paul's imprisonment, and by way of an addition, the conversion of the jailer and his household. Paul found himself in trouble, not directly because of his mission activity but because of the socioeconomic consequences of his miracle. Treated as a Jewish agitator, without any interrogation or trial, he was subjected to being whipped and sent to prison until the magistrates made a final decision. However, even in such adverse conditions, with the help of divine providence, he was able to convert the prison's jailer. When the magistrates decided to free him, Paul surprisingly claimed his Roman citizenship, which put the city's authorities in an extremely difficult position. After satisfying Paul's claim, they expelled him from the city. Nevertheless, Paul left some converts there.

[177] J. Schnabel, *Exegetical Commentary on the New Testament, Acts*, 694–695.

Luke's narrative first of all shows the difficulty of the mission to the Gentiles, resulting from prejudice toward the Jews, which was the main reason for Paul's troubles. In such an environment, the protection of the Roman law granted to all Roman citizens and those who possessed Roman citizenship not only had advantages but also became a basic requirement, as it enabled Paul to use the rights given by the Roman law during the mission in the non-Jewish world. Even in such difficult circumstances, the mission in the city brought some positive results.

1.4. In Thessalonica (Acts 17:1–9)

Luke, after the extended narrative of Paul's mission in Philippi, gives a short account of his work in Thessalonica.[178] Paul chose this city due to presence of the Jewish community that was large enough to maintain a synagogue (v. 1).[179] According to his modus operandi, he entered the synagogue and, using the scripture, proclaimed Jesus as the resurrected Messiah (v. 2).[180] The simple kerygma was not sufficient to convince the Thessalonians, and consequently, he had to explain and argue why the Messiah had to suffer and be raised

---

[178] The distance from Philippi to Thessalonica is 144 km, which would take about five days on foot. Thessalonica is located on the Thermaic Gulf on the west of the Chalcidice Peninsula, between two rivers: the River Axios to the west, and the River Strymon to the east. The city was founded in the fourth century BC by Greeks, and it prospered as a center of trade until it fell under Roman domination in 168 BC. At this period, the city became the capital of one of four Macedonian districts. R. S. Ascough, "Thessalonica," in *Dictionary of the Bible*, ed. D. N. Freedman (Grand Rapids: Eerdmans, 2000), 1300–1301.

[179] On the Jewish community in Thessalonica, see I. Levinskaya, *The Book of Acts in its First-Century Setting. Diaspora Setting*, vol. 5 (Grand Rapids: Eerdmans, 1996), 154–157.

[180] The information that Paul was teaching in the synagogue for three weeks does not necessarily indicate the length of his mission in Thessalonica, as this information may refer only to the time of his teaching in the synagogue and not to his activity in the city. C. R. Holladay, *Acts. A commentary* (Louisville: Westminster John Knox Press, 2016), 333.

from the dead.[181] In doing so, Paul specified that the Messiah is Jesus of Nazareth (v. 3).[182] In this very schematic fashion, Luke presents Paul's approach to proclaiming Jesus as the Messiah to the Diaspora Jews, who were greatly influenced by Hellenistic thought, even if this was not commonly preferred, due to the more popular image of the Messiah as a victorious king.[183]

The more challenging issue was the notion of "the resurrected Messiah," as not all Jews believed in the resurrection of the body, and few, if any, in a resurrected Messiah, which is an idea that has little basis in scripture. The main message of Luke concerns the intellectual opposition to the kerygma proclaimed by Paul, as well as the rationalistic approach of the Thessalonian Jews to the idea of a resurrected Messiah. Although the results of his mission were not a significant success—only some Jews became believers—Luke presents it as being successful, as a significant number of Greeks and even some very influential women of Thessalonica (who may have been God-fearers) became Paul's followers (v. 4).[184] It is not certain which group of converts—Jews, Greeks, or the influential women—was the cause of the Jews' jealousy,[185] but the hostility against Paul, probably abetted by rebels and other malcontents, led to rioting and

---

[181] Witherington states that Paul used a rhetorical syllogistic form called *enthymeme*. B. Witherington III, *The Acts of the Apostles*, 504–505.

[182] Paul's syllogism is the following: the first premise—Messiah must suffer, died, and rose again; the second premise—Jesus suffered, died, and was resurrected; the conclusion—Jesus is the Messiah; cf. B. Witherington III, *The Acts of the Apostles*, 505.

[183] L. T. Johnson, *The Acts of the Apostles*, 305.

[184] In the narrative concerning the mission to the Gentiles, Luke frequently amplified the importance of women. This pattern is found especially in the account of the second mission journey; cf. Acts 16:12–15; 17:4; 17:12; 17:34; 18:1.

[185] Jealousy as the motive for the Jews' action against Paul has been mentioned in the account of the mission in Pisidian Antioch (Acts 13:45), where the influential women (probably God-fearers) of the city are also listed (Acts 13:50). It is another pattern used by Luke to describe some aspects of Paul's mission to God-fearers—namely, Gentiles—who, to some extent, were associated with the local synagogue, without converting to Judaism, which was on par with the mission efforts the Jews of the Diaspora.

disturbance in the city. In a city such as Thessalonica, capital of Macedonia, a district of the Roman Empire, this was considered a major crime.[186] This information, together with verse 8, where Luke informs us that the crowd and the city's officials joined on the side of the Jews, indicates the considerable power and influence of the Jews in the city. The official accusation against Paul and those who were helping him became a political issue, in which Paul was presented as a political agitator who proclaimed a king different than Caesar (vv. 6–7). Since the accusers named the king (Jesus) proclaimed by Paul, it is valid to suppose that they shaped the accusation in political terms, despite the fact that Paul's teaching about the Messiah was strictly religious. It is probably for this reason that Pauls' friend, Jason's bail was sufficient to solve the critical situation.[187] Luke presents the Jews' opposition as being the direct reason for the end of Paul's mission in Thessalonica (Acts 17:10).

Conclusion

Luke presents Paul as the missionary to the Jews, whose activity, although with a mixture of success and failure, nevertheless had a deep impact on Gentiles, including influential women. Probably his success in approaching the Gentiles was the reason for the Jews' accusation of political agitation against Paul, which consequently led to his departure from the city. Luke's narrative concerning the

[186] Luke calls the Greeks who supported the Jews ἀγοραίων ἄνδρας (*people of the marketplace*), a rather negative expression, referring to people without permanent work, malcontents who quite often acted as agitators, serving their benefactors for a monetary reward.

[187] Luke's laconic narrative does not include a defense by Jason that would be sufficiently convincing to overrule the accusation; instead, Luke says: καὶ λαβόντες τὸ ἱκανὸν παρὰ τοῦ Ἰάσονος καὶ τῶν λοιπῶν (*Then they made Jason and the others post bond and let them go*) (Acts 17:9 NIV), which says that the bail paid by Jason and other members of messianic movement was accepted by the local authority, not only as sufficient recompense for the disturbances caused by Paul's behavior but also as an appropriate guarantee for Paul's future behavior, which was the critical factor in overruling the case.

mission in Thessalonica, as will be the case in Berea, underlines the Jewish persecution of Paul, rooted in their jealousy, because of the success of his mission.

1.5. In Berea (Acts 17:10–15)

Luke's account concerning Paul's activity in Berea is even shorter and more schematic than that of Thessalonica, but some new and important items of information concerning his mission in the region of Macedonia are given. The first concerns the urgent manner of Paul and Silas leaving Thessalonica by, showing how serious the riot had been, and that Jason's bail only succeeded in calming the situation but did not solve the problem.[188] After two or three days, they reached Berea, and following their usual mission pattern, they entered the synagogue to proclaim the kerygma.[189] Nothing is written about Paul's mission strategy in Berea, but from the few hints given (v. 11), we can suppose that it was similar to that in Thessalonica (proclaiming the suffering and Resurrected Messiah who is Jesus). The large Jewish community had its own synagogue, and Paul and Silas were able to follow their usual modus operandi and encounter fellow Jews living in the city when they gathered to pray on the Sabbath.[190] Luke describes the Berean Jews as εὐγενέστεροι—*more noble-minded*—than the Thessalonian Jews (Acts 17:11). Luke lists some reasons for this evaluation: they readily accepted Paul's message (v. 11), and they compared Paul's message with the scripture in order to see if his teaching was true. Luke portrays them as zealous

[188] Undertaking travel by night was hazardous due to the high possibility of being attacked by robbers. By indicating the time of travel, Luke underlined the danger in which Paul found himself in Thessalonian.

[189] The city of Berea was located 80 km from Thessalonica in the foothills of Mt. Bermion. During Roman rule, the city was an important center of the imperial cult and the location of the headquarters of the Macedonian confederation. R. S. Ascough, "Berea," in *Dictionary of the Bible*, ed. D. N. Freedman (Grand Rapids: Eerdmans, 2000), 167–168.

[190] According to Jewett, the mission in Berea could have lasted even two months. R. Jewett, *Chronology of Paul Life* (Philadelphia: Fortress Press, 1979), 59–61.

orthodox Jews, for whom the Torah was the central foundation of their lives (Acts 17:11). This presentation of the Berean Jews suggests that they found echoes of Paul's teaching in the Torah, and when they found that the Torah seemed to confirm Paul's teaching, they were open to making a positive response to Paul's message. As a result of this intellectual process, they accepted Paul's kerygma and became believers (Acts 17:12). Although nothing is written about Gentiles or Paul's work among them, Luke, in his summary regarding the mission in Berea, includes the information that many influential Greek men and women also became believers.[191]

In the second part of the narrative of the mission in Berea (Acts 17:13–15), Luke gives an account of Jewish opposition to Paul. This opposition did not come from Berean Jews but was initiated by Jews from Thessalonica, probably the same group that drove Paul from their city.[192] The phrase "some of them went there too, agitating the crowds and stirring them up" (Acts 17:13 NIV) suggests that the opposition to Paul in Berea followed the same pattern as that in Thessalonica (v. 13). Because of the schematic nature of the narrative concerning the anti-Paul movement in the city, we can only assume that the opposition was similar to that in Thessalonica. Since the group opposing Paul was the same as in Thessalonica, this strongly suggests that the opposition was not spontaneous but was planned by a strongly motivated group of people. It is possible to suppose that Paul's mission in these two Macedonia cities was seen by the Thessalonian Jews in terms of competition. The real level of danger

---

[191] Luke wrote nothing about Paul's activity among Gentiles in Berea, nor is there any mention of conflict between Paul and the Jews in Berea. The information concerning the conversion of Gentile men and women (Acts 17:12) strongly suggests that these were God-fearers associated with the local synagogue. The only name of a disciple from Berea known to us is Sopater, who is mentioned in Acts 20:4.

[192] There are some similarities between the attitudes of the Jews in Thessalonia and Pisidian Antioch (Acts 14:19–20). It is possible that this fomenting of antagonism in the local society against Paul by a very determined group of opponents is another pattern in Luke's narrative that shows the modus operandi of the Jewish opponents.

is shown by the swift reaction of the disciples in Berea, who not only helped Paul to flee from the city but also assisted him along the way to Athens.[193]

Conclusion

Luke presents the mission in Berea as a great success, due mostly to their attitude toward Paul's kerygma, where searching for truth with an open mind and heart resulted in many being converted. This fruitful work, however, was interrupted by Jews from Thessalonica, who came to Berea to oppose Paul in a manner similar to that used in their own city. Their action is presented as being the direct reason for the end of the mission effort in Berea.

1.6. In Athens (Acts 17:16–34)

Paul, persecuted in Berea by opponents from Thessalonica, was forced to flee as far as Athens.[194] Protected by disciples from Berea, Paul reached Athens with a strong desire to undertake mission activity in the city. His coworkers Silas and Timothy arrived later (Acts 17:15), and while waiting for them, Paul visited the city. He was reminded everywhere of the idolatry of the Athenians (Acts 17:16). They worshipped not only gods known to them but even unknown gods, whom they nevertheless respected, probably due to their respect for pluralism (Acts 17:22–23). Although the city was famous for religious pluralism, this should not be taken to imply that the Athenians took religion lightly. On the contrary, they were a very religious people.[195] The issues of idolatry and religious pluralism

---

193 Acts 17:14 suggests that Paul intended to travel the 56 km to Athens by sea but Acts 17:15 implies that he took the longer (450 km) land route. This second possibility is the more likely. H. Conzelmann, *Acts of the Apostles*, 136.

194 The journey of about 450 km, which he made by foot, would have taken more than two weeks.

195 Paul's statement in Acts 17:22 is not an affirmation of the Athenians' idolatry; it should be read as sarcastic word play; cf. B. Witherington III, *The Acts of the*

became (very soon according to Luke) the main topic of discussion between Paul and many different social groups in the city (Acts 17:17). The narrative of Acts presents Paul in discussion with Jews and God-fearers in the synagogue during their meetings on the Sabbath. He also engaged Gentiles in debate on their understanding of the divinity. Passing conversation sometimes led to serious academic discussions with philosophers, but these scorned Paul's knowledge and understanding as inferior and shallow (Acts 17:18, 31).[196] This activity brought attention to Paul and his teaching, and the leaders of the city invited him to give a public speech in the Areopagus, in order to clarify details in his teaching on the basis of which they might decide whether or not he might continue with his discussions (Acts 17:1–20).[197] Those who brought Paul before the court in Athens are referred to as "others," who disagreed with his religious convictions. This may suggest that Paul's open criticism of idolatry met with opposition from Athenian fundamentalist groups who favored religious pluralism.[198] The "others" probably considered Paul's

---

Apostles, 520.

[196] The philosophers who were involved in discussion with Paul were, according to Luke, members of the Epicurean and Stoic philosophical schools. Although the account is very laconic, it contains enough information to allow us to see them as representing Greek materialism. The Epicureans accepted the existence of gods but as material in essence. This essence has no connection with the human world, and as a concept, it is radically different from the Jewish concept of God. For the Epicureans, the aim of human life is to pursue pleasure, understood as freedom from pain, disturbing passions, or superstitious fear. The Stoics accepted the idea of god as being an essential part of the world, dwelling in each existing being, giving reason and order to the whole creation. The main aim of human life, for the Stoics, is to live in accordance with nature. In practice, this means a subordination to reason as being the fundamental principle that creates the perfect world. In this perfect world, which seeks a harmony of various elements, the division caused by human emotions and self-sufficiency must be avoided.

[197] The Areopagus was not just a meeting place; it was also the location of "the main administrative body of the city" and "the chief court of Athens." D. W. J. Gill and C. Gempf, *The Book of Acts in its First-Century Setting* vol. 2 (Grand Rapids: Eerdmans, 1994), 447–448.

[198] The phrase *τί ἂν θέλοι ὁ σπερμολόγος οὖτος λέγειν* Zerwick translates as "what on earth is he trying to say?"; cf. M. Zerwick and M. Grosvenor, *A Grammatical*

teaching not only as being new and inferior, due to the fragmentary knowledge on which it was based, but also as being intolerant and offensive toward the existing religious status quo in the city (Acts 17:19–20). For these reasons it is unlikely that their invitation was merely an expression of polite hospitality; it was interpreted as a kind of interrogation.[199]

Whatever was the true reason, it gave Paul the opportunity to give a speech at the very heart of Greek culture—philosophy and religion. Considering that in Luke's narrative, this speech is the only speech that Paul gives during the second mission journey, which lasted about three years, it is reasonable to suspect that the speech is a product of Luke's narrative concept. The speech can be read as presenting how Paul proclaimed the kerygma to Gentiles who had not yet been exposed to Jewish monotheism.[200]

When Paul delivered his speech on the Areopagus, he was aware that his teaching would be to the Athenians' ears (vv. 19–21), and that his speech was of crucial importance, as his mission efforts in the city would depend on whether it was accepted or refused.[201] This time, he was more concerned with obtaining permission to proclaim the kerygma than with his own safety.[202] In order to receive this permission, he had to deliver a speech that would meet the level of expectation of the audience. For this reason, Luke presents Paul as a professional Greek orator, adhering to the rhetorical standards of a Greek speech.[203] The speech begins (Acts 17:22) with an *exordium*

Analysis of the Greek New Testament (Rome: Biblical Institute Press, 1996), 409.

199 Bruce thinks that it was an interrogation. F. F. Bruce, *The Acts of the Apostles*, 331–332.

200 Because the interpretation of the speech is examined in appendix 3 at the end of the book, our main focus here is to show the rhetorical skills shown by Paul.

201 E. J. Schnabel, *Exegetical Commentary on the New Testament. Acts*, 728.

202 Note that despite Paul's irritation mentioned in Acts 17:16, the following narrative of Acts 17:17–18 concerns Paul's involvement in arguing with many different Gentiles.

203 For the structure, we follow, in general, that proposed by Witherington III, but with a different explanation of the absence of a *narratio*. B. Witherington III, *The Acts of the Apostles*, 518.

(ἄνδρες Ἀθηναῖοι), and it includes a *captatio benevolentiae* (κατὰ πάντα ὡς δεισιδαιμονεστέρους ὑμᾶς θεωρῶ), which is the normal way to catch the attention and goodwill of the audience. Mention of the deep religious awareness for which the Athenians were renowned (vv. 22–23) would no doubt meet with the approval of the audience. The proof of this, as used by Paul, also included his noting that there was a space for his teaching within the existing Greek religious system that acknowledged the existence of gods unknown to them. Using this "gate," Paul presents himself as a teacher who proclaims to them a God whom they worship without knowing him. Here, Paul proceeds to present a God not yet known to the Athenians. This God is the only God, the Creator and source of all existing things, who surpassed this material world and who needs nothing from the subjects he created (vv. 24–25). He is the Creator of human beings who are subordinated to him, and because of which, human beings are obliged to search for him (vv. 26–28).[204] The conclusion of Paul's creationism leads to the affirmation that human beings are the offspring of God (v. 29). This dignity should prevent human beings from turning to idolatry (v. 29).[205] Paul even insists that it is the will of God that all humankind must abandon idolatry in order to find him (v. 30).[206] Neglect of this call will bring severe punishment on the day of judgment, executed by the chosen one who was raised from the dead by God (v. 31).[207]

At this point, his speech was interrupted and rejected (v. 32).[208] As the main reason for their rejection, Luke gives the teaching concerning resurrection of the human body, despite the fact that the main aim of Paul's speech was a critique of the Athenians' idolatry.

---

[204] Paul remains, at this point, in a position that could possibly be accepted philosophically by the Athenians.

[205] At this point, Paul goes back to the controversy regarding idolatry presented in Acts 17:16–17.

[206] Here, Paul requests that they convert to monotheism.

[207] Paul now attempts to teach the concept of the Messiah.

[208] As a result, Paul was not allowed to undertake mission activity in Athens, which explains the brevity of Luke's account.

Paul lost his philosophical debate against idolatry due to his use of the argument based on the resurrection of the body. This was a concept that was foreign to all the Greek religious or philosophical systems.

Conclusion

According to Luke's narrative, during the stay in Athens, Paul focused on the problem of the Athenians' idolatry, which was a direct reason for Paul's irritation and his arguing with Jews, God-fearers, Athenians philosophers, and other inhabitants of Athens. Surprisingly, although Luke mentions the synagogue, he writes almost nothing about Paul's activity among the Jews in Athens. It is more probable that this aspect of Paul's activity was not a point of major interest to Luke than that Paul did not undertake any mission to the Diaspora Jews in the city. Luke's account concerning the second mission journey is focused on the mission to the Gentiles, although during this period, Paul also regularly proclaimed a resurrected Jesus to the Jews. In the account concerning Athens, the two major problems encountered were the religious system that accepted the notion of idolatry, and the philosophical system that excluded the idea of the resurrection of the body. Against these at the center of Paul's teaching lay the concept of monotheism and belief in the resurrected Messiah.[209] In the narrative on the mission in Athens, Paul is presented as one whose mission is impossible.

1.7. In Corinth (Acts 18:1–17)

After the unsuccessful mission in Athens, Paul went southwest to Corinth, which was about seventy-eight kilometers from Athens. This city was established in 44 BC by Julius Caesar as *Colonia laus*

209 In the context of the Athenians' idolatry, greater attention seems to be given to the first.

Iulia Corinthiensis.[210] Located between the Corinthian Gulf with the harbor in Lechaeum, and the Saronic Gulf with the harbor in Cenchrea, the city was the most important location between Europe and Asia, making it an important commercial center.[211] Its strategical economic position led to its becoming the administrative center of the province of Achaia.[212] The population of the city consisted mostly of Greeks and Romans, and the majority were freedmen and slaves.[213] As a wealthy city, Corinth attracted people of many cultures and religions, making it a melting pot of religious and cultural diversity.[214] Unlike Athens, Corinth was multicultural place, but it resembled Athens in the diversity of religions.[215] There was a large community of Diaspora Jews who had a synagogue, as is indicated in Acts 18: 8.[216] The city also had a dubious "fame" for immoral behavior, which

---

[210] Corinth was a Greek city founded in the fifth century BC. It grew in importance and wealth until it was destroyed by the Romans, led by the consul Lucius Mummius in 146 BC. After that, the city lay in ruins for almost one hundred years, inhabited but without importance, until it was rebuilt by the Romans as a colony in 44 BC.

[211] J. M. McRay, "Corinth," in *Dictionary of New Testament Background*, eds. A. Craig, A. Eavens, S. E. Porter (Downers Grove/Leicester: InterVarsity Press, 2000), 227–231.

[212] Archeological excavations in the forum of the city suggest that during 27 BC–AD 44, Corinth was an administrative center of Achaia. Luke's account in Acts 18:12 seems to confirm this; cf. D. W. G. Gill, "Achaia," *The Book of Acts in Its First-Century Setting*, eds. D. W. G. Gill and C. Gempf, 448–450.

[213] Inscriptions contain Roman and Greek names of inhabitants of the city. Another source that attests the account in Acts is 1 Corinthians 18:7–8; cf. Collins R.F., *First Corinthians* (Collegeville: The Liturgical Press, 1999), 21–23.

[214] J. Wiseman, *The Land of Ancient Corinth: Studies in Mediterranean Archeology*, vol. 50 (Göteberg, 1978), 11–12.

[215] The most famous were a sanctuary of Asclepius, the temple of Athena, a temple of Apollo, a sanctuary of Demeter and Persephone, and a temple for imperial cult; cf. J.M. McRay, *Corinth*, 228–229. Luke, in Acts 18:4, explicitly mentions a Jewish synagogue.

[216] The Jewish community in Corinth included groups from different social rank. There were Jews who possessed Roman citizenship; Jews who were sent as slaves to Corinth by Vespasian after the Jewish War; and Jewish freedmen, workers, and merchants. B. Witherington III, *Conflict & Community in Corinth. A*

became proverbial.[217] The time of Paul's visit to the city is related to the Roman official Gallio, the proconsul of Achaia (Acts 18:12), who held the office for no longer than a year and a half.[218]

Luke's narrative concerning Paul's mission in Corinth differs from the narrative concerning another cities Paul visited during the second mission journey. The narrative of Acts, until Paul's mission in Corinth, is dynamic, with frequently changing situations (Acts 16:6–40); it is sometimes dramatic (Acts 17:1–9) or intriguing (Acts 17:16–31), but the account of the mission in Corinth seems to be presented in a more static manner. First, Luke informs us of Paul's introduction to the city, where he met some Jews from Rome who practiced the same trade as Paul, and they gave him work and a place to stay (Acts 18:1–4). It is the first time that Luke mentions directly Paul's physical labor for a living. Paul is referred to as a "leatherworker," which should be understood as "tentmaker."[219] This information is very important for describing Paul's economic circumstances during the mission journey, which is often overlooked in portraits of Paul.[220] Also, for the first time, Paul's life is presented as settled, where he has a house and work, and his mission activity is restricted to teaching in the synagogue on the Sabbath (Acts 18:4). However, after Silas and Timothy finally joined Paul in Corinth, he left his work and devoted himself entirely to mission activity, which tells us indirectly

---

Socio-Rhetorical Commentary on 1 and 2 Corinthians (Grand Rapids/Cambridge: Eerdmans, 1995), 24–28.

217 "Korynt [Corinth]," in *Leksykon Biblijny [Lexikon zur Bible]*, eds. F. Reinecker and G. Maier (Warsaw: Vocatio, 1994), 368.

218 Based on information provided in Acts 18:11–12 and Acts 18:24–9:1, it is possible to determine the period of Paul's mission in Corinth, which took place most probably between AD June 50 and April 51.

Most probably, Gallio held the office of proconsul of Achaia between AD June 51 and April 52; cf. R. F. Collins, *First Corinthians*, 23–24.

219 E. J. Schnabel, *Exegetical Commentary on the New Testament. Acts*, 728.

220 This criticism extends to the not infrequent lack of detail in accounts of Paul's mission referring to time, distance, topography, economic aspects, and the physical effort involved in the missionary work.

that the financial support of the mission team was transferred to his coworkers (v. 5).

The primary targets of his mission were Jews and God-fearers (v. 4), which was a practice corresponding to his usual modus operandi.[221] Paul's work involved two steps: first, proclaiming the kerygma (Jesus is the Messiah), and then, proving that the kerygma is in accordance with Jewish tradition (v. 5). In the case of the Jews, his work was generally without success, as they did not accept Paul's kerygma. As a result, Paul abandoned his mission activity in the synagogue (despite the fact that Crispus, who was in charge of the synagogue's affairs, became a believer in Jesus, the Messiah), and moved into the neighboring house of a Greek convert to Judaism, Titus Justus (Acts 18:6–7). Paul's words, as related by Luke—"Your blood be on your own heads! I am innocent of it. From now on I will go to the Gentiles" (Acts 18:6 NIV)—are of crucial importance for understanding how Luke wants to present Paul's identity.[222] The first statement, "Your blood be on your own heads," indicates where the responsibility lies; in this case, with the Jews who opposed Paul's kerygma. It also includes indication of potential consequences for their action. The second statement, "I am innocent of it" (Acts 18:6 NIV), expresses his lack of responsibility for the Jews' ignorance regarding recognition of Jesus as the Messiah.

It is not the case that Paul neglected proclaiming the kerygma to the Jews; on the contrary, it is the Jews who did not want to listen to his kerygma. Paul first proclaimed the kerygma to the Jews, but their resistance forced him to make the third statement, "From now

---

[221] Schnabel's interpretation of the term "Greeks" in Acts 18:14, as referring to Greeks whom Paul encountered in daily life on a business basis, can be accepted as a possibility. If so, Acts 18:4 will function as a general statement concerning Paul's mission in Corinth. E. J. Schnabel, *Exegetical Commentary on the New Testament. Acts*, 758. The fact that Luke specifically limited the place of Paul's activity to the synagogue, without even suggesting other options, remains problematic.

[222] A similar statement is given in Paul's speech at Pisidian Antioch (Acts 13:46), where it is more elaborated: "We had to speak the word of God to you first. Since you reject it and do not consider yourselves worthy of eternal life, we now turn to the Gentiles" (Acts 13:46 NIV).

on I will go to the Gentiles" (Acts 18:6 NIV). It does not mean that Paul abandoned the mission to the Jews, but he changed the place of his activities from the synagogue to the house of Titus Justus.[223] It is important to interpret his statements in the particular context (the lack of the possibility to continue the mission in the synagogue), rather than in a general context (Paul was called to become a missionary to Gentiles). These three statements show Paul's deep interest in the mission to the Diaspora Jews but also his great disappointment at the Jews' resistance.

According to Luke's general pattern, Paul's mission to the Gentiles in Corinth was a consequence of the Jews' rejection of his mission, which is the background in which Luke wants to see Paul's mission to Gentiles, not only in this city but in general elsewhere. However, it is not Luke's aim to present Paul as one who abandons the mission to the Jews; rather, he wants to show him as one who has expanded his mission also to the Gentiles, as a result of particular circumstances.

The short and schematic narrative of Paul's work in Corinth contains also a record of a kind of epiphany of Jesus to Paul in a dream (Acts 18:9), the message of which seems to be direct instruction and assurance, with an exposition of the purpose of the mission. The epiphany begins with two orders: one is a prohibition (*do not be afraid*), and the second is a direct order for action that is presented in both a positive (*but speak*) and negative way (*and do not be silence*) (Acts 18:9 NIV). These orders seem to indicate some kind of psychological break in Paul, which may have been caused by his disappointment, as presented in verse 6. Paul is afraid and, as a result he, is silent, suggesting that he may have stopped proclaiming the kerygma. His condition seems to be the reason for the epiphany, and the orders are intended to change the present state of things. Verse 10 contains a therapy aimed at driving Paul out of the present impasse. To achieve the aim Jesus assures Paul about his permanent presence with Paul: "I am with you," and a guarantee for his safety: "and no one is going to attack and harm you" (Acts 18:10 NIV). The first

223 W. S. Kurz, *Acts of the Apostles*, 281–282.

consolation implies Paul's doubts about the meaning of this mission and his thinking of leaving Corinth. The meaning of verse 11, "So Paul stayed in Corinth for a year and a half, teaching them the word of God" (Acts 18:11 NIV), comes out better if we understand that Paul's actually continuing in Corinth had not, for a time, been intended.

But Paul is not alone, and Paul's mission is not his mission only; he is with Jesus, and his mission is Jesus's mission. Because of this, Jesus guarantees Paul his physical safety, which strongly suggests there was a real threat aimed at Paul.[224] In this way, Paul is assured not only of his safety but also about the fruitful results of his mission in the city. "Because I have many people in this city" (Acts 18:10 NIV) is a statement that implies Paul's doubt after the incident presented in verse 6. The epiphany brought positive results, and Paul returned to mission activity in the city for the next year and a half.

The narrative of Paul's trial before Gallio (Acts 18:12–17) attests that a real threat against Paul's life existed in Corinth. Jews of Corinth succeeded in putting Paul on trial (Acts 18:12), based on the weak accusation: "This man," they charged, "is persuading the people to worship God in ways contrary to the law" (Acts 18:13 NIV).[225] The accusation is presented as a problem within the Jewish community, which automatically disqualified it as the subject of interest in the Roman juridical system, since the local Roman officials did not judge on the religious questions of any minority groups.[226] Gallio's strict following of this regulation worked in Paul's favor, and it can

---

[224] It may refer to the group of Paul's opponents in Corinth. This, however, is not certain because the threat is only presented in a very general manner. D. G. Peterson, *The Acts of the Apostles*, 513–515.

[225] It is debatable if the term "law" here refers to the Mosaic Law or to Roman law. C. S. Keener, *Acts. An Exegetical Commentary,* vol. 3, 2772–2773. In our opinion, the term refers to the Mosaic Law because the noun *God* is used in the singular, indicating that it comes from a monotheistic context. The reference also to worshipping God against the law directly suggests the religious character of the law. It is also important to note that Gallio refused to accept an accusation based on religious controversies: "But since it involves questions about words and names and your own law" (Acts 18:15 NIV).

[226] H. Conzelmann, *Acts of the Apostles*, 153.

be understood as an example, given by Luke, of Jesus fulfilling his promise to Paul (Acts 18:9–11). The Roman authorities did not recognize Paul's action as criminal and treated it as a question that pertained strictly to the Jewish community, nor did the Jewish community in Corinth (despite the fact that they possessed *Jewish politeuma* that, according to Roman law, allowed them to judge religious matters by themselves) undertake any organized action against Paul, so he could continue his mission activity with considerable freedom.

According to Luke's narrative, Corinth was the first and only city, during the entire second mission journey, where Paul left without being forced to do so by circumstances. Luke suggests that Paul decided to finish the mission and to go back to Antioch (Acts 18:18). On the way back, Paul made a brief stop at Ephesus, where he proclaimed the kerygma to the Jews, with apparently promising effect, as Paul expressed his willingness to undertake a mission in the city "if it is God's will" (Acts 18:19–22 NIV). This account is a connecting link in Luke's narrative composition between the account of the second mission journey and the third mission journey, which almost exclusively concerns Paul's activity in Ephesus. After Corinth, it is another place of promise, where proclaiming the kerygma will bear fruit.[227]

---

[227] Conzelmann assumes that Luke's narrative of Paul's visit to Ephesus (Acts 18:19–21) is intended to present Paul as the first preacher in the city. According to him, Luke knows that Paul's short stay in Ephesus was not a beginning of proclaiming kerygma in this city, and for this reason, he includes, before the narrative regarding the third mission journey (Acts 18:23–21:16), a short preparative section concerning the mission activity of Apollos in Ephesus (Acts 18:24–28), which also presents the mission activity of Priscilla and Aquila in the city (Acts 18:26). H. Conzelmann, *Acts of the Apostles*, 155–156. In our opinion, this is not supported by the text, which clearly refers to Paul's trip to Syria (Acts 18:18), as well as the lack of an intention on his part to stay longer in Ephesus (Acts 18:20). Paul's activity in Ephesus on his way back to Syria must be taken as a chance encounter with Jews in the city, caused by need to wait for a ship. Luke's intention in including this event should be related to his narrative strategy, according to which, at the end of a particular narrative, he introduces a topic

Luke ends the narrative with information that Paul reached Caesarea and went up to Jerusalem, where he visited the community, and finally went to Syrian Antioch (Acts 18:22). The purpose of his visiting the community in Jerusalem remains a matter of speculation that depends on scholars' general perspective on Paul.[228] However, in the context of Paul's visit to Jerusalem, "I will come back if it is God's will" (Acts 18:21 NIV) may indicate merely his wish to work in Ephesus, or it may show Paul's anxiety regarding his visiting Jerusalem. Luke, in this way, can connect the end of the second mission journey with the end of the third mission journey, in order to underline the constant threat that was connected with Paul's presence in Jerusalem. It may equally be intended to show Jesus's continued protection of Paul.[229] Luke's real purpose may be difficult to uncover, but we can be certain that Luke does not write without some purpose.

Conclusion

Paul's mission in Corinth is the first in the whole account of the mission journeys where Paul was forced by Jewish opposition, stemming from the synagogue, to operate mostly within a Gentile environment. Jewish rejection and opposition caused him distress, to the point that it required intervention by Jesus. Luke, in a characteristic manner, presents Paul as being in great distress during the mission in Corinth. In this way, Luke shows again the truth—known to the reader (Acts 9:15–16) but still not directly revealed to Paul—that he is only a tool in Jesus's hands, useful to carry out the order given to the disciples (Acts 1:8).[230] Paul is just a human being who, without God's strength, is confronted with the limitation of his own power, but he

---

that will be the subject of the following narrative (cf. Acts 14:15–17 with Acts 17:22–31).

[228] D. G. Peterson, *The Acts of the Apostles*, 521–522.

[229] The first possibility seems to be the more acceptable.

[230] Schwarz, considering Acts 13:47, argues that the phrase "to ends of the earth" (Acts 1:8) refers to Paul's mission to the Gentiles. D. R. Schwartz, *Reading the First Century* (Tübingen: Mohr Siebeck, 2013), 172–174.

is constantly supported by his Lord, who, in order to protect his own servant, uses even the political structure of this world.

2. Fulfilling a Promise (Acts 18:23–21:16)

The next stage of Luke's presentation of Paul is the third mission journey (Acts 18:23–21:16), which almost exclusively narrates Paul's mission in Ephesus (Acts 18:23–19:40) and his return to Jerusalem from Macedonia (Acts 20:1–21:16). The narrative begins with Paul's journey to Ephesus, which is mentioned in Acts 18:23 (specifically) and Acts 19:1 (in a very general manner). The second account only tells us that Paul walked the 1330 kilometers through the highlands, without details or interpretation by the narrator. The first account is more useful for reconstructing Paul's journey to Ephesus because it mentions two regions that he passed through—Galatia and Phrygia—which are the regions that Paul visited during the second mission journey (Acts 16:6).[231] Considering that in the narrative of Acts, Luke often uses a pattern of brief information, mentioning an issue whose full meaning may be deduced based on information that has already been given, it is possible to assume that Paul, on his way to Ephesus, not only visited Galatia and Phrygia but also those places he had visited during the first mission journey. The information given in Acts 18:23 is more than a simple geographic reference because it shows one of Paul's characteristics; namely, his care for the Christian communities that he established.[232]

The first mission encounter of Paul in Ephesus, as recorded by Luke, concerns "some disciples," whose identification is unclear.[233]

---

[231] Note the same pattern in the information regarding Paul's trip to Macedonia, including also the places visited by Paul during his first mission journey.

[232] This information helps us understand Luke's placing the speech at Miletus, addressed to the elders of the church in Ephesus, at the end of the third mission journey and again at the end of Paul's mission career (as far as we know it). Paul will not visit Ephesus on the road to his new mission destination.

[233] Concerning the possible interpretation of the term *some disciples* in Acts 19:1, cf. Schnabel: E. J. Schnabel, *Exegetical Commentary on the New Testament. Acts*,

Usually, Luke uses term *disciple* in reference to Christians, but these disciples not only have not yet received the Holy Spirit, but they have not even heard about the Holy Spirit (Acts 19:2), which shows that their belief differed from that of Christians. They knew only about John's baptism for the forgiveness of sins (Acts 19:3–4), which strongly suggests that they followed John the Baptist as the Messiah. However, more important than their identity, for Luke, is that they became Christian by the work of Paul, who used the argument that John himself announced that Messiah will come after him (v. 4). This brought them to baptism in the name of Jesus (Acts 19:5), which was followed by their receiving the Holy Spirit (Acts 19:6).[234] This kind of audience appears here for the first time in Luke's narrative and surely is not accidental.[235] At the end of the narrative concerning these "disciples," Luke adds that their number was "about twelve," where the term *about* reflects Luke's usage with numbers, and *twelve* includes a symbolic reference to Israel.[236] Does Luke imply that these "disciples" were people of God in some kind of transit state between Israel and New Israel? If this is the case, Paul's work is presented in terms similar to that of Phillip in Samaria (Acts 8:4–7).[237]

On Paul's mission in Ephesus, the narrative is a short and schematic description of Paul's mission activity among Jews and Gentiles (Acts 19:8–10). The narrative is a kind of summary de facto that concerns the events known to the reader from Luke's narrative concerning Paul's mission in Corinth. Paul followed his modus operandi of proclaiming to and convincing the Jews in the synagogue (Acts 19:8). This mission continued for three months, amounting to twelve meetings, and it ended with Paul's departure

---

787–788.

[234] L. T. Johnson, *The Acts of the Apostles*, 337–338.

[235] We can assume that the disciples of John were Jews, making Luke's account the first in which a distinction is made between the Jews and the Jewish followers of John the Baptist.

[236] W. S. Kurz, *Acts of the Apostles*, 281–282.

[237] Note the presence of miracles in both accounts (Acts 8:7; 19:11–12). Also, it is important to note that the account in Acts 19:11–16 has some similarity (in meaning) with the account in Acts 8:9–13.

from this synagogue, due to the stubbornness of some Jews (Acts 19:9). Paul and some of his disciples, probably those Jews and God-fearers who had come to the faith in Jesus, find a new place to meet in "the hall of Tyrannus." This may be simply a reference to a public building, or it may refer to a community that gathered in the house of Tyrannus (Acts 19:9).[238]

As was the case of the mission in Corinth, Paul was proclaiming the kerygma in a Gentile environment, but this does not automatically mean that he abandoned the mission to Corinth's Jews, since verse 10 informs not only about the period of his work (two years) but also about places (Asia), and the ethnic groups (Jews and Gentiles) to whom his kerygma was addressed. These general indications are all that Luke gives his readers about the mission in Ephesus. It shows Luke's approach to the narrative concerning this stage of Paul's activity; he focuses on particular problems that will show some peculiarities of the mission in a Gentile environment (Acts 19:11–40), rather than on aspects of Paul's attitude toward mission work that already were presented in the preceding narratives.

The peculiarities of Paul's mission in Ephesus lay in the socioreligious effects of his activity and occasioned by "some imitators" (Acts 19:3–16). When in the first (Acts 13:8–20) and second (Acts 16:16–24) mission journey, Luke recorded a particular miracle worked by Paul. In the case of the third mission journey, he refers generally to many miracles (Acts 19:11–12) without mention of any miracle in particular. Paul's miracles and healing ability made a considerable impact on local society, and some Jewish imitators emerged (Acts 19:13–14), who lacked faith in Jesus (v. 13) and tried to heal people in the same way as Paul. These were readily noticed by the local community (Acts 19:17), who responded to these with great respect (in fear or in awe) and glorified the name of Jesus.[239] In this way, Luke indicates Paul's extremely successful mission in Ephesus. Luke does not focus on Paul but concentrates exclusively on Jesus's

238 E. J. Schnabel, *Exegetical Commentary on the New Testament. Acts*, 791–792.

239 All these three futures (to know; to respond; to glorify) are typical of Luke elements used to describe a miracle. L.T. Johnson, *The Acts of the Apostles*, 341.

glory. This kind of presentation shows Luke's perspective on Paul, who is the servant of Jesus, sent to work for his glory, where the source of his power is identified as the Lord Jesus.

In the narrative concerning the miracles, Luke includes one important item of information that those who came to faith in Jesus included—those who practiced magic. The information concerning the public confession of sins and the burning of books detailing magic practices (which involved huge personal loss of many), among many other aspects, such as the strong faith of the converts and their radicalism, shows the great impact of Paul's mission on the society of Ephesus.

This impact was not without a response from those who suffered economic loss because of Paul's successful mission work.[240] Luke suggests that the opposition of Demetrius and the Ephesian craftsmen occurred just before Paul planned to leave the city in order to visit the regions of Macedonia and Achaia (where he was active during the second mission journey), as well as to extend the mission and undertake work in Rome (Acts 19:21).[241] An argument to show that this was his plan is his sending the coworkers to Macedonia, probably to make the necessary preparations (Acts 19:22).[242] All these were planned before, as part of his return to Jerusalem,[243] which may seem surprising because Macedonia, Achaia, and Rome lay in the

---

240 This economic reason for aggressive opposition against Paul allows us to see some similarities with the problem in Philippi (Acts 16:16–24).

241 Luke directly indicates that Paul's leaving Ephesus was not caused by the riot of Demetrius, which gives the event a special function in Luke's narrative. H. Conzelmann, *Acts of the Apostles*, 164.

242 Luke does not inform us about the purpose of sending Timothy and Erastus to Macedonia (which *de facto* was for making a collection for Jerusalem), but we know this from Paul's letters (1 Cor. 4:16–17; 16:8–18–11). D. G. Peterson, *The Acts of the Apostles*, 543–544.

243 A reason for Paul's ending the work in Ephesus and going back to Jerusalem is not given here by Luke, but it will be mentioned later in Paul's speech before Felix (Acts 24:17).

opposite direction from Jerusalem.[244] A visit to Macedonia and Achaia raised no serious problem, even if Luke does not provide information concerning the true reason. He indicates that the reason was not the riot of Demetrius. From his letters, we know that he wished to visit places where he had earlier worked, and they were not far from Ephesus.[245] A real problem would emerge if after visiting Achaia and before going Jerusalem, Paul visited to Rome. However, Luke does not tell us of Paul visiting Rome after visiting Achaia; on the contrary, he described Paul's journey back through Macedonia and Asia to Jerusalem.[246] The phrase "After I have been there, he said, I must visit Rome also" (Acts 19:21 NIV) suggests that after Paul visited Jerusalem, his intention was to undertake a trip to Rome (another mission journey). Luke's narrative may be interpreted in two ways: at this point, Paul was not aware of the potential danger of his visit to Jerusalem, and he had a real plan to undertake a mission in Rome and Spain; or Luke is giving an itinerary for the last part of Acts (Acts 21–28) regarding Paul's imprisonment, during which Paul

[244] It is highly possible that Luke, in this way, indicates the beginning of the narrative section concerning Paul's visit to Jerusalem and his imprisonment, where other events (Paul's visit to Achaia and Macedonia, as well as his return to Jerusalem) are treated as preparatory units. The phrase "Paul decided to go to Jerusalem" (Acts 19:21 NIV) may refer to his own decision (decision within himself) or to a decision taken under an inspiration of the Holy Spirit (even if the term *holy* is not used here). Parts of Paul's speech in Miletus (Acts 20:21–22) strongly suggest the second possibility. The phrase "I must visit Rome also" in Acts 19:21 (NIV) suggests Paul's wish to work in Rome, but Luke's narrative ends with Paul's arrival in Rome and only gives a very schematic introduction to his activity there. Similarly, Acts 21:22 may indicate the end of his narrative concerning Paul's mission activities, and Acts 21:23 may indicate the beginning of the narrative section concerning Paul's imprisonment.

[245] Paul's visit to Achaia had much in common with the situation in Corinth (1 Cor. 4:14–21), but basic ground concerns the collection for brothers in Jerusalem, as Romans 15:26 directly exposes it. However, Luke wrote nothing about of these two reasons.

[246] Romans 15:22–26 mentions Paul's wish to visit Rome on his way to Spain, after he delivered the collection from Macedonia and Achaia to the brothers in Jerusalem.

will complete the task he was elected for (including the visit to Rome, although in a drastically different form than he initially intended).[247]

In the account of Demetrius's riot (Acts 19:23–40), Luke hardly mentions Paul. He is mentioned for the first time in the speech of Demetrius (Acts 19:26–27), where indirect accusations against Paul are listed.[248] From them, we learn that Paul's mission activity was successful not only in Ephesus but also throughout Asia Minor. The second accusation was that Paul successfully convinced many people that god's images are not God. The final accusation directly presents Paul's activity as being a threat to the economic and religious prosperity of Ephesus. All of this was known to the reader from Acts 19:11–20, but here, they are presented in the form of an accusation. The second time Paul's name is mentioned, it is in the context of Paul's coworkers Gaius and Aristarchus being dragged to the theater of the city (Acts 19:30). Luke notes that Paul wished to involve himself in the danger, but he was not allowed by his disciples. Luke does not explain the purpose of Paul's attempt, but it may be assumed that he wished to save his coworkers.[249]

According to Luke's narrative, the riot of Demetrius is not directly connected with Paul's decision to leave Ephesus and go to Macedonia and Greece (Acts 19:21–22; 20:1). Although the visit to Greece took at least few months, Luke decided to write nothing more than giving a simple account of his going to Greece and that Paul passed through the region of Macedonia and Achaia, where his activities were limited to encouraging and exhorting the disciples dwelling in these regions (Acts 20:2).[250] Concerning the stay in Greece, Luke indicates only the length of time (three months), saying nothing about the places Paul visited or his activities.[251] Paul planned to go to Syria from Greece,

---

[247] C. S. Kenner, *Acts. An Exegetical Commentary,* vol. 3, 2860.

[248] Concerning the speech of Demetrius and the speech of the town clerk, cf. appendix 4 and appendix 5 at the end of the book.

[249] E. J. Schnabel, *Exegetical Commentary on the New Testament. Acts*, 806.

[250] The collection for the community in Jerusalem is not mentioned.

[251] Luke does not mention Corinth or problems that existed in that community, although he undoubtedly, knew about them, as the plural personal pronoun in

but a Jewish plot against him makes this plan impossible to realize, which forced him to walk through Macedonia (Acts 20:3) to Troas (Acts 20:5).[252]

Luke named his companions and their places of origin, which shows that they come from places where Paul worked during his three mission journeys.[253] Some of them went ahead to Troas, probably in order to make some preparations before Paul came (Acts 20:6) after his short stay in Philippi, where Luke joined him. In Philippi, Paul and his companions celebrated the Feast of Unleavened Bread, which started the next day (15–21 Nisan) after the Feast of the Passover (14 Nisan). Luke tells us that the voyage from Philippi to Troas took five days and that they spent one week there before they traveled to Miletus (Acts 20:6). We can understand from this that Paul was in a hurry to reach Jerusalem before the Feast of Pentecost (Acts 20:16).[254]

The account of one-week stay in Troas is limited by Luke to only one event: Paul's teaching the day after the Sabbath, with the main focus on the resurrection of the dead boy named Eutychus (Acts 20:7–12). According to Luke's narrative, the believers in Troas gathered to "break bread," which refers to their sharing a meal as a community, a common practice in the Christian communities, including that in

---

Acts 20:6 suggests. More information concerning this trip of Paul is provided in the letters to the Corinthians (1 Cor. 16:5; 2 Cor. 1:16; 2:12–13; 7:5. 13–16; 8:1–5).

[252] Again, Luke gives no specification concerning the Jewish plot or the place where it occurred. It can be deduced from Paul's letters that the event concerned the Jews from Corinth. This is attested also by Luke's account of Paul's trial before Gallio (Acts 18:12–17). E. J. Schnabel, *Exegetical Commentary on the New Testament. Acts*, 832–833.

[253] The seven names (Sopater son of Pyeehus, Aristarchus, Secundus, Gaius, Timothy, Tychnicus, Trophimus) from four places (Berea, Thessalonica, Derbe, Asia) are sometimes taken as indicating men representing the churches that contributed to the collection. However, Luke does not mention the collection in his narrative (Acts 20:1–38). Even more striking is the fact that among the seven names there are no representatives from Corinth and Philippi, two cities that contributed to the collection.

[254] Paul's hurry probably relates to the collection for the Jerusalem community, which Paul wanted to deliver before the Feast of Pentecost. However, Luke does not mention this in the narrative here.

Troas. It was the last day of Paul's stay in the city, and for this reason, he prolonged his speech until midnight, which may seem unusual but was accepted by the community, due to the circumstances.[255] After the background is mentioned, Luke proceeds with the main theme of his narrative concerning the visit in Troas; namely, the accidental death of Eutychus, the boy or young man, aged between eight and twenty-eight years old—the two different terms (παῖς in verse 12 and νεανίσκος in verse 9) that Luke used allow for a wide range.[256]

Eutychus was asleep, fell from the third story to the ground below, and was picked up dead (Acts 20:9). Then, Paul did several actions: he went down; he threw himself upon the dead boy; he put his arms around him; he said, "Don't be alarmed"; he said, "He's alive!" (Acts 20:10 NIV), which brought Eutychus back to life (Acts 20:12). Luke presents this miracle in a strange manner, considering that verse 11 returns to the topic of Paul's long sermon. Lack of any kind of reaction, such as glorifying God's name or even a simple notice of the event as being miraculous or reference to Paul's extraordinary power, results in the narrative being very peculiar. While Luke presents Paul as a person capable of acting like the prophets (1 Kings 17:19–22, 2; 2 Kings 4:34–35), or Jesus (Luke 7:11–15; 8:49–51; John 11:38–44),

---

[255] This unusually long sermon may show, in Luke's presentation, Paul's total devotion to proclaiming and teaching. However, it is also possible to understand this information as a preparation for the speech in Miletus, where the aspect of Paul's working for the churches (Acts 20:31) is strongly underlined. In this case, the information will serve as proof (for the readers) of Paul's statements in the speech to the elders of the community of Ephesus.

[256] The Greek term νεανίσκος (*young man*) in the LXX is used to translate the Hebrew term נַעַר and בָּחוּר (*nahar* and *bahur*). In the New Testament, the term defines a young man (Matt. 19:20, 22; Mark 14:51; 16:5; Luke 7:14; Acts 2:17; 1 John 2:13–14) or a young servant (Acts 5:10). Use of the term νεανίσκος by Luke is imprecise. In Acts 23:17–18:22, Luke uses the term νεανίας for the nephew of Paul. However, in Acts 23:22, when speaking further about the nephew of Paul, he uses the term νεανίσκος. In this case, the use of both terms is consistent with the division of age presented by Philo. However, in another place (Acts 20:9, 12), where Luke speaks about the same person (Eutychus), he uses first the term νεανίας (Acts 20:9) and then the term παῖς (Acts 20:12). In this case, Luke uses the division of age in a manner that is different from Philo.

or Peter (Acts 9:36–41), placing him on a rank with the greatest, he nevertheless passes over the event as something casual, a kind of servant's work without any expectation of praise or reward.[257]

The next part of the narrative regarding the third mission journey concerns Paul's visit to Miletus, the city where Luke placed Paul's only speech during the entire mission. The narrative begins with a report on the journey. Paul walked alone, the distance of about fifty kilometers, from Troas to Assos, where he met the companions who traveled the same distance (seventy kilometers) by sea (Acts 20:13).[258] From Assos to Miletus, they traveled (Acts 20:14), passing by Ephesus without visiting it because of hurrying on the way to Jerusalem (v. 16). The reason Luke gives is not convincing for some scholars, who argue that meeting the elders from Ephesus in Miletus would require more time than if Paul were to stop in Ephesus.[259] However, considering Luke's narrative of the voyage to Rome (Acts 27), it is possible to assume that it was not easy to find a ship sailing to one's destination of choice in a short time.[260] Even more, Acts 20:38 suggests that some arrangement has been made.[261]

---

[257] It is extremely important to note this presentation, since, in our opinion, this is the most important characteristic in Luke's perspective on Paul (cf. Acts 9:15–16).

[258] Luke does not offer a reason for Paul's decision. For some highly speculative explanations, cf. a list of scholars' proposals presented by Keener. C. S. Keener, *Acts. An Exegetical Commentary,* vol. 3, 2980–2983. Perhaps Paul was still afraid of a potential plot on his life in Ephesus.

[259] H. Conzelmann, *Acts of the Apostles*, 171.

[260] The harbor of Miletus was more likely to have a ship than was that of Ephesus, due to its geographical location that was more accessible for ships from Achaia. To suppose that Luke knew the true reason (Paul did not think it safe to enter Ephesus) is highly speculative. Luke specifically indicates that the riot of Demetrius was not a reason for Paul's leaving Ephesus, and the riot was solved by the local authorities, which leaves little room to suspect the continued existence of opposition against Paul. Acts 21:27 and Acts 24:8–18–19 concern Jews from Asia whom Luke did not directly mention as part of the riot in Ephesus, which is presented by Luke as involving the Gentiles.

[261] Kurz rightly points to the fact that Paul spent much of the time between the Feast of Passover and the Feast of Pentecost (fifty days) in Macedonia and Asia. W. S. Kurz, *Acts of the Apostles*, 307. Concerning the information regarding Paul's

The second part of the narrative concerns the meeting (Acts 20:7–38), where the major topic is Paul's speech to the elders of the community of Ephesus (Acts 20:18–35). Luke informs us that after arriving in Miletus, Paul sent messengers to call the elders of the church in Ephesus to meet him in Miletus (Acts 20:17). This information suggests a spontaneous decision by Paul, rather than a well-planned meeting. The reader will learn a reason for this meeting from the content of the speech. The speech is placed at the end of Luke's account of the third mission journey (Acts 18:23–21:16). It is at the center of the subsection concerning Paul's journey to Jerusalem (Acts 20:1–21:16). It is preceded by the account of Paul's visit to Macedonia (Acts 20:1–16), and it is followed by the narrative regarding his voyage to Jerusalem (Acts 21:1–16). The speech's structure can be readily determined on the basis of the content, rather than on the basis of the formal rhetorical elements.[262] The speech seems to be a farewell speech, or at least Luke purposely uses some elements of this kind of a speech in order to create a conclusion for accounts of not only the third mission journey but most probably for all Paul's mission journeys.

Most of the verses concern Paul (Acts 20:18–21, 33–35), which is a sign that Luke is presenting some important characteristic of Paul.[263] The narrative regarding Paul falls into three sections: Paul's mission

---

traveling provided by Luke (Acts 20:6–7; 20:13; 20:15; 20:17; 21:2; 21:4; 21:7), it is possible to conclude that Paul spent at least twenty-eight days of the fifty days in traveling, which indicates that he spent no more than three weeks in Achaia. This attests to Luke's use of the term *in a hurry*.

262 Scholars differ in their evaluations of the speech. For example, Dibelius is of the opinion that the speech is an *encomium*. M. Dibelius, *Studies in the Acts of the Apostles* (London: SCM Press, 1956), 155–158. For Watson, the speech is an example of epideictic rhetoric. D. F. Watson, "Paul's Speech to the Ephesian Elders (Acts 20:17–38): Epideictic Rhetoric of Farewell," in *Persuasive Artistry: Studies in Honor of George A. Kennedy*, ed. D. F. Watson (Sheffield: Sheffield Academic Press, 1991), 184–208. Witherington III takes the speech to be an example of deliberative rhetoric. B. Witherington III, *The Acts of the Apostles*, 613–614.

263 Kurichianil sees similarities between the speech and some speeches found in the Old Testament (Josh. 23:2–16, 1 Sam. 12:1–25, 1 Kings 2:1–9). J. Kurichianil, "The Speeches in the Acts and The Old Testament," *InThSt* 17 (2/1980): 181–186.

in Ephesus (Acts 20:18–21); Paul's plan to return to Jerusalem (Acts 20:22–24); and the economic aspects of Paul's mission activity (Acts 20:33–35).[264]

The speech is addressed to the elders of the community in Ephesus, specifically invited by Paul to hear his last dispositions (Acts 20:17). Paul, ignoring the rhetorical rules, proceeds immediately to present the example of his own mission activity in Ephesus (20:18–21).[265] In Acts 20:18, by way of an opening statement, Luke presents Paul's conviction that the elders were well informed about his life during the mission in Asia Minor.[266] In this speech, Paul is an example that serves as a point of reference and a point of direction. Paul's constant and unchanging conduct during his long stay in Asia is summed up in the following verses. Acts 20:19 shows the hardship of the mission in the region caused by the Jewish plot against him. This is new information that, until now, Luke has not mentioned in his account of the third mission journey.[267] This opposition was the reason for his tears; for him, it was a time of permanent testing (Acts 20:19). While describing the hardship of the mission, the impression given is that this condition of trial was not something occasional but permanent.[268]

Despite the circumstances, Paul humbly served his Lord.[269] The

---

[264] The section concerning the community in Ephesus (Acts 20:25–32) can be divided into three parts: the first contains Paul's teaching about the elders' responsibility for the community in Ephesus (Acts 20:25–28); the second refers to dangers that might challenge the community (Acts 20:29–31); and the third contains Paul's words of encouragement addressed to the elders of the community (Acts 20:31–32).

[265] C. S. Keener, *Acts. An Exegetical Commentary*, vol. 3, 3005.

[266] The same rhetorical phrase is used in 1 Thess. 1:5.

[267] This may be connected with information in Acts 20:9, where the Jews' opposition to Paul in Ephesus is briefly mentioned, or it may refer to other incidents of opposition in Asia Minor that were not recorded by Luke.

[268] This kind of description of the third mission journey is not included in the narrative concerning Paul's activity in Ephesus and Asia Minor.

[269] Paul's self-description is that of a faithful servant of Jesus, the Lord. The three expressions used—ταπεινοφροσύνης καὶ δακρύων καὶ πειρασμῶν (*humility, and sorrows and trials*)—serve to underline his faithfulness. They are key words that sum up all the suffering experienced during his service. Similar expressions

meaning of the verse is that Paul faithfully served the Lord, despite great personal cost.[270] In the midst of this unfavorable condition (Acts 20:20), Paul has not neglected his duties toward the elders and believers of the community in Ephesus, who always intended to advance their progress in the faith.[271] He raised them up by proclaiming the kerygma and teaching them a correct interpretation of the Gospel, both in public and in private.[272] Mention of proclaiming and teaching is intended here to show Paul's holistic approach to mission work, from spreading of the kerygma to explaining it in order to lead to correct understanding. All his efforts were directed toward leading Jews and Greeks to repentance and to belief in Jesus the Lord (Acts 20:20). This statement indicates the purpose of Paul's service as the servant of the Lord among the inhabitants of Asia Minor, but it also shows the main purpose of his activity.[273] There was no difference between Jews and Gentiles in Paul's mission work (Acts 20:21).[274] In this way, Luke, in Acts 20:20–21, presents his overview of this characteristic of Paul's missions.[275]

---

can be found in Paul's letters (Rom. 8:35–39; 1 Cor. 4:11–13; 2 Cor. 4:8–18–13; 6:3–10; 11:23–28).

[270] The statement "by the plots of my Jewish opponents" (Acts 20:19 NIV) should be taken as a general reference to opposition in Asia Minor and not specifically to the Ephesian Jews. Luke indicates opposition from the Jews in Acts 19:9, but he excludes the Jews from participating in the riot caused by Demetrius (Acts 19:21–40). Neil, *The Acts of the Apostles,* 213.

[271] The potential accusation against Paul, regarding a neglect of his duty, is offered by Watson as a reason for Paul's amplifying his zealous service of the communities. The positive background in which Paul's speech is placed, however, suggests a progressive presentation of the summary regarding Paul's mission attitude, which should be seen as another of Luke's ways to present his own perspective on Paul. D. F. Watson, "Paul's Speech to the Ephesian Elders," 197.

[272] This statement indicates the many public speeches and private instruction Paul gave to the Jews in Ephesus and Asian Minor. Indication of the places shows that Paul taught not only in the synagogues and the hall of Tyrannus but also in private houses (Acts 19:8–9).

[273] Fitzmyer, *The Acts of the Apostles*, 677.

[274] In accordance with Paul's *modus operandi* his mission activity was first addressed to Jews, and then to Gentiles, as Acts 20:21 indicates.

[275] Johnson, *The Acts of the Apostles*, 361.

The narrative of Acts 20:18–21 presents Paul's mission attitude, which serves as an example for the elders; it also forms the basis on which the whole speech is built, since most of the following narrative (Acts 20:28–32) refers to topics presented in the account of Paul's attitude (Acts 20:18–21).[276] The elders knew Paul's teaching and his lifestyle, and that can serve as an example the elders should follow when they find themselves in circumstances similar to those under which Paul had to work.[277]

After presenting this summary of Paul's mission in Asia Minor, Luke gives Paul's reason for calling the elders to Miletus. In the first part of the speech, Paul recounts his mission in Ephesus and Asia (Acts 20:18–21), but now, he expresses his feelings concerning the visit to Jerusalem (Acts 20:22–24). The readers of Acts have been already informed about Paul's plans (Acts 20:3, 16), which make it possible to assume that the elders of the Ephesus church also knew about his decision; until verse 25, they still did not realize that it would be the last time they would see Paul. In this part of his speech, Paul gives the reason for his decision, making the Holy Spirit as the agent of his decision when he says, νῦν ἰδοὺ δεδεμένος ἐγὼ τῷ πνεύματι [and now, compelled by the Spirit, I am going to Jerusalem] (Acts 20:22 NIV).[278] The decision was not based on his personal conviction but was made out of obedience to divine guidance. Paul's doubt concerning his visit to Jerusalem shows his awareness of a potential danger in the visit, while also showing the subordination

---

[276] Several aspects of Paul's character are presented by S. C. Barton, "Paul as Missionary and Pastor," in *The Cambridge Companion to St. Paul*, ed. J. G. Dunn (Cambridge: Cambridge University Press, 2004), 34–48.

[277] Dodd thinks that the speech (Acts 20:18–35) shows strong influence of Paul's language, as found in his epistles, which suggests that Luke had access to at least some of his epistles. C. H. Dodd, *Apostolic Preaching and its Developments* (New York: Harper & Brothers Publisher, 1944), 18–19.

[278] Among many topics used by Luke to present Paul in the narrative of Acts, the topic of the guidance of the Holy Spirit for Paul during his mission seems to be one of the most important in creating the portrait of Paul. This topic is presented in Acts 9:17; Acts 13:2, 4, 9; Acts 16:6–7, 18; Acts 20:23.

of his anxiety to the will of the Holy Spirit.[279] Luke develops this motive by saying, τὸ πνεῦμα τὸ ἅγιον κατὰ πόλιν διαμαρτύρεταί μοι [in every city the Holy Spirit warns] (Acts 20:23 NIV), which directly suggests that Paul's doubt does not regard the possibility of the persecution, which seems to be naturally included by the will of the Holy Spirit in each of Paul's missions, and rather points to a kind of persecution (Acts 20:23).[280]

The term *warns me* (indicative present active) gives the statements general character about opposition toward Paul during his entire mission career.[281] Despite his own experience and the testimony of the Holy Spirit (Acts 20:23), Paul is determined to obey the Holy Spirit by understanding the expected captivity and oppression in Jerusalem as part of God's plan, which he is willing to fulfill (Acts 20:24). Paul seems to be aware of the potential cost of his visit to Jerusalem, which may also include his own life, but he cares more about accomplishing the ministry to which he was appointed by the Lord Jesus (Acts 9:15–16).[282] Acts 20:24 indicates that Paul understands his life as the "course," which has a definite purpose that must be fulfilled. This

---

[279] Paul's statement refers to persecution in Jerusalem, which is consciously expected by Paul. This kind of narrative leads some scholars to note a parallel with Jesus's passion. Johnson, *The Acts of the Apostles*, 361; Keener, *Acts. An Exegetical Commentary,* vol. 3, 3015. However, Paul was not executed in Jerusalem, and there is no account of Paul's death in Acts, which weakens the analogy. A more appropriate point of comparison would be to understand the statement as referring to the Jews' rejection of Paul in the way that the Jews rejected Jesus in Jerusalem.

[280] Paul refers to the "imprisonment" and "hardships" he expected in Jerusalem but without further specification. Luke, in his narrative strategy, will justify Paul's doubt by employing a device of prophecy (Acts 21:4, 11–14), as well as by the narrative regarding Paul's imprisonment in Jerusalem (Acts 21:27–23:11), which will be more specific about imprisonment and hardships.

[281] Because the agent who makes the order (Acts 20:22) and the agent who testifies (Acts 20:23) are the same (the Holy Spirit), this interpretation seems to be the more accurate. Witherington III, *The Acts of the Apostles*, 620. For the term *chains* in Paul's letters, cf. Phil. 1:7, 13–14, 17; Philem. 13. For the term *afflictions* in the letters, cf. 2 Cor. 1:4; 2:4; 4:17; 6:4; Phil. 1:17; 1 Thess. 3:7.

[282] This declaration is also found in his letters: Rom. 5:15; 1 Cor. 1:17; 3:13; 9:24–27; 2 Cor. 5:18; Gal. 1:12; 1 Thess. 2:9; Phil. 2:16.

course for him is ministry, understood as "an official commissioning for a particular task."[283] This ministry was given to him by the Lord Jesus, whom he accepted as his Lord, the owner of his life and works. This ministry concerns "bearing witness," which here is limited particularly to proclaiming the kerygma. This kerygma concerns "God's grace" (Acts 20:24 NIV), which her means the resurrected Messiah, who is fulfilment of God's promise given to the ancestors. This kerygma was proclaimed by Paul (Acts 20:24 NIV) to Diaspora Jews and to Gentiles but not to the inhabitants of Jerusalem.

Although the speech is placed at the end of Paul's third mission journey and, at the same time, at the end of all Paul's mission activity recorded by Luke, Paul seems convinced that he still has not accomplished the Lord's order, and to do that, it is necessary for him to proclaim the kerygma to the Jews in Jerusalem.[284] After giving the necessary background, which contains an evaluation of Paul's mission activity during the third mission journey (Acts 20:18–21) and Paul's understanding as being the servant of the Lord Jesus (Acts 20:22–24), Luke continues with Paul's teaching concerning the elders of the church in Ephesus (Acts 20:25–32). The reason for calling the elders to Miletus and for the teaching concerning their service for community is presented as the formal statement regarding his final departure from Ephesus (Acts 20:25), which means that Paul will

[283] E. J. Schnabel, *Exegetical Commentary on the New Testament. Acts*, 842.

[284] The mention of Israel as the last in Acts 9:15 has little significance for the interpretation of this passage. Acts 22:17–22 indicates Paul's desire to undertake the mission in Jerusalem immediately after his return to the city from Damascus, but this was not in accordance to the Lord's will (Acts 22:18, 21). According to that plan, Paul must first undertake his mission activity among the Jews of the Diaspora living outside Palestine, and following that, he also must approach the Gentiles. After establishing Christian communities of Jews and Gentiles in many parts of the Roman Empire, he finally will be prepared for his last mission among the Jews of Palestine. It is worth noting that Luke's narrative shows that during the mission in Jerusalem after his conversion, Paul proclaimed the kerygma to Diaspora Jews in Jerusalem (Acts 9:28–29), but the mission to Palestinian Jews was left until the last part of the narrative in Acts.

not meet the elders again.[285] The nurture that Paul had provided for a long time would not be available anymore, which was a new reality of the community in Ephesus.[286]

Since Paul no longer would provide for the community, the elders must take responsible for the believers (Acts 20:26). This statement is a transfer of the responsibility for the community from Paul to the elders. It means that during his stay in Ephesus, Paul took responsibility for proclaiming, preaching, and teaching, but he could do so no longer. This does not mean that Paul left the elders unprepared for taking over the responsibility because he had prepared them for this task by teaching (Acts 20:27) about God's plan of salvation, which here means salvation in the name of Jesus, the Messiah.[287] From Acts 20:28, Paul turns to several particular issues relating to leadership of the community.[288] Among these, the first concerns the need for permanent development, which regards the elders as well as the entire community. This task is the most important duty of the elders, who were established by the Holy Spirit to become "overseers," looking for the unity of the community and protecting the true teaching. The term ἐπίσκοπος (*overseer*) here has its Hellenistic meaning, rather than the later postapostolic hierarchical sense, and it refers to various social and political offices, including

---

[285] Comparing the information contained in the letter to Romans (Rom. 15:24–28) with Luke's account of Paul's perspective regarding Paul's future activities, radical differences can be detected.

[286] After Paul presented some information regarding his life among the Christians in Ephesus (Acts 20:18), he now offers some self-evaluation of his proclaiming the kerygma (Acts 20:25), which contains suggestions addressed to the elders on their relationship with the community's members.

[287] This statement is a slight variation of the statement found in Acts 20:20. H. Conzelmann, *Acts of the Apostles*, 174.

[288] Acts 20:28 contains an important statement that is variously interpreted by scholars with regard to its reference. For Conzelmann, Acts 20:28 is "paraenesis for the postapostolic age." H. Conzelmann, *Acts of the Apostles*, 174–175. For Johnson, Acts 20:28 comes from the apostolic age. L. T. Johnson, *The Acts of the Apostles*, 362–363.

the office of educator.[289] Education, understood here as proclaiming and teaching (Acts 20:20, 27), is Paul's main concern; he uses the imperative form "take heed to" to show the importance of this task. As Paul was chosen by the Lord to proclaim the kerygma to both Jews and Gentiles; in a similar manner, the elders are chosen by the Holy Spirit to be the shepherds of "God's church," which is an expression indicating their duty toward the community; in a sense, closer to the Jewish tradition (God is the shepherd, and Israel is God's flock) than to the contemporary Greek image of shepherds in general.[290] This statement concerns the function of the elders within the community, which refers to their administrative position. They have a responsibility for a community that belongs to God, since God obtained it by the blood of Jesus, the faithful servant.[291] The unusual phrase underlines that the community in Ephesus, which the elders are obliged to look after, is something that belongs to God himself, which gives crucial importance to their duty.[292] Paul's words in verse 28 are not just advice; they contain, in brief, a very advanced ecclesiological teaching concerning the nature of the Christian community, from which the prerogatives and obligations of the elders devolve.[293] However, in the context of the following verses (Acts 20:29–31), these words may be additionally understood as a kind of hidden warning for the elders concerning some possible

---

[289] The term ἐπίσκοπος is used by Paul in the context of his self-evaluation concerning the duty of proclaiming and defending the kerygma, and it is not to be understood in its later ecclesiastical and hierarchic sense (Acts 20:26–27).

[290] C. S. Keener, *Acts. An Exegetical Commentary*, vol. 3, 3033–3040.

[291] Concerning the problem of interpreting the phrase "which he bought with his own blood" (Acts 20:28 NIV), cf. E. J. Schnabel, *Exegetical Commentary on the New Testament. Acts*, 846–847.

[292] The phrase "God's church" has soteriological meaning, and despite the fact that it is placed in the particular context of the community in Ephesus, it takes a general meaning, referring to all communities. W. Neil, *The Acts of the Apostles*, 214.

[293] The community is called "the church of God, which he bought with his own blood" (Acts 20:28 NIV), which is an unusual phrase in the New Testament, referring to the Christian community. The pronoun *his* does not refer to God, but to his servant Jesus. The elders are duty-bound to guard the communities, which belong to God because of the price paid by Jesus.

difficulties that they are about to face. More detailed information related to the order given in verse 28, "keep watch over yourselves and all the flock" (Acts 20:28 NIV), is given in verses 29–30, where verse 29 gives the meaning of the phrase "keep watch over yourselves and all the flock" (Acts 20:28 NIV), regarding the elders' obligation to keep watch over the community because they will be confronted with aggressive propaganda by false prophets from outside, who will attempt to destroy the community (Acts 20:29).[294] This will happen after Paul's ἄφιξις (departure), a term that may refer to Paul's leaving Asia Minor, which would suggest that problems are about to come; it may be understood as a euphemism for Paul's death, which would indicate that the attack will come sometime in the future, but it certainly will come.[295] Acts 20:30 presents another danger for the community in Ephesus, which will come from within the community. The elders have to "keep watch over yourselves" (Acts 20:28 NIV), which means that the time will come when some of those who were chosen by the Holy Spirit to be the overseers, looking after the whole flock, will begin to deceive, tearing apart the community in order to draw believers away as their own followers (Acts 20:30).[296] Their action will be deliberate, motivated by personal interest and contrary

---

[294] The phrase ἐγὼ οἶδα (I have known) used in the perfect tense, indicating that the action has already taken place, shows Paul's certainty about the organized and systematic attempt to destroy the Christian communities. Although this has not yet occurred in Ephesus, it most probably happened in other places. J. B. Lightfoot, *The Acts of the Apostles*, 265.

[295] Although the second interpretation is generally accepted, Witherington III refers to Paul's departure from Asia Minor. B. Witherington III, *The Acts of the Apostles*, 624.

[296] In Acts 20:17 the phrase πρεσβυτέρους τῆς ἐκκλησίας (the elders of the church) (Acts 20:17 NIV) is modified in Acts 20:28 (NIV) into ἐπισκόπους ποιμαίνειν τὴν ἐκκλησίαν (overseers (bishops), the shepherds of the church). Conzelmann interprets this change as indicating a postapostolic origin for this *paraenesis*. H. Conzelmann, *Acts of the Apostles*, 174. Concerning the term ἐπίσκοπος, cf. H. W. Beyer, "ἐπίσκοπος," in *TDNT*, vol. 2 (Grand Rapids: Eerdmans, 1973), 608–622. Luke specifically indicates that the elders were elected to be overseers, not by Paul but by the Holy Spirit. B. Witherington III, *The Acts of the Apostles*, 623.

to their duty of looking over the flock.[297] Looking to themselves, which is grounded in reasons presented in Acts 20:30, and looking out for the community, which is grounded in reasons presented in Acts 20:29, is the basic obligation for those to whom the future of God's church in the region was entrusted.[298] The dangers from outside (Acts 20:29) and from within (Acts 20:30) are here named by Paul as the biggest challenge for the *overseers*, who take full responsibility for the fate of the local community.[299] Because of these two threats, the elders must constantly watch over themselves and the flock in order to fulfill their task (Acts 20:31); if they fail, the existence of the community will be in danger.[300] He calls on them to be permanently vigilant, day and night. They should conduct themselves in the same way Paul did during his three years in Ephesus, when he was always on guard, looking after them and instructing them.[301] The instruction did not concern theoretical issues and was most probably provoked by some unbecoming behavior on the part of the elders, which was the reason for Paul's anguish.

These words of Paul show his awareness of the difficulty involved

---

[297] This statement does not refer to all overseers but only to certain individuals. C. S. Keener, *Acts. An Exegetical Commentary*, vol. 3, 3045. The private interests of some elders contrast greatly with the idea of God's church as the community in which the elders are just shepherds of God's flocks (Acts 20:28). It is possible that this statement by Paul is based on Paul's experience with the community in Corinth.

[298] Concerning the textual problems of Acts 20:28, cf. B. M. Metzger, *The Text of the New Testament* (Oxford: Oxford University Press, 1979), 234–236.

[299] S. Walton, *Leadership and Lifestyle. The Portrait of Paul in the Miletus Speech and 1 Thessalonians* (Cambridge: Cambridge University Press, 2000), 81–82.

[300] The use of term γρηγορέω (watch, keep awake) in the context of Acts 20:29–31 may suggest that Paul was thinking in terms of immanent eschatology. A similar term is used by Paul in 1 Thessalonians 5:6.

[301] Here, Paul returns to using his own example as the standard for the elders' attitudes and conduct in service of the community. Paul's mention of the need for permanent admonishing may indicate indirectly the problems in changing old habits and learning a new Christian lifestyle by members of the community in Ephesus. The context suggests that the duty to admonish is the responsibility of the elders. F. F. Bruce, *The, Book of the Acts*, 93–394.

in ceding the responsibility for the community in Ephesus to the elders. It will not be an easy task, and not everyone will be properly prepared for it, which is a reason why Paul commits those who, until now, were under his care to the protection of God and his Word. The elders cooperated with Paul in successfully building the community during his time in the city, but now they must commit themselves to the service of God and his Gospel in order to continue building up the identity and stability of the community in Ephesus.[302] It is only by cooperating with God and the Gospel, as proclaimed by Paul, that they may accomplish the tasks for which they had been chosen (Acts 20:32).[303] Verse 32, in which he entrusts the elders to God, is the climax of Paul's transmission to the elders the responsibility for the community in Ephesus.[304]

In the fourth and the last part of the speech (Acts 20:32–35), Luke gives Paul's self-presentation regarding his attitude toward material goods. This is given to show the elders correct conduct in the matter of material goods and has an exemplary character. Paul's exposition contains three different aspects of the issue. The first (Acts 20:32) regards the reason for Paul's service to the community, which was never motivated by a desire to possess the goods belonging to the believers who were under his care.[305] The desire regards not only the wish to take the goods of the flock but probably also any demand for compensation for service to the community.[306] Indirectly, Paul calls on the elders to follow his example and avoid every material motivation in their service to the community in Ephesus. The second aspect concerns the way in which he earned the money necessary for living (Acts 20:33). Paul earned this by manual work undertaken during his mission work in Asia Minor in order to provide for his

[302] L. T. Johnson, *The Acts of the Apostles*, 364; W. Neil, *The Acts of the Apostles*, 215.

[303] In order to be recognized and accepted by the faithful believers of Jesus, the elders of the community must fulfill this condition.

[304] C. S. Keener, *Acts. An Exegetical Commentary*, vol. 3, 3053.

[305] J. A. Fitzmyer, *The Acts of the Apostles*, 681.

[306] For exposition of Paul as the example for community life and leadership, cf. S. Walton, *Leadership and Lifestyle*, 82–84.

own needs as well as for needs of his coworkers (Acts 20:34).[307] Indirectly, Paul instructed the elders that they should work to provide the necessary material support for themselves (and probably for their families) and not take advantage of the community.[308] The third aspect refers to assistance to those in need.[309] Paul sees the work as a source of financial stability, which first serves to support himself and those who are his coworkers but also makes it possible to help those who are unable to secure their own needs (Acts 20:35).[310] Paul refers to his own example, which was known to the elders, although Luke does not mention this in the narrative regarding Paul's mission in Ephesus. This attitude, according to Paul, is in accordance with Jesus's teaching, even though the quotation is not found in the Gospels, but it is attested by Lucan tradition as being the common practice among the believers in Jesus (Acts 4:32–37). Indirectly, Paul instructs the elders that they have to use their possessions to assist members of the community who are in need.[311] In reality, in Acts 20:33–35, Paul, in an indirect manner, focuses on the social obligation of the elders, who must serve the community without expectation of reward; instead, they must work for their own needs, but they also are

[307] This is new information that was not mentioned in Luke's narrative of the mission in Ephesus (unlike the narrative concerning the mission in Corinth during the second mission journey). For similar statements, cf. 1 Cor. 4:12; 9:15–18; 1 Thess. 4:1 1; 2 Thess. 3:6–10.

[308] C. S. Keener, *Acts. An Exegetical Commentary*, vol. 3, 3060.

[309] Note a gradual escalation of the requirements Paul expected from the elders of the Ephesus community, starting with *do not use the goods of the believers; earn money by your own work; use your money for those in need.*

[310] Luke uses the term ἀσθενέω (to be weak, powerless) in reference to physical illness (Luke 4:40; 5:5; 12:27). Paul, in his letters, refers it to spiritual weakness and mental incapacity (1 Cor. 4:12; 2 Cor. 12:10; Gal. 4:11; 2 Tim. 2:6). A comparison of Acts 21:35 with the sayings of Jesus is provided in a study by R. F. O'Toole, "What Role Does Jesus' Saying in Acts 20, 35 Play in Paul's Address to the Ephesian Elders?" *Bib* 75 (1994): 329–249.

[311] The texts of the Gospels do not support Paul's statement that the phrase "it is more blessed in giving than in receiving" (Acts 20:35 NIV) is a *logion* of Jesus. On the contrary, it seems that the phrase is a Greek aphorism. However, a similar expression can be found in Luke 12:23. H. Conzelmann, *Acts of the Apostles*, 171.

obliged to share their possessions in order to secure the daily needs of the believers.[312] Luke presents Paul as the man who fulfilled these demanding obligations and who expected the same conduct from those to whom he entrusted responsibility for the community, which was built by him.

The last part of the narrative of the third mission journey concerns Paul's return to Jerusalem (Acts 21:1–16), which, due to Luke's being in the company of Paul, contains much detailed and useful information about the journey itself but hardly mentions Paul. The name of Paul first appears in the context of a weeklong stay at Tyre, where the believers thought the Spirit warned him not to go to Jerusalem. For some reason, however, Paul ignored their advice. The second time Paul's name is mentioned is in the context of his stay in the house of Philip in Caesarea (Acts 21:11–16). During the stay, the prophet Agabus from Judea foretold Paul's imprisonment in Jerusalem, which caused the believers and Paul's coworkers to oppose his return to the city (Acts 21:12, 14). Their reaction disconcerted Paul, probably because he expected their encouragement in this time of great distress. Paul is alone in the strong conviction that he is ready to be imprisoned or even to die in the name of Jesus. These words of Paul are the climax of Luke's narrative regarding the persecution expected in Jerusalem, which began with Paul's confession during the speech in Miletus (Acts 20:22–24), followed by the warning by the believers from Tyre (Acts 21:4), and ended with Paul's statement provoked by the believers in Caesarea.[313]

Luke's perspective indirectly shows some important characteristics of Paul, who is about to walk into the lion's den. The first concerns his conviction that it is necessary for him to enter Jerusalem, and in the narrative, this is underlined by invoking divine assurance in his decision and the arguments of the believers who oppose him (Acts 20:22–23; 21:4, 11).[314] The second concerns Paul's full consciousness

---

[312] S. Walton, *Leadership and Lifestyle*, 82–84.

[313] H. Conzelmann, *Acts of the Apostles*, 178.

[314] Probably for this reason, Luke excludes from the narrative any mention of the collection for the believers in Jerusalem.

of the real danger, and at the same time, his willingness to obey the will of the Lord, which is the most important characteristic in Luke's perspective on Paul. The third concerns the fact that from now on, Paul will be forced to face the hardship of imprisonment alone. His coworkers do not understand, or they do not accept his decision, and after his imprisonment, they are limited in the way in which they can support him in his fight against the judicial machine (Acts 23:16; 24:23; 27:1).[315] This last characteristic explains why, in the narrative of Paul's imprisonment and trials, Luke hardly mentions the believers in Jerusalem, Caesarea, and Rome.[316]

Conclusion

The narrative concerning the third mission journey (Acts 18:23–21:16) contains two major sections: Paul's mission in Ephesus (Acts 18:23–40), and his visit to Macedonia and Greece, as well as his journey home (Acts 20:1–21:16). Although the first part contains some new and important information that contributes to Luke's perspective on Paul, the most important information is placed in the second part of the narrative, especially in Paul's speech in Miletus, which ends the narrative of the third mission journey. Much is contained in the farewell speech, but the main purpose is to show Paul's achievements during his mission activity in Asia Minor. In fact, the reader can learn more about Paul's achievements in Ephesus from the speech than from Luke's narrative regarding the mission, which is just a very schematic summary.

In the narrative concerning the third mission journey, Luke chooses the speech as the place to indicate four aspects of Paul's character as a missionary. The first aspect concerns his mission

[315] Although the help provided for Paul is only briefly mentioned by Luke, Paul's two years of imprisonment in Caesarea required great effort by the Caesarean believers.

[316] Luke's narrative regarding Paul's visit to James may be taken as an exception, but this is presented as an event preceding the arrest.

attitude (Acts 20:18–21), which is characterized by his total devotion to the task for which he was appointed. The second aspect concerns Paul's self-consciousness regarding the circumstances in which he is operating, as well as a deeply theologized interpretation of his service (Acts 20:22–24). The third aspect shows Paul in his relationship with the fruits of his mission works; namely, those who are to succeed him in working for the community (Acts 20:25–30). The advice given to the elders shows Paul's recognition of the responsibility of the leaders. The fourth aspect shows Paul's attitude toward compensation for his mission work (Acts 20:31–35). The first (A) and fourth (A^1) aspects are related to each other and form a bracket around the main topic of the speech, which is the expectation of the persecution of Paul (B) and of the community in Ephesus (B^1). This structure of the speech is a characteristic of Luke's design to prepare the reader for the following narrative, while at the same time presenting some characteristic aspects of Paul. Luke does this at the end of each narrative section regarding a specific period of Paul's life.

3. Walking into the Lion's Den (Acts 21:1–26)

When Paul and his companions finally reached Jerusalem, they found hospitality in the house of Mnason, a Jew of the Diaspora from Cyprus (Acts 21:16).[317] At the beginning of the narrative of Paul's visit to Jerusalem, Luke indicates that the community in Jerusalem welcomed him very warmly (Acts 21:17), but he offers no further information about their relationship. On the second day after Paul's arrival in the city (Acts 21:17–18), he paid a visit to James, the leader of the Jerusalem community.[318] Luke says nothing about the real reason for the visit, but the fact that the elders of the

[317] Mention of another Jew of the Diaspora suggests that Paul's network in Jerusalem was mostly within this group.

[318] Note that Luke still says nothing about the collection. Concerning the possible interpretation of this fact, cf. E. J. Schnabel, *Exegetical Commentary on the New Testament. Acts*, 871.

Jerusalem community were also present (Acts 21:18) may suggest that the meeting had a semi-official character and was not just a courtesy visit. However, Luke attempts to present Paul in an independent manner, not as a person subordinated to the Jerusalem community. Luke mentions Paul's account regarding the mission among Gentiles (Acts 21:18–19), which, judging from the reaction of the audience (Acts 21:20), contained optimistic information that focused on the successes of his mission. Paul's account caused the elders to praise God for Paul's achievement (Acts 21:20), but they did not praise Paul himself, and in their reply (Acts 21:20–25), they expressed their misgivings concerning Paul's stay in Jerusalem. This is a serious issue they wished to resolve.

James's speech begins with an *exordium* addressed only to Paul (not to the other visitors), who is called "brother." This is a formal greeting that indicates that the one addressed is accepted by the speaker.[319] The following *narratio* (Acts 21:20–21) presents the elders' understanding of the present attitudes in the Jerusalem community (Acts 21:20), which is generally negative in its evaluation of his mission attitude (Acts 21:21).[320] In verse 20, the elders, in a very direct way, show the current consensus existing in the Jerusalem community, where the believers in Jesus continuing to follow Jewish tradition and preserve the Mosaic Law. The term πάντες (all) shows that this was the common practice in Jerusalem, which was followed also by the elders.[321]

The Jewish Christians living in Jerusalem do not consider themselves to be non-Jews, nor do they consider it necessary to live in any way different from Jews who are not believers in Jesus.[322] They stress the fact that thousands of Jews who believe in Jesus are

---

[319] M. I. Soards, *The Speeches in Acts. Their Content, Context, and Concerns* (Louisville: Westminster/Knox, 1994), 110. Note the opposite situation during the Paul's trial before the Sanhedrin (Acts 23:1).

[320] The subject of Acts 21:20 and Acts 21:21 is the same Jewish Christians. H. Conzelmann, *Acts of the Apostles*, 180.

[321] D. G. Peterson, *The Acts of the Apostles*, 585–586.

[322] C. S. Keener, *Acts. An Exegetical Commentary*, vol. 3, 3119–3124.

zealously obeying the Law. Their words are not just intended as information; they indicate the problem that they are about to discuss. Their statement serves as a preparation of the basis for a critique of Paul's teaching, which is seen as contrary to the consensus of the Jerusalem community (Acts 21:21). The issue concerns a problem within the Jerusalem community, which, according to the elders' speech, involves three groups that hold different positions. The first group is formed by Jewish Christians still following the Mosaic Law (Acts 21:20). The second is represented by Paul, who is accused of encouraging Jewish Christians and Diaspora Jews to abandon the Mosaic Law.[323] The third group acts as a mediator between these two groups and consists of James and the elders. The mediators present the most problematic issue of Paul's teaching that can scarcely be accepted in Jerusalem. Paul is "famous" among Jewish Christians in Jerusalem as the one who teaches Jews in the Diaspora to abandon the Mosaic Law (the first accusation) by abandoning the signs of the covenant (the second accusation) and by encouraging them to change Jewish traditions (the third accusation).[324] Acts 21:22 is the *propositio* of the speech, in which the mediators use a rhetorical question to point toward the solution. The effect of the rhetorical question is strengthened by the mediators' mention regarding the possibility (including elements of a real threat) that Paul's arrival in Jerusalem will be not hidden for long, and when the Jewish Christians come to know of it, the problem will become real within the Jerusalem community.[325]

---

[323] The mediators take no side in the dispute. This is attested by the fact that they use the third-person plural pronoun when speaking about Jewish Christians from Jerusalem, and the second-person singular when speaking about Paul. It shows their attempt to prevent a potential conflict between members of the Jerusalem community. J. A. Fitzmyer, *The Acts of the Apostles*, 693.

[324] Sanders is of the opinion that the Gentiles mentioned in Acts 21:21 are not "God-fearers" but are Jews living among Gentiles. J. T. Sanders, "Who is a Jew and Who is a Gentile in the Book of Acts," *NTS* 37 (1991): 447.

[325] Acts 21:22 indicates that the elders in the Jerusalem community took seriously the possible danger of Paul's visit. This conviction prompted their speech and their strong request that Paul act according to their suggestions (Acts 21:23–24). A question arises about their motivation: were they concerned for Paul's life, or

In this way, the mediators not only put considerable pressure on Paul, but they also indirectly insinuate that Paul held a responsibility for the whole situation.[326] Certainly, the mediators persuaded Paul, asking him to act in order to convince the Jewish Christians in Jerusalem that the rumor about him is not true. Acts 21:23–24 is the *probatio* of the speech, where a solution to the rhetorical question is given by the mediators (those who asked the question) in a very

---

were they merely attempting to avoid possible conflict within the community? Acts 21:24b, containing the solution of the problem, seems to support the second possibility; namely, Jewish Christians in Jerusalem might act against Paul. The most suitable solution for them was that Paul perform something in public that would convince his opponents that their suspicions toward Paul were unfounded, and to achieve this, they ordered Paul to follow the ritual of purification, obligatory for those returning from abroad, and also to make a financial contribution to four believers from Jerusalem who wished to fulfil their Nazarite vows. This attitude of Paul should, in their estimation, convince his opponents within the Jewish Christian community that he had not abandoned the Mosaic Law, nor had he spoken against circumcision and Jewish tradition. In this way, the Jews in Jerusalem would be shown that all accusations against Paul and his mission among the Diaspora Jews were unfounded (Acts 21:24).

326 Acts 21:22 expresses the common opinion of Jewish Christians in Jerusalem—that Paul, during the missions, taught Jews to abandon Judaism by calling on Jews to abandon the traditions of the ancestors. From the evidence of Paul's letters, this widespread opinion can be dismissed and should be taken as indicating anti-Paul propaganda. But a question arises concerning the source of the propaganda. According to one theory, many opponents who actively challenged Paul during his missions did not restrict their activities to the local community but also spread, with considerable success, their criticism to neighboring cities and even to Jews in Jerusalem when they went on pilgrimage to the city. It is possible but still highly speculative that their opinions were reported to the authorities of the Temple. It is also thought that there was a lack of real knowledge about Paul's teaching on the part of the Jerusalem community. Acts 21:21 suggests that the community did not yet know Paul's teaching concerning the relationship between the Law and the faith, or if they knew it, they failed to understand and comprehend it correctly, but this seems very unlikely, given the length of time that elapsed since the Council of Jerusalem. Luke's narrative presents the elders in a neutral light, as those who present the opinion of others, which points to others in the Jerusalem community (Jewish Christians who opposed Paul in Antioch and during the Council of Jerusalem) who were the declared antagonists of Paul.

authoritative manner.[327] Paul, together with the four Jewish Christians from the Jerusalem community, must perform the ritual purification, according to the Law. This is the elders' solution for avoiding conflict within the community in Jerusalem. The final verse (Acts 21:25) is the *peroratio* of the speech, which seems to have little in common with the content of the speech. It refers to teaching concerning food regulations, and it is addressed to Gentiles as part of the decree of the Council of Jerusalem.[328] Considering the fact that Paul and the elders took part in the council, this information seems unnecessary.[329] However, the use of ἐπεστείλαμεν (*we wrote*—using the first-person plural) suggests that this commonly known information is used here by the elders as their final argument addressed to Paul, which should convince him to act according to their wish. Acts 21:25 does not introduce a new topic of the speech because it is the end of the speech, and the topic is not elaborated. However, the elders' repetition of some parts of the decree of the Council of Jerusalem concerning the Gentiles contributes to the topic of this speech.[330] Acts 21:25 should be read as the final argument of the elders in their presentation of a solution for a problem. In the rhetorical strategy of the elders, the quotation of the decree attests that the Jerusalem community respected the different cultural background of Gentile Christians

[327] Paul, together with the four Jewish Christians from the Jerusalem church, must perform ritual purification, according to the Mosaic Law. This is the elders' solution to convince Jewish Christian in Jerusalem that Paul not only personally obeys the Mosaic Law but also financially helps other Jewish Christian to perform the ritual.

[328] The quoted part of the decree has some modifications (Acts 15:20, 29).

[329] Witherington III thinks that the aim of the narrative in Acts 21:20–25 is to indicate to the reader that the accusations against Paul were the result of his mission to the Gentiles and the negative evaluation of this by the Diaspora Jews, rather than by Jewish Christian criticism of Paul's teaching. B. Witherington III, *The Acts of the Apostles*, 650–651.

[330] This version of the decree shows that Gentiles are not obliged to obey the Mosaic Law and follow Jewish customs, but they are obliged to refrain from all acts related to idolatry (Acts 15:29). Note that in Acts 21:25, the order of prohibition has been changed, in comparison to Acts 15:28–29), and it does not include the Golden Rule. L. T. Johnson, *The Acts of the Apostles*, 376.

and, for this reason, requires from them respect of those parts of the Mosaic Law that are necessary to maintain unity (particularly, unity at the table) between Gentile Christians and Jewish Christians. This understanding of Gentiles' differences is a considerable compromise by the Jewish Christians, but it also is a very compelling argument on the part of the elders to convince Paul to attend the purification ritual.[331] If even Gentile Christians are obliged to respect some part of the Mosaic Law, then it seems logical that the Jewish Christians are obliged to continue obeying the Law.

The message that the elders want to give Paul is that Jewish Christians should follow the Mosaic Law and the ancient traditions, particularly in places and communities that are dominated by Christians with a Jewish background.[332] Luke's narrative suggests that the elders' arguments convinced Paul and helped him to understand the specific nature of the community in Jerusalem. Paul acquiesced to the request of the elders, purified himself, and went to the Temple to report that he had carried out the ritual (Acts 21:26).

Conclusion

The narrative concerning Paul's visit to James, which consists, for the most part, of the elders' speech, shows that Paul was a controversial person in the circle of Jewish Christians from the Jerusalem community. This kind of presentation is not new in Luke's narrative, and it is in accord with other narratives concerning the relationship between Paul and the Jerusalem community (Acts 9:26–30; 15:1–6).[333]

---

331 H. Conzelmann, *Acts of the Apostles*, 180. Actually, Luke does not inform us if Paul was planning to follow the ritual obligatory for all Jews returning from abroad.

332 However, not all that is required of Jewish Christians is also required of Gentile Christians. E. J. Schnabel, *Exegetical Commentary*, 877.

333 Despite the fact that the speech is given in the house of James, Luke does not directly point to James as the author of the speech; rather, he indicates the elders of the Jerusalem communities as the authors of the speech. Then, in Miletus, Paul was speaking to the elders of the Ephesus community; here in Jerusalem,

The narrative presents the elders as the mediators between Paul and his opponents, who were Jewish Christian in Jerusalem. The task of the elder was to avoid conflict within the community, something that was expected to emerge due to Paul's reputation. This reputation was spread among the Jewish Christian in Jerusalem, partly by Diaspora Jews, who came annually to the city for the feasts, and partly by those members of the Jerusalem community who came into conflict with Paul due to differences of opinion on issues related to their understanding of the New Israel.

For the most part the controversy about Paul and his teaching was based on a misunderstanding of the true meaning of Paul's teaching, concerning some topics that were of critical importance for Paul's interpretation of the realization, in Jesus, of the messianic promises, but also were extremely sensitive for Jewish Christians who were still strongly rooted in Jewish tradition.[334] In Luke's narrative concerning Paul's imprisonment in Jerusalem, the speech functions as a preparation that clarifies the relationship between the Jerusalem community and Paul, before entering into the account about events leading to Paul's imprisonment. Some Jewish Christians were aware of controversy surrounding the person of Paul, which creates suspicion concerning Paul's interpretation of the scripture and his attitude towards Mosaic Law. The content of James's speech gives no basis to assume that the elders believed the accusations against Paul, but they were aware that some believers in Jerusalem found Paul's teaching and behavior as a Jew to be wanting.

The aim of the elders' speech was to prevent potential conflict within the community, which naturally would involve Paul and could also endanger his life. The aim of the speech was to require an action from Paul that would prove his respect and obedience to the

---

the elders of the community are speaking to Paul. This observation may expose another of Luke's perspectives on Paul.

Schnabel thinks that James's speech is Luke's attempt to avoid every possibility of connecting James with Paul's arrest. E. J. Schnabel, *Exegetical Commentary*, 811–812.

334 J. A. Fitzmyer, *The Acts of the Apostles*, 692.

Mosaic Law and tradition (Acts 21:24). His action, in their opinion, should convince the skeptics among the Jewish Christians that the accusations made against Paul were false. According to the account of Acts, Paul, from the beginning to the end of his mission career, had to face suspicion, accusation, misunderstanding, and difficulties coming from not only Jews but also from Jewish Christians, and the community in Jerusalem, at least in part, was no exception.[335] The function of the speech in Luke's narrative strategy is to show that the community in Jerusalem took no action against Paul and was not involved in the event leading to Paul's imprisonment (Acts 21:27–40), despite the suspicions concerning Paul within the community.[336] The elders ensured Paul's presence among the Jewish Christians in Jerusalem, but according to Luke's narrative, their action was limited only to the group of Jewish Christian and contributed nothing to protect him from the antagonistic attitude of the Diaspora Jews.

4. Paul in Chains (Acts 21:27–28:31)

Luke's narrative concerning Paul's imprisonment is developed in four stages, where importance is given to the place of the events and the persons involved, allowing us to make the following division: imprisonment in Jerusalem (Acts 21:27–23:35); imprisonment in Caesarea (Acts 24:1–26:32); voyage to Rome (Acts 27:1–28:16); imprisonment in Rome (Acts 28:17–31). Because the narrative forms the end of the book of Acts, it is to be expected that Luke used it as the final stage in developing his portrait of Paul. Information regarding Paul's life that has not yet been presented by Luke is collected into this narrative, at times in order to conclude a presentation that was

[335] This aspect of Paul's biography is even stronger attested by Paul's writings; cf. Gal. 2.

[336] The next section, the events at the Jerusalem Temple, begins with the indication of the initiators of Paul's arrest, which does not include the members of the Jerusalem community (Acts 21:27). Concerning this problem, cf. L. T. Johnson, *The Acts of the Apostles*, 377–380.

begun but left incomplete, but in some cases, in order to show a new aspect of Paul.

4.1. Imprisonment in Jerusalem (Acts 21:27–23:35)

The narrative regarding this stage of Paul's imprisonment contains the following events: the incident in the Temple (Acts 21:27–22:30); the trial before the Sanhedrin (Acts 23:1–11); the plot against Paul (Acts 23:12–35). These events occurred in a Jewish setting, with the participation of the Roman soldiers. The narrative gives the reasons for the rejection of Paul by the Jews of Jerusalem.

4.1.1. The incident in the Temple (Acts 21:27–22:30)

The incident in the Temple is the beginning of the narrative concerning Paul's imprisonment in Jerusalem (Acts 21:27–23:34), and it comprises two subsections: the Jews seize Paul (Acts 21:27–40); Paul's speech to the Jews in the Temple (Acts 22:1–29). After Luke's exclusion in the speech of the elders of Jewish Christians in Jerusalem from being the opponents of Paul, he now specifies the passage of time (one week) between Paul's visit to James and the incident in the Temple, in order to separate these two events that have nothing in common. Acts 21:27 indicates the place of the incident as being one of the inner courts of the Temple, frequented by Paul after the completion of the seven days of his purification ritual. It also identifies those acting against Paul as Jews from Asia Minor, who were in Jerusalem for the Feast of Pentecost.[337] They recognized Paul and accused him of teaching against the nation (Israel), the Mosaic Law, and the Jerusalem Temple (Acts 21:28).[338]

The accusation goes from the general (the nation), through the

[337] Acts 21:29 suggests that among the Jews from Asia Minor, there were also Jews from Ephesus.

[338] The accusation against Paul's teaching has a universal character because the accusers emphasized that Paul spread his teaching everywhere and to everyone (Jews and Gentiles).

more specific (the Mosaic Law), to the particular (the Temple), with a gradual increase of emotion.[339] The general accusation refers more to Paul's teaching (Acts 14:1–2; 17:3–5; 18:5–8; 19:8–10) that divided Jewish communities in the Diaspora than to his propaganda against the Jews in general. The specific accusation concerns the Mosaic Law, and it is similar to that contained in the objections presented by the elders in the preceding narrative (Acts 21:21). The particular accusation concerns the Temple where the incident takes place, which is the most sensitive issue if the context of this accusation (the Pentecost Feast) is taken into consideration. The last accusation is immediately reinforced by the false conviction that Paul has brought into the inner part of the Temple a Gentile, Trophimus. This would be an act of profaning the Temple, punishable by death. The succeeding narrative suggests that this last accusation played the most significant role in the development of the incident.

A large number of Jews, alerted by these accusations, turned on Paul (Acts 21:30), seized him, then dragged him out of the inner court of the Temple in order to kill him (Acts 21:31). This intent is repeated by Luke in verse 32 and verse 36. Luke clearly indicates that if the incident had run its course, Paul would have died at the hands of the Jews, but the involvement of the Romans soldiers, who evidently misunderstood the situation, thinking that Paul was the leader of a riot against Rome (Acts 21:31–38), saved him from immediate death but initiated what would be, for Paul, a long road of interrogations.

In the barracks, Paul identified himself to the Romans, where we learn the new information concerning his citizenship of Tarsus (Acts 21:37–39).[340] By correcting the Romans' wrong assumption,

[339] Note some similarities with the accusation against Stephen (Acts 6:13–14).

[340] In Acts 21:39, Paul claims to possess the citizenship of a Greek city, which naturally implies that he inherited this from his parents. Considering that his parents were Jews and Pharisees, there are some reasons to doubt that his parents, in fact, obtained that privilege. The first doubt is raised by the circumstances in which Paul declared that he possessed citizenship of the Greek city. He made this claim to distance himself from being considered the Egyptian troublemaker that the Romans thought they had arrested. The second doubt comes from whether it was possible for Jews to acquire citizenship in Greek cities. Several requirements

Paul forced the soldiers to search for another reason to explain the riot in the city (Acts 21:30), and in order to find it, permission was given for Paul to give a speech to clarify the whole situation.[341] This speech is an important part of the narrative concerning Paul's imprisonment (Acts 21:27–28:31), and due to its apologetic character, it contains a brief, unique account of Paul's life that includes much information (Acts 22:17–21) that cannot be found elsewhere in the New Testament, even in Paul's own writings.[342] This gives this speech a particular importance, both for the information it contains and for its contribution to our understanding of Luke's portrait of Paul.

The speech is a very much elaborated apology, containing an account of Paul's life from his birth until the revelation in the Jerusalem Temple, at which point the speech is interrupted by the audience and is left incomplete.[343] For this reason, from a rhetorical point of view, the speech is reduced only to two parts: a short *exordium* (Acts 22:1) and an extensive *narratio* (Acts 22:3–21).[344] Paul addresses Jews in Aramaic, the vernacular of the inhabitants of Jerusalem, which comes as a surprise to the audience, who expect this Jew from the

related to the citizenship were in direct opposition to Jewish conviction. While it was possible for a Jew to acquire the citizenship in the cities (*polites*), it required considerable wealth and a degree of Hellenization. M. H. Williams, *The Jews Among the Greeks & Romans. A Diasporan Sourcebook* (London: Johns Hopkins University Press, 1998), 107–111. These requirements made it almost impossible for religious Jews to obtain the citizenship. Another possibility lay in the entire community of Jews possessing the citizenship. Because it is only Flavius Josephus who mentions the possibility of obtaining the citizenship by an entire Jewish community (*Ant.* XIX, 278–285; *Pros Apion* II, 39–40), it is doubtful whether Jewish communities, as a group, could possess the citizenship of Greek cities.

341 E. J. Schnabel, *Exegetical Commentary*, 898.

342 For more information concerning the speeches and their social context, cf. J. Neyrey, "The Forensic Defense Speech and Paul's Trial Speeches in Acts 22–26: Form and Function," in *Luke-Acts: New Perspectives from the Society of Biblical Literature Seminar*, ed. C. H. Talbert (New York: Crossroad, 1984), 210–224; F. Veltman, "The Defense Speeches of Paul in Acts," in *Perspectives on Luke-Acts*, ed. C. H. Talbert (Edinburgh: T&T Clark, 1978), 253–256.

343 L. T. Johnson, *The Acts of the Apostles*, 393.

344 B. Witherington III, *The Acts of the Apostles*, 666–668.

Diaspora to speak in the same language as his accusers, the Jews from Asia Minor (Acts 22:2).[345] He not only speaks in Aramaic, but he also uses the correct form of greeting when addressing the audience, and phrases such as "my brothers, my fathers" show an identification of the speaker with the audience, making his speech more convincing (Acts 22:1).[346]

The following words, "ἀκούσατέ μου τῆς πρὸς ὑμᾶς νυνὶ ἀπολογίας [listen now to my defense]" (Acts 22:1 NIV), directly indicates the purpose of Paul's speech, which is to defend himself against an accusation. Although the accusation is not directly indicated here, it is known to the reader from the narrative preceding the speech (Acts 21:27–29), and it includes all three elements that prove that Paul had renounced Judaism (Acts 21:28). This short *exordium* contains two important points that clarify that the event was a strictly a Jewish problem (even if Romans are partly involved): the speaker and his audience belong to the same ethnic and religious group; and Paul has to make an apology to his countrymen because of doubts concerning his orthodoxy. The second part of the speech (*narratio*) consists of four subsections, where each, in a chronological and a logical way, concerns four periods of Paul's life until his first visit to Jerusalem after his conversion.[347]

The first subsection refers to the period from Paul's birth in Tarsus to his active involvement in the persecution of the new

---

[345] The fact that Paul silenced the crowd and then began to speak to them was already presented in Acts 21:40 and Acts 22:2 should be taken as a simple repetition, intended to underline the attention of the crowd. In Acts 22:2, Luke connected the crowd's attention with Paul's speaking in Aramaic, which suggests that by speaking in Aramaic, Paul not only got their attention but also their sympathy. R. J. Cassidy, *Society and Politics in the Acts of the Apostles* (New York: Orbis, 1987), 96–144; L. T. Johnson, *The Acts of the Apostles*, 387.

[346] This speech shows some similarities with the speech of Stephen in the manner of addressing the crowd and in its context (Acts 7:2). C. S. Keener, *Acts. An Exegetical Commentary*, vol. 3, 3204.

[347] Some scholars doubt the relevance of analyzing the speech according to Greek rhetorical standards; cf. B. Witherington III, *The Acts of the Apostles,* 665–668.

messianic movement within Judaism (Acts 22:3–5).[348] It is a short résumé of Paul's life from his birth in Cilicia until his escape from Damascus. For the second time (the first time in Acts 21:39), Luke informs us that Paul was a Diaspora Jew, born in Tarsus in Cilicia.[349] Although Paul was not a Palestinian Jew, he was raised in Jerusalem, where he was educated in the Mosaic Law by the Hillelite Gamaliel, the most famous teacher among the Pharisees.[350] His study of the Mosaic Law is described as ἀκρίβεια (exact), which shows the high level of Paul's knowledge of the Law.[351] His intellectual preparation was supplemented by his religious zeal in serving the only God (Acts 22:3). Paul compares his zeal to that of the opponents he is addressing,[352] which in this context refers to his former uncompromising attitude toward anything that seemed to be in opposition to Judaism. In the same way that the crowd is now convinced of Paul's guilt, he was convinced of the guilt of Jesus's followers. Such conviction led Paul

---

[348] The information contained in this part of the speech agrees with that given in Acts 8:1–3; 9:1–2; Gal. 1:13; Phil. 3:5–6.

[349] This information may have been intended to earn the sympathy of Diaspora Jews.

[350] There is no contradiction between the information that Paul was raised in Jerusalem and the information presented in Galatians 1:22 because they concern different periods of Paul's life and are placed in different contexts. L. T. Johnson, *The Acts of the Apostles*, 387–388. Similar biographical statements can be found in Stephen's speech (Acts 7:20–22). For an extensive account on Gamaliel, cf. C. S. Keener, *Acts. An Exegetical Commentary*, vol. 3, 3215–3221.

[351] The inclusion at the beginning of the speech of such biographical information is an *encomium* intended to establish the speaker as a credible person who shares values similar to those of his audience. E. J. Schnabel, *Exegetical Commentary*, 899–901.

[352] Paul's praise of their zeal for Judaism serves as a *captatio benevolentiae*, which, in this particular context, is designed to counterbalance their initial negative evaluation of Paul as an opponent of God. In this particular narrative, reference to the Jews' zeal may serve also as a form of preparing the hearers for Paul's presentation of himself as a zealous Jew who has persecuted a new sect within Judaism, which he had considered to be opposed to God and a threat to Judaism. In the context of Acts 21:7–11, this *captatio benevolentiae* may be intended as a veiled insinuation of the crowd's wrongdoing toward Paul. D. G. Peterson, *The Acts of the Apostles,* 596–597.

to participate in their persecution with the same determination and purpose as the crowd now showed toward Paul (Acts 22:4).[353] His strong conviction that the messianic movement was dangerous to Judaism and his boundless zeal led him to be involved in a large-scale effort aimed at the destruction of Jesus's followers, not only in Jerusalem but wherever there were Jews (Acts 22:5).[354]

The importance of Paul's involvement in this persecution is underlined by the fact that the high priest and the elders encouraged him to continue his persecution, not only in Jerusalem and Judea but also in places where they had no jurisdiction, such as Damascus in Syria.[355] They granted him letters of reference for the Jews in the Diaspora, ordering them to assist Paul in his search for the followers of Jesus, who may have found shelter in Damascus. In this way, Paul presents himself as a Jew with the same zeal for God now shown by the crowd. This was a tactic that would earn him the sympathy of the crowd, but at the same time, this mention of zeal serves as a preparation for the following stage of the narrative (Acts 22:6–11), which shows how wrong he had been in his conviction and also insinuates that the zeal of the crowd is misdirected.

The second subsection (Acts 22:6–11) refers to the event in Damascus. After a very schematic account about Paul's own youth that mostly underlines his active participation in the persecution of

353 The term τὴν ὁδὸν means literally *this way*, but here, it is a technical term that refers to the messianic movement established by Jesus of Nazareth (Acts 9:2; 19:9, 23). Lucan Paul assumes that the crowd was familiar with the meaning of this technical term. Information regarding Saul's persecution of the Way can be found also in Paul's letters (1 Cor 15:9; Gal. 1:13–14; Phil. 3:6), where his zealous service of God is presented as being the reason for his action. L. T. Johnson, *The Acts of the Apostles*, 388.

354 The statement in Acts 9:1 (NIV), "Saul was still breathing out murderous threats against the Lord's disciples," is the most extreme expression of Saul's determination to destroy the messianic movement.

355 The accounts in Acts 22:5 and Acts 9:2 concern the same event, but they contain some small differences. Concerning these differences, cf. H. Conzelmann, *Acts of the Apostles*, 187. Saul's zeal in persecution is presented in terms that would amplify Paul's credibility, with reference made to the authorities of the Jerusalem Temple as witnesses.

the messianic movement, now, in the second subsection of the speech (Acts 22:6–11), he refers to the events that turned him from being a persecutor into becoming a follower. The event is commonly called the revelation of Jesus to Paul on the road to Damascus, or more briefly, "Paul's conversion," or also Paul's call to the mission to Gentiles.[356] At the beginning of this part (Acts 22:6), Paul provides three aspects concerning the event: the place ("near Damascus"), the time ("noon"), and the form of revelation ("suddenly, a bright light from heaven flashed around me") (Acts 22:6 NIV).[357] The power of the revelation made Paul subordinate himself to the light (the visible sign of the revelation) by falling to the ground (Acts 22:7). In this position, Paul heard a voice speaking to him in the form of rhetorical question that is, in effect, an accusation: "Saul, Saul, why do you persecute me?" (Acts 22:7 NIV).[358]

In this position of subordination, Paul interacts with the superior power, asking him for self-identification. The subject of the revelation identifies himself as Jesus of Nazareth, which means that the one who

---

[356] The account of Paul's conversion is already known to the reader from Acts 9:1–7, where Luke, with a considerable degree of accuracy, gave a coherent description of several events that led to Paul's conversion. Probably for this reason, the account of Paul's conversion presented in Paul's speech is brief and schematic, but it contains some differences in emphasis that have a critical importance for understanding the aim of the entire speech. M. E. Rosenblatt, "Recurring Narration as a Lukan Literary Convention in Acts: Paul's Jerusalem Speech in Acts 22:1–22," in *New Views on Luke and Acts*, ed. Richard E. (Collegeville: Liturgical Press, 1990), 94–105.

[357] The first aspect indicates the place in which the revelation occurred. The event took place outside Palestine in a foreign land, near the capital of the Syrian Province. The second aspect indicates the time of the revelation. It happened at midday, thus indicating its divine origin by excluding the possibility that it was a vision in a dream. The third aspect indicates the source of the light and its nature. It was not the light of the sun, but it was the light of God's glory coming from heaven (Acts 22:9, 11). J. A. Fitzmyer, *The Acts of the Apostles*, 705.

[358] In narrative of the revelation, there are some differences between the narrative of Acts 22:6 and that of Acts 9:2; cf. L.T. Johnson, *The Acts of the Apostles*, 388. In Acts 22:6–11 and Acts 26:13, the unnaturally bright light is a manifestation of Jesus's heavenly glory. C. S. Keener, *Acts. An Exegetical Commentary*, vol. 3, 3229.

was considered to be dead is not only living but is also in the presence of God in glory, and those who believe in him as the resurrected Messiah were in the right, and Paul was mistaken in his convictions about the Resurrection and his understanding of the Messiah. Paul's failure to recognize Jesus as the Messiah led him to persecution of those who recognized Jesus, which makes Paul an opponent of the Messiah, God's anointed one.[359] The dialogue between Paul and Jesus (Acts 22:8) presents, in a schematic way, the whole process leading to Paul's conversion, beginning with his request to the revelator for self-identification, followed by the answer of the revelator, and ending with Paul's recognition of his wrongdoing.[360]

The dialogue between Paul and Jesus is continued in Acts 22:10, but it now moves to another stage of the relationship between Paul and Jesus because Paul has accepted that Jesus is the Lord, to whom he will offer service.[361] Although Acts 22:8 indicates the moment

---

[359] Witherington III, *The Acts of the Apostles*, 671. In Acts 22:8, the subject of the revelation presents himself as "Jesus of Nazareth," but in Acts 9:5 and Acts 26:14, he presents himself with the common Jewish name "Jesus."

[360] Before this revelation, Paul does not yet believe in Jesus's Resurrection. The question concerning the identity of the voice was a direct reason for the unexpected answer that it was Jesus of Nazareth who appeared to him. This answer, together with the experience of the revelation, changed Paul's thinking regarding both the general question of the Resurrection and the particular question concerning the resurrected Messiah. Jesus's answer also indicates Paul's antagonism towards Jesus, since acting against Jesus's believers is equated with acting against Jesus himself, who appeared to Paul in heavenly glory. It is possible that here, Luke includes Paul's teaching concerning an understanding of the Christian Church as the body of Jesus Christ (1 Cor. 12:12–31). Acts 22:7–8 shows some similarities with the revelation to Moses on Mount Sinai. In both cases there are some identical elements: an unnatural event, a voice, a question concerning the name, an answer to the question with the giving of instructions. It is possible that Luke consciously intended these similarities in order to indicate that God is the main agent who chooses people for particular tasks.

[361] In the narrative concerning the revelation, Acts 22:6–8 gives the circumstances in which Paul acknowledges his wrongdoing toward Jesus and consequently toward Jesus's followers. Acts 22:10, which is the second part of the dialogue, shows Paul's subordination to Jesus, the Lord. In this context, Acts 22:9, which seems to interrupt the dialogue between Jesus and Saul, may serve as an indication

when Paul considers himself mistaken about Jesus, the Messiah raised by God, and in Acts 22:10, he chooses Jesus as his Lord to whom he subordinates his life, this radical change was not the result of his own personal deliberation in his recognition of the truth; it was exclusively the result of divine revelation and Paul's being chosen by Jesus. Paul, who began believing in Jesus as the resurrected Messiah, not only subordinated himself to Jesus but also asked for direction in his new life. The instructions given by the Lord are reduced to two simple orders: "get up" and "go," with an indication of the direction (Damascus). Paul is also assured that someone in the city will reveal God's task for him (Acts 22:10).

The dialogue between Paul and Jesus concerning his life after this revelation contains the very important assertion that all that happened to him is a part of God's plan for Paul that already had been decided and gradually would be revealed to him.[362] The first step in this plan is Paul's conversion from being a persecutor of

---

of the change in the character of the relationship between Jesus and Saul, from one of antagonism (Acts 22:6–8) to one of subordination (Acts 22:10).

[362] Although Acts 22:10 indicates that the Lord promised Saul to reveal "everything" to him after he entered Damascus, the term "everything" is, in fact, considerably restricted because in the narrative of Acts 22:12–16, Saul learned from Ananias only those things that were necessary for his joining the messianic movement (Acts 9:1–19; 22:12–16). Even the real purpose for Saul's conversion, known to readers from Acts 9:15–16, is here reduced to a very general statement regarding Saul's witness to Jesus. According to a statement included in Luke's account of Paul outside the Temple, the real purpose of his service to the new Lord was revealed to him in the Jerusalem Temple, three years after his conversion and by the Lord himself but not by Ananias. Some things that the reader already knows from Acts 9:10–16, the crowd learned from Paul's speech (Acts 22:17–21). The differences between the accounts must been seen in the context of the different purpose of each narrative. In Acts 9:10–19, interest lies in the baptism of Saul, whereas Acts 22:17–21 is a presentation of the divine origin of Paul's mission to the Gentiles. The future form of the verb ὑποδείκνυμι suggests an unspecified time in the future when the action will occur. The hardship of bearing witness to Jesus in a Jewish setting, beginning in Damascus, is revealed to Saul. In Jerusalem, Jesus reveals to Saul his commission to work among the Gentiles. If this is the case, the reason for sending Saul to the Gentiles was the rejection of his teaching by the Palestine Jews. This is then a criticism leveled at the crowd.

the messianic movement to becoming a follower of this movement. Lucan Paul underlines that his conversion is God's work; despite Paul's wrongdoing, God has chosen him as his useful servant. In this way, Paul insists that all that he was doing was God's will; this idea will be more fully developed in the last subsection of the speech (Acts 22:17–21).

The narrative of this subsection also contains two additional items of information. Paul's companions saw the sign of the revelation, but they did not participate in the dialogue. The revelation was a private event, although it was attested by a wider public.[363] The second item (Acts 22:11) concerns Paul's physical condition after the revelation; he was temporarily blind. Acts 22:11 shows that the revelation was a real event of divine origin, which caused a temporary physical illness for Paul.[364] In general terms, the information contained in this subsection agrees with Luke's account found in Acts 9:3–9, although some details are presented in a different order with considerable modification.

The third part (Acts 22:12–16) refers to the relationship between Paul and Ananias, the man who probably baptized Paul.[365] After the revelation, Paul spent three years in Damascus, but in his speech,

---

363 Paul's companions probably saw him speaking, but they did not comprehend the dialogue, which confines the revelation to Paul. According to Acts 9:7, Paul's companions heard the voice, but they saw nothing. This seems to differ from Acts 22:9, but in both cases, the companions are passive observers of the event. Concerning the differences between Acts 22:9 and Acts 9:7, cf. C. S. Keener, *Acts. An Exegetical Commentary*, vol. 3, 3230–2231.

364 Although Johnson translates the phrase δόξης τοῦ φωτὸς as "glory of the light," arguing that there is "thematic association throughout the work between light and the glory of God," this phrase should be translated as "brightness of the light" because both the context of the revelation and the effect of revelation are strictly physical. L. T. Jonson, *The Acts of the Apostles*, 389.

365 The subsection refers to Luke's narrative regarding the event presented in Acts 9:10–19 in a more elaborated form. For this reason, the narrative of Acts 22:12–16 can be understood as being a summary of Acts 9:10–19 with regard to the narrative, but in the context and purpose of the speech, it should be considered as a development of Acts 9:10–19.

Paul refers only to Ananias's revelation of God's plan for him.[366] Acts 22:12 indicates that Jesus sent a Jew named Ananias to visit Paul, and he became the first man in Damascus who approached Paul and consequently led him to baptism.[367] Ananias, whose reputation among local Jews was well known, was not only a Diaspora Jew but also a follower of Jesus, trusted by his Lord, but Paul, in his speech, presents him as a devout man living according to the Mosaic Law, well respected by the local Jews, and probably one of their leaders.[368] He visited Paul for a precise purpose that included many interrelated aspects. In Acts 22:13, Ananias addressed Paul as "brother," which must be taken as a sign of recognition of Paul as a "fellow Jew," and then he cured Paul's temporary blindness with a simple command.[369] This, however, was not the most important task that Ananias had to perform because Ananias's main role was to give testimony concerning Paul. This testimony, beginning with Acts 22:14, includes some traditional Jewish expressions that indicate Paul was at one with Jewish tradition; there also were statements concerning Paul's future fate.

The first is the phrase "the God of our ancestors" (Acts 22:14 NIV), indicating that all events related to Paul are in accordance with Jewish tradition, in which people were chosen by God for particular tasks. Paul's case is not extraordinary, and he was chosen by God long before his conversion. Even when he was still a persecutor of Jesus, Paul was chosen by God to become his useful instrument,

---

366 The term *conversion* does not refer here to "changing religion" but to changing his own conviction concerning Jesus as the resurrected Messiah.

367 In Acts 9:10, Ananias is described as "a disciple" (of Jesus), but in Acts 22:12, he is described as "a devout follower of the Law." The change is probably required by the contexts in which the phrases are used: in Acts 9:10, it was appropriate to use the term *disciples*, but in the context of Paul's apologetical speech, this would be highly improper. The reader of the Acts could understand the change between Acts 9:10 and Acts 22:12, as the followers of Jesus are also followers of the Mosaic Law. L. T. Johnson, *The Acts of the Apostles*, 389.

368 Note that Paul makes no distinction between Jews and Jews believing in Jesus.

369 The term ἀναβλέπω (look up) can be understand in different ways. Concerning the possibilities, cf. B. Witherington III, *The Acts of the Apostles*, 672.

ready to be used later, following three acts of God that were revealed to him gradually: "to know his will," "to see the Righteous One," and "and to hear words from his mouth" (Acts 22:14 NIV).[370] It means that the will of God, for Paul, was to experience the resurrected Jesus, here called "the Righteous One".[371] Indirectly, Paul says that by God's work, he, the former persecutor of Jesus's believers, met Jesus in order to understand his own wrongdoing and to get to know the truth. All these elements were intended to prepare Paul to give testimony to his own experience of meeting the risen Jesus and to spread the knowledge he learned during the revelation.[372] This was intended for all people, not only for Jews who were in a covenant with God (but until verse 21, this is not explicitly revealed).

In Acts 22:12–15, Ananias reveals to Paul God's plan for him, and in Acts 22:16, he encourages Paul to accept this task by joining the messianic movement. The expression τί μέλλεις (*why delay?*) might suggest Paul's doubts regarding Ananias's proposition, but this expression together with other expressions used by Ananias ("get up," "be baptized," "wash your sins by calling on his name") (Acts 22:16 NIV) can be seen as parts of one formula that describes the

---

[370] Ananias, during the dialogue with Saul, presents Jesus in Acts 22:14 as "the Righteous One," who fulfilled the will of God (Acts 3:14; 7:52), which is more specific than Ananias's presentation of Jesus in Acts 9:17 as "the Lord Jesus." In the speech, Ananias's words are addressed to Paul, but in the narrative concept of the speech, Paul used it to give witness, in an indirect way before the reader and possibly also before the crowd, that Jesus is the Righteous One, using an expression that was very meaningful both for Jews and Christians. J. A. Fitzmyer, *The Acts of the Apostles*, 706–707.

[371] This term (the Righteous One), taken from the tradition of the prophet Isaiah, has a messianic connotation.

[372] Ananias gives three dimensions relating to the conversion of Saul: the first concerns the God of Israel who chose him; the second regards the purpose of his being chosen—namely, to experience Jesus the resurrected Messiah; the third regards Saul's subordination to Jesus as his disciple. E. J. Schnabel, *Exegetical Commentary*, 904–905. This presentation of Ananias is very close to that presented by Paul in his letter to the Galatians (Gal. 1:11–12).

early Christian baptism rite.[373] This interpretation fits well with the use of verbs in the imperative aorist form, which here do not indicate psychological or physical pressure.[374] Paul, in this part of the speech, attempts to convince the audience that his joining the messianic movement was a consequence of following of God's will, as it was revealed to him by Ananias, a pious Diaspora Jew from Damascus.

The fourth subsection (Acts 22:17–21) concerns Paul's visit to Jerusalem after his conversion, which is narrated also in Acts 9:10–19. These two versions of the same event, however, are very different. This part of Paul's speech in the Temple contains information that is absent not only from Acts 9:10–19 but also is not attested by Paul's writings, and because of this, the versions are often considered in mutual contradiction. The narrative of the last subsection of the speech (Acts 22:17–21) refers to Paul's revelation that occurred in the Temple. Paul's visit to Jerusalem is mentioned also in Acts 9:10–19 but without reference to the revelation, which makes this part of Paul's speech take on a specific purpose in Luke's narrative strategy.

---

[373] L. T. Johnson, *The Acts of the Apostles*, 390. Acts 22:16 may suggest that Paul could still have some doubts concerning his joining the messianic movement, but according to Conzelmann, Acts 22:16 could be a "cultic formula used within initiation rites," and in this case it does not express Paul's dilemma. H. Conzelmann, *Acts of the Apostles*, 187. We exclude both interpretations because of the context of the speech. Acts 22:16 is Ananias's encouragement addressed to Saul, and also to the reader, possibly including the crowd, to accept Jesus as the way to attain forgiveness.

Scholars are divided on the question of Ananias being the person who baptized Saul. Concerning this problem, cf. F. F. Bruce, *The Book of the Acts*, 417–418; C. S. Keener, *Acts. An Exegetical Commentary*, vol. 3, 3234–3235; B. Witherington III, *The Acts of the Apostles*, 672.

We argue for the interpretation that Paul was baptized by Ananias. Luke, in Acts 9:18, uses the passive voice (καὶ ἀναστὰς ἐβαπτίσθη), and in Acts 22:16, a middle voice (Ἀναστὰς βάπτισαι καὶ ἀπόλουσαι τὰς ἁμαρτίας σου), with reference to the baptism.

[374] The name of Jesus is not explicitly mentioned in Acts 22:16, but the interpretation of the third-person singular pronoun is self-evident and is required by the context of the speech. The verbs βάπτισαι καὶ ἀπόλουσαι, which are both used in the imperative aorist form, confirm that the phase refers to baptism.

The accounts (Acts 9:1–9; Acts 22:6–11) concerning the event on the road to Damascus are almost identical, and the accounts (Acts 9:10–19) referring to Paul's association with Ananias in Damascus are generally similar, but the accounts (Acts 9:26–30; Acts 22:17–21) regarding Paul's visit to Jerusalem are focused on different aspects of this event, where the narrative of Acts 9:26–30 concentrates on Paul's social relations with the inhabitants of Jerusalem, and the narrative of Acts 22:17–21 gives attention to Paul's private revelation during this visit.[375] In this speech, Paul—regarding his first visit to Jerusalem after his conversion, after simply stating that he went to Jerusalem—turned directly to the event in the Temple, which is the only de facto topic in this narrative.[376]

Acts 22:17 indicates that in the Temple, Paul had a vision (literally, "I fell into a trance") while praying. This information shows his devotion and piety in relation to the Temple, but it can probably be understood as a direct response to the accusation by the Diaspora Jews against Paul in Acts 21:28, where teaching against the Temple and defiling the Temple are mentioned. Paul joined the messianic movement without severing his relationship to the Temple, which continued to be for him a place for prayer and worship of the God of Israel. During a routine prayer in the Temple, Paul had a vision, and the vision saw him. The personal pronoun *him* can be interpreted differently, depending on the background of the hearers and readers.[377] In the narrative of Acts 22:17–21, Luke uses the personal pronouns with undefined meaning. Use of the first-person singular pronoun (ἐμοῦ) and the third-person singular (αὐτὸν) in Acts 22:18 suggests that the subject of the revelation can be God (which was probably the understanding of the audience), or it can refer to Jesus (which

---

375 We consider these two versions of the narrative of Paul's visit to Jerusalem as being complementary, rather than contradictory.

376 The narrative of Acts 22:17–21 completely omitted Saul's three-year stay in Damascus. L. T. Johnson, *The Acts of the Apostles*, 390.

377 B. Witherington III, *The Acts of the Apostles*, 673–674.

was probably Paul's intention).[378] The same concerns the use of the verb εἶπεν (third-person singular) in Acts 22:21. Jesus's first order given to Paul during the vision concerns his leaving Jerusalem immediately, which presupposes that the inhabitants of the city will reject his testimony about the resurrected Messiah.[379] Surprisingly, Paul opposes this order and argues with the Lord.[380] Paul argues his case with extensive reference to his activities as the persecutor of the messianic movement. He underlines the fact that the citizens of Jerusalem know about his activities, including his imprisoning Jesus's believers and publicly punishing the messianic Jews (Acts 22:19). Paul, as a zealous Jew, passively participated in the stoning of Stephen, with full affirmation of this punishment (Acts 22:20).[381] These arguments are in accordance with Luke's initial introduction of Paul in Acts 7:58–8:3. The device of arguing with God is often used to affirm the correct position of the speaker (as in the case of Peter in Acts 10:13–16), and it is so used by Luke in the narrative.

Considering the background of the speech, Paul's self-presentation

---

378 In Acts 22:16, Paul was thinking about Jesus, which is an interpretation strongly supported by the following narrative (Acts 22:17–21). However, it is possible that the crowd, hearing this pronoun, thought it referred to God. This supposition is based on fact that if they interpreted the pronoun in the same way as Paul, the opposition toward Paul would occur at this point of Paul's speech, not after statement presented in Acts 22:21.

379 The account in Acts 22:17–21 differs from the account in Acts 9:26–30. Acts 9:26–30 focuses on the relationship between Paul and the inhabitants of Jerusalem (both Jews and the messianic Jews); in Acts 22:17–21, Paul concentrates on his determination to undertake the mission among the Jews of Jerusalem, but this was prohibited by divine power, due to the fact that Jerusalem rejected Paul. L. T. Johnson, *The Acts of the Apostles*, 390.

380 Probably the term *Lord* in Acts 22:19 takes a different meaning for Paul (Jesus) than for the crowd (God). J. A. Fitzmyer, "κύριος," in *EDNT*, vol. 2, 328–331. However, the reader of Acts understood the term in the same way as Lucan Paul.

381 In Acts 22:19, Paul uses the phrase "those who believed in you," and in Acts 22:20, he uses the phrase "when the blood of your martyr Stephen was shed" (Acts 22:20 NIV). Both of these phrases refer to events well known to the inhabitants of Jerusalem. If, until now, the crowd thought the reference was to God, at this point (Acts 22:19–20) it became clear to them that Paul refers to Jesus of Nazareth as the divine one.

as the one who stands for the Jews of Jerusalem, even if it contradicts the will of the Lord, placed him among those greatest prophets who stood for the nation, and here, it may be an indirect answer to the accusation in Acts 21:28 that Paul acted against the nation.[382] Considering the context in which the speech was given, this part of the speech has a strategic function as a rhetorical device used to gain a minimum of sympathy for Paul from the his opponents. Although the strategy was promising (as Acts 22:22 may suggest), it did not bring the expected effect, not because of the presentation of the vision itself but because of Jesus's highly provocative last statement, given in Acts 22:21, that suddenly changed the mood of the crowd to one of open hostility and brought Paul's speech to an unexpected end.[383] The second part of the Lord's order presented in Acts 22:21 contains Paul's being sent not only out of Jerusalem without a mission to the Jews of Palestine or to the regions outside Palestine, or without a mission to the Diaspora Jews but to foreign lands to undertake a mission to the Gentiles. In Acts 22:18, the Lord's order is attested by the negative response of the Jews to Paul's kerygma, but the order presented in Acts 22:21 completely overlooks Paul mission to the Jews.[384] This kind of statement, where Paul, in the Temple, received from the Lord—for the Jews, this meant from God—a direct order to work for the Gentiles is something that could be accepted by Jesus's followers (the readers) but hardly by the audience, the Jews in Jerusalem. Placing the vision and the order in the Temple is clearly intended to show the divine origin of Paul's mission among the Gentiles. Although from Paul's perspective (and that of the readers), this exposition is very convincing and is a sufficient response to the initial accusation presented in Acts 21:28, from the Jews' perspective,

---

382 The account of Acts 22:17–21 shows that Paul's mission to the Gentiles is subsequent to his mission to the Jews, and this interpretation is attested by Paul's modus operandi of preaching first to the Jews; that is one of the most important characteristics in Luke's presentation of Paul in the Acts. A similar opinion is offered by M. F. Bird, *An Anomalous Jew* (Grand Rapids: Eerdmans, 2016), 90.

383 H. Conzelmann, *Acts of the Apostles*, 188.

384 This agrees with Acts 9:15.

this is blasphemy in the very suggestion that God favors the Gentiles over the Jews and making this take place in the Jerusalem Temple. It is clearly a rejection of the traditions held in esteem by the Jews.[385] The fact that, according to Luke's account, at this stage Paul's speech is interrupted supports this interpretation (Acts 22:22).[386] Because the order from Acts 22:18, 21, in a direct way, is in opposition to the Acts narrative regarding Paul's mission activities, where Paul's modus operandi, without exception, is to favor Jews before Gentiles, the question about a reason for such provocative statement by Lucan Paul seems to be a crucial point in Luke's perspective on Paul. It is clear that the reason for the rejection of Paul by the Palestine Jews was his mission to the Gentiles and his spreading a teaching that could not possibly be accepted by mainstream Judaism, but it is less clear how well the Jews understood Paul's mission and teaching. Luke's narrative shows the Jews as strongly opposed to any notion that God could, at the same time, be both the God of Israel and the God of the Gentiles (Acts 22:22). Luke's narrative in Acts shows that this is possible and that it became a reality through the messianic movement. Paul, together with Peter and others, plays a significant role in overcoming the prejudice of the Jews, but for all of them, the task would bring great hardship.

Conclusion

Because this speech is the first of three speeches (Acts 22:1–21; 23:1, 6; 23:26–30) concerning Paul's imprisonment in Jerusalem (Acts 21:27–23:35), Luke placed it in the narrative context of the Jews' strong opposition to Paul, intended toward his elimination (Acts 21:31). His life was saved by the Roman soldiers who were confused

[385] Jesus's statement in Acts 22:18 contains a very critical evaluation of Jerusalem Jews in regard to their conversion. H. Conzelmann, *Acts of the Apostles*, 188; C. S. Keener, *Acts. An Exegetical Commentary*, vol. 3, 3228.

[386] Acts 22:22 is not the only case in Acts where Luke uses interruption of the speech as a literary device. J. D. Garroway, "'Apostolic Irresistibility' and the Interrupted Speeches in Acts," *CBQ* 74 (2012): 739.

by the sudden riot in the city and arrested Paul as the main suspect for the disturbance. They then, in order to clarify the situation, allowed him to make the speech (Acts 21:39–40), which consists of four parts (Acts 22:1–5; 22:6–11; 22:12–16; 22:17–21). All four subsections combine to form a progressive apology, with each subsection designed by Luke as a separate unit concerning a particular stage of Paul's life. The whole offers, at the same time, a portrait of Paul and an answer to the accusation made in Acts 21:28. The first part of the speech (Acts 22:1–5) serves to present Paul as a religious, zealous, and faithful Diaspora Jew, closely related to Jerusalem, not only by the fact that he was educated in Jerusalem but also by the fact that in order to defend true Judaism, he had persecuted, with personal conviction, the new sect of messianic Jews, commonly called "the Way." Indirectly, this subsection functions as an answer to the accusation regarding Paul's teaching against Mosaic Law. Luke's message is that Paul has not deviated from the Law.

The second part describes the reason for the drastic change in Paul's life: from being a persecutor of the messianic movement, he became a member of this movement. The reason is God's intervention, thus making Paul's conversion of divine origin, rather than being his own deliberate decision. Jesus's revelation to Paul ended his antagonism and changed him into a servant of the Lord, with whom he was previously fighting (Acts 22:10). Indirectly, this subsection contains a response to the possible conclusion that may be drawn from three accusations presented in Acts 21:28 (Paul's acts against the nation, the Law, and the Temple) that Paul actually fights God when he fights the Way.

The third part of the speech serves to inform Paul about God's plan for him, which includes the information that the former persecutor of the messianic movement has become himself one of the followers of Jesus by baptism and that he will serve the Lord by giving testimony to the revelation he has experienced. The person who assisted Paul in joining the movement and who revealed to him the purpose of this election was Ananias, the pious Jew of solid reputation. Indirectly, this subsection serves as an answer to the accusation concerning

Paul's teaching against the Mosaic Law (Acts 21:28) because his mission activity is addressed to all people (and especially Gentiles) on direct orders from Jesus himself.

The fourth part of the speech aims at indicating clearly that Paul's mission to the Gentiles was of divine origin, and this was revealed to Paul in the Temple during his vision. It was the Lord himself who chose Paul for the mission to the Gentiles. The message given to Paul by Ananias, in general terms as a mission to all people, is here specified as being a mission to the Gentiles and is an order given by the Lord, who knows that Paul will not succeed among the Jews in Jerusalem but will succeed among the Gentiles. From the beginning, the aim of God's plan concerning the conversion of Paul was to make him the apostle to the Gentiles, without, however, excluding Paul's mission to the Diaspora Jews. Paul mission to the Gentiles was not his own choice, but it was a consequence of his obedience to the Lord. Indirectly, this subsection serves as a response to the accusation regarding Paul as teaching against the nation and the Temple; it shows Paul's will to proclaim the kerygma to the Jews, and the Lord's order for the mission to the Gentiles was given in the Jerusalem Temple.

Strong opposition to Paul was raised by the Diaspora Jews (Acts 21:27) and spread among the Jews in all Jerusalem, leading to disturbance in the city that was noted by the Roman soldiers. Paul was arrested by the Romans on suspicion of causing political agitation, but in order to calm the anger of the crowd, they allowed Paul to speak. If the Romans had hoped that Paul's speech—which they did not understand (v. 24)—would clarify the situation and restore peace, they were surprised by a sudden explosion of anger. The Jews in Jerusalem did not accept Paul's statement (Acts 22:21) that the mission to the Gentiles, to which he was committed, was the will of the Lord, who revealed it to him in the Temple.[387] This statement, from the Jews' perspective, confirmed the accusations against Paul presented by the Jews from Asia Minor (Acts 21:28). In this way, Luke shows that the real reason for Paul's imprisonment

[387] Johnson, *The Acts of the Apostles*, 394.

was his rejection by his fellow countrymen. Since the speech did not solve the problem for the Romans, they took him to the barracks in order to ascertain the truth by using forcible compulsion (Acts 22:24). It forced Paul to reveal his Roman citizenship, which waived him from being scourged (Acts 22:25–29). In these circumstances of being rejected by the Jews and being held in suspicion by the Romans, Paul's Roman citizenship was revealed, and from this time, Paul became subject to the Roman judicial system. The speech and the narrative (Acts 22:22–29) are carefully and skillfully crafted by Luke in these sociopolitical backgrounds, which serve as the basis for developing the narratives concerning Paul's imprisonment in Jerusalem.

4.1.2. The interrogation before the Sanhedrin (Acts 23:1–11)

Since the speech in the Temple and initial interrogation of Paul did not clarify for Romans the present situation, the Roman authorities were left with no choice but to ask the Sanhedrin for their opinion about the case (Acts 22:30).[388] It is unlikely that the Romans could force the Sanhedrin to assemble, but probably it was in the best interest of both sides that a solution be found, as the incident took place in the Temple during the Feast of Pentecost.[389] However, Luke

---

388 The use of the term κρίνομαι ("I am judged"—Acts 23:3) directly indicates that Lucan Paul considers this to be a trial. However, the context of the event, as well as the Romans' purpose for Paul's presentation before the Sanhedrin, points to clarification but not judgment, which allows us to accept the position of Witherington III, who prefers to refer to the event as an interrogation before the Sanhedrin but not as a trial. B. Witherington III, *The Acts of the Apostles,* 684–686.

389 It seems that the tribune was convinced that Paul was not guilty of any crime against Roman law, which left it no other possibility than to suppose an offense by Paul against the Mosaic Law. This gives it the right to convene the Sanhedrin (cf. *Ant.* 20, 202) to clarify a case that could not be clarified otherwise by Romans (Acts 22:26–29). The tribune put its hopes on the Sanhedrin, the highest authority that could possibly clarify the case. Although from Luke's narrative perspective, the interrogation was a trial, it is unlikely that the tribune submitted a Roman citizen to the jurisdiction of the Sanhedrin. Since the incident was initiated in

presents this event not as an interrogation before the Sanhedrin but as a trial before the Sanhedrin (Acts 23:3, 6). This approach serves Luke's narrative purpose to present Paul as a Jew rejected by his own countrymen, both by the citizens of Jerusalem and by the authority of the Temple.

The speech—in fact, there are two attempts made, but neither is developed beyond the exordium—is addressed to the members of the Sanhedrin, and it goes directly into Paul's apology (Acts 22:30). The way in which Paul begins the speech strongly suggests its apologetic character, and its main aim is to attempt to present himself as a faithful Jew (Acts 23:1). Following the rhetorical custom, Paul addressed the Sanhedrin in the exordium as ἄνδρες ἀδελφοί (*brothers*), which, despite its common use in greetings, is intended here to show the relationship of brotherhood between Paul and the members of the Sanhedrin.[390] Indirectly, this beginning of the speech shows Paul's real conviction—that he considered himself to be a true Jew. Paul first considered the situation (Acts 23:1) and then chose the right rhetorical strategy that would assure acceptance of this apology by the Sanhedrin, as well as provide convincing proof to the tribune that this case was strictly confined to Jewish religious controversy and did not constitute a threat to the peace in the city.

The following part of the exordium contains Paul's statement regarding an evaluation of his life as being a faithful and conscientious servant of God. Paul's self-evaluation was designed as the basis for the apology, and in his estimation, it should have been accepted and convinced the Sanhedrin that he was a Jew living according to the Mosaic Law, and consequently, he deserved to be heard by the authorities of the Temple where whole problem started.[391] The speech,

---

the Temple, and the Romans could not determine the reason for the unrest, the Temple authority was the only body capable of determining Paul's guilt in terms of the Mosaic Law.

[390] This greeting is a common form of address in Acts (Acts 4:8; 7:2). W. Neil, *The Acts of the Apostles*, 226–227.

[391] In the three statements, Paul shows his conviction that by obeying the Law, he lives according to the will of God; he was convinced that his conduct was right;

however, was interrupted by the high priest, who ordered that Paul be beaten (Acts 23:2).[392] It was a direct sign that the Sanhedrin did not accept Paul's statement, and because the speech was not continued, this act of the high priest may be considered as a rejection of Paul. The reason for the rejection of Paul may have had some connection with the incident in the Temple, or it may have been related to Paul's perceived betrayal of Judaism by supporting the messianic movement, or it may have reflected the generally negative evaluation by Jews from the Diaspora and from Jerusalem.[393]

To this rejection, Paul answered with a rejection of the high priest, expressing a formula used in a curse (v. 3), which, according to the Mosaic Law, was a grave offense.[394] It was Paul's reaction to his unexpected humiliation. This reaction included not only cursing the high priest, but it also contains the accusation against the high priest concerning his conduct. Although, the high priest was about to judge Paul according to Mosaic Law, however, he also ordered to punish Paul in way violating this Law. Although Paul's curse is a

and he had no doubt about his way of living, not only in the past but also in the present situation. J. G. Schnabel, *Exegetical Commentary*, 924–925.

392 Luke presents Paul's intended speech (Acts 23:1) before the Sanhedrin as an unsuccessful attempt, in which Paul is involved in an unfriendly debate with the Sanhedrin (Acts 23:2–6), which adequately shows the reader the antagonism of the Temple authorities toward Paul, particularly in the high priest's sharp rejection of Paul's claim to be a zealous Jew. This rejection would determine Paul's strategy, as presented in Acts 23:6.

393 Although Luke does not name the high priest, from the writings of Josephus, it is possible not only to identify the high priest as Ananias (in office from AD 47 until 59), about whom Josephus was very critical, but also to learn additional details that show him as more concerned with politics than with religion. He was appointed by Herod of Chalcis (*Ant.* 20.5.2) and during his time in office, he was very loyal to the Roman administration; also, during the Jewish-Roman war, he collaborated with the Romans, which was the immediate reason for his eventual assassination. C. S. Keener, *Acts. An Exegetical Commentary*, vol. 3, 3268–2270. The high priest Ananias is accused by Josephus of constant injustice and violation of the Mosaic Law, but as well as playing a part in ambushing of Samaritan pilgrimages (*Bell*, 2.243, 2.426–29, 2.441–442). T. L. Johnson, *The Acts of the Apostles*, 396.

394 H. Conzelmann, *Acts of the Apostles*, 192.

response to his humiliation by the high priest, Acts 23:4 shows that Paul's action was considered a violation of the Mosaic Law, which excluded the right to oppose the high priest, as expressed explicitly in Exodus 22:47.[395] This fact was instantly pointed out to Paul by the Sanhedrin, which, in the context of his action, was unlikely to accept his statement presented in Acts 23:1. Paul offered a prompt apology for his behavior, explaining (unconvincingly) his ignorance concerning the person of the high priest (Acts 23:5). His apology was underlined by quoting the relevant passage of scripture (Exod. 22:47), which shows Paul's keen knowledge of the Mosaic Law. However, his apology should be recognized as an irrelevant excuse because Paul knew that Ananias spent a long time in office, and the place of the high priest was exhibited, which makes it almost impossible not to recognize his rank.[396]

Paul's accusation (Acts 23:3) is addressed to one person, most probably to the high priest, who will make the final judgment, and not just to someone from the Sanhedrin.[397] It is also possible to take Paul's apology as being ironic: "Brothers, I did not realize that he was the high priest" (Acts 23:5 NIV), related to the improper conduct of the high Priest, who should himself obey the Mosaic Law, but he acted otherwise.[398] In Luke's narrative, this event not only shows Paul as a Jew who respects the Mosaic Law (unlike the high priest), but also it shows Paul's awareness that the Sanhedrin (as a body) was not clearly on his side.[399] According to Luke's narrative, at that moment, Paul reevaluated the situation (Acts 23:6), and he adopted a new strategy in which, unlike the previous attempt, he sought to win some supporters to his side in the Sanhedrin. Paul begins the speech by carefully

---

395 H. Le Cornu and J. Shulam, *A Commentary on the Jewish Roots of Acts*, vol. 1–2 (Jerusalem: Academon, 2003), 1244.

396 The fact that Paul looked intently at the Sanhedrin (Acts 23:1) should exclude the possibility that he did not recognize the high priest. H. Conzelmann, *Acts of the Apostles*, 192.

397 E. J. Schnabel, *Exegetical Commentary*, 927–928.

398 T. L. Johnson, *The Acts of the Apostles*, 397.

399 I. H. Marshall, *The Acts of the Apostles* (Grand Rapids: Eerdmans, 1980), 361–362.

choosing the group to which he is about to address a new message. The speech (in fact, a second attempt to make the speech) begins again with a one-word exordium (*brothers*), which is immediately followed by a peroration ("I am a Pharisee, descended from Pharisees. I stand on trial because of the hope of the resurrection of the dead") (Acts 23:6 NIV), where the new biographical information (for the readers) is presented.[400]

Paul's statement that he is a Pharisee, the son of Pharisees, creates some problems when we consider that they lived outside Judea, where rigorous observance of the Mosaic Law, as required for Pharisees, would have been difficult.[401] The self-presentation as a Pharisee, together with mention of the theoretical issue of resurrection, is now presented as being the immediate reason for his interrogation (Acts 23:6).[402] In this way, Paul won over the sympathy and support of the

---

[400] Paul's statement, "I am a Pharisee, descended from Pharisees" (Acts 23:6 NIV), is disputed among scholars, particularly because of the suspicion that it would be impossible to live as a strict Pharisee in the Diaspora. For a review of opinions, cf. J. Murphy-O'Connor, *Paul: A Critical Life* (Oxford: Oxford University Press, 1996), 56–59; W. Rakocy, *Pawel Apostol* [*The Apostle Paul*] (Czestochowa: Święty Paweł, 2003), 42–44; B. Witherington III, *The Acts of the Apostles,* 689–691.

[401] Presenting himself as a zealous Jew at this time did not produce the desired result, which was the direct reason for Paul's changing his defense strategy. After his claim was rejected by all participants, Paul attempted to use the differences between Sadducees and Pharisees within the Sanhedrin regarding the question of the resurrection of the dead. Paul's claim to be a Pharisee who believed in the resurrection of the dead turned out to be a master move that probably saved his life. According to Luke's narrative, the Sanhedrin surprisingly lost sight of the purpose of the meeting, as being intended to uncover the cause of the disturbance in the Temple, and turned to a theological debate about the Resurrection, angels, and spirits, in which the Pharisees sided with Paul. Luke's narrative seems to be strongly influenced by the theological perspective in which the Pharisees are the closest faction to Christians, with whom they share some similarities in theological teaching. However, Luke does no more than imply a general similarity.

[402] Peterson thinks that Paul's strategy in the narrative should not be seen not as a clever move intended to wrest some advantage from very ambivalent circumstances; rather, Luke intended to draw attention to a minor theological problem within Judaism, which, following further specification in Acts 26:6–8,

Pharisees in the Sanhedrin, who accepted the controversial teaching concerning the resurrection of the dead. This time, his strategy worked, causing a rift within the Sanhedrin (Acts 23:7–9) because the Pharisees and the Sadducees were opposed on this debated issue (Acts 23:7–9).[403] The move to change the subject of the speech from the particular problem of the incident in the Temple to the more general question concerning the resurrection of the dead turned the interrogation into a heated religious discussion (Acts 23:7–10). The Sanhedrin, divided on this controversy, was incapable of continuing the interrogation, and the growing aggressive attitude toward Paul forced the Romans to save the Roman citizen by taking him back to the fortress (Acts 23:10). Although the tribune's expectation was not fulfilled, the development led to his concluding that the problem surrounding Paul was strictly a Jewish religious matter and had no political or social implications.

Conclusion

These fragments of attempted speeches, although incomplete in structure and content, play a very important function in Luke's presentation of Paul, not only by giving new information and introducing a new theological issue that will play an important role in a following narrative but also by finally clarifying the relationship between Paul and the Jews of Jerusalem.[404] The fragmentary character of the speeches makes it impossible to determine what the intended main topic is, and it allows for the suspicion that Luke intended more than one message in these fragments of speeches. The first message concerns Paul's being rejected by the Jews. After Acts 22:22, where Luke's informs us that the crowd in Jerusalem rejected Paul because

22–23, was established as the main doctrinal issue that caused the rejection of Paul's kerygma by the authorities of the Temple and by Jews in general. D. G. Peterson, *The Acts of the Apostles*, 615–616.

[403] J. A. Fitzmyer, *The Acts of the Apostles*, 718.

[404] In Paul's speech to the Jews of Rome (Acts 28:17–20), Luke will again address the topic of the relationship between Paul and the Jews of Jerusalem.

of his claim that his mission to Gentiles was ordered by God himself (Acts 22:21–23), this is now also rejected by the Sanhedrin, who did not accept his self-presentation of being a righteous Jew (Acts 23:1–2). In this way, Luke makes a general but final statement regarding the relationship between Paul and Palestinian Jews. Paul was totally rejected by the citizens of Jerusalem and the Sanhedrin, the official leaders of Judaism.

The second message concerns Paul's relationship with Roman officials on the local level; in this case, specifically Claudius Lysias. Roman soldiers, obeying orders, saved Paul from being killed by the crowd. Clarification of Paul's case before the crowd ended in failure and an escalation of antagonism toward Paul. Clarification of the case in "the Roman way" became impossible because of Paul's Roman citizenship, which left the Roman officials with no alternative other than to ask the Sanhedrin to interrogate Paul in the presence of the Roman officials. During the interrogation Paul found that the Sanhedrin was antagonistic in his regard, forcing him to create a division in the Sanhedrin, which rendered that body incapable of reaching a conclusion. Consequently, Paul, although arrested as a Roman citizen, was under the protection of the Romans, who again saved his life when disagreement among the Jews turned into open conflict that put Paul's life at risk (Acts 23:10).

In in his narrative, Luke uses this interrogation and the following narrative, concerning a plot against Paul (Acts 21:12–35), as two initial indicators that prepare the narrative, concerning the legal trials that will conclude with Paul's appealing to Caesar. The third message concerns a new theological topic that, until now, was absent from the narrative regarding the accusation against Paul; now, Luke suddenly presents it as being Paul's recognition of the true reason for his persecution. Although Luke, in his narrative, several times presents many different kinds of accusation against Paul, Paul's own point of view is now presented for the first time. According to Paul's understanding, the reason for his being persecuted by the Jews was not his forsaking Judaism (Acts 21:28) or his service to the Gentiles but his proclaiming of the Resurrection.[405] This reason, which is of a strictly theological character, will become, in the following narrative, the main argument presented by Paul to the Romans officials, in order to show the strictly religious character of his case.[406]

The fourth message regards the movement of Paul's case from being a strictly Jewish matter, in which the Romans are only involved secondarily, to becoming a strictly Roman judicial case involving Jewish religion controversy, in which one of the feuding parties possesses Roman citizenship. Luke's narrative of Paul's arrest in Jerusalem has a progressive character, where the first speech (Acts 21:1–21) indicates that the Jews of Jerusalem rejected Paul's claim regarding his mission to the Gentiles as being God's order, and the second speech (Acts 23:1.6) shows that the Sanhedrin rejected Paul's claim as a faithful servant of God. These speeches concentrate on the negative aspects of the relationship between Paul and Jerusalem, preparing the way for the final "speech" in the narrative of Paul's imprisonment in Jerusalem, which takes the form of the official letter of the Roman soldier. Here, for the first time in Acts, the Roman's opinion of Paul's case will be presented.[407] Before the final speech in this section is exposed, Luke presents the background, justifying the writing of such a letter (Acts 23:12–22).

---

405 Although Paul presents the topic of the resurrection of the dead in a general manner, both he and the Sanhedrin were aware of Paul's understanding of the idea and its application in Paul's teaching. The indication of this teaching as being the direct reason for Paul's troubles reflects Paul's overall mission activity, rather than the event in the Temple itself. However, from here on, Lucan Paul will present this teaching as the main reason for Paul's imprisonment, in order to highlight Paul's place as the witness to the resurrected Messiah.

406 Luke's narrative of the interrogation before the Sanhedrin clearly suggests that the Pharisees are the closest party to the Christian movement because they also believe in the resurrection of the dead.

407 During the trial before the procurator Felix, Paul will use the fact that the Sanhedrin did not reach a conclusion during Paul's interrogation (Acts 24:20–21).

4.1.3. The plot against Paul (Acts 23:12–30)

Between the account of Paul's interrogation before the Sanhedrin and the narrative concerning the plot against Paul, Luke mentions the appearance of the Lord to Paul in a vision (Acts 23:11). The message from the Lord is one of exhortation, encouraging Paul. It begins with the phrase "take courage" (Acts 23:11 NIV), which suggests that the experience before the Sanhedrin was a challenging event for Paul. This is followed by praise of Paul's testimony in Jerusalem, which refers to his speech in the Temple, as well as the speech before the Sanhedrin. The praise indicates the value of Paul's witness to the Lord in Jerusalem, but it is not the end of Paul's struggle because the Lord requires similar testimony from him before the Roman officials. In this way, Luke assures the reader that Paul will survive the Jewish hostility in Jerusalem, and at the same time, he indicates that the final point of the narrative of Paul's imprisonment is his appeal to Caesar.

After this brief preparatory unit, Luke goes on to narrate the Jewish plot against Paul (Acts 23:12–35), which shows the level of danger in which Paul found himself after the interrogation before the Sanhedrin. Verse 12 shows that the Jews intended to kill Paul, which in itself is nothing new (cf. Acts 21:31, 36), but this time, it was a plot involving a large group of extremely determined men, who took an oath to fast until they achieved their goal of eliminating Paul (Acts 23:13–14). The plot seems to have been an independent product of zealous Jews, but it was supported by the Sanhedrin, which was supposed to play a part in it by asking the Roman officials to hold another interrogation (Acts 23:15–16). The plot was apparently not a great secret, if Paul's relatives learned about it and could warn Paul by his nephew (Acts 23:16). This information is interesting for at least two reasons. Paul's relatives were living in Jerusalem, yet Paul lodged in the house of Mnason of Cyprus (Acts 21:16); whereas Paul's family were actively involved, members of the Jerusalem community are nowhere mentioned. The tribune learned about the plot from Paul's nephew (Acts 23:20–21) and immediately undertook the necessary arrangements to avoid a possible conflict between the Roman soldiers and the Jewish assassins. His decision was motivated by pragmatic concerns more than by concern for the life of one Jew with Roman citizenship.[408] Sending Paul to Caesarea was the simplest solution, but the decision indicates the level of risk involved.

Forced by circumstances, Claudius Lysias sent Paul to Caesarea in order to avoid turning the disturbance caused by Paul's case into a riot against the Romans. Together with the prisoner, he had to send a report about Paul's case. This report (Acts 23:23–30) contains the first official clarification of Paul's case by the Roman authorities. Lysias, describing the circumstances of Paul's case, underlines several items of information: the fact that the Roman soldier saved Paul, who was attacked by Jews who intended to kill him (Acts 23:27). Paul's Roman citizenship is noted (Acts 23:27). Lysias followed proper protocol by investigating the case in cooperation with the local authority, the Sanhedrin (Acts 23:28), which helped him to conclude that Paul's

[408] Note the credibility of Luke's information regarding the number of the soldiers sent to Caesarea with Paul, not just for Paul's security but more probably and primarily for reinforcement of the Roman troops (Acts 23:31–32) in the Jerusalem. Scholars usually interpret the number of soldiers (470 in total) as being unrealistic and think that the inflated number is intended to establish Paul's importance. Considering that Paul's case occurred during the Feast of Pentecost, however, and that Romans always treated the Jewish feasts as a "state of emergency," the number of soldiers and their specification by Luke strongly suggests that the numbers are real and not a narrative exaggeration. Luke refers to Lysias as a *tribunus millitum*, who was in charge of a cohort, the standard military unit of the Roman legion. Luke's specification of the numbers sent corresponds with what is known of the *cohortes equitatae*. B. Rankov, "Military Force," in *The Cambridge History of Greek and Roman Warfare*, vol. 2, eds. P. Sabin, H. van Wees, and M. Whitby (Cambridge: Cambridge University Press, 2007), 54. Lysias sent about half of his soldiers to secure a safe way to the sea at Antipatris, which suggests that the threat of attack was real. From Antipatris to Caesarea, only seventy of the cavalries (which would not be of great use in Jerusalem) continued on the way, but the infantry returning to Jerusalem (vv. 31–32).

That the number of Jewish assassins was more than forty (Acts 23:13, 21) shows that the affair involving Paul could possibly turn into a larger riot in Jerusalem if the assassins acted, and it suggests that they planned (Acts 23:15) to attack the Roman soldiers who were escorting Paul to the Sanhedrin, which *de facto* would be considered a riot against the Romans.

case was strictly concerned with the Mosaic Law (Acts 23:29). Lysias excludes Paul's guilt in any crime against Roman law (Acts 23:30). The plot against Paul is presented as the reason for sending the prisoner to the procurator (Acts 23:29). The Jewish accusers were informed by Lysias about the proper and legal way to solve the problem between them and the prisoner (Acts 23:30). Paul and the report were delivered to the prefect, who accepted Lysias's report and confirmed his jurisdiction over Paul's case (Acts 23:33–35). Most of the information contained in Lysias' report is already known to the reader. The most important new information regards the stipulation that Paul's case is a Jewish religious issue and the exclusion of any crimes against Roman law. This will form the basis of the entire narrative of Paul's trials.

4.2. Caesarea (Acts 23:31–26:32)

The narrative concerning the plot against Paul (Acts 23:12–30) ends the period of Paul's imprisonment in Jerusalem, which consisted of interrogations intended to clarify Paul's case, and ended with Lysias's statement in his report that the matter was strictly a Jewish religious issue. Luke signals a new section in the narrative not only by changing the place to Caesarea but also by advancing the narrative to the level of the trials. Two trials take place during Paul's imprisonment in Caesarea, which are distinguished by the names of the procurators involved.

4.2.1. The trial before Felix (Acts 23:31–24:27)

The trial before Felix took place five days after Paul's arrival in Caesarea. This haste may indicate the scale of the problem. The accusers were the high priest himself and some other elders. They availed themselves of the service of a professional rhetorician, Tertullus (Acts 24:2).[409] He gave a speech in a highly rhetorical

[409] The mention of the Resurrection in Acts 24:15 may suggest that one of Paul's accusers was perhaps a Pharisee. However, there is a difference in the

manner. In the *propositio* of the speech (Acts 24:5), Paul's crime was outlined and supported by a *probatio* (Acts 24:6), in which Paul is accused of a capital offense in his attempt to desecrate the Temple.[410] In the proposito, Tertullus presents Paul as a dangerous man, who is like a plague spreading through the whole world and causing disturbance among the Jews because he is a leader of the sect of the Nazarenes.[411] Tertullus's accusation shows the perspective of a Judaism official (the Sanhedrin) on the new sect within Judaism called the Nazarenes.[412] By using the qualifier, *the Nazarenes*, Tertullus indicates the marginal nature of the sect rooted in the region of Galilee, which was not recognized by mainstream Judaism. However, by Pauls' activity, according to Tertullus, this sect takes responsibility for causing riots among Jews throughout the world, thus bringing the religious issue to a sociopolitical level. Although Tertullus attempts to avoid direct indication of Jesus of Nazareth as the Messiah, Felix, who was probably experienced in Jewish matters, fully understands the semantic force of this term and its sociopolitical

---

understanding of the term *resurrection of the dead* between Paul, who speaks about the universal resurrection of both good and bad, and the Pharisees, who accepted the resurrection only of the good (Josephus, *Bell* 2.163 and probably *Ant.* 18.14). B. Witherington III, *The Acts of the Apostles,* 711.

[410] The western text has an addition between verse 6 and verse 8: "but Lysias the tribune came and took him away from us with great violence, ordering those accusing him to come before you." B. M. Metzger, *A Textual Commentary*, 434. For a proposal of a different construction of the speech, cf. O. Padilla, *The Speeches of Outsiders in Acts. Poetics, Theology, and Historiography* (Cambridge: Cambridge University Press, 2008), 218.

[411] The use of the active aorist of the verb εὑρίσκω ("find") shows that the accusers (Jews) find Paul to be a danger to Jewish society and the *Pax Romana.* After prolonged investigation, they call him τὸν ἄνδρα τοῦτον λοιμὸν ("this man a perfect pest"), which is equivalent to calling him an evil man. L. T. Johnson, *The Acts of the Apostles*, 410–411.

[412] The term Ναζωραῖος (appearing in the plural only in Acts 24:5) refers to one who believes in Jesus of Nazareth as the resurrected Messiah and is a direct reference to the Christian movement.

connotations.[413] Tertullus is incorrect in making Paul to be the leader of the sect, but it is indicative of Paul's zeal in proclaiming Jesus's teaching.[414] In Tertullus's account, Paul is the most active among the members of the sect in spreading the teaching that divided Jews throughout the world. This general accusation is made more specific in the accusation against Paul, regarding his attempt to desecrate the Temple, which, for Jews, was a crime punishable by death. We know from Josephus (*Ant.* 20.115–120) that Roman officials also showed little tolerance toward those who defiled the Jerusalem Temple. Tertullus's last remark shows that this part of the accusation was the main reason for Paul's arrest and this trial. Surprisingly, Lucan Tertullus did not offer any proof or present witnesses, leaving the task of confirming the accusation to Felix in his interrogation.

Following Roman practice, after the speech of the accuser containing a clearly presented accusation against Paul, the apostle was given the opportunity to defend himself. In Luke's narrative, Paul's defense (Acts 24:10–21) is placed immediately after Tertullus's speech (Acts 24:2–9). It contains Paul's answer to the accusations, with little attention given to the second particular accusation (Acts 24:6) but with an extended answer to the first general accusation (Acts 24:5). The speech begins with a short exordium containing a *captatio benevolentiae* (Acts 24:10), which in contrast to the exordium of Tertullus's speech, is a eulogy of Felix and is of critical importance.[415] Paul's speech does not contain praise of Felix, and the *captatio benevolentiae* is reduced to a simple statement to show

[413] Tertullus's presentation of Paul as the leader of the Nazarenes, with the additional information regarding the disturbances caused by them among Jews around the world, is probably intended to connect the case of Paul with recent disturbances caused by the Egyptians, mentioned in Acts 21:38.

[414] Calling Paul πρωτοστάτην ("leader"—a hapax legomenon of the New Testament) is another attempt by Tertullus to connect Paul's case with the problem caused by the Egyptians.

[415] The combination of the *captatio benevolentiae* in Tertullus's speech with *captatio benevolentiae* in Paul's speech shows not only the difference in attitude of the speakers and the convincing power of their arguments, but it also serves Luke in order to present Felix's personality.

Felix's competence to judge rightly in Jewish cases.[416] The statement contains three details concerning the procurator. Felix had been in office for a long time. The office of procurator required that, on occasion, he act as judge.[417] This makes him a judge with great experience and knowledge about Mosaic Law and Jewish tradition, as well as about the socioreligious background of the people, who are subject to him as judge.[418] The third detail concerns Paul's expectation of receiving a just judgment. These words of Paul may be taken as a development of the *captatio benevolentiae*, aimed at earning Felix's favor, but it may also contain a concealed irony on Luke's part directed at Felix, if the nonbiblical testimony concerning Felix's quality of judging is taken into consideration.[419]

The next part of the speech is a short *narratio* (Acts 24:11), indicating that the period of Paul's stay in Jerusalem (seven days) was too short to allow for all the problems, of which Paul is accused, to have taken place.[420] This is an important move in Paul's defense because the general accusation of Tertullus regarding Paul's activity around the world was skillfully reduced by Paul to a local perspective (only Jerusalem), which is the de facto main concern for Felix. Paul not only states that he is a newcomer to Jerusalem, which makes it more or less impossible that he was involved in all the disturbances in Jerusalem of which he was accused, but also that the main reason

---

[416] H. Conzelmann, *Acts of the Apostles*, 199.

[417] After Pilate (AD 26–36), Felix was the second longest to serve as procurator (AD 52–60). H. Conzelmann, *Acts of the Apostles*, 199; J. A. Fitzmyer, *The Acts of the Apostles*, 735.

[418] The procurator's wife was Jewish (Acts 24:24), which may explain Drusilla's interest in Paul's teaching (Acts 24:25).

[419] The suggestion that Felix was open to being bribed (Acts 24:26) is also attested by Josephus in *Bell*, 2.272–274.

[420] Information regarding Paul's one-week stay in Jerusalem serves to prove that he did not have time to commit the crimes he was accused, rather than it is indicating a possibly easy review of his stay in Jerusalem because the context is Paul's trial before Felix but not the preparatory investigation. H. Conzelmann, *Acts of the Apostles*, 199.

for his coming to the city was of a religious nature.[421] Paul's remark that this information can be easily verified by Felix should be taken as a suggestion that the trial be brought to a proper conclusion, rather than as a suggestion that Felix should undertake a new investigation in Jerusalem.[422]

In the next part of the speech, the *propositio* (Acts 24:12), Paul asserts his innocence of inciting the Jews of Jerusalem, which was the second accusation of Tertullus. Paul affirmed in verse 11 that he spent only seven days in Jerusalem, which would be too short a time for him to have committed the crimes of which he was accused by the Sanhedrin. He denied three kinds of action regarding disturbing the peace of the city.[423] The first is Paul's behavior in the Temple in debate and argument that may cause disturbance in this place. The second is Paul's agitation in the synagogues of Jerusalem. The third is Paul's agitation in the city. With reference to Tertullus's accusation, Paul claims that there are no witnesses to prove his wrongdoing in the city, in the synagogues, or in the Temple (Acts 24:12). Paul, in fact, insists on his lack of guilt in terms of Roman law (Acts 24:13).[424] In this way, Paul rebutted Tertullus's attempt to present his case as a question involving Roman law. This secured Paul's position because the Roman procurators were very sensitive to accusations regarding activity to incite the people of Jerusalem (especially during the times of festivals), which often caused serious problems for them (Acts 21:38).

---

421 The other reason for Paul's coming to Jerusalem—namely, with a donation for the poor in Jerusalem—is mentioned in Acts 24:17, but this is not yet expressed in Acts 24:11, due to the general character of the information given here.

422 Paul uses the same rhetoric as Tertullus in Acts 24:8. M. L. Soards, *The Speeches in Acts*, 118.

423 Paul confines himself to the particular case of Jerusalem (Acts 24:12), but Tertullus's accusation is general and extends to the whole world (Acts 24:5). C. S. Keener, *Acts. An Exegetical Commentary*, vol. 4, 3395–3396.

424 Paul's answer to Tertullus's accusation is reduced to the question of his disturbing the peace in Jerusalem, which makes Tertullus's accusation seen as more rhetorical than substantive. D. G. Peterson, *The Acts of the Apostles*, 633–634.

In the following part of the speech, the *probatio* (Acts 24:13–20), Paul answers Tertullus's first accusation concerning Paul's religious activities (Acts 24:5–6). To judge from its length alone, this is the most important section in Luke's narrative of the trial. He begins with a conclusion that the Sanhedrin, represented by Tertullus, is unable to offer evidence supporting the accusation regarding Paul's causing disturbance in Jerusalem (Acts 24:13), making it unwarranted to find him guilty of something semipolitical without adequate proof (Acts 24:8).[425] In other words, Paul insists that Tertullus's arguments in Acts 24:6. 8 must be dismissed due to lack of evidence.[426] Paul does not deny all the statements presented by Tertullus; although he firmly denies the accusation of disturbing the peace in Jerusalem, he seems to confirm some aspects of Tertullus's accusation regarding Paul's religious activities.[427] This part of his apologetic speech (Acts 24:14–21) refers to the accusation that Paul is a "ringleader of the sect of the Nazarenes" (Acts 24:5), which Tertullus presents as being a worldwide rebellious movement, causing disturbance among Jews.

Paul confirms that he belongs to the community of Nazarenes, which the Sanhedrin called a sect (a qualifier that implied lack of recognition), but for him, it is the Way, in which he is serving the God of Israel.[428] This statement indicates Paul's conviction that the Way is, for him, a part of Judaism (Acts 24:14).[429] As proof of his claim, he shows that as a member of the Way, he follows the same tradition of Judaism (the Mosaic Law and prophets). Paul does not agree with qualifying the Way as a sect separated from Judaism, as he sees the Way as one of the many groups within Judaism in which he has chosen to serve the God of Israel in accordance with the teaching

---

425 L. T. Johnson, *The Acts of the Apostles*, 412.

426 Paul's answer (Acts 24:13) concerns the particular issue; namely, the social disturbances in Jerusalem. For this reason, it does not regard the entire accusation presented by Tertullus.

427 D. G. Peterson, *The Acts of the Apostles*, 635.

428 There is no reference by Paul to the accusation that he was a leader of the "sect of Nazarenes."

429 The term *the Way* describes the Christian movement, which, for Paul, is the fulfilment of Judaism. H. Conzelmann, *Acts of the Apostles*, 199.

of the Torah (Acts 24:14). Paul is a member (not the leader) of the Way, a group within Judaism who, like the Pharisees, believe in the resurrection of the dead. In this way, Paul makes a link between the Way and one of the most influential groups in Judaism, the Pharisees, who share a similar conviction regarding resurrection (Acts 24:15). The purpose of making the link is to present the most important teaching for the Way, the Resurrection of Jesus, as a question that was accepted by at least some groups within Judaism. Bringing up the topic of the resurrection of the dead is an answer to the accusation that Paul belonged to the sect of Nazarenes (Acts 24:6), where Tertullus, without specifying the meaning of the term, referred to "Nazarenes" with a very negative connotation and with a distinct purpose.

Luke, very skillfully, without directly showing it, presents the strictly religious issue of the Resurrection as being the main cause of controversy between mainstream Judaism and the Way. Luke does not mention directly the resurrected Messiah, neither in Tertullus's accusation nor in Paul's answer. In the circumstances, in a trial before a Roman official with long experience in Jewish affairs, it could not be predicted how the mention of the resurrected Messiah would be interpreted by any of the parties involved. Felix might have recognized the allusion to the Way as referring to the group believing in Jesus of Nazareth, the resurrected Messiah, and probably for this reason, Lucan Paul, in his answer, presented the issue of resurrection in a general manner, avoiding, in this way, any particular association of the issue. His presentation of the Way's belief regarding the hope of resurrection of all people, good and evil, as the link between the Way and mainstream Judaism, is a generalization of the issue because this teaching was characteristic of the Pharisees, not by the entirety of Judaism.

During the narrative regarding Paul's trial, the issue of the Resurrection (usually presented in general terms but with a strong particular connotation) gradually becomes, in Luke's narrative, the most distinct reason for Paul's troubles. It begins with a general presentation of the issue during Paul's interrogation before the Sanhedrin (Acts 23:6) and ends with a direct presentation of Christ as the resurrected one (Acts 26:23). Paul's apology continues with the statement that faith in the resurrection of all people, the righteous and the wicked, is, for him, the main reason behind his attempt to offer due service to God and conduct his life for the benefit of all people (Acts 24:16).[430] Lucan Paul attempts to give a positive image of the messianic movement as a balance to Tertullus's negative presentation of "the Nazarenes" sect and to present the Way as contributing to society, with the possible insinuation that it should be recognized by Felix as "the more legitimate form of Judaism."[431] In Acts 24:17, Paul affirms his good conduct toward God and his fellow humans by giving two reasons for his coming to Jerusalem: bringing financial assistance to Jews in Jerusalem (without mentioning any specifics) and his making an offering to God. The second reason has been partly mentioned in Acts 24:11, where Paul speaks about "worship of God" as his purpose for coming to the city.[432] This information given in Acts 24:11 is supplemented with new details in Acts 24:17. In Acts 24:11, he says that he came to Jerusalem for twelve days before, but in Acts 24:17, he adds that this took place many years after the last visit, which minimalizes the possibility of Paul's causing disturbance in the city.

Acts 24:17 contains the information that, until now, was not

[430] Answering the accusation regarding his belonging to the Way, Lucan Paul actually describes the character of the movement. This characteristic contains several aspects that show a clear relation to Judaism. Paul underlines in Acts 24:14 that the movement worships the God of the fathers (the God of Judaism), respecting the prophets and the Mosaic Law (the scripture). The movement also shares the faith in the resurrection of dead that is accepted by some parties of Judaism (Acts 24:15), and this conviction is the solid ground for their lifestyle (Acts 24:16). The strictly theocentric character of Paul's presentation that overlooks all Christological reference is to be noted. D. G. Peterson, *The Acts of Apostles*, 635–636.

[431] L. T. Johnson, *The Acts of the Apostles*, 412–413.

[432] The main aim of Paul's argument was to present the movement as a part of Judaism (Acts 24:14–16), which automatically excludes the possibility that a member of the movement could possibly attempt to profane the Jerusalem Temple. Acts 24:12 introduces the topic elaborated in Acts 24:17–19 and Acts 24:19 concludes the argument presented in Acts 24:13–16.

revealed by Luke, who, in verse 11, mentions only worshipping of God as the reason for his coming, but in verse 17, he adds financial assistance to the nation as being the purpose of his visit.[433] The indication of the additional reason for Paul's coming to Jerusalem serves to testify the statement in Acts 24:16.[434] In Acts 24:17–18, Paul gives the account of his arrest in the Temple, which is generally in accordance with the narrative of Acts 21:27–31. Paul underlines that in the Temple, there was no problem between him and the crowd that could provoke the disturbance, and also, there was no direct interaction between him and the authorities of the Temple.[435] The disturbance was initiated by some Jews from Asia Minor who acted against Paul, accusing him of issues regarding Jewish religious matters and verbally and physically harassing him.[436]

This presentation allows Paul to undermine the right of the Sanhedrin to accuse him about the event in the Temple, in which they were not involved.[437] From the beginning until the end of the event, the Temple authorities were not present, and they were not eyewitnesses, who could prove the accusation presented in Acts 24:6.

---

[433] Mention of the financial aid for the Jews in Jerusalem is only fleeting, but we know more about it from Paul's writings (Rom. 15:25–32; 1 Cor. 16:1–4; 2 Cor. 8–9; Gal. 2:10). He calls "the saints in Jerusalem" the Jewish Christians in Jerusalem. H. Conzelmann, *Acts of the Apostles*, 199.

[434] Mention of the collection (Acts 24:17) is very fleeting and is not referred to elsewhere in Acts. It was probably mentioned here as a necessary preparation for the statement concerning Felix's attitude (Acts 24:26). C. S. Keener, *Acts. An Exegetical Commentary*, vol. 4, 3409–3412.

[435] In this way, Paul shows the lack of coherence in Tertullus's accusation. M. L. Soards, *The Speeches in Acts*, 119.

[436] Luke's narrative clearly shows the strictly religious purpose of Paul's visit to the Temple, even though he also informs us about the social circumstances of Paul's action (Acts 21:21–24). E. J. Schnabel, *Exegetical Commentary*, 961.

[437] Acts 24:14 shows that the accusers are unable to present a convincing argument to support their accusation; Acts 24:19 goes even further, claiming lack of a legal basis for the Sanhedrin to play the role of accuser because they were not eyewitnesses to the incident in the Temple. J. A. Fitzmyer, *The Acts of the Apostles*, 737. In such a case, according to Roman law, the trial should be abandoned. C. S. Keener, *Acts. An Exegetical Commentary*, vol. 4, 3418–3420.

The only accusers who can accuse Paul before Felix about crimes against Mosaic Law (Acts 21:27–28) are Jews from the Diaspora in Asia Minor (Acts 24:19), something that seriously complicated the case, if not even making it impossible. The actual accusers were Paul's opponents during the interrogation before the Sanhedrin (Acts 22:30–23:10). However, based on the narrative of Acts 23:1–10, the readers know that no accusation against Paul was formulated that the Sanhedrin could present to Felix (Acts 24:20). Also, the procurator knows from Lysias's report that Paul was accused by the Sanhedrin of crimes against Mosaic Law, with no further specification. Paul skillfully makes a reference to the event, only schematically known to Felix, which indicates that the Sanhedrin found no proof of Paul's guilt, as there was no formal accusation and consequently no decision, and at the same time, it suggests that the only controversy between Paul and the Sanhedrin concerned the issue of the resurrection of the dead.[438] The fact that the interrogation concluded unexpectedly with a heated quarrel over the issue of the Resurrection (Acts 23:9) ironically becomes the only issue that the Sanhedrin can use as an accusation during the trial before Felix.[439] However, an accusation based on one religious issue was the last thing that Tertullus would wish to achieve by his speech, as it would mean that he lost the case. The Roman procurator would hardly judge a Roman citizen on an accusation concerning a Jewish religious matter.

Paul's answer (Acts 24:14–21) to the accusations (Acts 24:2–8) achieved two important aims. The first is that Tertullus's accusations, presented as relating to a political issue, were successfully moved by Paul to the level of religious controversy. The second is that the legal right of the Sanhedrin to act as Paul's accusers was undermined, as they were not involved in the Temple event. Luke also attained his aim in the narrative by establishing that the issue of the resurrection of the dead was the only accusation that the Sanhedrin could possibly

---

[438] D. G. Peterson, *The Acts of the Apostles*, 637–638.

[439] Here, Lucan Paul tactfully overlooks the information concerning his offending the high priest (Acts 23:2–5).

lay against Paul, and even on this issue, the Sanhedrin was unable to formulate a clear accusation and find him guilty.

Despite Paul's convincing apology, Felix postponed his decision, officially due to the need to check the Sanhedrin's accusations and Paul's apology with Lysias's personal testimony concerning the event (Acts 24:22).[440] But Luke indirectly suggests that it could be that Felix's own knowledge about the Way meant that he correctly understood the main point of Paul's apology. This was also, most probably, the reason for the procurator's order that Paul be given special treatment, with considerable freedom to meet the friends who provided assistance to him (Acts 24:23). The fleeting information in verse 22 regarding Felix's knowledge of the Way indicates that the procurator and his wife often listened to Paul's teaching about the faith of those who believed in Jesus the Messiah (Acts 24:24). However, Paul's teaching concerning some moral issues, situated in terms of responsibility during the eschatological judgment, were not accepted by the procurator (Acts 24:25). As well as his limited interest in the teaching about the Way, Felix also had an interest in making financial profit from Paul's situation (Acts 24:26). For the two years until the end of his time in office, Felix neither freed Paul—probably because he was waiting for a bribe!—nor judged in favor of the Sanhedrin (Acts 24:27).[441]

Conclusion

Paul's apologetic speeches, together with Tertullus's accusing speech, constitute the main body of the narrative of the trial before Felix.[442] This narrative is supplemented with a brief explanation of the two

[440] The narrative of Acts 23:26–30 tells us (almost casually) that the accusers lost the case.

[441] Luke's narratives (Acts 24:17, 26) leave no doubt about Felix's being susceptible to being bribed. B. Witherington III, *The Acts of the Apostles,* 715–716.

[442] The account of Paul's trial before Felix is almost completely dominated by the two speeches, and other matter outside the speeches is reduced to Acts 24:1–2a, and Acts 24:10a, 22–23.

reasons why Felix adjourned the trial (Acts 24:22–27). Although the official reason was the need to interrogate the tribune, Lysias (v. 22b), the procurator's decision, according to Luke, was strongly influenced by his knowledge concerning the Way (Acts 24:22a), as well as his desire for a bribe (Acts 24:27). The two speeches (Acts 24:2–8; Acts 24:10–21) are highly informative concerning Paul's first official trial before the Roman procurator of Judea, who at that time was Felix. The trial was an *extra ordinem* process, where the accusers and the accused were present and had an opportunity to present the accusation (by the Sanhedrin) and the apology (by Paul). Tertullus, who represented the accusers, presented in his speech (Acts 24:2–8) three main accusations, designed to present Paul's case as having a political character. Paul answered the accusation in the second speech (Acts 24:10–21), in which he successfully defended himself against the accusations by showing the strongly religious character of the accusers' arguments (Acts 24:21), which could not be proved, even by the relevant eyewitnesses (Acts 24:13).

In the narrative regarding Paul's first trial (Acts 24:1–27), Luke successfully indicates Paul's innocence. When Lysias's report (Acts 23:29) concerning Paul's case, based on his investigation in Jerusalem, freed Paul from any crime against Roman law, the trial before Felix shows that the Sanhedrin had no adequate reason to accuse Paul in political terms (Acts 24:11–13. 17–19), and the only accusation that they might possibly present concerned a religious issue—the resurrection of the dead. In this way, Lucan Paul established that the issue of resurrection, until now treated as a general issue, was, in fact, the main reason for his being persecuted by the Jews. Felix, however, though he had the authority and was well acquainted with Jewish thought (Acts 24:22), failed to declare Paul innocent, neglected Paul's apology, and, for less than proper reasons, left Paul in prison for the next two years.

In the narrative of the trial before Felix, Luke advanced his presentation of Paul, leaving aside the rather passive apologetic attitude that characterized Paul in the narrative of the Jerusalem period for a more aggressive stance that would dominate the account of the Caesarea period. During the first official trial, Lucan Paul, with surprising ease, shows the irrelevance of the accusers' arguments. In addition, Paul gives a well-designed and professionally presented witness to the Way. It is probably the most noteworthy presentation of Paul's witness recorded by Luke, in which he shows his pride in being a servant of God, actively involved in the messianic movement. This involvement not only has a positive effect on Paul himself but also contributes to society in the assistance he brings to the poor. Paul indirectly claims that the only reason for rejection of the Way may lie in the rejection of faith in the resurrection, which actually meant the Resurrection of Jesus, the Messiah.

4.2.2. The trial before Festus (Acts 25:1–26:32)

The procurator Felix left Paul's case unsolved until the end of his time in office in Judea, and his successor had to reactivate the case. Festus succeeded Felix in the late 50s (he died in office in AD 60).[443] He was newcomer to Judea, with little knowledge of the culture, religion, and problems of the Jews, who became, to some extent, his subjects (Acts 25:18–19). Naturally, he first paid a visit to Jerusalem in order to meet the Sanhedrin, the Jewish authority that would be indispensable for Festus's success in the office (Acts 25:1). According to Luke's narrative, the high priest and the most powerful Jews (Acts 25:2) introduced Paul's case to Festus, asking him to transfer Paul to Jerusalem, probably under the pretext of holding another interrogation, but in reality in order to assassinate Paul on the road (Acts 25:3). The account shows that after two years, the attitude of the Jews in Jerusalem toward Paul had not changed at all, and they were still intent on executing him. Festus, however, most probably adhering to the principle that a Roman citizen should be interrogated or judged before Roman officials rather than acting out of any real knowledge regarding the case, submitted Paul to trial in Caesarea

[443] Little is known about Festus as the procurator of Judea, and the beginning of his office is difficult to establish. The years 54, 56, or 59 are suggested. D. G. Peterson, *The Acts of the Apostles* (Grand Rapids, 2009), 642–643.

(Acts 25:4–5). The second trial of Paul took place at the end of the second week of Festus's being procurator of Judea (Acts 25:6).

The account of the trial before Festus is a continuation of the narrative of the trial before Felix (Acts 24:1–23), and it marks the beginning of a new chapter in the narrative of Paul's imprisonment.[444] Luke, in his narrative, gives no detail either about the Jewish accusers or the content of their accusation. Surprisingly, he does not include the speech of the accusers but proceeds immediately with Paul's speech. Rather than being a speech in self-defense, Paul attempts to argue the case for a just trial for himself. Luke mentions, only in very general terms, that the accusers (this time, the Jews themselves and not a professional orator) presented "serious accusations" but without convincing proof (Acts 25:7). This strongly suggests that the accusations during the trial before Festus were similar to those presented by the Jews in the trial before Felix.[445] It is probably for this reason that Luke enters directly with Paul's speech, and this also is in a reduced form (Acts 25:8). Paul denied that he broke Mosaic Law or defiled the Jerusalem Temple. He also rejected the

---

[444] Concerning the trial before Festus, Luke only fleetingly presents the accusation against Paul, and he gives scant attention to Paul's answer to the accusation. This very reduced presentation is caused by two reasons. The first is that both the accusation and the defense had already been presented in the narrative of the trial before Felix, and since little had changed in the meantime, it was unnecessary to repeat the material. The second reason is the progressive character of the narrative regarding the trial before Festus, in which Luke's main focus is now concerned with the reasons for Paul's appeals to Caesar. C. S. Keener, *Acts. An Exegetical Commentary*, vol. 4, 345–3457.

[445] Acts 25:7 tells us that the Jews presented "serious accusations" against Paul, without offering any specifics. These accusations may be indirectly deduced from Paul's defense in Acts 25:8. F. F. Bruce, *The Book of Acts*, 451–452. Compared to the accusations made during the trial before Felix (Acts 24:10–21), only the last "speaking against Caesar" shows anything new in the accusers' strategy. Concerning this accusation, with the exception of Acts 17:7, which concerns events in Ephesus where no solid proof was offered, there is nothing to indicate Paul's opposition to the emperor. The accusation is very general, and for this reason, it would be very hard to prove. E. J. Schnabel, *Exegetical Commentary*, 989.

accusation that he committed a crime against "the person of Caesar." This refers to Roman law in general, rather than to any particular crime against Caesar himself. The schematic account shows Luke's narrative approach in which he avoids repetition, but it is also an indication of what the accusations made during the trial before Festus were.[446] There is some slight modification of the previous accusation, which is reduced here to only one word: *Caesar* (referring to the Roman law), but there is no substantive change.[447] This presentation of Paul's defense during the trial before Festus, in which the narrative is reduced to his final assertion of innocence in regard to both Mosaic Law and Roman law, serves to underline the truth (that is obvious to the reader) that Paul cannot be sentenced on the basis of the accusation presented by the Jews. Paul's statement in Acts 25:8 should end his trial before Festus because he argued convincingly that all the accusations against him were not rooted in facts, and the accusers did not present new evidence beyond what had already been presented and answered during the trial before Felix (Acts 25:7).

Although the logical conclusion after Paul's defense should be his acquittal, as had happened in the trial before Felix (Acts 24:27), Festus is about to hand over a Roman citizen to the jurisdiction of the Sanhedrin, on the condition that Paul would agree (Acts 25:9).[448]

---

[446] Because the account of the trial before Festus begins at the point where the narrative concerning the trial before Felix ended, these two narratives should be taken as complementary, continuing the same topic. This would also explain the lack of a narrative concerning the accusation and Paul's defense in the section on the trial before Festus. H. Conzelmann, *Acts of the Apostles*, 203.

[447] The accusation that Paul was acting against Caesar, which here probably refers to acting against Roman law, relates better with the narrative concerning Paul's appeal to Caesar. In his appeal, Paul refers twice to the name of Caesar (Acts 25:10a, 11b).

[448] Festus's approval of Paul's appealing to Caesar comes as a surprise, as he initially seemed to favor the Jews and put his own interest before the rights of the Roman citizen, Paul. Considering the narrative of Acts 25:24–27 where Festus expresses his own problem regarding the legal reason for accepting the appeal, Luke's presentation of the trial before Festus is peculiar, and it lacks coherence. It is hardly possible that Luke was not conscious of this, and his narrative seems to have been purposely created in this way. Luke presents both procurators (Felix

Despite Festus's ignorance regarding the sociopolitical context in Judaea, he obviously should have known that a Roman citizen, who was not found guilty of crimes either against Mosaic Law or Roman law, could not be turned over to Jewish jurisdiction. His attempt to get around the law by adding a condition was an unjust way of solving the issue because it put Paul's case in a new context that clearly favored the accusers over the prisoner. In both trials, Luke makes clear the true reason for the procurator's attitude. Festus wished to win over the cooperation of the Jewish leaders in exchange for his favor in Paul's case. Such behavior by the procurator, in which he ignores, out of self-interest, the rights of a Roman citizen is used by Luke to express a negative judgment on the functioning of the Roman juridical system at the local level, where, in many cases, the prisoner was forced to request a trial before Caesar.[449] The procurator Felix, after hearing Paul's apology, adjourned the case (Acts 24:22), leaving Paul in prison for two years, despite being convinced of his innocence.

Similarly, the procurator Festus, although convinced by Paul's defense, was prepared to cede the case to Jewish jurisdiction in order to avoid a possible conflict with the Jews and merely included the condition that Paul accept this arrangement (Acts 25:9).[450] Both cases are used by Luke in his narrative to show to the reader the weakness of the local Roman juridical system that depended on the will of procurator. These accounts at the same time show both the corruption in Roman legal practice and the Jews' determination to

---

and Festus) in negative terms that are in accord with other nonbiblical sources. Josephus, in his writings, presents both procurators as being ill-disposed toward the Jews (Felix: *Bell.* 2. 247–270; *Ant.* 20.137–182. Festus: *Bell.* 2.271–272; *Ant.* 20.182–200). Luke shows the wrongdoing of both procurators and the unjust attitude of local Roman officials that forced Paul to seek justice in Rome. C. S. Keener, *Acts. An Exegetical Commentary*, vol. 4, 3457.

449 H. Conzelmann, *Acts of the Apostles*, 203.

450 Acts 25:11 strongly suggests that Paul was perfectly aware of the potential consequences of a trial in Jerusalem, if he should agree to Festus's proposal. This interpretation is confirmed by Luke's direct presentation of the Sanhedrin's intentions in Acts 25:3.

solve for themselves that case of Paul. Paul's later assertion that he did not come to Rome to accuse the nation (Acts 28:19) is a reflection of the overlap of motivations that resulted in Paul's making his appeal to Caesar. Paul, very forthright in his rejection of Festus's "proposals" (Acts 25:10–11) emphasized that he, as a Roman citizen, was subject to the Roman judicial system, which guaranteed him the right to be judged by Caesar in Rome (Acts 25:10–11). His answer is reinforced by the phrase "I am now standing before Caesar's court" (Acts 25:10 NIV), which, in this particular context, should be interpreted as a direct rebuke to Festus, rather than stating the obvious—that Festus is the legal and official representative of Caesar.[451]

Paul had not committed offenses against Mosaic Law; hence, there was no reason for him to be judged by the Sanhedrin (Acts 25:10).[452] In this context, Paul's statement concerning his willingness

---

[451] The context of Acts 19:21 and Acts 23:11, where Luke uses the term *must*, and its use in Acts 25:10 (οὗ με δεῖ κρίνεσθαι—*I must be tried*) strongly suggests his wish for the trial before Caesar in Rome; this wish will be directly shown in his official appeal to Caesar (Acts 25:11b). F. F. Bruce, *The Book of Acts*, 453.

[452] Paul's statement in Acts 25:10 assumes that Festus is aware of Paul's innocence of crimes against the Roman law and the Mosaic Law. However, the preceding narrative does not affirm Paul's assumption because Festus heard about Paul's crimes from the Jews during his visit to Jerusalem (Acts 25:2), but he did not hear Paul's apology. The narrative indicates that before the trial (Acts 25:1, 6) Festus had no knowledge about Paul's case. There is no information about Festus's knowledge of Lysias's report, which leaves no possibility other than our assuming that Festus was familiar with the official records of Paul's trial before Felix. However, even this possibility must be questioned because it is unthinkable that, in the report, Felix should include proof of Paul's innocence and then leave him in prison for the next two years. Festus's speech before King Herod Agrippa II (Acts 25:14–21) shows that during the trial, Festus found Paul to be innocent of any crime (Acts 25:18). In these contexts, Paul's statement in Acts 25:10 may be interpreted as an ironic rebuke of Festus's lack of sufficient understanding of the real situation. C. S. Keener, *Acts. An Exegetical Commentary*, vol. 4, 3461. A more preferable explanation, however, seems to be that Luke's short and schematic narrative containing the accusation and the reply to it, does not repeat the detailed information that has been presented in the narrative concerning the trial before Felix; instead, it proceeds with the general statement that applies both to the trial before Felix and that before Festus.

to accept the penalty, should his guilt be proven (Acts 25:11), concerns only the crime against Roman law.[453] In this way, Paul indirectly indicates that he wishes to be judged exclusively by the Roman authorities.[454] In the last part of verse 11, for the second time, Paul directly indicates that the Jewish accusations against Paul were not proved, and consequently, there is no reason for a trial before the Sanhedrin.[455] Paul does not directly show his disagreement with Festus's proposal, but this disagreement is indirectly shown by his request for a trial before Caesar (Acts 25:11c).[456] The narrative of the trial before Festus concentrates on the relationship between Festus and Paul, in which power and right are opposed. The injustice of the one is confronted by Paul's effort to save his life.[457] Festus, despite his power, had to admit the right of the Roman citizen, protected by Roman law, to request a trial before Caesar (Acts 25:12).[458]

---

[453] Mention of a possible penalty of death is made here in very general terms, and it can refer either to the Roman law or the Mosaic Law. In the context, the second is the more probable.

[454] From the perspective of Luke's narrative, the two trials before the Roman authorities are the way in which Jesus's plan for Paul was realized. P. W. Walaskay, *And So We Came to Rome*, 58.

[455] In Acts 25:11, Paul reminds the Roman official of his duty to protect the rights of the Roman citizens, even if it should complicate the relations between the procurator and his Jewish subjects. Festus's favor (χαρίσασθαι) toward the Jews, caused by his private interests, is in sharp conflict with his duty. In this context, Paul's statement may be interpreted as a rebuke. F. F. Bruce, *The Book of the Acts*, 452–454.

[456] Submitting Paul to a trial before the Sanhedrin in Jerusalem (cf. Acts 23:14–16) would mean death for Paul, most probably even before the trial would begin. D. G. Peterson, *The Acts of the Apostles*, 646.

[457] Although the appeal to Caesar was the right of a Roman citizen, it could not be invoked automatically; it was dependent on the good will of the local officials. In Paul's case, Festus consulted with his advisers before he granted the appeal, which suggests that Festus had some doubts regarding the issue. Or it may be Luke's preparation for the topic presented in Acts 25:13–27. B. Witherington III, *The Acts of the Apostles*, 723.

[458] If Acts 25:12 concerns Festus's doubts about Paul's appeal, it would show significant lack of knowledge on the part of the procurator concerning correct procedure. B. Witherington III, *The Acts of the Apostles*, 722. However,

Conclusion

Paul's speech during the trial before Festus contains two parts: the first is Paul's apology to the accusations of the Jews, which actually are not presented here.[459] This apology is reduced to one statement declaring his innocence of crimes against Mosaic Law as well as Roman law (Acts 25:8). The second part of the speech contains Paul's answer to Festus's "proposal" concerning the trial before the Sanhedrin in Jerusalem. The structure of this part is chiastic (A-B-A¹), where A (Acts 25:9) and A¹ (Acts 25:12) contain the words of Festus, creating a kind of bracket for whole section, and B is a considerably elaborated form of Paul's apologetic speech (Acts 25:10–11). This short analysis shows Paul's argument as being the most relevant for Luke's narrative purpose. Luke's main concern is to present a reason for Paul's appeal to Caesar. Luke's previous narratives (the trials before Felix and Festus) prepared the ground for the final climax of the trials section, where Paul presents and evaluates the circumstance that forced him to seek help in Rome. During two years of imprisonment and two trials, Paul (according to Luke) defends himself from all form of accusations (Acts 25:8). However, this fact, as well as Paul's Roman citizenship, does not change his unfavorable position in the eyes of the Roman officials or in the eyes of the accusers. Paradoxically, in the final combat during the period of the Caesarea imprisonment, Paul had to fight against the procurator Festus, who put his own interests before the interest of the Roman citizen.[460] Paul's speech directly addressed Festus's unjust attitude, and at the same time, it is Paul's desperate attempt to save his life while being boldly critical of the Roman procurator's neglect of his duty. Paul used his rights as a Roman citizen to request a trial

considering Festus's practical approach in Paul's case, it is possible to suppose that the consultation concerned the potential consequences of approval or refusal. A. Fernando, *Acts*, NIVAC (Grand Rapids 1998), 593.

[459] Scholars present various structures for this section; cf. M. L. Soards, *The Speeches in Acts*, 119–120.

[460] C. S. Keener, *Acts. An Exegetical Commentary*, vol. 4, 3450.

in Rome (Acts 25:11) because although he was able to convince the procurators of his innocence, he was not able to earn their favor. In this speech by Paul, Luke makes a highly critical evaluation of the local officials of Roman administration, something he shares with other historians of the time. Considering the fact that the Gospel and Acts were dedicated to Theophilus, this approach is hardly accidental. Luke presents Paul as the victim of the Sanhedrin's hatred and the procurators' failings in their office.[461] From the theological perspective, Paul's appeal to Caesar is another step in the realization of Jesus's plan for Paul, which will be realized in several, sometimes very strange, sociopolitical circumstances (Acts 23:11).[462]

4.2.3. Paul's speech before King Agrippa II (Acts 26:1–32)

The second subsection in the narrative of Paul's trial before Festus (Acts 25:13–27) consists of two speeches of the procurator Festus, which have a preparatory character in Luke's arrangement. These two speeches (Acts 25:14–21; 25:24–27) do not offer new information that might contribute to the presentation of Paul, but since they are in the form of direct statements by the procurator, they clarify the legal status of the apostle. Although all the factual statements are already known to the reader from the preceding narrative, the speeches underline Paul's innocence in the context of his appeal to Caesar. Festus has to attest his acceptance of Paul's appeal in a report concerning the prisoner's crimes and the conclusions reached in the trials. In fact, he was unable to reach any conclusion due to his lack of knowledge about the socioreligious context relating to the case. For this reason, Festus sought the help of Agrippa II. Festus's

---

[461] The unjust attitude of the Sanhedrin will again be used by Paul in his presentation of the relationship between him and the Sanhedrin during the meeting with the Jewish elders in Rome (Acts 28:19).

[462] Paul's meeting with the Jews living in Rome may be simply a result of Paul's modus operandi, or it may show his awareness of the sensitive situation in which the Jewish community in Rome was placed (Acts 28:19). B. Witherington III, *The Acts of the Apostles*, 724–726.

two speeches are not of great importance for the information they contain, but they are necessary for the narrative structure of Acts, as they preceded Paul's speech before the king, which, in Luke's strategy, is of critical importance in his presentation of Paul. In the first speech, Festus explains that Paul's case was left unsolved by the previous procurator, Felix, which tactfully exonerates Festus of responsibility for the present state of things (Acts 25:14). Immediately, he adds that the case was reactivated by Jews in Jerusalem who pressed for a condemnation of Paul (Acts 25:15), thus again taking the responsibility away from Festus. In the next verses, Festus first presents the actions that led to the trial (Acts 25:16–17) and the result of the trial, which found the arguments of the accusers to be irrelevant (Acts 25:18). He found that the case concerned a Jewish religious controversy concerning a certain Jesus, who was dead, but Paul insisted that he was alive (Acts 25:19). In Acts 25:20, Festus offers his inability to solve the problem as the reason for his offering Paul the possibility of a trial before the Sanhedrin in Jerusalem, to which Paul, in answer, requested a trial before Caesar (Acts 25:21). The narrative of Acts 25:19–21 shows Festus to be totally ignorant in matters concerning the socioreligious reality in Judaea.

Festus's second speech (Acts 25:24–27) contains no information about Paul not already given in the first speech, with the exception of Festus's reason for gathering the most influential people of Caesarea, together with Agrippa II and his wife, in order to hear Paul's speech (Acts 25:26–27). However, the information regarding Paul that was presented in the first speech in a narrative manner is given here in the form of statements. The first regards the many Jews who accused Paul, asking Festus for the penalty of death for him (Acts 25:24). In this way, in the narrative regarding Paul's imprisonment, Luke explicitly presents the Jews from Jerusalem (the Sanhedrin) as the main antagonists of Paul, causing the trial before the procurators that would eventually lead to the trial before Caesar. Paul, who at the beginning of Luke's narrative was supported by the Sanhedrin in his persecution of the Way, at the end of the narrative is presented as one persecuted by his former mentors because of his belonging to the Way. The second statement (Acts 25:25) asserts Paul's innocence of any crime that would deserve the death penalty. The general character of the statement does not specify which law is intended by Festus, but while it was most probably the Roman law, this may also be extended to mean the Mosaic Law, based on Festus's statement in Acts 25:19, where he uses the term "enquiry" but not the term "crime," describing the main issue of disagreement between Paul and the Sanhedrin, which was the resurrected Messiah.

After this preparation (Acts 25:13–27), Luke brings the narrative regarding Paul's imprisonment to its climax, with Paul's proclaiming the kerygma to the king of the Jews. Although Paul's speech is presented by Luke as a public event, because it was given in the meeting chamber of the procurator's residence, with the most important guests present (Festus, Herod Agrippa II and Bernice, the tribunes, and the notables of Caesarea), it was addressed to Agrippa II, giving it a personal character that is underlined also by several mentions of the name of the king (Acts 26:2, 7, 19, 27). The speech is an example of forensic rhetoric, delivered before the king in highly rhetorical terms.[463] The speech begins with an exordium (Acts 26:2–3), containing a *captatio benevolentiae* addressed, surprisingly, only to the king.[464] Acts 26:2 indicates that the king (not Festus, who should be in charge of this interrogation) gave Paul permission to proceed with his defense. It is the first time in Luke's narrative that Paul proclaims the kerygma to the king of the Jews alone, and consequently, Agrippa is in charge of Paul's interrogation, since formally (according to Festus's previous speech) he is the only one capable of giving an authoritative answer to Festus's dilemma (Acts 25:26).

In the following *exordium* (Acts 26:2–3), two statements are presented regarding Paul's present situation: Jews, not Romans, are Paul's accusers. This may seem to be a statement of basic fact, but

---

[463] For a detailed rhetorical analysis of the speech, cf. W. R. Long, "The Trial of Paul in the Book of Acts: History, Literary, and Theological Considerations," (Ph.D. diss., Brown University, 1982), 237–239.

[464] M. L. Soards, *The Speech in Acts*, 122–126.

Paul is alluding to the reality that he was handed over by the Jews to the Roman authorities. In this context, the second statement, where Paul considers himself fortunate to defend himself before a competent judge, who is the king of Jews, shows his disappointment with trials between the procurators.[465] Indirectly, this statement contains a critique of both the Sanhedrin's and the Roman procurators' handing of the case.[466] In Acts 26:3, Paul explains further his statement concerning his good fortune, which, for him, means to have the opportunity to present his case before Herod Agrippa II, the king of the Jews, and a person who is familiar with the customs and traditions of the nation. This extends to a knowledge of past and present controversial issues in religion and politics. The most relevant point is his knowledge about tension within Judaism regarding also the case of the sect called Nazarenes.[467] Although this is only the *captatio benevolentiae* aimed at earning the attention and good will of the person(s) addressed, Paul expresses a recognition that Herod Agrippa II is the right person to judge the truth of his case.[468]

---

[465] Although Paul says that he is about to give an apology, the content of the speech does not support this claim, because most of the speech is a presentation of the kerygma from several perspectives, all aimed at the conversion of the king. Paul's claim regarding his apology is more an amplification of the *captatio benevolentiae*, where Paul recognizes Herod Agrippa II as the competent judge. This also is an indirect allusion to Festus as lacking competence to judge Paul.

[466] The competence of Herod Agrippa II concerns the fact that he is a Jew with knowledge of Jewish society and religion, as opposed to Festus, the Roman official, whose ignorance of the society and the religion of his subjects was clear. B. W. Winter, "Official Proceedings and the Forensic Speeches in Acts 24–26," in *The Book of Acts in Its First-Century Setting,* vol. 1, eds. B. W. Winter and A. D. Clarke (Grand Rapids: Eerdmans, 1993), 329.

[467] The content of Paul's speech suggests that Agrippa II was familiar with the Christian movement. There is no introduction to the movement (unlike Paul's approach in the speech before Felix in Acts 24:24–25), but Paul proceeds directly with an account of his life as a zealous Jew and a member of a movement that aims at the fulfillment of God's promises given to the Jewish nation. C. J. A. Hickling, "The Portrait of Paul in Acts 26," in *Les Actes des Apôtres: Traditions, redaction, théologie*, ed. J. Kremer (Leuven: Leuven University Press, 1979), 499–503.

[468] L. T. Johnson, *The Acts of the Apostles*, 432.

In the *narratio* (Acts 26:4–21) of the speech, Luke exposes another extensive account of Paul's biography. It contains three related sections referring to specific periods of Paul's life: Paul's youth in Jerusalem (Acts 26:4–11); Paul's life in Damascus (Acts 26:12–18); and Paul's mission journeys (Acts 26:19–23). The first section in the *narratio* of the speech (Acts 26:4–11) concerns mostly an account of Paul's life in Jerusalem (before the event at Damascus), with special attention given to his activities as the persecutor of believers in Jesus (Acts 26:6–11). Paul presents himself as somebody who was well known to the Jews in Jerusalem.[469] The knowledge also includes information regarding his origin, where he informs that from his youth, he lived in Jerusalem, which indirectly tells us that Paul was not born in Jerusalem (Palestine) and that he was a Diaspora Jew who came to the city to further his education.[470] Despite his origin, Paul attempts to underline his close relationship with Palestinian Judaism by using expressions such as *from youth*, *from the beginning*, and *from the start*, which amplify his claim of being a zealous servant in service of God. Another way of showing his connection with Palestinian Judaism is the claim of belonging to the sect of the Pharisees (Acts 26:5), which directly indicates his zeal for service to God, which was a characteristic claim of the Pharisees.[471] The use of the aorist tense of the verb ζάω indirectly shows that this period of his life belongs to the past, and he no longer counts himself as a Pharisee, or that after his conversion, he is no longer recognized by the Pharisees as one of their members and a truly devout Jew. The second possibility is the more

---

[469] Although commonly, Paul is called the apostle to the Gentiles, Luke consistently presents Paul's modus operandi as being always initially directed to the Jews. S. Kim, *The Origin of Paul's Gospel* (Grand Rapids: Eerdmans, 1981), 62.

[470] In Acts 26, Paul presents himself in a manner that differs slightly from that in Acts 22:3. J. A. Fitzmyer, *The Acts of the Apostles*, 756.

[471] The present tense of ζάω in Acts 23:6 may seem surprising if we consider that now Paul is a follower of Jesus, and he actually discontinued the way of living characteristic of the Pharisees after the event at Damascus. However, the issue concerns the resurrection of dead, the teaching shared by Pharisees and by Jesus's followers, and so his conviction remains unchanged (except for the idea of the resurrected Messiah). E. J. Schnabel, *Exegetical Commentary*, 1003.

likely because of Paul's additional statement, expressing doubt about the Jews who would acknowledge his past as a Pharisee (Acts 25:5).

After establishing the most positive picture of his youth, Paul continues with his present situation which, although it is less favorable for him, he evaluates in a highly theological perspective. In Acts 26:6, Paul directly gives the reason for his imprisonment, which is his hope, based on the promise that God has been given to the chosen nation. Although this statement is directly connected to this particular interrogation, it naturally refers also to all the other trials he has experienced (the trial before the Sanhedrin—Acts 23:1–11—and the trials before the Roman procurators—Acts 24:1–23; Acts 25:1–12).[472] Paul does not specify to which promise of God he is referring, but for Agrippa and the Jews present, it is clear that he refers to the promise of sending the Messiah to Israel, despite the fact that identity of the Messiah is still unrevealed.[473] The topic of God's promise is further developed in Acts 26:7, where Paul shows it to be something of critical importance for all zealous Jews.[474] Paul naturally includes himself among them, as is seen in his use of "our twelve tribes" (Acts 26:7 NIV), which also means that it concerns

---

472 It is hardly accidental that the topic of "God's promise" is the main theme in both Paul's first speech (Acts 13:7) and his last (Acts 26:6) in the section regarding his trials. C. S. Keener, *Acts. An Exegetical Commentary*, vol. 4, 3500.

473 Paul's understanding of God's promise will be clearly presented in Acts 26:8–9. For this reason, the relationship between God's promise and the resurrection of the dead is not yet clarified here.

474 In Acts 26:7, Paul's teaching regarding God's promise concerns the resurrection of dead, and it may refer to two different aspects that are related to this eschatological event. The interpretation of God's promise as the resurrection may refer to individual resurrection (Acts 26:8), which was partly accepted in Judaism but only by the Pharisees. However, it also may refer to "the resurrection of Israel," understood as the free kingdom of Israel, which was expected by all Jews. Although the second interpretation of resurrection is irrelevant to Luke's narrative strategy in the speech, it would point to the Jewish mainstream political interpretation of the term. Paul, speaking about resurrection of dead in general, uses his own experience (Acts 26:9), which he considers to be the fulfillment of God's promise (Acts 26:6–7). This interpretation, according to Lucan Paul, is the direct reason for Paul's imprisonment.

Jews believing in Jesus as the Messiah.[475] Nevertheless, the promise itself is still not yet clearly defined by Paul for the audience.

Surprisingly, Paul clams that his hope, which comes from this promise, is the reason for his trial, due to his particular interpretation of the promise. This particular interpretation of God's promise has something in common with the possibility that God raises the dead (Acts 26:8). As a Pharisee, Paul is surprised that some Jews exclude this possibility, and for this reason, his rhetorical question is addressed to those who do not believe in the resurrection of the dead, including King Agrippa (cf. Acts 26:28).[476] Despite the fact that Acts 26:6–7 does not state clearly to which of God's promises Paul refers, the preceding narrative of Paul's trials (Acts 23:6; 24:14–15; 25:19), as well as the following account of this speech (Acts 26:8–9), strongly connect God's promise with belief in the resurrection of the dead, which is here probably narrowed further by Lucan Paul to refer to the resurrection of one specific person.[477] The rhetorical question presented in Acts 26:8 indirectly indicates that Paul understands God's promise as a fulfilled reality, which was realized in a manner that was unexpected by Jews, including Paul himself. By melding the widely accepted idea of the Messiah with the less acceptable idea of the resurrection of the dead, Paul introduces, in his speech, a new concept—namely, "the resurrected Messiah". Acts 26:6–7

---

[475] Paul's mention of his belonging to the Pharisees' sect (Acts 26:5) may serve as a connecting link between this religious group believing in resurrection and being recognized by mainstream Judaism, and the Nazarene sect that believes in the resurrected Messiah and, for that reason, was not recognized by mainstream Judaism. Although, the relatively new teaching concerning the resurrection of the dead was acceptable to Judaism (2 Macc. 7:9), it was not a required teaching. The teaching about the resurrected Messiah, however, was something entirely new and was not readily accepted in mainstream Judaism. L. T. Johnson, *The Acts of the Apostles*, 432.

[476] L. T. Johnson, *The Acts of the Apostles*, 432.

[477] Acts 26:8 finally makes clear the meaning of the phrase *God's promise* (2 Macc. 7:9; Dan. 12:13). The fact that it is expressed in the form of a rhetorical question may suggest a lack of common consensus regarding Paul's interpretation. J. A. Fitzmyer, *The Acts of the Apostles*, 756.

suggests that Paul's hope in God's promise is identical with the Jews' understanding of this promise, but Acts 26:8 clearly shows a fundamental difference in the interpretation of God's promise—for Jews, it refers to the Messiah; for Paul, it refers to the resurrected Messiah.

In Luke's narrative concept, the rhetorical question here has another purpose: to prepare the background for transferring the narrative regarding Paul's own struggle with such a strange realization of God's promise (Acts 26:9–11). The next part of the speech (Acts 26:9–11) contains an account of Paul's activities as a persecutor of the Way. To the audience mentioned in Acts 26:8, Paul presents his own example of misunderstanding the teaching regarding Jesus of Nazareth and his followers. This serves as a challenge to Paul's audience on the teaching concerning the resurrected Messiah. Acts 26:9 directly refers to the past period in Paul's life, when he was also wrongly convinced about the need to persecute those who spread the kerygma that Jesus of Nazareth is the resurrected Messiah.[478] This conviction led him to oppose, with every means, the believers in Jesus. Acts 26:10 contains Paul's confession that he persecuted Jesus's followers in Jerusalem. The short description of the persecution shows some

---

[478] Paul does not offer a reason for his conviction that led him to persecute those who believed that Jesus was not only the Messiah but also was the resurrected Messiah but Acts 26:8 indirectly points to the issue of Jesus's Resurrection as the reason for Saul's conviction. Because Paul claimed to be a Pharisee, and the Pharisees believed in the resurrection of the dead, Paul necessarily shared this conviction of the Pharisees. For this reason, Saul's conviction that led him to persecute Jesus's followers does not derive from the issue of the resurrection of the dead in general but from the claim that Jesus of Nazareth is the Messiah, resurrected by God. This claim involves two elements: the first is the recognition of Jesus as the Messiah by God himself by raising him from the dead; the second is the rejection of Jesus of Nazareth as the Messiah by mainstream Judaism (including the Pharisees). God's act affirms the claim of Jesus's followers, which thereby makes the rejection of Jesus by mainstream Judaism to be wrong. Acts 26:9 contains Paul's confession that he, as a zealous Jew, considered the messianic movement as a deviation from true Judaism, and because of that, he chose open hostility to Jesus's followers as the way to protect Judaism from this evil. B. Witherington III, *The Acts of the Apostles,* 741.

characteristics of his action. His action was not only authorized by the high priests of the Temple, but he was also given special authority. He had power to imprison all followers of the Way. Following arrest, they were brought for judgment before the Sanhedrin, which in some cases resulted in the death penalty. Paul himself acquiesced to this when he cast a vote against them.[479] This description of Paul's action as persecutor leaves no doubt about Luke's intention to present this stage of Paul's life not as an individual zealous Jew but as somebody acting with the authority of the Sanhedrin and intent on eliminating the Way from Judaism.[480]

The detailed description of Paul's "career" as the persecutor continues in Acts 26:11, where his actions in the synagogues are indicated. It seems that the actions in the synagogues are different from those presented in Acts 26:10 because here, the aim of the action was to convince adherents to abandon their faith in Jesus. This action was not limited only to synagogues of Jerusalem but extended also to synagogues outside the city.[481] Paul's activities were undertaken

[479] The phrase τε αὐτῶν κατήνεγκα ψῆφον (I cast my vote against them) (Acts 26:10 NIV), which is absent from the other narratives, may suggest that Saul could be a member of the Sanhedrin. However, in the other narratives (Acts 7:58; 8:1; 22:20), while Paul is presented as actively persecuting Jesus's followers, he is never referred to as a member of the Sanhedrin. The interpretation of Acts 26:10 serves to show Saul's responsibility for wrongdoing, which was based on his particular understanding of showing zeal for Judaism. C. S. Keener, *Acts. An Exegetical Commentary*, vol. 4, 3506–3508.

[480] On the question of Saul's possible membership in the Sanhedrin, it must be noted that several regulations concerning membership in the Sanhedrin would rule out the possibility. The information provided in Acts 26:10 should be interpreted as referring to Saul's cooperation with the Sanhedrin, which included advising the Sanhedrin in cases involving members of the Way, especially on the interpretation of scripture by Jesus's followers, which in some cases differed from the official interpretation. It is also possible that his "experience" as persecutor was used by the Sanhedrin in planning and carrying out persecution (*to shut up*; *to give approval*; *to force*; *to pursue*) as Acts 26:10–11 seems to suggest. E. J. Schnabel, *Exegetical Commentary*, 1005–1006.

[481] Paul speaks of the synagogues as the places of his activity (Acts 26:11), which is information that shows two characteristics of his modus operandi. The first regards the public character of the punishment, and the second concerns

also in other cities, which supports the thesis that the persecutions were systematic. The modus operandi included also public physical punishment in order to make the believers of Jesus renounce their faith in him as the Messiah.[482] In order to amplify his zeal for Judaism and his uncompromising rejection of the Way, Paul shows the reason for his attitude, which resulted in furious rage toward those who blasphemed God by believing that Jesus is the resurrected Messiah (Acts 26:11).[483] After Paul has established his image of the zealous Jew, actively opposing the followers of the resurrected Messiah, he gives a short account of the event that forced him to change sides in the conflict in which he was involved. Acts 26:12 begins this new unit within Paul's speech (Acts 26:12–18), which indicates that Paul's activity in Jerusalem was terminated (or deferred) in order that he undertake persecution in other places (Acts 26:11) that had become shelters for those who fled the persecution in Jerusalem. Luke's narrative (Acts 26:11) suggests that Paul's journey to Damascus was not the only one of this type, but it was the one during which Paul's fate was changed.[484] Paul, the antagonist (described in Acts 26:11), with the authorization of the high priests of the Jerusalem Temple, goes to Damascus to search for the members of the Way.[485] Considering that the speech is given before King Herod Agrippa II,

---

the forcing of Jesus's believers to demand their faith in Jesus as the Messiah. Indirectly, it indicates that until the systematic persecution took place, Jesus followers either separated themselves from Judaism, or they were rejected by synagogues because of their messianic convictions.

[482] Paul presents the persecution against the Way as something strictly within Judaism, where he and his supporters were responding to a temporary problem that was recognized as being potentially dangerous to Judaism but not yet as a divisive force.

[483] E. J. Schnabel, *Exegetical Commentary*, 1007.

[484] The speech before King Herod Agrippa II contains the third account of Paul's conversion (Acts 9:1–9; 22:6–11). While the account agrees with the other two accounts, due to the circumstances in which the speech is given and its purpose, there are some minor discrepancies in the interpretation of the conversion. W. Neil, *The Acts of the Apostles*, 242.

[485] Bruce maintains that the term ἐν οἷς has two specifications: it may be a circumstantial reference, as in Luke 12:1, or a temporal reference, as in Acts

who possessed the right of superintending the Jerusalem Temple and appointing the high priest, Lucan Paul's mention of the authorization given by the Temple authorities emphasized the fact that he was not acting on his own behalf and that the official institution (the Temple) was also involved in the persecution.[486]

The narrative from Acts 26:13 contains Paul's account of the revelation he experienced on the road to Damascus. In general terms, the account, though it contains many specific details, is similar to previous ones given on the same topic that Luke already had presented in his narrative.[487] The account in Acts 26:13 refers to the light, which is used here as a sign of theophany. The terms used, "heavenly light" and "light of the sun," indicate not only the reality of the event—it was not a dream—but also underline the unnatural character of the event. The additional mention that the light also affected Paul's co-travelers shows that the event was not a private inner revelation but a public event. Acts 26:14 continues the description of the revelation in a way similar to the account presented in Acts 22:6–11 but with some new details. Paul and his companions fell to the ground after seeing the light from heaven. This may be intended to indicate that the testimony of the other travelers was some guarantee that it was a true revelation.[488]

The second new detail was that "the voice" (message) was

24:18. F. F. Bruce, *The Acts of the Apostles*, 500. The circumstantial reference is preferred.

[486] The use of the term *high priests* (plural) is explained variously by scholars. According to Fitzmyer, the term refers to the high priest and his council. J. A. Fitzmyer, *The Acts of the Apostles*, 758. According to Keener, the term refers to the entire house of the high priest. C. S. Keener, *Acts. An Exegetical Commentary*, vol. 4, 3510–3511. According to Witherington, the term refers to two high priests, the current officeholder and his predecessor. B. Witherington III, *The Acts of the Apostles*, 741.

[487] In substance, the account in Acts 9:2 of the speech before King Agrippa II only contains the addition of specifying the time of day. Other differences are merely stylistic. L. T. Johnson, *The Acts of the Apostles*, 435.

[488] Comparing the account of Acts 9:2, some details included in the conversion narrative of Acts 22:6–16 are absent here. D. G. Peterson, *The Acts of the Apostles*, 665–666.

addressed exclusively to Paul, who alone would hear it, despite the public character of the revelation. Despite the fact that the revealer spoke in Hebrew and addressed Paul by his Hebrew name, he used a rhetorical question and the Greek proverbial sentence.[489] The rhetorical question indicates that Paul actually persecutes the revealer, and this should be interpreted as the revealer's self-identification with his believers. This self-identification may be a theological statement by Luke: to act against the Way means acting against the revealer, who, in Paul's understanding at this point, was God, rather than Jesus of Nazareth. The Greek proverb shows the vanity of Paul's struggle against the Way, which, in this context, also indirectly indicates the divine origin of the movement, with the revealer becoming personally involved to protect the Way.[490] The identity of the revealer is given directly in Acts 26:15 in answer to Paul's question.[491] Although Paul asks the revealer to identify himself in a manner similar to Moses' experience (Ex 3:13–14), the revealer's answer is given in a much more direct manner than in Moses's case, as the revealer revealed himself as Jesus.[492] Paul did not believe in Jesus as the resurrected Messiah (Acts 26:9), which led him to oppose this blasphemous claim, but he now was facing a living Jesus, who revealed himself to Paul in God's glory.[493] Jesus' self-presentation is reinforced by a direct presentation of Paul's wrongdoing toward him. This was partly presented in Acts 26:14 but without making a direct connection to Jesus. The statement in Acts 26:15 indirectly shows the enmity between Paul and Jesus,

---

489 The proverb was well known in the Hellenistic world, but it is unknown in the extant Aramaic literature. F. F. Bruce, *The Acts of the Apostles*, 501.

490 F. S. Spencer, *Acts and Modern Literary Approaches*, 227.

491 Despite the addition of *Nazarene* to the name of the revealer (Jesus) in Acts 22:8, the accounts regarding the Jesus-Saul dialogue are identical. J. A. Fitzmyer, *The Acts of the Apostles*, 759.

492 Some scholars see similarity between the experiences of Paul and Moses. Moses met the living God on Mount Horeb, and Paul met the living Jesus on the road to Damascus. E. J. Schnabel, *Exegetical Commentary*, 1009.

493 Paul almost instantly calls Jesus "the Lord," which shows his unconditional surrender.

which had been indicated but now, in the context of the revelation, shows Paul to be guilty of acting against God.[494]

Despite Paul's obvious guilt, no penalty was handed down to him, which shows that the aim of the revelation was not to destroy him but to make him useful for the resurrected Messiah. Verse 16 begins a short subsection (Acts 26:16–18) containing a description of the reason for Paul's conversion, and the purpose of his was appointment.[495] The order to stand up from the ground, from a position of one defeated in battle, is the Lord's act of appointing Paul to the service of the Lord.[496] Paul's new status is to be servant and witness, with a single task to perform; namely, to give testimony to his experience of meeting the resurrected Messiah and to what will be revealed to him in the future.[497]

Jesus's appointment of Paul is a command, but it also contains a promise of protection for his servant. Verse 17 refers to the obligation undertaken by Jesus to protect Paul during his service. There is no assurance that Paul will not meet with hardship, but Jesus will rescue him from the opponents who will reject his witness and will even try

---

[494] The identification of the persecution of Jesus's followers directly with persecution of Jesus himself underlines the awareness that persecution of Jesus's believers, while being an act of obedience to the human will, was disobedience to God's will.

[495] When the account refers to Saul's guilt without mention of a sentence or penalty, it is similar to Exodus 3:7–22 For other possible similarities with the Old Testament, cf. C. S. Keener, *Acts. An Exegetical Commentary*, vol. 4, 3517; W. Neil, *The Acts of the Apostles*, 243–244.

[496] Conzelmann sees similarity here with Ezekiel 2:1–4. H. Conzelmann, *Acts of the Apostles*, 211. In Acts 26:16, the commission of Saul for service of the Lord is directly pronounced by Jesus, but in Acts 9:15, the commission is given to Saul through Ananias. A completely different version is found in Acts 22:14, where the commission is directly given by Jesus in the Temple, and it includes not only service to the Lord but also being his witness.

[497] The account gives two purposes to Jesus's revelation: it concludes the period of Saul's antagonism toward Jesus's followers, and it is the beginning of Saul's service to the Lord Jesus. The content of the service is here limited to one very general expression—"to give witness"—with the additional specification that the witness should include the past and future experiences of Saul.

to eliminate him.[498] Indirectly, Luke indicates that Paul's appointment will include risk and danger, but Paul will be under divine protection.[499] The object of Paul's service ("I am sending you to them") (Acts 26:17 NIV) is elaborated as including Jews who are in covenant with God, and Gentiles who do not have a covenant, which is a de facto reference to all people. In this way, Paul presents the essentials of the account of the revelation, during which Jesus himself appointed Paul to a mission, not only to the Jews but also to the Gentiles.[500] Paul's mission, which the Jews considered to be blasphemy (Acts 22:21–22), is nothing other than the realization of the Lord's order. After presenting the content of the order, Paul presents, in Acts 26:18, the purpose of his appointment to the mission. This purpose is presented in three different but complementary expressions: "to open their eyes and turn them from darkness to light, and from the power of Satan to God" (Acts 26:18 NIV). All three expressions have the image of conversion, which here means the process of changing the conviction from rejecting Jesus as the resurrected Messiah to that of affirming him.[501] Each of these expressions indicates the next logical step in a process of conversion, which begins with recognition (*to open their eyes*), which leads to action (*and return them from darkness to light*) in order to find fulfillment in the covenant with God (and *from the power of Satan to God*). The metaphor is an indirect indication that all people (both Jews and Gentile) are not walking according to God's will and that Paul's task is to bring back the Jews or show the way to the Gentiles, and thus, all will be reconciled and united with God.[502] This reconciliation, which here indicates the forgiveness of sins and justification by God (God accepts people), is only possible

---

498 Some similarities to the prophets can be drawn (Jer. 1:5–8; Isa. 42:7).

499 Mention here of divine protection for Saul is a new element in the narratives of Paul's conversion. E. J. Schnabel, *Exegetical Commentary*, 1010.

500 Acts 26:17 shows Jews and Gentiles as the objects of Saul's service to the Lord Jesus. B. Witherington III, *The Acts of the Apostles,* 744.

501 Use of metaphor is a common device in the Bible; cf. C. S. Keener, *Acts. An Exegetical Commentary*, vol. 4, 3520–3526.

502 According to Schnabel, the metaphors describe "the process and reality of conversion." E. J. Schnabel, *Exegetical Commentary*, 1010–1012.

by accepting Jesus of Nazareth as the resurrected Messiah.[503] This is required of Jews in order to faithfully serve God and of Gentiles in order to enter into the covenant with God. With this last sentence, Luke encapsulates the core of Paul's theology.

The third part of the speech is the *propositio* (Acts 26:19–23), which is a logical subsection in the speech, continuing Luke's presentation of Paul to the reader. In historical terms, it is Paul's self-presentation to the king. The first part of the speech presented Paul's life in Jerusalem, with special attention given to his zeal as a Jew (Acts 26:2–11). Then, in the second part, we learn the way in which Paul changed from the persecutor of the Way to become the follower of the Way (Acts 26:12–18). Now, in this part Paul is about to give a short schematic account of his mission activity after his conversion (Acts 26:19–23). Acts 26:19 begins with a repetition by Paul of his address to the king, which probably serves, in Luke's narrative, to indicate the crucial importance of this section. Paul first presents the reason for his mission activity, which was a direct consequence of his appointment as a servant of the Lord. Paul feels this obligation as an inner force that drives him to share his experience. Concerning the circumstances of the speech, Paul's account should be understood by King Agrippa II as having sufficient and logical reason, as it was based on private revelation, and it concerns obedience to the divine will.[504]

Herod was greatly influenced by Hellenism in his ways, but he

---

[503] Conversion, understood here as faith in Jesus as the resurrected Messiah, is an essential requirement for Jews to be forgiven and return to God, and for Gentiles, in order that they would be saved by entering into a covenant with God through Jesus. The perfect passive participle of ἁγιάζω (Acts 26:18) shows that faith in Jesus is fundamental to believers. D. G. Peterson, *The Acts of the Apostles*, 668–669.

[504] In Acts 26:19, ὀπτασία – *vision* is described as a "vision from heaven" (Acts 26:19 NIV), which according to the narrative of Acts 26:14–18, was Paul's inner experience of encounter with Jesus. B. Witherington III, *The Acts of the Apostles*, 746. The term ὀπτασία (*vision*) appears only infrequently in the New Testament (Acts 1:22; 24:23; 26:19; 1 Cor. 12:1). C. S. Keener, *Acts. An Exegetical Commentary*, vol. 4, 3527.

knew very well the teaching of Judaism regarding disobedience to God's will, together with the divine origin of the revelation and the appointment, and he knew that Paul's decision was acceptable and correct. Acts 26:19 indicates that the speech is developing into a new topic, and this is the last occasion in Acts that gives the most accurate presentation of Paul's understanding of his own conversion and his life after the revelation.[505] The consequence of Paul's obedience to the Lord's order was his mission activity, which, in Acts 26:20, is presented in a very short and schematic form.[506] In his account, Paul begins with sparse information, without any details concerning the mission activity in Damascus that took place immediately after his conversion. He then lists the mission in Jerusalem, without giving any details, and then his mission in Judea, which is, in fact, new information that is not found in the other narratives. He finally ends with information about his mission to the Gentiles, again without details.[507]

The general nature of this summary of Paul's mission activity, which lasted for at least ten years (including Damascus and Syrian Antioch), is evident. It probably reflects Jesus's order given to the disciples (Acts 1:8). Luke thus established, in the eyes of the king (and the readers), that Paul is one of the apostles (the apostle to Gentiles)

---

505 C. K. Barrett, *A Critical and Exegetical Commentary on the Acts of the Apostles* (Edinburgh: Bloomsbury T&T Clark, 1998), 1162; C. H. Talbert, *Reading Acts: A Literary and Theological Commentary on the Acts of the Apostles* (Macon: Smyth & Helwys Publishing, 2005), 208.

506 In general terms, apart from occasional new details, the summary agrees with Luke's narrative regarding Paul's mission journey.

507 Luke's account of Paul's missions in Damascus, Jerusalem, and to the Gentiles (Acts 9:20–22; Acts 9:26–29; Acts 13–20) is here (Acts 26:20), supplemented by information about Saul's activity in Judea. Acts 26:20 shows Paul's commission has some similarities with Jesus's commission to the twelve in Acts 1:8. E. J. Schnabel, *Exegetical Commentary*, 1012.

The information about Saul's activity in Judea is new and is not found in other accounts regarding Paul's mission activity. The new information poses some problems for interpretation. There are also some difficulties with the grammar of the passage. For an account of these, cf. M. Zerwick, M. Grosvenor, *A Grammatical Analysis of the Greek New Testament*, 445–446.

and shows him fulfilling the Lord's order given to the apostles.[508] Paul, in his mission to both Jews and Gentiles, used the method Jesus showed him, in a metaphorical way, when he was appointed (Acts 26:18). The three stages of the conversion process given in Acts 26:18 is now in Acts 26:20, given in more theological language. Here, Paul's use of the term *conversion* (understood as the changing of one's way of thinking) corresponds to the phrase "to open their eyes" in Acts 26:18. The phrase *turning to God* in Acts 26:20 corresponds to the phrase "to turn them from darkness to light" in Acts 26:18. Finally, the phrase "demonstrate their repentance by their deeds" (Acts 26:20) corresponds to the phrase "and from the power of Satan to God" in Acts 26:18.[509] In this way, Lucan Paul shows his understanding of Jesus's order. This understanding and fulfillment of the Lord's order is presented by Paul as the direct reason for the Jews' hostility toward him, which found its culmination in the event in the Jerusalem Temple (Acts 21:27–22: 29).[510]

Paul's mission to the Jews and the Gentiles earned him many enemies among the Jews (including the authorities of the Temple), who were determined to destroy him. When during his appointing of Paul to the mission, the Lord speaks about protecting him from the Jews and the Gentiles (Acts 26:17); here (Acts 26:21), only the Jews' hostility is mentioned, probably because reference is restricted to the event in the Temple. Indirectly, Paul rejects other accusations, whether political or religious, by pointing to the fact that his proclaiming the resurrected Messiah to all people is the only reason for the Jews'

---

[508] Acts 26:20 underlines Paul's presentation of himself to King Herod Agrippa II as a zealous Jew, spreading the kerygma about the resurrected Messiah, first to the Jews and then to the Gentiles.

[509] Acts 26:18 is very similar to Peter's teaching in Acts 3:19. L. T. Johnson, *The Acts of the Apostles*, 437–438.

[510] The term ἕνεκα τούτων (*for these reasons*) exposes Paul's proclaiming Jesus as the resurrected Messiah to the Jews and Gentiles as the respective reason for his persecution in Jerusalem. D. G. Peterson, *The Acts of the Apostles*, 670–671; B. Witherington III, *The Acts of the Apostles,* 746–747.

hatred toward Paul.[511] The conclusion of Paul's presentation of his present situation is that his zealous service to the Lord is the reason for his rejection by Jews. Despite the hostility of Jews and their determination to kill him, Paul always managed to escape from the Jews, which is the realization of the Lord's promise to protect his servant (Acts,26:17). This protection was given to Paul on many occasions during his mission journey. In this way, he was able to testify about the resurrected Messiah to many different groups. Now, however, in this particular context, the opportunity has been given to testify before King Herod Agrippa II, Festus, and other notables of Caesarea. This seems to be particularly important in Luke's account (Acts 26:22).[512]

At the beginning of the speech, Paul expressed his delight at getting the opportunity to defend himself before King Agrippa (Acts 26:2), and now, he clearly indicates his understanding that the real purpose of this interrogation is his proclaiming the kerygma to the king, which differs from Paul's initially declared purpose (Acts 26:2), as well as from Festus's purpose (Acts 25:26–27).[513] Lucan Paul is fully aware that this interrogation is a time for his "testifying" about the resurrected Messiah before King Herod Agrippa II. He sees the present state of his imprisonment as being part of God's due, to which he will be able to fulfill another element in his commission in the Lord's service (Acts 9:15).[514] Paul boldly claims that all his teaching

---

[511] Acts 26:22–23 contains Paul's teaching about Jesus the Messiah and the Savior that is presented as the only activity for which he is imprisoned. In the last words of Paul's apology, there is no reference to the initial accusation presented in Acts 21:28.

[512] In Acts 26:17, Jesus promised Paul constant assistance in his commission. Paul's claim in Acts 26:22—"but God has helped me" (Acts 26:22 NIV)—confirms fulfillment of the promise. J. A. Fitzmyer, *The Acts of the Apostles*, 761; C. S. Keener, *Acts. An Exegetical Commentary*, vol. 4, 3532.

[513] cf. D. G. Peterson, *The Acts of the Apostles*, 477–478.

[514] Although Paul's speech is presented as an apology, Paul uses the occasion to be a witness to Jesus the Messiah in the presence of the king. That the purpose of the speech was really to attempt to convert the king seems confirmed in Acts 26:24–29.

concerning the resurrected Messiah is in accord with Judaism and the scriptures. He thus rejects any suggestion of blasphemy and claims that his teaching fully conforms to Judaism (Acts 26:22).[515] Specifically, he points to prophecy concerning the Messiah in scripture (Acts 26:23).

Paul presents three central notions concerning the Messiah in the Bible. The first relates to the suffering of the Messiah, who must sacrifice himself for the nation, which is traditional teaching.[516] The second refers to the resurrection of the Messiah as being consonant with traditional teaching. The Messiah not only can suffer, but he also can be raised from the dead, as the first among many, leading to the eschatological resurrection of all the people.[517] The third is the universal character of the Messiah, who is no longer a Messiah for Jews alone but for all.[518] Indirectly, Paul indicates that the ideas of the suffering Messiah, the resurrected Messiah, and the universal Messiah, as proclaimed by him, amount to the proclamation of the fulfillment of God's promise (Acts 13:23).

Paul's statements (verse 23) were found to be annoying and irrational by Festus, who interrupted the speech, and his subsequent exchange with Paul was a heated debate.[519] The last three statements of Paul concerning the Messiah met with a strong emotional

---

[515] E. J. Schnabel, *Exegetical Commentary*, 1013. Herod Agrippa II was strongly influenced by Hellenism, but he was still a Jew and unlikely to find Paul's conception of the resurrected Messiah acceptable.

[516] The term παθητὸς (*subject to suffering*) refers to the possibility that the Messiah could suffer. L. T. Johnson, *The Acts of the Apostles*, 438. This claim of Paul is not attested by the Old Testament writings, which make the claim to be Lucan Paul, to be specific Christian interpretation of some writings regarding the Messiah (Isa. 53:1–9). J. A. Fitzmyer, *The Acts of the Apostles*, 761.

[517] This claim is not attested by the Old Testament writings. This claim may be based on specific interpretation of Isaiah 53:10–12. E. J. Schnabel, *Exegetical Commentary*, 1014.

[518] This universal approach is also presented in Acts 26:17–18, and it exposes the same idea that was presented by Simeon in Luke 2:32. The possible text of the Old Testament that may be grounds for this statement are Isaiah 42:6; 49:6; 51:4. C. S. Keener, *Acts. An Exegetical Commentary*, vol. 4, 3532–3533.

[519] L. T. Johnson, *The Acts of the Apostles*, 438.

reaction from Festus, with strong words addressed to Paul—"You are out of your mind, Paul!" (Acts 26:24 NIV).[520] Although it is not explicitly stated, the statements concerning the Resurrection of the Messiah probably triggered Festus's reaction, as the idea was totally unacceptable to Greco-Roman philosophy and culture.[521] The interruptions caused by Festus and King Agrippa (Acts 26:28) serve to show the impact of Paul's speech on the procurator and the king (Acts 26:27. 29).[522] Unlike Festus's excited reaction, Paul, in a respectful manner, denied that he was mad but was in full control of his senses and that what he was teaching was very reasonable.[523] This refers properly only to Paul's last teaching, but it seems to contain the most important theological teaching (Acts 26:22–23).[524] Paul's answer, which is, at the same time, a veiled rebuke of Festus (Acts 26:25), refers to the knowledge of Herod Agrippa as being the only listener who could comprehend the meaning of Paul's words (cf. Acts 26:3). The teaching, which for Festus was irrational, for Herod Agrippa II was the issue within Jewish society, about which he was very well informed, and that made him a reliable witness and judge of Paul. This praise of the king's competence, with Paul speaking

---

520 The speech (Acts 26:1–23) turned into a dialogue (Acts 26:24–29); then it was interrupted by Festus in Acts 26:24 and by Agrippa in Acts 26:28. This is the reason for which only Acts 26:2–23 is sometimes recognized as the speech. F. F. Bruce, *The Acts of the Apostles*, 440.

521 Since the reason for interrupting Paul's speech at Areopagus (Acts 17:22–34) was Paul's speaking about a judge who was resurrected from dead, it is possible to assume that the direct reason for Festus's reaction was Paul's teaching about resurrection.

522 Scholars are divided on the structure of the speech; cf. B.W. Winter, *Official Proceedings and the Forensic Speeches in Acts 24–26*, 329–330; C. S. Keener, *Acts. An Exegetical Commentary*, vol. 4, 3492–3494.

523 Festus's reaction (Acts 26:2–23) is the point in Luke's narrative where Paul's semi-apology (with some kerygmatic hints) becomes a direct kerygmatic "offensive" aimed at the king. C. S. Keener, *Acts. An Exegetical Commentary*, vol. 4, 3534–3535. W. Neil, *The Acts of the Apostles*, 245.

524 Some scholars refer the statements to facts from his life but not to Acts 26:22–23. L. T. Johnson, *The Acts of the Apostles*, 438.

directly only to the king, may be interpreted as an indirect rebuke of Festus.[525]

Leaving the procurator aside, Paul expresses his strong conviction regarding the king's knowledge about all that is related to Jesus of Nazareth and his teaching and deeds, as well as about the followers of Jesus, known commonly as Christians, because these had a strong impact on Jews in the kingdom of Agrippa II.[526] The king could hardly reject this affirmation of his own knowledge, and Agrippa unexpectedly found himself forced to choose between the tradition of Judaism or his Hellenistic education.[527] Given the place and the audience, the king was under pressure, and this was only increased by Paul's next rhetorical question (Acts 26:27).[528] To the rhetorical question addressed by Paul to the king, concerning possibility that the king believes in the prophets' words, Paul himself answered affirmatively.[529] To reach the goal at which the narrative is aimed, Luke makes two axiomatic assumptions: first, that the writings of prophets confirm the concept of the resurrected Messiah; and second, that king Herod Agrippa II is a zealous Jew who believes

---

[525] A. J. Malherbe, "Not in a Corner: Early Christian Apologetic in Acts 26:26," 147–163.

[526] The phrase "because it was not done in a corner" (Acts 26:26 NIV), used here by Paul, shows the significant attention that had been given to the messianic movement within Jewish society. E. J. Schnabel, *Exegetical Commentary*, 1016. The statement in Acts 26:26 established the messianic movement as historical fact. J. A. Fitzmyer, *The Acts of the Apostles*, 764.

[527] In Acts 26:2–29, where Paul's speech becomes a dialogue with the king, Luke shows his purpose in including the narrative of Paul's interrogation here.

[528] The logic in Paul's rhetorical question, which is a de facto trap for the king, begins from the fact that the king knows about the messianic movement, as well as the teaching of the prophets, and ends with the axiomatic supposition that these two factors would lead the king to share in Paul's conviction and believe in Jesus as the resurrected Messiah. C. S. Keener, *Acts. An Exegetical Commentary*, vol. 4, 3545. This logic assumes that some prophetic writings have a Christological interpretation. W. Neil, *The Acts of the Apostles*, 245.

[529] The fact that Lucan Paul himself answered the question shows its rhetorical function in Paul's dialogue with the king. Paul's attempt to convince the king failed in a manner like the rejection of Paul's teaching by the citizens of Athens.

in the prophets.[530] To Paul's question (Acts 26:27), the king answers ambiguously (Acts 26:28), the meaning of which depends on the reader's interpretation of the entire passage (Acts 26:19–29).

There are five possible ways to understand King Agrippa II's answer.[531] It can be understood in the affirmative—namely, that the king's recognizes Paul's arguments—but this did not lead him to make a final decision. It can be understood also as an ironic expression, offering no clear comment on Paul's teaching. It is possible also that Paul's arguments did not fully convince the king. According to the fourth interpretation, the king's words are an angry denial.[532] A final possibility if that this is an expression of the king's irritation, by which he escapes having to confirm or deny Paul's presentation, as presented in Acts 26:26–27.

After Festus disagreed with Paul's teaching (Acts 26:24), Paul attempted to gain the support of King Herod Agrippa II.[533] However, Paul answered his own rhetorical question (Acts 26:27) in a manner that strongly suggests an attempt to put considerable pressure on the king, and it hardly attests that the king was ready to give a positive evaluation of Paul's attempt or to lean toward Paul's side.[534] The king's words—"Do you think that in such a short time you can persuade me to be a Christian?" (Acts 26:28 NIV)—show his irritation, and this was probably the direct reason for ending the interrogation.[535] This

---

[530] Paul's high evaluation of the king's zeal for Judaism may be questionable. Such zeal on the part of Herod Agrippa II does not emerge in the nonbiblical sources that relate to the king.

[531] For some textual variants, cf. B. Witherington III, *The Acts of the Apostles*, 750.

[532] M. Zerwick and M. Grosvenor, *A Grammatical Analysis of the Greek*, 446–447.

[533] Luke often uses the device of interruption in his narrative (Acts 17:32; 22:1–5; 26:30). G. H. Horsley, "Speeches and Dialogue in Acts," *NTS* 32 (1986), 611.

[534] The trap in Paul's rhetorical question (Acts 26:27) lies in the fact that King Agrippa could either deny or affirm his knowledge of the prophets' teaching. To deny it would make him ignorant of his own religion and culture; to affirm it would make him a supporter of the messianic movement

[535] In Acts 26:28, the king does not refer to the messianic movement or to the sect of the Nazarenes, but he uses the term *Christian* that was given to the Way by the inhabitants of Syrian Antioch (Acts 11:26) to show the distinction between

reaction shows Herod Agrippa II is not on Paul's side concerning the issue of the resurrected Messiah.[536] It does not mean that he is totally against Paul (cf. Acts 26:32), but that on the particular issue question of the resurrected Messiah, the king feels very uncomfortable in the particular circumstances.[537]

Although Paul does not achieve his aim by his speech, Luke's use of Paul's speech achieves his narrative purpose. When we take into consideration the trial before Festus, Paul's speech before King Herod Agrippa II was not necessary because Paul's fate was already decided, and the interrogation itself did not throw any new light on Paul's case. Festus's presentation of his private problem can be understood on the private level (Acts 26:13–22), but on the public level, it seems to be self-indulgence for a display before his military subjects and the dignitaries of Caesarea (Acts 26:23–27). In this context, Luke's extended account of the interrogation was used not to show the *meritum* of the trial but to present the trial as the fulfillment of his commission (Acts 9:15).

Despite the fact that Paul's kerygma was rejected by the Sanhedrin, the religious authority (Acts 24:1–9; 25:1–7), and finally, also by the political authority, King Herod Agrippa II (Acts 26:28), Luke, in the narrative, presents Paul as the victor.[538] Paul openly expresses the hope that, eventually, Herod Agrippa II and all those who were present will find the way to faith.[539] Although he convinced neither the Sanhedrin nor King Herod Agrippa II, his kerygma about the

---

Jews believing in Jesus as the Christ, and Jews who do not believe in him. D. G. Peterson, *The Acts of the Apostles*, 676.

536 F. F. Bruce, *The Book of the Acts*, 471.

537 The attitude of King Herod Agrippa II (Acts 26:32), who is convinced of Paul's innocence, does not differ from the attitude of the Roman procurators Felix, and Festus, yet it did not affect Paul's fate.

538 B. Witherington III, *The Acts of the Apostles*, 752.

539 Despite the rejection of Paul's kerygma by Festus (directly) and by Herod Agrippa II (indirectly), Paul expresses his wish for the conversion of all those present at the interrogation. This shows his zeal as the witness to Jesus the Messiah, though faced with the impossibility of realizing it. L. T. Johnson, *The Acts of the Apostles*, 440.

resurrected Messiah nevertheless was planted in their ears, and this is probably the main reason for Lucan Paul's optimism concerning the future (Acts 26:29).[540] This hope extends beyond the present circumstances toward the day when Jews and Gentiles will believe in Jesus as the resurrected Messiah. In this way, Luke presents Paul as the witness who, due to God's providence and social circumstances, was able to bring his commission to a conclusion.[541]

Conclusion

In the narrative of Acts, Paul's speech before Herod Agrippa II gives Luke the opportunity to evaluate Paul's mission activities. According to Luke, Paul, by his speech to the king, fulfilled the last stage of his commission presented in Acts 9:15 (to give witness to the kings), which means the fulfillment of God's plan.[542] From the beginning of the narrative regarding Paul's interrogation, Luke does not disguise the fact that the king is the main target of Paul's speech. He also shows the main theological message addressed to the king regarding the resurrected Messiah.[543] This concept was not acceptable to Festus[544] and was also met with skepticism by the king, but Paul continued to hope. Despite, the fact that we learn almost nothing new about

[540] Luke's presentation of Paul's attempt to convert the elite of Jewish society shows the sharp differences between Paul's interpretation of the scripture and the teaching found in Palestinian Jewish literature. E. P. Sanders, *Paul and Palestinian Judaism*, 543–556. Also see K. Haacker, "Paul's Life," in *The Cambridge Companion to St Paul*, ed. J. G. Dunn (Cambridge: Cambridge University Press, 2004), 27–28.

[541] D. G. Peterson, *The Acts of the Apostles*, 676.

[542] M. L. Soards, *The Speech in Acts*, 122. According to Walaskay, Luke's narrative of Paul's trial before the Roman procurators and King Herod Agrippa II presents the entire event as another of "God's devices" in the realization of his plan, revealed to Paul by Jesus. P. W. Walaskay, *And So We Came to Rome*, 58.

[543] R. F. O'Toole, "Acts 26: The Christological Climax of Paul's Defense," *AB* 78 (Roma: Pontifical Biblical Institute, 1978).

[544] The Hellenistic background of Festus explains his reaction to Paul's teaching about resurrection in Acts 26:24.

Paul from Luke's narrative, this narrative plays an important role in the progression of Luke's presentation of Paul.[545] More than new information, what is important is the way in which Luke presents Paul, standing before the powers of this world in the persons of the Roman officials and the king of the Jews.

From the beginning of the narrative, Paul is presented in an extremely aggressive manner. This is seen especially in his address to the king (Acts 26:2–3), during which he (diplomatically) expresses his expectation that he will not receive fair judgment. This can be understood as an indirect criticism of Festus. Paul, with considerable self-confidence and ease, gives the account of his own activity as a persecutor, ending with the conclusion that it was caused by his rejection of Jesus as the resurrected Messiah. Another part of Paul's speech, regarding his conversion and its evaluation, serves Luke in presenting Paul as one who unconditionally subordinated himself to God's will, with full knowledge of what his service would entail (Acts 26:16–18). Paul's radical change was possible due only to his zealous service to God and to meeting the resurrected Jesus. Paul does not feel guilty about abandoning his previous conviction, but he is fascinated by his new commission. His conversion leads him to undertake mission activity now as witness to the resurrected Messiah, whereas he himself had been a persecutor of those who believed in Jesus.

Based on the background prepared in the speech, Paul finally launches into a strong critique of the king, putting him under considerable pressure in the circumstances of the interrogation and driving him to evade a straight answer. In the speech, Paul is a witness who knows no limit to his zeal for proclaiming Jesus as the resurrected Messiah.

---

[545] L. T. Johnson, *The Acts of the Apostles*, 440–443.

4.3. Voyage to Rome (Acts 27:1–28, 16)

The next step in Luke's narrative is Paul's voyage to Rome, which is the consequence of his appeal to Caesar.[546] Luke skillfully uses narrative devices, such as detailed descriptions, suspense, and eyewitness accounts, to create a vivid sense of the journey. While the journey itself is the main purpose of this section, it also contains three different kinds of relationships in which Paul was involved during the voyage.[547]

The first is the personal interrelationship between Paul and Julius, a centurion from the Augustan Cohort. The detailed presentation of Julius (Acts 27:1) indicates that there is something of importance in the information. The first note is the obvious one—that Julius was a Roman citizen—but we are also given his rank (the centurion), and the specific identification of the place of his service. The *Cohors Augusta* can be identified with *Cohors I Augusta Thracum Eguitala Civium Romanorum* or *Cohors I Augusta Ituraeorum* that was most probably in the service of Herod Agrippa II. It suggests cooperation between Festus, who sent Paul to Rome, and the king, who oversaw delivering the prisoners to Caesarea. The third-person-plural form of the verb *hand over* strongly suggests this.[548] The fact that Paul was not the only prisoner sent to Rome allows us to assume that the interrogation of Paul was not the only one in which Festus and the king took part together, but Luke's narrative is only interested in Paul's case.

The second time Julius is mentioned in Acts 27:3 shows him to be "kindly" disposed toward Paul, which may have been due merely to Julius's pragmatism (Paul's needs the provision for the voyage) or,

---

546 According to Acts 27:2, during Paul's voyage to Rome, he was accompanied by Luke and Aristarchus, which explains the detail given in the account (Acts 27:1–28:16). B. Rapske, "Paul's Helpers," in *The Book of Acts in Its First-Century Setting, vol. 3. Paul in Roman Custody*, 374.

547 The genre of the narrative of Paul's voyage to Rome is a subject of dispute among scholars; cf. E. J. Schnabel, *Exegetical Commentary*, 1030–1032.

548 A. Kyrychenko, *The Roman Army and the Expansion of the Gospel*, 4–43.

more likely, due to his sympathy toward Paul (as Acts 27:42–43). The account indicates that Paul had friends in Sidon, but unfortunately, Luke does not identify them. We cannot conclude that they were believers because in the case of believers, Luke usually uses the term *brothers*. The next mention of Julius (Acts 27:11) is in a dispute on whether the voyage should be continued during unfavorable weather conditions. Paul was not in favor (Acts 27:10), but the captain and the owner wished to go on, and for some reason, this was accepted by the centurion, who, trusting the opinion of experienced sailors, decided that the voyage was to continue. When this decision proved to be wrong and the voyagers had to struggle for survival, Luke again mentions Paul's advice to Julius on the danger that the ship would not survive if the sailors were allowed to flee (Acts 27:31–32). This time, Julius followed Paul's advice and took the necessary action to prevent the sailors from abandoning the ship, which saved the lives of all the travelers.

The last mention of Julius concerns his saving Paul's life (Acts 27:42–43) when, under the pressure of circumstances that made it possible for the prisoners to escape, the soldiers, according to regulation, were about to kill the prisoners. In order to save Paul, Julius found another solution. Luke's presentation of the relationship between Paul and Julius goes from initial kindness, through difference of opinion, to accepting advice to break the regulations in order to save Paul's life.

The second relationship concerns Paul and the inhabitants of the island of Malta (Acts 28:1–10). Paul and his co-travelers were shipwrecked and reached the island of Malta, where they were assisted by the local people. Again, Luke confines his narrative to events concerning Paul and an account concerning a snake (Acts 28:3–6). The inhabitants initially considered Paul to be a murderer—although he survived the sinking of the ship, the goddess of justice did not allow him to live because he was bitten by a snake (Acts

28:4).[549] When, as expected, he did not die, the inhabitants considered Paul to be a god because he survived not only the sinking of the ship but also the snake bite. This episode is similar to the events at Lystra (Acts 14:8–20), where local folk superstitions are presented. However, in this case, there is no attempt to make an offering for Paul, which explains the difference in Paul's reaction in Acts 14:14–18.

The second part of narrative on the stay in Malta concerns Paul's miracles. In the first account, the father of Publius, who was a leader on the island, was healed by Paul. Paul's healing local people in need of assistance represents a different case. Paul was honored in many ways for his good deeds, with special accent placed on the provision of the necessities needed for continuing the voyage (Acts 28:10). Luke's presentation of this relationship begins with the locals' judgment, based on the events, interpreted more in accord with local beliefs than on knowledge of Paul. This continues with their considering the possible divine nature of Paul and ends with their honoring him for his healing activity.

The third relationship concerns Paul and his co-travelers during the long and dangerous voyage to Rome (Acts 27:1–28:14). Because Luke was Paul's companion on the voyage, he gives not only a detailed account of this voyage but also makes considerable effort to present Paul's relationship with others, particularly with his co-travelers, during this stage of his imprisonment. Sailing on the Mediterranean Sea always involved considerable risk and danger, especially during the period from late autumn until early spring. Paul's journey by sea to Rome was no exception, and the hardship of this voyage was, for Luke, an excellent opportunity to present the psychological and spiritual characteristics of the main character in his narrative. Although the circumstances of the voyage were not conducive to including any extensive account of Paul's mission activity or theological thought, Luke nevertheless uses this time of suffering and struggle to present aspects of his character and

---

[549] The association between a snake and divine justice is attested by Greek mythology. E. J. Schnabel, *Exegetical Commentary*, 1050–1051.

convictions, with which he faced the dangers with hope and which gave him strength to comfort others. Paul's relationship with his co-travelers (treated here collectively) is most extensively elaborated in Paul's speeches and statements made at different stages of the voyage.

The narrative of the voyage contains only two direct statements and two short speeches by Paul, in which Luke condensed all that Paul spoke over the course of the four-months voyage to Rome.[550] The first statement, presented in verse 10, is related to Paul's speech in Acts 27:21–25. In the form of a warning, Paul gives his opinion concerning the risk involved in continuing the voyage under unfavorable weather conditions. This was based on common sense rather than any kind of prophetic inspiration, even though what he predicted would soon come to pass.[551] Paul's common sense, based on his own experience as a traveler, casts doubt on the competence of the captain and the owner. There is also room for the suspicion that they were simply irresponsible or motivated by greed. To underline his opinion Paul uses two arguments, the first regarding the loss of the ship and its cargo (Acts 28:19, 31, 41) and the second concerning the loss of life (Acts 28:20, 31, 42). In this way Luke prepares the background for the following narrative, which presents the consequences of their ignoring Paul's warning.

The second section (Acts 27:21–25), after the short introduction, contains an *epideictic* speech of Paul.[552] After addressing the voyagers (Acts 27:21), Paul refers to his advice (Acts 27:10) that was ignored by those in charge. This can be taken as indirect criticism of the owner

---

[550] S. M. Praeder, "Acts 27:1–28:16: Sea Voyages in Antient Literature and the Theology of Luke—Acts," *CBQ* 46 (1984), 683-706.

[551] Paul's warning in Acts 27:10 is sometimes categorized as prophetic (J. A. Fitzmyer, *The Acts of the Apostles*, 775) or as a commonsense statement. B. Witherington III, *The Acts of the Apostles,* 763. Concerning the whole narrative of Acts 27, the second interpretation seems to be more appropriate.

[552] The short speech (Acts 27:21–26) begins with an *exordium*, Acts 27:21a reduced to only the one-word πολλῆς. Then follows *narration*, containing only Acts 27:21b. Acts 27:22–24 is *probatio* of the speech that ends with *peroratio* (Acts 27:25–26).

and the captain or as a way to establish Paul's position.[553] Acts 27:21 indicates that the things that Paul had predicted have occurred. The voyagers are now in the middle of the storm for several days, without hope of surviving.[554] Paul talks about losing the cargo and ship's rigging, but he does not speak of lives being lost. In this situation, the words of comfort and encouragement were addressed to the co-travelers to sustain their hope and enable them to undertake what was needed.

In Acts 27:22, Paul addresses words of consolation to his co-travelers, urging them to be confident.[555] The good news concerning the safety of the helpless co-voyagers should be supported by some evidence to assure that behind the words, there is a real power that will fulfill the promise of the words.[556] In the case of Paul's words of consolation, the proof takes the form of prophecy: Paul claims that their deliverance was revealed to him by God's angel.[557] The information in Acts 27:24—that in the night, the angel of God stood before Paul and communicated God's will to him—serves to assure that revelation Paul is talking about is real divine intervention aimed at assisting them.[558] This divine power is described by Paul in an indirect way but is still understandable for the co-voyagers, since he informs them about three important aspects concerning the divine power.

The first aspect is that Paul belongs to God, which means that he believes in the one God, the God of Jews. The second aspect that also

---

[553] H. Conzelmann, *Acts of the Apostles*, 218.

[554] V. K. Robinson, "By Land and by Sea: The We-Passages and Ancient Literature and the Voyages," 215–242.

[555] The term παραινέω (*advice*, *urge*, *recommend*) is used only rarely in Acts (Acts 27:6, 22).

[556] F. F. Bruce, *The Book of the Acts*, 448.

[557] When Paul speaks about revelation, he usually refers to Jesus's revelation, such as in Acts 18:9–10 and Acts 23:1. Here, however, he is speaking about a revelation made through an angel of God. The non-Jewish context may have made this necessary. F. F. Bruce, *The Acts of the Apostles*, 521.

[558] The Greek technical term for *epiphany* is παρίστημι. H. Conzelmann, *Acts of the Apostles*, 219.

indicates Paul's relation to God concerns the fact that Paul worships this God, which means he not only believes in this God but also follows him zealously. The third aspect regards God's relationship to Paul that is shown in the assertion that this God speaks to Paul through his angel, which indicates an interactive and real relationship between Paul and God.[559] Paul actually presents the God of Israel as the one who will save all the voyagers. Since the voyagers were mostly Gentiles who, in their own religious systems, were familiar with the saving interventions of the gods, Paul's words could be acceptable.[560] More details concerning the message are given in Acts 27:24, where Paul gives the words revealed by the angel. The message is addressed to Paul in particular and not to all the voyagers. It begins with an admonition that is normal in such circumstances: "Do not be afraid" (Acts 27:24 NIV). While these are words of comfort for Paul, they also indicate that Paul too was overcome with fear. The second part of the message concentrates especially on Paul's safety. The words "Paul. You must stand trial before Caesar" (Acts 27:24 NIV) do not just refer to the necessity of the trial itself but also include the message that Paul will not die in his present desperate situation. Paul's life will be saved now because it is part of the Lord's plan for Paul.[561]

In Acts 23:11, when Jesus, in a time of distress, tells Paul, "You must also testify in Rome" (Acts 23:11 NIV), these words assured a positive outcome to the problems in Jerusalem. Now the angel of God, in a more specific manner, informs Paul that he must stand trial before Caesar, indicating a positive outcome to the difficulties encountered on the voyage. The third part of the message concerns the safety of all the travelers, who will be saved by the God of the

[559] J. A. Fitzmyer, *The Acts of the Apostles*, 777.

[560] H. Conzelmann, *Acts of the Apostles*, 219.

[561] There is a possible reference in Paul's argument (Acts 27:24) to Jesus's revelation in Acts 23:11. Jesus himself delivered the plans concerning Paul's witness in Rome, which, during the voyage to Rome, is used by Paul as an argument proving his claim concerning the safety of the travelers. C. S. Keener, *Acts. An Exegetical Commentary,* vol. 4, 3631.

Jews because of the divine plan for Paul.[562] God's saving all travelers is related to God's saving Paul. Because according to God's will, as presented by Luke, Paul's safety is guaranteed in order that he may safely reach Rome; the safety of those whose fate is connected to Paul's fate is guaranteed by God.[563]

Acts 27:25, which begins as an invocation (similar to that in Acts 27:21), is an encouragement and serves as a conclusion based on the angel's message.[564] First, he calls on the voyagers to rekindle their hope because they will not perish. Paul bases this confidence on his total trust that God keeps his promises. Acts 27:26 offers a possible way of realizing God's promise with Paul's conviction that, eventually, they will reach an island.[565] In the following narrative, the voyagers will find salvation on the island of Malta (Acts 28:1–10), which gives Paul's encouragement a semi prophetic character. But the reference to the island, while being a logical conclusion to the angel's message (Acts 27:23–24), is also preparation for the following narrative (Acts 27:39–28:10).

Another mention of the relationship between Paul and the co-voyagers is in Acts 27:31 (NIV)—"unless these men stay with the ship, you cannot be saved"—and shows Paul's common sense concerning the need for the sailors to stay with the ship to save the voyagers. Paul's opinion is given to the centurion, who this time takes Paul's advice more seriously than in Ac 27:10-11. In this way, Luke indicates a change in the relationship between Paul and the centurion, the final stage of which will be presented in Acts 27:42–43.

The last account concerning the relationship between Paul and

---

562 E. J. Schnabel, *Exegetical Commentary*, 1042–1043. In Acts 27:42–44, the centurion saves the lives of the prisoners to save Paul. Peterson is of the opinion that the travelers were saved because Paul prayed for their safety. D. G. Peterson, *The Acts of the Apostles*, 690.

563 Mils thinks that God's act of saving Paul's life may have been interpreted by the Gentile Christians as proof of Paul's innocence (Acts 28:1–6). G. B. Mils and G. Trompf, "Luke and Antiphon: The Theology of Acts 27–28 in the Light of Pagan Beliefs about Divine Retribution," 265.

564 C. S. Keener, *Acts. An Exegetical Commentary*, vol. 4, 3633.

565 B. Witherington III, *The Acts of the Apostles*, 770.

the voyagers contains Paul's second speech. Here again, he offers encouragement to the travelers at a time when they are abandoning hope and even neglecting what is basic (eating) for their salvation. Paul uses deliberative rhetoric to exhort the co-travelers to strengthen their hope in salvation and to ward off the destructive despair into which they were falling.[566] The speech begins directly with the narratio (Acts 27:33b), in which their present position is outlined. After Paul's speech of encouragement (Acts 27:21–26), the hope of the voyagers was again challenged by the event presented in Acts 27:27–32, and as a result, the condition of the voyagers was even worse than before, as not only had their hope faded, but even their basic instinct for survival was paralyzed. In a short propositio (Acts 27:34a), Paul urges them to take some food, which shows how serious and dangerous the situation had become.

The rest of Acts 27:34 is the probatio of the speech, here limited to a short sentence, in which taking some food is presented as the condition necessary to save themselves. The speech ends with a peroratio (Acts 27:34c), where again Paul expresses his assurance that all the travelers will survive.

Conclusion

The statements in Acts 27:10, together with the speeches in Acts 27:21–26 and in Acts 27:33–34, form a body of narrative regarding Luke's presentation of Paul during his voyage to Rome. Acts 27:10 introduces Paul as being alone in his being aware of the danger involved in continuing the voyage during unfavorable weather conditions, but his opinion is completely ignored at this stage of the narrative. This topic of Paul's objection to continuing the voyage is developed in the first speech in Acts 27:21–26, which is set in the context of the voyagers' despair, caused by the great storm. In this

[566] For more information about the speech and its historicity, cf. B. Witherington III, *The Acts of the Apostles,* 767–768.

context, Paul presents God's promise to save the travelers, which is closely connected with God's promise to save Paul.

Paul's first speech is followed by Acts 27:31, which contains Paul's advice to the centurion regarding the sailors' attempt to abandon the ship. It is the second mention (after Acts 27:10) of interaction between Paul and centurion, but now, contrary to Acts 27:10, the centurion agrees with Paul and acts according to his advice.[567] The statement presented in Acts 27:31 seems to be independent and additional, as it has no connection with the previous (Acts 27:21–26) nor the following speech (Acts 27:33–34). Between Paul's first speech (Acts 27:21–26) and second speech (Acts 27:33–34), Luke placed the narrative concerning the voyagers' struggle to survive for two weeks (Acts 27:27–30), which ended unsuccessfully and led to the sailors' attempt to abandon ship and the travelers, in order to save their own lives. In this context, Luke placed Paul's second speech (Acts 27:33–34), which develops the topic presented in the first speech (Acts 27:21–26) regarding God's promise to save Paul and his co-travelers, but here, it shows Paul's steadfast faith in God's promise.[568]

Acts 27:33 shows that the situation after the first speech (Acts 27:21–26) has not changed in the travelers' favor; they are now overcome by despair and refuse to eat, thus reducing to a minimum their chances of surviving, given also that they were in the middle of a violent storm. Acts 27:34 shows that Paul encouraged his co-travelers to eat in order to have strength to fight for their survival, as recovery of physical strength was the first step to recover their psychic strength, which was also increased by Paul's reminding them that, according to God's promise, everyone would survive (Acts 27:24–26).[569] Paul's second speech (Acts 27:33–34) has a conclusive

[567] Luke's narrative in Acts 27:10 and Acts 27:42–44 shows a special relationship between Paul and the centurion, for whom Paul became very a helpful support during the time of distress, both with advice and encouragement of the voyagers. C. S. Keener, *Acts. An Exegetical Commentary*, vol. 4, 3641.

[568] E. J. Schnabel, *Exegetical Commentary*, 1045.

[569] The phrase "not one of you will lose a single hair from his head" (Acts 27:34 NIV), which is reminiscent of the similar proverb in 1 Samuel 14:45, 2 Samuel

character, showing how Paul's unwavering faith in God's promise motivates him to undertake the actions that are necessary so that the promise can be fulfilled.

In this dramatic narrative within the voyage to Rome, Luke again presents Paul as the focus of the narrative, having the only source of strength and hope. Paul is the savior of the travelers. It was affected due to God's providence toward Paul that, in this particular case, included also all those whose fate was similar to Paul's. Paul's strength and hope comes from his believing in God, to whom he is giving the witness.

Paul does not go farther than presenting the God of Israel as the source of deliverance; mention of the messianic movement's kerygma is absent. The three kinds of Paul's relationships with others (the centurion, the inhabitants of Malta, and the co-voyagers) show the degree of his social empathy, which is in sharp contrast with his initial introduction in Acts 7:58–8:3.

4.4. In Rome (Acts 28:17–31)

The last section of Acts concerns the beginning of Paul's stay in Rome (Acts 28:17–31) and is presented mostly in three speeches that provide some interesting information about him. The speeches concern exclusively the relationships between Paul and the Jews of Rome. Other relationships, such as those between Paul and Jesus's believers in Rome, are reduced to a simple statement (Acts 28:15). Luke noted that the believers had heard about Paul's coming, which suggests that Paul himself or one of his coworkers had contacted them, probably to make some necessary preparations. They also went to meet Paul at least two days distant from the city, which gives both sides the opportunity to make themselves known. Luke also mentions Paul's reaction to this meeting—namely, he gives thanks to God and is encouraged—implying that Paul had felt some anxiety concerning his reception in Rome. This short and very schematic

14:11, and Luke 12:7; 21:18, was used by Paul to show his trust in the fulfillment of God's promise to save the travelers. J. A. Fitzmyer, *The Acts of the Apostles*, 777.

account regarding the relationships between Paul and the believers in Rome allows us to assume that it was characterized by friendship and cooperation. Another relationship is mentioned in Acts 28:16, but it is passed over fleetingly by Luke. This is the relationship between Paul and the Roman officials connected with his imprisonment. He was allowed to live by himself, guarded by soldiers. From this, it is possible to say that Paul was subject to *custodia militaris* (a lenient form of imprisonment), and hence, it seems that his case initially qualified as being less important, probably due to the contents of Festus's *littera dimissoria.* After presenting these two relationships, Luke proceeds to give an extensive account of the relationship between Paul and the Jews in Rome, which begins with Paul's speech to the elders of the Jewish community in Rome (Acts 28:17–20), containing a summarized account of his imprisonment. Since the details of Paul's imprisonment already have been presented in Luke's narrative (Acts 21:17–26:32), Paul here focuses on a short interpretation of the events that he assumes are known to the Jews in Rome. This apologetic speech to the elders of the Jewish community in Rome is of crucial importance for Paul, as his self-presentation would have an important influence on his fate.

On the third day—hence, immediately after his arrival in the capital—Paul called the elders of the Jewish community in Rome to visit him. This shows that the relationship between Paul and the Jews of Rome was of crucial importance to Paul and, for some reason, also to the Jews, as their acceptance of the invitation suggests. In Paul's first speech, he presents his reason for calling the Jews (Acts 28:20), and the speech of the elders of the Jewish community gives the reason for their acceptance of the invitation (Acts 28:22). Paul's speech (Acts 28:17–20) begins with an exordium (Acts 28:17b), in which Paul addresses the Jews as "brothers," thus identifying himself as a Jew. Paul's consciousness is attested by his using the phrase "people or against the customs" (Acts 28:17 NIV), where the term *people* refers to the Jewish nation, and the term *customs* refers to the Jewish lifestyle.[570] The following narratio contains Paul's affirmation of his innocence in regards to the accusation made against him by the Jews from Jerusalem, aimed at supporting his claim that his imprisonment in Jerusalem and Caesarea was unjust (Acts 28:17c). Paul insists that there was no reason for his imprisonment and that a greater injustice was committed when he was handed over to the Roman authorities. With this, Paul passes a very negative judgment on the authorities in Jerusalem, as handing over a countryman to the occupation forces was not acceptable to the Jews. The notice refers to Acts 21:27–23:22, but it is clear there that from the beginning, Paul was in the hands of the Romans, and they arrested him (Acts 21:31–33). Paul suggests that the Jews' attempt to eliminate Paul outside the Temple was the event that marked his arrest by the Jews, and the intervention by the Roman soldiers was a de facto act of the Jews handing him over to the Romans.[571] In his brief account of the imprisonment, Lucan Paul puts all responsibility for his appeal to Caesar on the Jewish authorities in Jerusalem (Acts 28:19). The arguments for his claim are given in the probatio of the speech (Acts 28:18–19a). Here, there are two contrasting attitudes toward Paul. One regards the relationship between Paul and the Romans, and it underlines the fact that the Romans found Paul innocent of any crimes that could justify a sentence of death (Acts 28:18). The second attitude concerns the relationship between Paul and the Jews in Jerusalem, in which the uncompromising, hostile attitude toward Paul comes to the fore (Acts 28:19a). Paul states that the Roman authorities examined him (referring to the trials before the two Roman procurators in Caesarea: Acts 23:23–26:32) and finally decided to release him. This statement does not agree with the narratives of the trials but is based on the final statement of King Herod Agrippa II, which (at least in an indirect

[570] The term λαός takes the meaning of "God's people," and it refers to Jews (Acts 2:47; 3:24; 4:10). L. T. Johnson, *The Acts of the Apostles*, 469.

[571] The Jews' action against Paul in the Temple and his being handed over to the Romans is sometimes interpreted as reflecting Jesus—being handed over to the Romans by the Sanhedrin. H. Conzelmann, *Acts of the Apostles*, 227. B. Witherington III, *The Acts of the Apostles,* 796–797.

way) was also shared by Festus (Acts 26:31–32). Although Paul's innocence of crimes against the Roman law is frequently expressed in the narrative of Acts, there is no indication that the procurators decided to free Paul.

At the same time, the issue of Paul's guilt before the Mosaic Law was uncertain in the eyes of Lysias and the procurators from the beginning, resulting in the case remaining unsolved until the interrogation before Herod Agrippa; it eventually led to Paul's direct appeal to Caesar. For these reasons, Paul's statement that both procurators, Felix and Festus, were ready to release him because they found no reason to sentence him to death serves to amplify the injustice of the Jews in Jerusalem, who requested the death penalty for Paul.[572] Paul presents this strong opposition of the Jews as the reason for his appeal for a trial in Rome (Acts 28:19). Luke briefly summarizes the narrative of the plot against Paul in Jerusalem (Acts 23:12–22) and the trial before Festus (Acts 25:1–12). The Jews' determination to kill Paul, and Festus's readiness to cooperate with the Jews, left Paul with no option but to avoid the sentence of the local Roman officials and appeal to the higher authority, according to the rights of Roman citizens.[573]

The phrase "I was compelled" (Acts 28:19 NIV) shows how dramatic Paul's situation had become; in order to save his life, he has to invoke the higher authority of Rome within a Jewish controversy, which naturally casts a shadow over the standing of the Jews of Jerusalem. This apologetic presentation is intended to assure the Jews in Rome that Paul's action is not targeting them, and it is not intended as a kind of accusation against Jews. This addition seems to be important if we consider the historical and social circumstances of the Jews in Rome. In general terms, they did not enjoy good

[572] Although Luke's narrative in Acts 23:23–26:32 does not present the Roman procurators in a positive light, in his speech to the Jews in Rome, Paul presents the procurators in a very positive light, overlooking their responsibility for Paul's fate. E. J. Schnabel, *Exegetical Commentary*, 1067.

[573] Based on some Jewish writings, it is generally understood that Jews did not allow Jews to be handed over to the Gentiles (11QT 64, 6–8).

standing, partly because of prejudice regarding their religion and social customs, and partly because of the disturbance their presence caused in many cities around the empire.[574] Also, in Rome, tensions within the Jewish community between Jews and Jews who believed in Jesus as the Messiah may have already developed, as is implied in Acts 28:22.[575] Paul's declaration in Acts 28:19 aims to avert the suspicion of the local Jewish community regarding his person and the reason for his coming to Rome.[576] Acts 28:20 clearly indicates that Paul's presentation of the circumstances and reason for his appeal to Caesar was the main purpose of his inviting the leaders of the local Jewish community. This invitation was also an opportunity for Paul to present himself as a Jew who shared the same mind in matters concerning the hope of Israel.[577]

---

[574] C. S. Keener, *Acts. An Exegetical Commentary*, vol. 4, 3740–3743.

[575] According to Luke's narrative, the Jews in Rome did know Paul personally, but they would have known that Paul was a member of the new sect within Judaism that was opposed by most Jews. In this context, the arrival of Paul, a member of that controversial sect, who probably intended to accuse his own nation before the Romans, would have been very inconvenient for them.

[576] The information that Paul called the elders of the Jewish community in Rome needs to be considered within the historical context of the position of the Jews in Rome after the reign of Claudius. By order of Claudius, the Jews were expelled from Rome during the period AD 49–53. C. S. Keener, *Acts. An Exegetical Commentary*, vol. 4, 3733–3738. Although the Jewish community in Rome was significantly large (between 20,000 and 30,000 people), it did not possess *politeuma*, and many different groups of Jews took care of their own affairs separately. This may explain the attitude of the Sanhedrin in not sending information concerning Paul's case. It also explains the problem to which Luke is refers in Acts 28:25. For this reason, it must be concluded that although they may have been influential because of their numbers, they did not have significant power in the capital.

[577] After placing the responsibility for his fate on the Jews from Jerusalem (Acts 28:17–19), Paul presents himself as being on the same side as the Jews from Rome. In this context, the phrase "the hope of Israel" (Acts 28:20 NIV) seems to be of crucial importance because the understanding of this phrase will influence the interpretation of the narrative in Acts 28:17–31. On the interpretation of the phrase, scholars are divided into three groups: the first group refers the phrase to the resurrection of the dead; the second group refers it to the messianic hope;

The addition that the hope of the whole of Israel is the reason for his imprisonment probably has a general character, and it refers to the general messianic idea circulated within Judaism, rather than to the particular Christian understanding of the messianic idea. While the second might be possible in light of Acts 23:6; 24:15; 26:22–23, nevertheless, the particular contents of the speech (Acts 28:23–25) strongly supports the first interpretation.[578] The messianic interpretation of Acts 28:20—namely, Paul's belief in the prophecy of the scripture regarding the appearance of the Messiah in way common for all Jews—should be preferred. This statement is attested by Paul's second speech to the elders (Acts 28:25–28), where Paul speaks about the kingdom of God (Acts 28:23), attempting to persuade Jews in Rome to believe in Jesus as the Messiah by using arguments from the scripture (the Mosaic Law and the prophets). The quotation used in this speech (Isa. 6:9–10) concerns the problem of the Jews' proverbial stubbornness in relation with God, but here, Lucan Paul uses it to expose the stubbornness of Jews in Rome regarding acceptance of Jesus as the Messiah.

Conclusion

In the narrative concerning the beginning of Paul's imprisonment in Rome, Luke continues the approach already used in the narrative regarding Paul's speech before King Herod Agrippa II and in the narrative concerning the voyage to Rome. Namely, Luke presents Paul as a very active person, who, despite unfavorable circumstances, is an initiator of the relationship between him and the local Jewish community. Paul's active approach may have been indicated or even required by the initial uncertainty of his position in Rome. Even if Paul would have known that Festus sent a letter to Rome, he certainly did not know its contents. He was also ignorant of any possible action

---

the third group refers it to the Messiah and the Resurrection. J. A. Fitzmyer, *The Acts of the Apostles*, 793.

[578] L. T. Johnson, *The Acts of the Apostles*, 469.

taken by the Jews from Jerusalem, which could include their sending an accuser to Rome, sending a letter to Rome, using influence on Caesar's court, or using the local community to fight against Paul.

Paul's first speech to the elders of the Jewish communities in Rome points to the last possibility as the one that Paul considered most likely. The fact that Paul does not begin his meeting with the elders with a simple discussion or by posing questions that might show their attitude toward him but with a direct apology on his own behalf betrays considerable worry on his part (Acts 28:17, 19). Paul was not confident about the Roman Jews' positive reaction to him, and for this reason, he chose to expose his conflict with Jews in Jerusalem as the past event that no longer existed, despite its being a direct reason for his appeal to Caesar.[579] This strategy would be risky if the Jews in Rome were contacted by the Jews from Jerusalem, but Luke knows things that Paul probably did not.

The direct result of Paul's speech is the knowledge about the surprisingly passive attitude of the Sanhedrin, who did not even inform the Jews in Rome about Paul's case.[580] This meant some relief for Paul because it meant that the Jews in Jerusalem had finally abandoned their intent to kill Paul. Paul's invitation to the elders does not only clarify Paul's good attitude toward Jews in Rome, but it also opens a possibility for Paul to proclaim the kerygma to the local Jewish communities, which, according to Luke's narrative, was indicated by Jewish suspicion about the sect to which Paul belonging.[581]

The Jews' suspicion shows their knowledge about the Christian movement, as well as their negative evaluation of the movement. In this way, Luke prepared the ground for the narrative regarding the

---

[579] J. A. Fitzmyer, *The Acts of the Apostles*, 790.

[580] According to Luke's narrative, the recognition of Paul's situation in Rome and especially the attitude of Jewish communities in Rome toward Paul was very important, as it could influence the mode and manner of his stay in the city and his trial. However, according to Luke, it was beginning of the events that led to the second purpose of Paul's encounter with Jews; namely, his proclaiming the kerygma to them (Acts 28:23). D. G. Peterson, *The Acts of the Apostles*, 709.

[581] W. Neil, *The Acts of the Apostles*, 257.

partial rejection of his kerygma by the Jews of Rome. The critical evaluation regarding the Jews from Rome who opposed Paul's kerygma may also have a more general character and be reviewed as Luke's final criticism of Jews rejecting Jesus as the resurrected Messiah. Although Paul is now a prisoner in Rome, as a witness to the resurrected Jesus, his situation does not change significantly when compared with his mission activity, when he still enjoyed his freedom. He continues to proclaim the kerygma to the Jews, and this kerygma is not accepted by them all.

 3

LUKE'S PORTRAITS OF PAUL

Introduction

In this chapter, based on the results of the analyses provided in chapter 1 and chapter 2, we will present Luke's perspective on Paul, which here means the way in which Luke presented to the reader the person and life of Paul. It is not the case that Luke just worked on sources available to him in order to give an accurate account of Paul's life; rather, his personal encounter with Paul and various sources (written and oral) had created Luke's understanding of the apostle to the Gentiles, which, during the process of writing Acts, was shaped into a particular perspective that the author desired to be comprehended and accepted by the reader. Recognition of this perspective may help in some cases to look from different perspectives on the issues regarding the differences in the Lucan presentation of Paul and Paul's self-presentation in his letters.[582] The Lucan perspective on Paul was skillfully, gradually, and with unbroken consequence exposed in the

---

[582] Incapability to recognize the author's rights to particular perspectives on an elaborated subject often leads one to accuse the author of using an "unhistorical approach," which is a common mistake made by many eminent scholars, who expect from Luke a "modern historical approach." Another problem concerns differences between a primary source and a secondary source, where usually, the primary source is preferred, even if the author presents his personal perspective on the particular event. Many accurate examples on these issues can be found in the monography of Marguerat. D. Marguerat, *The First Christian Historian*, 1–25.

narrative of Acts, from the very first account (Acts 7:58) until the last word.[583] In general terms, we will follow the narrative of Acts in its exposition of Luke's presentation, with one exception—the period of Saul's life as the persecutor and the neophyte, which, in a general manner, is presented at the beginning of the narrative regarding Saul, but it is later complemented by new information contained in Paul's speeches. This new information will be connected to the primary narrative (Acts 9–13). Luke's perspective will be divided into three periods, where the first one concerns Saul from his appearance as the persecutor until the end of the first mission journey (Acts 7:58–14:28), the second regards the period of Paul's mission activities (Acts 15:1–20:38), and the third concerns the period of his imprisonment (Acts 21:1–28:31). Each of these periods has its own specific goal, but all of them are, in Luke's narrative, necessary stages in the development of Paul's presentation.

1. Paul, the Anointed One

In this part, we will expose Luke's perspective on Saul, from his activities as the persecutor until the end of the mission journey with Barnabas. In the first subsection, "The Persecutor," the life of Saul will be presented from his appearance in the narrative as the persecutor until his expedition to Damascus. In the second subsection, "The Convert," Luke's presentation of Saul's conversion will be exposed.[584] The third subsection, "The Neophyte," shows Saul's activities in Damascus after his conversion. The fourth subsection, "Persona non grata," exposes the relationship between Paul and the disciples in Jerusalem after Paul's conversion. The fifth subsection, "The Apprentice," concerns Paul's cooperation with Barnabas in

[583] On hypothetical reconstruction of Luke's work in the Acts of the Apostles, cf. W. A. Strange, *The Problem of the Text of Acts* (Cambridge: Cambridge University Press, 2005), 167–189.

[584] A short summary of Saul's life before conversion is presented by Wilson, with special attention on the role of grace in the conversion. S. G. Wilson, *The Gentiles and the Gentiles Mission in Luke—Acts*, 154–161.

Syrian Antioch. The sixth and final subsection, "The First Mission Experience," regards Paul's activities during his so-called first mission journey.

1.1. The Persecutor

Luke starts the presentation of Paul not from his birth but from his active life in Jerusalem, when he was still called Saul.[585] He is introduced to the reader on the occasion of a very dramatic event (the stoning of Stephen), where he seems to at least passively participate in the public execution of Stephen, a Jew executed due to his religious convictions, which were different from those shared by Saul and mainstream Judaism (Acts 9:58). The presentation seems to be neutral, but it instantly places Saul on one side of the conflict, and this is determined not by his emotions, social relations, or personal enmity but by his deep intellectual conviction (not yet fully exposed), which placed him on the opposite side of Stephen (Acts 8:1). It would be too much to say that Saul started the systematic persecution against Jesus's followers, but Luke directly points to him as the one (probably not the only one) who precisely clarified the aim of the persecution and the way it should be carried out (Acts 8:3).[586] The aim was the annihilation of the movement, and a way to achieve this goal was to destroy the household communities through the imprisonment of believers, both women and men. Until now, Luke concentrates his narrative on the facts regarding Saul (external characteristics), with little attention paid to his emotions and feelings. However, this aspect will very soon be complemented.

In the second presentation of Saul, Luke makes great progress in comparing his first presentation of Saul, as he places him not only on the other side of Stephen but also on the most extreme side as an antagonist of the followers of the Way. Luke describes Saul's feelings

[585] In the narrative of Acts, Luke uses the name "Paul" from Acts 13:13. However, before he gives the account regarding the meeting of Sergius Paulus, he informs readers that Saul was also called Paul (Acts 13:9).

[586] E. P. Sanders, *Paul. The Apostle's Life, Letters, and Thought*, 18–19.

with the words, "Saul was still breathing out murderous threats against the Lord's disciples" (Acts 9:1 NIV), which undoubtedly underlines his radicalization that reached levels of extreme hatred.[587] The external manifestation of this feeling was his decision to persecute Jesus's followers, who fled from Palestine. Luke, at this point, ends the introductory presentation of Saul, which, although it is very schematic and general in form, sufficiently describes Saul's case.

Lucan Paul, in his speeches, details a little bit more about this period (Acts 22:3–4; Acts 26:9–11). During the speech to the crowd in the Temple, Paul confessed to his actions, which Luke already has mentioned in Acts 8:3. Here, however, this action is amplified by Lucan Paul through the phrase "I persecuted the followers of this Way to their death" (Acts 22:4 NIV), which directly exposes his involvement in actions against Jesus's believers that, in some cases, led to their deaths.[588] Although the extension of his involvement stays a matter of different interpretations and many discussions, the fact that Saul consciously acts against the Way in order to completely destroy this movement may (but not necessarily) mean that he personally participated in the destruction of some individuals, leaving no doubt about his responsibility. This seems to be attested by the gradually amplified expressions used in Acts to describe Saul's actions. In Acts 7:58, Saul was just standing; in Acts 8:1, Saul agreed with taking action against Stephen; in Acts 8:3, he was destroying the community of Jesus's followers; in Acts 9:1, he wants to kill them; in Acts 22:4, he persecuted followers of the Way to death; in Acts 22:5, his action is attested by the Sanhedrin; also in Acts 22:5, he extended the persecution to foreign lands. Lucan Paul's frank confession in Acts 22:4–5 functions in his speech not as self-condemnation but as proof that attests to his zealous service to God, which he mentioned

[587] D. B. Capes, R. Reeves, and E. R. Richards, *Rediscovering Paul. An Introduction to His World, Letters, and Theology*, 59–60.

[588] K. Haccker, Paul's Life, 22–23.

in Acts 22:3.[589] All negative aspects exposed in this speech serve to underline his wrong conviction regarding the Way as an offense to God on one hand, and his persecution of the Way as right service to God on the other.[590] However, Luke also used this part of the speech to develop Saul's negative characteristics in order to expose the most important aspect of his theology: God's grace.

The second speech containing Paul's self-evaluation regarding his youth is given before King Herod Agrippa II (Acts 26:1–23). The speech contains the longest account of Paul's life that considers his activities as a persecutor (Acts 26:9–11), but even more interesting is the context in which this confession has been situated. It is stated in the context of Paul's rhetorical question regarding the resurrection of the dead (Acts 26:8), which is an extremally important aspect, giving Paul's confession about his involvement as a persecutor a theological reason.[591] This is the only place where Saul's conviction regarding the resurrection of the dead as a teaching was not accepted by him, despite his Pharisaic connections (Acts 26:9).

According to Luke's perspective on Paul, Saul, until his experience on the road to Damascus, did not accept the kerygma proclaimed by the Way, which concerned the idea of the resurrected Messiah.[592] This conviction was most probably the reason for his opposition to the messianic sect that claimed Jesus of Nazareth not only to be the Messiah but to be the resurrected Messiah.[593] In this context, Lucan Paul exposes another new aspect that concerns his

---

[589] Murphy-O'Connor wrote: "He was completely dedicated to, and totally involved in, what was for him a habitual activity." J. Murphy-O'Connor, *Paul. A Critical Life*, 67.

[590] L. T. Johnson, *The Acts of the Apostles*, 393.

[591] Wright rightly supposes that Saul's antagonism toward the new messianic movement and its claim was generated by the Temple circle, rather than by the Gamaliel school. N. T. Wright, *Paul. A Biography* (New York: Harper-Collins Publishers, 2018), 37–39.

[592] R. E. Picirilli, *Paul the Apostle. Missionary, Martyr, Theologian* (Chicago: Moody Publishers, 2017), 52–53.

[593] B. Witherington III, *The Paul Quest. The Renewed Search for the Jew of Tarsus* (Leicester: InterVarsity Press, 1998), 59.

cooperation with the Sanhedrin during his activities in Jerusalem (Acts 26:10). Until now, this aspect could be supposed only from the texts, but here, it is directly shown that Saul was not acting on his own; he was part of a more complex and systematic action supervised by the Temple authorities. It makes Saul to be an ideologically and religiously motivated "instrument" in the hands of the Sanhedrin, and that information puts into question Saul's responsibility for the persecution on a drastically different level. Saul takes responsibility for joining the persecutors' movement and for very active participation in it but not for the initiation of the persecution.[594] Saul's prerogatives as a persecutor, supported by the Sanhedrin, concerns the mandate to imprison Jesus's followers and to vote for the death penalty in some cases (Acts 26:10). It does not automatically mean that Saul was a member of the Sanhedrin, although he had rights to vote; rather, it indicates his very close cooperation with the Temple authority as a consequence of the prerogative he received from them (Acts 26:10).

Acts 26:10 presents Saul's most drastic attitude toward Jesus's followers, which should be understood as the most extreme attitude, rather than a standard procedure. The standard actions Saul undertakes are present in the next verse (Acts 26:11), and it concerns his persecution of Jesus's followers among Jews who gather in the synagogues in order to persuade them to blaspheme, which, in this case, means to deny their faith in Jesus as the resurrected Messiah. This information puts a new light on Saul's presentation, since Luke's narrative (Acts 26:11) shows him as the defender of the true Judaism, who, under his zealous service to God, fights against a new teaching, which according to his conviction was blasphemy to the only God. Luke's literary skills are shown in the term used by Lucan Paul, who speaks about forcing Jesus's followers to "blaspheme," indicating that Paul now believes in the teaching, which many years earlier Saul

[594] The statement that the Sanhedrin opposed the new messianic movement is indirectly exposed in very critical statements toward the Sanhedrin and the Temple (in general), contained in Stephen's speech. O. Padilla, *The Acts of the Apostles*, 163–165.

absolutely did not believe.[595] For Lucan Saul, it was blasphemy that Jesus's followers claimed that Jesus was the resurrected Messiah, and for Lucan Paul, it is blasphemy to force Jesus's followers to deny their faith in Jesus, the resurrected Messiah. Between these two extreme points, there is a very well-elaborated narrative that, in a sufficient way, will expose the whole process of this transformation.

There is still one more important aspect of the Lucan presentation of Saul, which regards Saul's hatred toward Jesus's followers. It is used by Luke to describe Saul (Acts 9:1–2), and it is used by Lucan Paul to describe Saul's activities (Acts 26:11). It exposes an emotional aspect of Saul's activities, where a low level of tolerance for diversity within the same religion and an extremely strong conviction about his own understanding of true Judaism resulted in a hatred towards the "others."

Summing up: Luke presents Saul's involvement in the persecution of Jesus's followers as the result of his hatred toward the Way, which was rooted in his religious conviction and understood as protection of true Judaism. Although the presentation is fragmentary and generalized in its character, it clearly—but without unnecessary elaboration of controversial subjects—exposes Saul's wrongdoing and misunderstanding of the true zeal for God.

1.2. The Convert

Luke's initial introduction of Saul is clear enough to understand that Saul was very strongly determined to achieve his aim, and the support of the Sanhedrin made him a man that ordinary followers of Jesus could not easily stop. In this way, Luke, in his narrative, makes a space for divine intervention, which aimed not to destroy Saul but

[595] Interesting is Zetterholm's suggestion that besides the theological reason for Saul's involvement in persecution activities, of considerable influence was also the political situation in Judea. M. Zetterholm, *Approaches to* Paul, 16–17.

to convert him.[596] The event at Damascus, like the presentation of Saul, is elaborated by Luke in three progressing narratives (Acts 9:3–19; Acts 22:6–16; Acts 26:12–18), where each of them exposes some new aspects of Luke's perspective on Paul.

The first narrative is a Lucan account of things that happened to Saul on the road to Damascus (Acts 9:3–19). During the trip, Saul suddenly was struck by a light from heaven that knocked him down onto the ground, which is a literary way of exposing his defeat (vv. 3–4). As a defeated subject, Saul was asked a question (v. 4), which, due to the lack of an answer, should be taken as a rhetorical one (at least at this stage of the narrative). Instead of giving an answer, Saul himself asked for identification of the superior force, which he accepted as the Lord (v. 5). The force identified himself as Jesus, who immediately exposed Saul's guilt and gave him the first order (v. 6). Saul's defeat is attested by his temporary physical disorder that caused his dependence on his co-travelers (Acts 9:8).[597] The narrative leaves no doubt that Saul was defeated by Jesus himself, which makes Jesus the force that stopped Saul's persecution activities. In this way, the first purpose of the divine intervention was achieved.

In order to achieve the second purpose of the divine intervention, Ananias's subordination to Jesus's order was necessary (Acts 9:17);

[596] In this particular case, the conversion concerns accepting Jesus as the resurrected Messiah. G. Boccaccini, "The Tree Paths to Salvation of Paul the Jew," in *Paul the Jew. Rereading the Apostle as the Figure of the Second Temple Judaism*, eds. G. Boccaccini and C. S. Segovia (Minneapolis: Fortress Press, 2016), 4–5. Some Jewish scholars of the New Testament interpreted the term *conversion* in its religious meaning. E. Lizorkin-Eyzenberg, *The Jewish Apostle Paul* (Middletown, 2021), 16–20.

[597] Ashton puts three classical questions regarding the event at Damascus (Call or conversion? What really happened at Damascus? What is the reason for transformation into Jesus's disciples?), and then he gives elaborate answers to them. Concerning the conversion, Ashton rightly understood it in the sense of an inner changing, rather than a changing of religion. However, he does not point to the fact that the event at Damascus starts the process of Saul's changing rather than fulfilling it. The direct reason for beginning of inner conversion process of Saul was Saul's announcer with resurrected Jesus in his divine glory. J. Ashton, *The Religion of the Paul the Apostle* (London: Yale University Press 2000), 73–79.

this allowed for the acceptance of the defeated Saul among Jesus's followers at Damascus. Ananias's doubts were an opportunity to expose the second purpose of the divine intervention, which concerns Saul's conversion and his anointing as the witness to Jesus as the resurrected Messiah, sent to the Gentiles, kings, and Jews (Acts 9:15–16). The first step in the realization of this task was Saul's baptism (Acts 9:18). In the narrative regarding Saul's encounter with Ananias, Ananias is very active in order to heal Saul (contrary to physical blindness), to fill him with the Holy Spirit (contrary to his hatred), and finally to baptize him. Contrary to Ananias, Saul is completely passive. This may indicate that Luke wants to show the importance of the Damascus community (Ananias) acting on behalf of Jesus in the process of Saul's conversion. The source of Saul's conversion was Jesus, and the Damascus community played a considerable role in transforming the revelation into practical action.[598]

This initial Lucan presentation of the event at Damascus is complemented by Lucan Paul in his speech at the Jerusalem Temple (Acts 22:3–21), where Paul refers to his experience at Damascus (Acts 22:6–16). Concerning the vision of Jesus, the narrative, despite minor differences, provides an account similar to that found in Acts 9:1–9 in regard to the Lucan presentation of Paul. However, there are three small additions that expose some nuances, where the first concerns Jesus's self-presentation, which here is extended to form "Jesus of Nazareth" in order to inform the audience that Saul met Jesus of Nazareth after the persecution, which is information indirectly referring to the Resurrection of Jesus.

The second difference is something more than a nuance because it presents Saul as an acting agent, asking his Lord for dispositions (Acts 22:10). This information complements the account of Saul's

[598] Dunn, in his book regarding the new perspective on Paul, analyzes also the "conversion of Saul" in order to determine how this event should be interpreted. Among others, Dunn offers a hypothesis that the conversion should be understood as a change "from denial to affirmation of Jesus as Messiah." This is a very correct interpretation of the event at Damascus, which we also accept. J. D. G. Dunn, *The New Perspective on Paul*, 350–353.

subordination to Jesus, presented in Acts 9:5 (passive attitude of Saul), by exposing his willingness to obey the will of the Lord. Then, Saul's subordination to Jesus in Acts 9:5 is presented as an effect of defeat that includes unconditional surrendering; the account of Acts 22:10 presents it in terms of deliberative subordination, probably connected with the recognition of his wrongdoing. The third difference regards the thing that Saul will learn at Damascus.[599] In Acts 9:6, Saul is told that at Damascus, he will learn what he must do, which is a very general statement. However, in Acts 22:10, Saul is told that at Damascus, "you will be told all that you have been assigned to do" (Acts 22:10 NIV), which indicates Saul's election for a special task. Although Acts 9:16 presents similar information regarding Saul, it is told to Ananias but not to Saul. Lucan Paul, in Acts 22:10, shows his consciousness concerning the election for some already determined purpose. This aspect is further elaborated by Luke in the narrative regarding Saul's encounter with Ananias, which, compared to Acts 9:10–19, contains many new details that significantly progress Lucan Paul's presentation of Saul.

Ananias, in his speech to Saul, revealed that Saul was chosen by God, and this decision was made in order that he would know the will of God (Acts 22:14), which indirectly shows that Saul did not know God's will, or at least what he knew and what he believed were not God's will. Placing this general statement in its particular context, it was not the will of God that Saul should persecute the Way, and consequently, Saul's actions were based on his own will or at least on a misunderstanding of zealous service to God. In a positive way, Luke indicates that Saul, despite his wrongdoing, was "designed" to recognize one day the true will of God. Lucan Ananias quite precisely defines what the expression "the will of God" means for Saul. First, it means that Saul must meet (see) the rightness one, who is Jesus of Nazareth, and second, he must hear his voice, which in

[599] Concerning the disciples at Damascus, worthy of consideration is Bruce's research regarding the Zadokite Work and its possible influence on Saul during his process of conversion. F. F. Bruce, *Paul. Apostle of the Heart Set Free* (Grand Rapids: Eerdmans 1977), 76–82.

both cases concerns a physical appearance. Then the meeting with Jesus is expressed by the light from heaven (Acts 9:3; Acts 22:9), and the hearing of Jesus's voice is indicated by Jesus's direct speech to Saul (Acts 9:4-6; Acts 22:8–10). This account, on the one hand, attests that Saul met the resurrected Jesus, and this event was the basic factor in Saul's conversion; on other hand, it supports Paul's claim found in Galatians 1:17–18. Since the meeting with Jesus, Saul will become the witness of the resurrected Messiah, Jesus from Nazareth, who will give testimony to all people (note the universal character of the mission mandate). His testimony must contain two aspects, where the first one concerns Saul meeting with the resurrected Jesus, and the second concerns teaching, which Saul learned from the resurrected Jesus. These two aspects are the basic elements of Saul's kerygma, where the meeting with Jesus concerns his uncompromised teaching that Jesus is the resurrected Messiah, and the teaching learned from Jesus concerns the theological aspects of Paul's kerygma.[600] In this way, Luke exposes the details regarding Saul's election, but this exposition is not yet completed.

The third account regarding Saul's conversion (Acts 26:12–18) is a part of Paul's speech before King Herod Agrippa II (Acts 26:2–23) and, despite few details (of secondary value for Luke's presentation of Saul), agrees with the two other accounts in general terms. However, the account focuses particularly on Jesus's response to Saul's question regarding Jesus's identity, which, compared to the other two accounts (Acts 9:4-6; Acts 22:7-8:11), is extensively elaborated (Acts 26:15–18).[601] Here, Jesus gives a detailed explanation to Saul, not only about himself but also about the purpose (v. 16) of Saul's election (similar to Acts 22:14–15), the constant protection of Saul by Jesus (v. 17), and the aim of Saul's mission work (v. 18). Concerning the election of Saul, Lucan Jesus himself declares that his epiphany works to

[600] The contents of Paul's letters prove this statement, as Paul's theology seems to be entirely built on Jesus's cross and evaluated from the perspective of Jesus's Resurrection.

[601] The third account (Acts 26:12–18) takes on a conclusive character within the group of three accounts concerning the purpose of Paul's election.

make Saul his own servant, who will act as the witness to things he has already experienced and things that have not yet been revealed to him (Acts 26:16).

While Ananias was speaking generally about God, who predestined Saul to see the resurrected Jesus and give witness to what he had seen (Acts 22:14–15), here, Saul is presented as the servant of Jesus, as the witness to Jesus, and as the addressee of Jesus's revelations.[602] It makes Acts 26:16 the place where Lucan Saul is anointed by Jesus himself for the apostle's dignity, which is naturally supported by Paul's claim from Galatians 1:17–18. Saul, as both the servant and the witness, is appointed to proclaim the mission addressed to Jews and Gentiles, which was given to him by Jesus, who also promised his constant protection during Saul's mission activities (Acts 26:17).[603] This is another example of Luke's theological axiom regarding Paul's mission appointment, where the mission to the Jews is listed first (primary aim) and the mission to the Gentiles second (secondary aim), although Paul will be remembered as the apostle to the Gentiles.[604] Lucan Jesus determined not only the target of Saul's activities but also the purpose of his mission, which was to convince both Jews and Gentiles that Jesus is the resurrected Messiah, the only Savior through whom human sin can be forgiven and salvation be achieved (Acts 26:18).

In this way, Luke, in three narratives regarding the same event, progresses the presentation of Saul's election from a simple exposition of the event, leading to the conversion of a persecutor (Acts 9:5–6),

---

602 It is important to recognize that Luke gives a very general account in Acts 9:1–19 about simple facts and statements regarding Saul's election. However, Lucan Paul, in his speeches (Acts 22:3–21; 26:2–23), presents an advanced interpretation of the election, based on his experiences and evaluations.

603 W. S. Kurtz, *Acts of the Apostles*, 358–359.

604 Concerning Luke's perspective on Paul's mission to the Gentiles, we should use the title "the apostle *also* to the Gentiles," rather than just "the apostle to the Gentiles," which is directly attested by Paul's letters rather than by Luke's narrative, whose purpose is directed at the Jews as the first and primary aim of Paul's mission, according to Lucan Paul's modus operandi (first Jews and then Gentiles).

with very general information regarding his election and its purpose, to the slightly more detailed Lucan Ananias's account (Acts 22:14–16), where divine predestination regarding Saul's election and its purpose is exposed, to the last account (Acts 26:16–18), where Lucan Jesus exposes the universal character of Saul's election (for Jews and Gentiles) and the theological aim of his appointment (salvation by the faith in Jesus).[605] This presentation serves for the following narrative of Acts, where the realization of this election will be gradually and consequently presented by Luke in order to give not only a historical account concerning Paul's mission but also to make his picture of Paul more coherent.

Summing up: Luke, in his three narratives, directly indicates that Saul was chosen by Jesus, who anointed him for an already determined task. The purpose of the divine intervention was not limited to defeating a persecutor but also to make use of him by slowly but consequently transforming him into one of the most important persons on the side of the Way.

1.3. The Neophyte

After his conversion, Saul spent three years in Damascus, but this period of his life was not of special interest for Luke, who dedicated only seven verses (Acts 9:19–25) of the narrative to this period. Lucan Paul hardly mentions Damascus in his speech and even then, only in an extremely laconic manner (Acts 26:20). In reality, the reader is left only with Luke's evaluation of Saul's activities at Damascus, which also is subordinated to the main aim of the Lucan narrative that is a presentation of Paul. According to Luke's account, Saul had to stay with disciples at Damascus for a few days (Acts 9:19), most probably due to his psychophysical condition. This information suggests that after his temporary physical indisposition, he was capable of

[605] Hanges rightly points to the fact that Acts 9:1–19 and two other accounts regarding Saul's conversion work to legitimize Paul and his mission. J. C. Hanges, *Paul, Founder of Churches*, 443.

living on his own, and this statement may also refer to his mission activities. His immediate involvement in spreading the kerygma directly underlines his neophyte zealotry and indirectly exposes the deepness and radical character of his conversion, restricted here to faith in Jesus as the resurrected Messiah. This belief became the teaching he was spreading in synagogues, which shows the basic modus operandi of Saul, who first addressed the kerygma to Jews, and it is an attitude that stays unchanged until the very last account regarding Paul that is recorded by Luke.

Concerning his teaching, Saul spread among the Jews that Jesus is the Son of God (Acts 9:20), which naturally was a highly controversial claim that could be accepted by Jews but that exposed, theologically, a very advanced evaluation of Jesus of Nazareth.[606] Due to this kind of teaching, Saul very quickly became a controversial person within Jewish society at Damascus, a group that was extremely puzzled by the fact that the former persecutor was himself spreading the teaching of those he previously had persecuted (Acts 9:21–22).[607] In this way, Luke indirectly shows Saul's activities as a reason for division within the Jewish community, which, after considerable time, will result in an attempt to exterminate Saul (Acts 9:23). The reason for the decision to kill Saul was his teaching regarding Jesus as the Messiah,

---

[606] At that point, Schnabel argues that although Saul, during his activities in Jerusalem, did not believe in Jesus the Messiah, he knows about him from encounters with Jesus's followers, which became useful in his later recognition of Jesus as the Son of God after the revelation. However, in our opinion, Acts 9:20 should be taken as a Lucan theological summary regarding Paul's recognition (but not Saul's recognition) of Jesus's true nature. E. J. Schnabel, *Exegetical Commentary on the New Testament*. Acts, 451–453.

[607] The information in Acts 9:22 about Paul's teaching that Jesus is the Messiah by any means seems to be more accurate to the context of the narrative and the social effect of this teaching than the very general statement in Acts 9:20 about Paul's teaching that Jesus is the Son of God. L. T. Johnson, *The Acts of the Apostles*, 170–171.

which, according to Luke's narrative, had a much stronger impact on the Jewish community than the claim presented in Acts 9:20.[608]

Striking is that the claim that "Jesus is the Messiah," which was nothing more than a very controversial statement within Jewish discourses, caused a more severe response from the side of the Jews than the claim that "Jesus is the Son of God," which should have been taken by the Jews as blasphemy. These two claims obviously are not identical, which raise a question regarding Luke's reason for including two different claims in his rather short account regarding Saul's mission activities at Damascus, where the claim "the Son of God" may hardly be recognized as the most frequently used term by Saul/Paul in Acts, although it is quite common in Paul's letters. The term is used in Acts for the very first time in Acts 9:20, immediately after the account of Saul's baptism (Acts 9:18–19), which may support the supposition that Luke included, characteristic of Paul, the title "the Son of God" in order to show that this conviction was part of Paul's evaluation of Jesus of Nazareth from the very moment of his conversion. This probably reached a much deeper level than only the recognition of Jesus as the resurrected Messiah and Lord. Despite the speculation, Luke clearly indicates that Saul, after his conversion, believed that Jesus was "the Son of God" and "the resurrected Messiah."[609] These were elements of Saul's faith in Jesus that he was sharing with the Jews in Damascus. Because the results of his mission are not detailed in the narrative, however, it is possible that Saul achieved very little, if anything at all, in terms

---

[608] Schnabel points to three facts that attest to Saul's claim about Jesus the Messiah, where the first one is Saul's experience; the second one is God's promises for Israel included in the scripture; and the third is the prophecies. E. J. Schnabel, *Exegetical Commentary on the New Testament*. Acts, 454.

[609] In this context, significantly important is the observation of Crossan and Reed, despite the fact that it concerns a different topic: "our basic argument is that the New Testament content and sequence has literally and figuratively *framed* Paul by locating those seven authentic Pauline letters after Luke's Acts of the Apostles, which corrects Paul's story *before* we read him, and among or before those inauthentic letters, which correct Paul's theology *after* we have read him." J. D. Crossan and J. L. Reed, *In Search of Paul*, 106.

of mission success, which is a statement supported by the fact that the second account (Acts 22) says nothing about Damascus, and the third account (Acts 26) is limited to simply mentioning that Saul proclaimed the kerygma at Damascus.

Summing up: The Lucan narrative regarding Saul at Damascus exposes his neophyte faith (two titles regarding Jesus), rather than offering a solid account about his mission in Damascus for three years.

1.4. Persona non Grata

The next aspect of the Lucan presentation of Paul is his relationship with Jerusalem after his conversion, which concerns his relationship with Jesus's followers and with their opponents. Lucan Saul, who had left Jerusalem as a persecutor of the Way, returned to the city after three years as a member of the Way, which is an extreme reversal that must have brought about inevitable consequences.[610] Concerning his relationship with Jesus's disciples, Saul most probably held the hope that his conversion would change everything and that the Jerusalem community would easily and seamlessly overcome their prejudice toward his past persecution activities (Acts 9:26). Luke, in a very gentle manner, exposed the harsh reality of the relationship between the community and Saul, which was marked by fear, disbelief in Saul's conversion, and avoidance of him on the side of the community, and with naive expectations of the community on the side of Saul.

His problem with earning the trust of the community may have been more difficult than Luke wants to admit, but the most important point is that Saul was accepted within the community only because of Barnabas's intervention—he acted on behalf of Saul, convincing them about his conversion (Acts 9:27). This indicates that Barnabas

[610] It is striking that according to the Lucan narrative, Saul/Paul's mission activities, from the very beginning until the end, mostly concerned urban societies. W. A. Meeks, *The First Urban Christians* (New Haven: Yale University Press, 2003), 32–50.

was the first person from the Jerusalem community who, for some reason (not mentioned by Luke), trusted Saul and gave him a second chance, or at least Barnabas was the most important among those who accepted Saul because in the following narrative of Acts, Barnabas became the main mentor of Saul on his way to growing in status as a well-prepared missionary. Barnabas's guarantee made it possible for Saul to stay among members of the community and act freely as a member of the Way. However, it did not necessarily mean that all suspicions or controversies regarding Saul immediately disappeared, once and forever, as James's speech to Paul (Acts 21:20–25) seems to indicate that, several years later, the problems with Paul, although of a different character, were still the subject of discussions.

Although it seems that the narrative concentrates mostly on the relationship between Saul and the community, Luke also provides some information about Saul's relationship with the Jews of Jerusalem, which here is limited only to his mission activities among them (Acts 9:28–29). The narrative attests that Saul was acting as a member of the Jerusalem community, freely and boldly giving testimony about Jesus as the resurrected Messiah (Acts 9:28). Luke probably narrowed the target of Saul's activities only to Greek-speaking Jews, possibly the same group that Saul was connected with three years earlier and who now became Saul's mission target and his most dedicated adversaries.[611] Since Luke mentioned only the negative results of Saul's mission (the Hellenist intents and attempt to kill him), it is possible to assume that there was little positive impact from his activities, or at least at this stage of the narrative regarding the

[611] Concerning Saul's relationship with the Diaspora Jews, Saul's educational background (bilingualism and biculturalism) predisposed him to work with Jews who had preserved their religion but significantly lost their original language and sense for contemporary Jewish culture. Before his conversion, Saul shared the same religious convictions with the Diaspora Jews, who appreciated his service for them. However, after his conversion, his religious convictions became an issue that caused Saul to face rejection by the Diaspora Jews visiting Jerusalem. Concerning the issue of Saul/Paul's bilingualism and biculturalism, cf. K. Ehrensperger, *Paul at the Crossroads of Culture* (London: Bloomsbury T&T Clark, 2013).

presentation of Paul, Luke consciously omitted indicating the results. The second possibility is not likely because the community had to send Saul out of Jerusalem in order to save his life, which indirectly indicates that the community suffered serious problems caused by Saul's activities in the city (Acts 9:30).

Luke's accounts strongly suggest that Saul was a problematic person for the community.[612] There were problems with his acceptance within the community, and after his acceptance, there were problems with his activities as a member of the community. Acts 9:31 may suggest that Saul's disappearance from Palestine brought peace to communities dwelling in the regions of Judea, Galilee, and Samaria. If it is so, Luke makes a very critical evaluation not only of Saul's activities as a persecutor but also of Saul's mission activities undertaken immediately after his conversion.[613]

Saul's visit to Jerusalem after the years spent at Damascus is also mentioned by Lucan Paul in Paul's speeches, where in the speech before King Herod Agrippa II, the visit to Jerusalem is only mentioned (Acts 26:20), and in Paul's speech in the Temple, the account of Saul's visit to Jerusalem is focused entirely on his private revelation (Acts 22:17–21). In his speech in the Temple, Paul omitted his problem at Damascus and directly gave an account about his visit to Jerusalem after his conversion.[614] The account is almost entirely built on dialogue between Jesus and Saul during his prayer in the Temple, and for this reason, it does not provide direct information regarding the relationship between Saul and the Jews of Jerusalem; it indirectly allows us, however, to draw some conclusions. Regarding the relationship between Lucan Saul and the Jews of Jerusalem,

[612] Luke mostly suggests that Paul's preaching was the main reason for his persecution, which is information that, in an indirect way, may concern (even at this stage of Luke's narrative) the problem of the relationship between "Paul's version of Christianity" and the "Jewish version of Christianity," as Tabor calls it. J. D. Tabor, *Paul and Jesus*, 6.

[613] Concerning Acts 21:10–1, which details the considerable suspicions of the Jerusalem community regarding Paul, which were still in existence even several years later. K. Haacker, "Paul's Life," 25.

[614] L. T. Johnson, *The Acts of the Apostles*, 390.

the dialogue exposes the naive hopes of the neophyte, who, with a considerable level of stubbornness, argues with his Lord that his conviction concerning the mission to the Jews in Jerusalem is logical, and it augurs positive results simply because he was a persecutor of Jesus's disciples, and now he himself believes in Jesus (Acts 9:19–20). Positively, the account shows Saul's determination in proclaiming the kerygma to the Jews, as well as his constant conviction regarding his Jewishness (the issue that was doubted by his opponents).[615] However, more important for Luke's presentation of Paul are Jesus's orders addressed to Saul, where the first one includes the statement that Saul's proclaiming of the kerygma to the Jews in Jerusalem will be not accepted by them, and for this reason, he must immediately leave the city (Acts 22:18). Although the dialogue (Acts 22:17–21) within the speech (Acts 22:3–21) has its own particular purpose, connecting to the apologetic aim of the speech, this particular information (Acts 22:18) provides details that are complementary to the account of Acts 9:28–30. In this context, Saul's successful mission in Jerusalem was not part of the Lord's plan for Saul, which is a theological interpretation of the event that is presented in Acts 9:28–30 on a socioreligious level.[616] The true plan for Paul is revealed to him later by Jesus, and it includes his mission to the Gentiles (Acts 22:21). In some way, this information is also complementary to Luke's account regarding the sending of Saul to his hometown (Acts 9:30) because it indirectly means the definite end of his activities in Jerusalem, which is in accordance with Luke's narrative strategy of Acts.

Summing up: Luke's narrative suggests that after his conversion, Saul was persona non grata in Jerusalem, which, in regard to his relationship with the disciples in Jerusalem, means the community was suspicious of Saul, and his presence brought troubles for them. In regard to his relationship with the Jews in Jerusalem, it means confusing the activities of the "traitor."

---

615 H. Conzelmann, *Acts of the Apostles*, 188.

616 C. S. Keener, *Acts. An Exegetical Commentary*, vol. 3, 3228.

1.5. The Apprentice

In the narrative of Acts, Saul disappeared for a while (Acts 9:31–11:25) and again appeared in the account regarding Barnabas's mission activities in Syrian Antioch (Acts 11:19–30). The city became a promising place for spreading the kerygma, not only to Jews but also to Gentiles (Acts 11:19–21); actually, Acts is presented as the first community of Jesus's followers consisting of Jews and Gentiles. Luke's narrative strongly suggests that the successful work of Barnabas in Antioch somehow is linked to his visit to Tarsus in order to find Saul, whom Luke deactivated from his narrative in order to reactivate him on a new level and in a different context.[617]

In fact, the period of Saul's "deactivation," which commonly is named the "unknown years of Paul's life," may even have reached seven years. Again, it is Barnabas who gave Saul a hand by inviting him as a coworker in the Antioch community (Acts 11:26). The cooperation continued with considerable success for one year, and it probably contributed to distinguishing, within the Jewish community in the city, the Messianic Jews, who associated with Gentiles, from the Jews, who did not do that, as the narrative seems to suggest it (Acts 11:26). Antioch became, for Saul, the place of his apprentice period under the supervision of Barnabas, which definitively contributed to the development of his skills in successfully proclaiming the kerygma.[618] Luke consciously presents Barnabas as Saul's most important patron, who helped him to both find his place within and

---

617 This approach strongly suggests that Luke, in his narrative, evaluates Saul/Paul's mission activities according to the following schema: rather unsuccessful mission attempts among Palestinian Judaism and considerably successful work among Diaspora Jews and Gentiles.

618 Pollock rightly states that according to Luke's narrative, the Antioch community was extraordinarily blessed with talented leaders, as even the main focus of Luke concerns Barnabas and Saul. Based on the leaders named by Luke, it is possible to conclude that community was characterized by background diversity that greatly contributed to creating one strong community, based on the same faith but characterized by its multicultural origin. J. Pollock, *The Apostle. A Life of Paul* (Colorado Springs: David Cook, 1985), 63–64.

to contribute to the community (Acts 11:26, 30). This is the very first time in the narrative of Acts when, because of his mission attempts, Saul is not forced to run away in order to save his life. In this context, it is important to notice that Luke determined the group to whom Saul addressed his teaching (the believers), which may explain the reason for this rather exceptional case. Luke presents this one year of cooperation with the very successful missionary Barnabas as the final point in Saul's preparation for fulfilling the task for which he was appointed.

In the next narrative regarding Saul, he will be a member of the mission team sent by the Antioch community to Cyprus. The laconic information regarding Barnabas and Saul's visit to Jerusalem with a contribution to the community (Acts 11:30) does not indicate that Saul suffered some troubles during the stay with Barnabas in Jerusalem (Acts 12:25), as even the information is placed in the context of the persecution of the Jerusalem community.[619]

Summing up: the only account recorded in Acts regarding Saul's mission in Syrian Antioch serves to present the way in which Luke reactivated him to mission work in the city, but this time under the supervision of an experienced missionary (Barnabas) and as part of the group that Luke called "teachers" and "prophets" (Acts 13:1).[620] This presentation indirectly highlights the significant improvement of Saul's ability to fulfill the will of his Lord.

---

[619] Luke's narrative regarding Saul's one-year mission work in Syrian Antioch reveals his conscious attempt to present "Saul's breaking-in period" in possibly the most idyllic fashion. Probably for this reason, Luke reduces information regarding Barnabas and Saul's visit to Jerusalem to the merit of travel, leaving aside all unpleasant events that possibly could have happened. Less possible is the hypothesis that Luke's narrative suffered from a lack of details concerning this trip.

[620] Murphy-O'Connor rightly suggests that the community at Syrian Antioch became the "hometown" for Saul/Paul. J. Murphy-O'Connor, *Paul. A Critical Life*, 95.

1.6. The First Mission Experience

From Acts 13, Luke's Acts of the Apostles turns almost exclusively into the Acts of Paul, who became the main agent and whose activities serve to help the author expose several aspects related to spreading the kerygma and the progressive development of the Christian movement. The transformation of Saul into Paul, however, has a progressive character in the Lucan narrative, and for this reason, the account regarding the so-called first mission journey of Paul is of crucial importance to Luke's presentation of Paul, as it is during this mission that Luke decides that the pupil (Saul) will end his apprenticeship under his mentor (Barnabas) and is now ready to fulfill the task for which he was appointed.[621]

Concerning the mission journey itself, Luke directly states the divine origin of the mission, which was initiated by the Holy Spirit (during the spiritual retreat) as a direct mission order that went as far as to name participants (Acts 13:2). In this way, Luke indicates that the first mission journey was the action in which Saul participated as an important member of the community, but it does not undermine the fact that the mission was the official mission of the Antioch church. Luke's narrative strongly suggests that the Barnabas and Saul team was the only team sent to Cyprus (Acts 13:4), which excludes the possibility that other teams were made and sent to other places. Since from Acts 13 the narrative focuses particularly on Paul, it is possible that the account of Acts 13:1–4 is only one part of wider activities provided by the Antioch community, which is a supposition that may be attested to by Luke's general characteristic of the community presented in Acts 11:19–21. Indirectly, Luke suggests that Saul's participating in the mission was possible only because of

[621] After several failed mission attempts and the neophyte Saul's successful cooperation with Barnabas at Syrian Antioch, Luke presents the next step for Saul in his preparation to fulfill Jesus's order. Cyprus was well known to Barnabas but probably hardly to Saul, which made this mission journey a real challenge for Saul but also a kind of graduation exam.

his cooperation with Barnabas, who, at least during the first part of the mission, is presented as the leader of the team.

Striking is the way in which Luke treats the narrative regarding the mission activities on Cyprus, which are reduced to a very general summary (Acts 13:5–6) in order to expose the particular event of the meeting with Sergius Paulus, the governor of Cyprus (Acts 13:7–8, 12).[622] The fact that the governor accepted the teaching (Acts 13:12), which followed extraordinary wonders (Acts 13:11–12), is usually taken as Paul's first spectacular success in the mission to the Gentiles, though this was not necessarily the aim Luke wanted to point out. Luke's narrative does not directly point to Saul as the main mentor in the process of Paulus's belief, making the success in Cyprus to be the success of the team but not exclusively the success of Saul. Luke precisely indicates that Sergius Paulus was "amazed by the teaching of the Lord," and he wanted to hear this teaching from Saul and Barnabas, as Acts 13:7–8 indicates it. However, Luke also directly indicates that the wonder performed by Saul was a direct impulse that convinced the governor (Acts 13:12). This allows us to suppose that Luke's interest in this narrative is with regard to Saul's miracle skills, which Luke will further detail in the following narrative of Acts (Acts 16:18; 20:9–12). This is the first account in Acts that shows Saul's extraordinary power, which is the third (after teacher and prophet) characteristic that exposes Paul's inner capability.

The next stage of the narrative regarding the mission concerns activities undertaken by the team in the regions of Pamphylia and Pisidia, and it starts with an extremely important change in the author's perspective on the mission team; namely, that beginning in Acts 13:13, the name of Saul is replaced by the name Paul, and this name usually is placed before the name of Barnabas. This is the

[622] This narrative clearly shows Luke's lack of interest in the mission activities among Diaspora Jews on Cyprus, which is overwhelmed by the main concern of this mission journey that concerns activities in the regions of Pisidia and Pamphylia, with a special focus on Pisidian Antioch, where Luke placed Paul's speech to Diaspora Jews, which seems to be the main aim of the entire narrative.

place in the narrative of Acts where Lucan Paul was born.[623] This is indicated not only by placing Paul's name before Barnabas's name, but also by Luke's using the second name of Saul, which he knew from the beginning (it is indicated by Acts 13:9) but did not use until now, in order to emphasize the precise point when Saul became an independent missionary. This idea is directly stated in Acts 13:13, where Luke starts the narrative regarding the mission in the region of Pamphylia with the phrase, "Paul and his companion," which shows the crucial change of perspective. It is possible that this change serves Luke's narrative purpose of presenting Paul, rather than indicating the true state of the matter.

Immediately after this change in narrative, Luke places Paul as the main speaker in Pisidian Antioch. It is possible that this speech (Acts 13:16–41) is the reason for which Luke suddenly changed the focus of his narrative from Barnabas to Paul. This is Paul's main speech during his mission activities that is addressed to Diaspora Jews and God-fearers, and it should be understood as an example of Paul's way of proclaiming the kerygma to this kind of audience, rather than taken as an exact record of the particular speech given at Pisidian Antioch.[624]

The structure of the speech exposes Luke's perspective on Paul's proclaiming the kerygma to Jews, which always starts with references to God's choosing of the nation, placed in the historical context, and

[623] In this way, Luke directly indicates that Saul became Paul, who would fulfill Jesus's order. From now on, the narrative will focus on Paul, the witness to the resurrected Messiah, who gradually is realizing his mission mandate. The exposition of Paul serves Luke's narrative strategy, and it probably has nothing in common with "Mark's problem."

[624] In the narrative concerning the first mission journey, there is also another "unwitting speech" at Lystra, which should be credited to Paul and Barnabas, if following Luke's narrative (Acts 14:14). At least the beginning of the speech should be treated in this way. However, the latter part of the speech is very similar to part of Paul's speech at the Areopagus, which clearly indicates Luke's narrative purpose, which aims at connecting these two speeches addressed to the strictly Gentile audience in order to expose the way Paul approached audiences with no Jewish background.

heads toward a desirable point, which in this case is the promise given to King David (Acts 13:16–22).[625] The second step in the speech is the presentation of the claim that Jesus is the fulfillment of the promise given to King David (Acts 13:23), regarding the Savior of Israel. The witnesses to this claim are John the Baptist (Acts 13:25), Paul and his companions (Acts 13:26), God, who resurrected Jesus from the dead (Acts 13:30–33), and Jesus's disciples (Acts 13:31). The third step regards the argument for teaching about the resurrection of the dead (Acts 13:33–37), which is supported by the authority of the Old Testament's texts. The fourth step regards Paul's aim of proclaiming that Jesus is the salvation of Israel (Acts 13:38–40). In this way, the Lucan narrative presents Paul as a Jew who believes in Jesus as the Savior of Israel, who connects his kerygma with the teaching and tradition of Judaism, which naturally testifies its continuity and integrity with Judaism.[626]

Lucan Paul does not spread something new that has no connection to Judaism; rather, he presents his own interpretation of the realization of God's promises that can be found in the scriptures. He always will proclaim to Jews that Jesus is the realization of God's promise given to Israel (Acts 13:22–23), which, in this particular case, regards the salvation of the nation. Concerning salvation, Lucan Paul presents what, for Jews, is his most controversial thesis—that salvation (the forgiveness of sins) can be obtained only by faith in Jesus as the Savior, and it cannot be obtained fully by observing Mosaic Law. For Jews, this thesis became the common reason for accusing Paul of abandoning the Law. Paul's kerygma to the Jews is supplemented by his argument of the thesis, where the contradiction between the rejection of Jesus by the Jews from Jerusalem and the fact that God resurrected Jesus (Acts 13:27–32) serves as the main argument that testifies that Paul's claim is adjusted, first by God's action, as well

---

[625] For a relationship between the content of the speech and Paul's letters, cf. T. R. Schreiner, *Paul, Apostle of God's Glory in Christ. Paulin Theology* (Downers Grove: IVP Academic, 2020), 67–82.

[626] R. A. Erric and G. M. Lamsa, *Aramaic Light on the Acts of the Apostles*, 118–119.

as by the testimonies of the witnesses, which also play an important role (Acts 13:24–30).

Since Luke recorded none of Saul's speech, it is impossible to compare Paul's speech to the Jews and God-fearers with Saul's speech to the Jews. However, it is possible to compare the results of Saul's speeches with the results of Paul's speeches.[627] Concerning the first case, few successes are mentioned, which may testify to the inadequate way of proclaiming the kerygma. Concerning the second case, four important results are mentioned, where the first regards the Jews attracted by Paul's teaching, who followed him and took instructions from him (Acts 13:43). The second result regards the great interest of the inhabitants of the city (probably including also Gentiles) in Paul's teaching, which caused a split within the Jewish community, leading to open opposition to Paul's teaching (Acts 13:45). The third result regards Paul and Barnabas's decision to extend the mission also to the Gentiles (Acts 13:46). Striking is that the reason for their decision is of a negative nature; namely, the rejection of the Paul's teaching by some Jews. The fourth result regards the persecution of Paul and Barnabas by some Jews (Acts 13:50–52). These four aspects may be found in all narratives regarding Paul's proclaiming the kerygma to Diaspora Jews, which makes them general characteristics of Luke's perspective on Paul's missions to the Jews. This statement is attested by following the narrative concerning the mission in Iconium (Acts 14:1–7), where all four aspects are used in order to create a short and very schematic account.

The last part of the account regarding the mission details the events that occurred in Lystra (Acts 14:8–20), which serves in the

[627] This comparison will hardly expose the real state of affairs; rather, it shows Luke's paradigmatic approach in his perspective on Paul, where Saul's period is a time of many mistakes, unexpected conversion, constant struggling, and growing up to become Paul, which presents Saul as a man in progress. Lucan Paul is a successful missionary who, despite all controversies about him and his teaching, failures in mission works, troubles in relations with Jews and Gentiles, or his own temper, is fulfilling the task he was called for, which makes him both the most influential and most controversial servant of Jesus among the many mentioned in the New Testament.

Lucan narrative to indicate Paul's healing skills (Acts 14:8–10) and to expose a preparatory unity regarding the problem connected with the mission to the Gentiles (Acts 14:11–18). Paul's miracle was interpreted by local rural society according to their polytheistic religious system, and that caused them to attempt to deify Barnabas and Paul. Their opposition to this attempt was an occasion to give a speech, the first one addressed to a strictly Gentile audience, which Luke attributes to Barnabas and Paul (Acts 14:14). If the speech was delivered in the way Luke recorded it, it is possible that the speech was given by Paul, as Acts 14:12 seems to suggest.[628] A large part of this speech will be repeated in Paul's speech at Areopagus (Acts 17:22–31). The speech does not go farther than teaching about the one and only God (Acts 14:15), which, in this case, is an introduction to Judaism and is necessary background that must be acknowledged by the audience in order for them to comprehend the kerygma.[629] Luke's summary that the speech convinced the audience may be interpreted as a success (Acts 14:18).

The last aspect of the mission to the Diaspora Jews concerns the persecution of Paul (but not of Barnabas) by some Jews (Acts 14:19–20). This aspect was already mentioned in Acts 13:50–51, and it was similar to the persecution experienced by Saul in Damascus or in Jerusalem. However, in the narrative of the persecution in

---

[628] Although Luke wrote in Acts 14:14, Ἀκούσαντες δὲ οἱ ἀπόστολοι Βαρναβᾶς καὶ Παῦλος διαρρήξαντες τὰ ἱμάτια αὐτῶν ἐξεπήδησαν εἰς τὸν ὄχλον κράζοντες [but when the apostles Barnabas and Paul heard of this, they tore their clothes and rushed out into the crowd, shouting] (Acts 14:14 NIV), which clearly indicates a rash and impulsive action on the side of the missionaries, where their main concern was to prevent blasphemy, Luke turned this cry of desperation into a semi-developed speech in order to prepare literary ground for the narrative concerning his mission in Athena.

[629] Lucan Paul's speeches at Lystra and at Areopagus introduce the monotheistic concept of God as it was developed by Judaism, with one critical difference regarding theophany and the roots of Jewish monotheism and the indirect way of acknowledging God by the Gentiles through his creation. This exposition is very closely related to Paul's teaching regarding acknowledging God through creation, presented in Romans 1.

Lystra, Luke presents Paul as the victim of an attempted stoning, done by some Jews from different places (Antioch and Iconium).[630] This aspect of Paul's mission activities (especially the second mission journey) will be an important element of Luke's perspective on Paul.

Summing up: Luke's account of the first mission journey is the place where Saul not only turns into the Paul, but, as Paul, he instantly becomes a fully developed missionary and a witness, acting according to his modus operandi with great skills and successful results. He also experiences various hardships connected to mission work, which seems to be in accordance with Jesus's exposition in Acts 9:16.

2. Paul, the Witness

2.1. The Protector of the Gospel's Truth

The narrative concerning the so-called Jerusalem Council (Acts 15) has its own purpose in Acts, and it serves as the preparatory unit for the narrative regarding the mission to the Gentiles. However, this narrative also contains an important part of Luke's presentation of Paul's doctrinal convictions and reflects Paul's theological teachings found in his letters.[631] Namely, the issue of salvation for Gentile

---

630 The pattern of a group zealously devoted to persecuting Paul, not only in their hometown but also in other places, will be frequently used in the narrative of Acts. This pattern allows Luke to present mostly the Jews' persecution of Paul as a systematic action rather than a spontaneous one, which may have been consciously created as an antithesis to Saul's past life as a persecutor (Saul was persecuting Jews following Jesus, and Paul is now persecuted by Jews who do not follow Jesus).

631 Placing the narrative regarding the Jerusalem Council after the narrative of the Antioch community's mission on Cyprus (the first mission journey) and before the narrative concerning the second mission journey is the result of Luke's narrative strategy rather than strict historical accuracy. Although the problem of the so-called "Gentile Christians" was elaborated by Luke in the narrative of Acts 10–11 that concerned the encounter of Peter and Cornelius's house and relates to the basic issue of Gentiles' election by God, in the narrative concerning

Christians is the main reason for the very strong, intense. and impossible-to-solve confrontation between the position presented by Paul and Barnabas and their opponents, named as the brothers from Judea (Acts 15:1). The crisis that caused the Jerusalem Council concerns the most crucial issue for the future of the Christian movement, which can be simplified to one question: in order to be saved, is it necessary for Gentiles who believe in Jesus to first join Judaism and then become a member of the Christian faction within Judaism? An affirmative answer (the position of the brothers from Judea) would result in the statement that "there is no salvation outside Judaism."

In the context of Paul's speech in Pisidian Antioch, where Jesus is presented as the "Salvation for Israel," this opinion seems accepted by Paul as appropriate for Jews also living outside Judea. However, in regard to Gentiles, Paul (as well as Barnabas) was of the opinion that the statement could not be accepted by any means. This kind of controversy most probably contributed to the creation of, in the later period, the coherent doctrinal teaching known as "salvation by faith." However, Luke's aim concerns the presentation of Paul as the one who went one step farther than Peter did by accepting Gentile believers among Jewish believers. Lucan Paul is a man who stands for the considerable independence of Gentile Christians from the obligations of Judaism, which still were in effect for the Jewish Christian. In this way, Lucan Paul made Judaism contribute to the world, instead of excluding it from the world. Due to Paul's efforts, something that was part of Judaism's tradition and, because of that, was valuable only for those inside this religious system became

---

the Jerusalem Council, the Gentile issue is placed on the dogmatic or theological level. In this way, Luke prepares to attest Lucan Paul's approach to mission work among the Gentiles, where proselytism to Judaism is axiomatically excluded, with accordance to Paul's teaching in his letters. The role of Paul and Barnabas is rather marginalized in the narrative concerning the council; however, Luke presents them as the very first stones that caused the real avalanche of rolling stones (the Jerusalem Council), which is a fact that attests well to Luke's knowledge about Paul's teaching on this matter.

valuable for those from outside, without any conditions. The fact that the decree of the council presents a practical solution rather than a doctrinal one suggests that the problem itself was reduced to the level of a practical issue, making possible the coexistence of Jewish and Gentile Christians (Acts 15:28–29) and putting little attention to the initial problem regarding Gentile Christians' salvation. Although Luke gave Paul and Barnabas a little space in the narrative of the council, he precisely indicates that the position presented by Paul and Barnabas was accepted, and both missionaries were recognized by the Jerusalem authorities (Acts 15:25–26), which is information of special importance in relation to Paul, due to the undermining of his authority by his opponents.[632]

Summing up: in the narrative regarding the Jerusalem Council, Luke made another step in his presentation of Paul, this time exposing his doctrinal contribution to developing the Christian movement.

2.2. Going on His Own

The short narrative regarding a controversy between Paul and Barnabas (Acts 15:36–41) serves in the narrative of Acts as an indicator that points to the event that ends Paul's cooperation with Barnabas, marking Paul's full independence in mission activities. The narrative indirectly shows that Barnabas and Mark went to revisit Cyprus, which rather exposes a static approach to mission work (development of already existing communities), but at the same time, Paul and his coworker Silas started a mission journey without a determined goal, which indicates an attitude open for many possibilities (as the narrative of the second mission journey will attest to by putting considerable focus on the guidance of the Holy Spirit in progressing Paul's mission to the Gentiles).[633] This laconic

[632] Averky (Taushev), *The Acts of the Apostles* (Jordanville, New York: Holy Trinity Seminary Press, 2020), 74–75.

[633] Although the account regarding the second mission journey focuses mostly on Paul's achievement among Gentiles, Paul's modus operandi (first Jew and then

information, contrasting the attitude of both groups, suggests the progressive character of Paul mission's that became the main topic of the Acts' narrative, contrary to Barnabas's mission that received no attention in Luke's narrative. In this way, Luke smoothly switches exclusively to the narrative regarding his main hero (Paul), and he probably also suggests to readers which way was more promising.

Another topic that relates to this narrative concerns the reason for the split, where Paul is presented as the one who created the problem by contesting the candidacy of Mark (who was useful during the mission in Cyprus, as Acts 13:5 suggests it), based on his absence during the mission in Pisidia and Panphilia because Mark "deserted them," as Lucan Paul harshly named it.[634] Although Luke wrote nothing about Mark's reason for discontinuing his work with Barnabas and Paul (Acts 13:13), Lucan Paul's extremely negative evaluation of Mark (Acts 15:38) suggests that Mark's decision deeply harmed Paul's feelings. It is impossible to determine closer what harm may have existed, but it was something that Paul and Barnabas evaluated radically differently, to the extent that Barnabas, "the man of consolation," was ready to involve himself in the sharp disagreement with the man for whom he had much understanding and good will.

Does Barnabas just disagree with Paul's evaluations of Mark, or does he prefer the bond of kinship before the bond of coworkers? The sharp disagreement between them, although strange, should not surprise one in the context of Acts 15:2, which exposes that this kind of communication problem within Christian communities was common. It may be assumed that Paul, as one of the more controversial

---

Gentiles) stays unchanged. K. Ehrensperger, *Paul at the Crossroad of Culture*, 219–221.

[634] We share the opinion that Mark's decision has something to do with the extension of the mission journey to the regions of Panphilia and Pisidia, which probably were not included in the initial mission plan regarding Cyprus alone. If it is so, Mark's presence in revisiting Cyprus could again cause problems with revisiting the regions of Panphilia and Pisidia (which were the first goal of the Paul and Silas's mission).

brothers, was often involved in temporary disagreements similar to this one. However, Luke used this event to profile his narrative on Paul exclusively in order to indicate indirectly that Paul, although still a member of the Syrian Antioch community, started his own "independent" mission activities.[635]

Summing up: Luke presents the disagreement between Paul and Barnabas as the main reason for their split and their creating two different mission groups that acted for the same reason but headed for different targets. However, he does not put responsibility on Paul or on Barnabas; he introduces a new quality (Paul's independence) that came into existence as a result of this problem.

2.3. Paul, Leading by the Holy Spirit

Like the narrative regarding the so-called first mission journey, the second mission journey, although based on historical events, is presented in Acts in a literary way that serves Luke's narrative purpose rather than as an exact historical record. Luke's narrative in Acts 16:1–18:17 is dedicated to Paul's mission to the Gentiles (although the mission to the Jews is still Paul's modus operandi), which takes on both a general and universal character, despite the fact that it refers to particular historical events. Luke's narrative approach allows him to present several aspects of Paul's characteristics as the apostle to the Gentiles, creating in this way another huge contribution to his very complex presentation of Paul.

The first aspect regards his attitude toward communities that he established during his first mission journey (Acts 16:1–5). Lucan Paul seems to have had no problem with visiting Lystra, the city where he suffered persecution (Luke's narrative does not mention a similar

[635] The end of the narrative regarding Paul's second mission journey includes the name of Syrian Antioch (Acts 18:18, 22) but does not contain Paul's report about his mission given to the Antioch community, contrary to the end of the narrative regarding the first mission journey (Acts 14:26–28), where such a report is included.

incident during his second visitation), concentrating the account on the first fruits of his mission, namely Timothy.[636] The story of Timothy shows Paul's flexibility in his adoption of the existing regulations, where he gives priority to the context in his application of the rules before giving the rules any dogmatic immunity. Paul was against the obligation of circumcision for those Gentiles who wanted to become Christian, but he was not against circumcision in the case of Christian Gentiles who, for practical purposes (not dogmatic), accepted circumcision (Acts 16:3).[637] The information about Paul's propaganda regarding the Jerusalem Council's decree (mentioned only once in Acts) should be taken not only in relation to a single case but as the general rule in his mission to the Gentiles (Acts 16:4). It means that, in regard to mission activities among the Gentiles, Lucan Paul employs a practical approach, where minimal and only indispensable obligations of Mosaic Law should be applied to Gentile Christians.

Luke's narrative suggests that Paul had some plans regarding the regions where he would like to spread the kerygma.[638] However, Luke shows that Paul subordinated himself to the will of the Holy Spirit,

---

[636] Acts 14:19 exposes Jews from Pisidian Antioch and Iconium as instigators of Paul's stoning, which may explain the lack of similar problems during his second visit to the city, and indirectly frees, to some extent, the local community's responsibility for their actions. L. T. Johnson, *The Acts of the Apostles*, 252–253.

[637] This is the only case recorded in Acts, which makes it an exceptional one, forced by particular circumstances and purpose. Lucan Paul understood and respected the fact that an uncircumcised member of the mission team would be reason for rejection of the kerygma spreading to Diaspora Jews, according to his modus operandi. I. W. Oliver, "The "Historical Paul" and the Paul of Acts. Which is more Jewish?" in *Paul the Jew*, eds. G. Boccaccini and C. A. Segovia (Minneapolis: Fortress Press, 2016), 54–57.

[638] The first plan concerns mission work in Asia Minor, which will be the place of Paul's mission work during the third mission journey, although right now, it is not allowed by the Holy Spirit. The second plan concerns work in Galatia and Phrygia, which was realized and brought considerable success, as Acts 18:23 suggests. The third plan concerns mission work in Mysia and Bithynia, but it was not allowed by the Spirit of Jesus. Definitively, Luke's narrative directs Paul's mission work to the northwest in order to reach Macedonia. H. Conzelmann, *Acts of the Apostles*, 126.

who, in the narrative regarding the mission to the Gentiles, takes responsibility for guiding Paul in such a way that he would be able to fulfill Jesus's plan for him (Acts 9:15–16). Although, Paul would like to work in regions where Jewish communities were present (Acts 16:6–8), the Holy Spirit's prohibition and the dream vision determined his will to spread the kerygma in Macedonia (Acts 16:10). Until now, Luke's narrative runs fast and exposes a high degree of schematization and an approach more appropriate for a summary than for narrative, but from Troas, where Paul met Luke, the narrative slows down, becoming very detailed, and it includes a considerable level of emotional intensity.

The information that Paul started in Philippi in his first mission activities in Macedonia highlights his general strategy in his mission to the Gentiles, where he preferred large cities with mixed cultures and religious backgrounds (Roman colonies). The lack of a considerably large and strong Jewish community in the city naturally worked in Paul's favor in his mission to the Gentiles and brought significant results among higher classes of the city's society (Acts 16:15, 33). In the case of Lydia, the context of her conversion is positive (Acts 16:14–15); in case of unnamed jailer, however, the context is negative (Acts 16:20–34), and it concerns Paul's first imprisonment. Luke presents Paul and Silas as missionaries facing a society that does not share their religious values and social standards. The indication that they are Jews sounds more like prejudice than an argument connected with the context of the problem (Acts 16:16–19). The main issue, however, on which Luke wants to focus is the fact that Paul's mission activities and their results violate the interests of some social groups (Acts 16:19) in an indirect way, which naturally leads to an unwelcome and defensive attitude toward Paul and Silas.

A similar situation takes place in the narrative of the third mission journey (Acts 19:18–40). The fact that Paul and Silas, based on a simple accusation, were beaten with rods strongly suggests that anti-Jewish sentiments played a considerable part for the magistrates in judging the case (Acts 16:22–24). Indirectly, Luke points to the anti-Jewish attitude of some Gentiles as the factor that makes the proclaiming of the kerygma by Jewish missionaries a considerably difficult and dangerous task. Paul and Silas's activities in the city were hardly welcome, as the flooding and imprisonment (Acts 16:22–23) and the somewhat nervous behavior of the city's authority (Acts 16:39) strongly indicates.[639] Luke complements the picture of Paul being persecuted by the local society because of the harm Paul's activities caused them, as well as the anti-Jewish prejudices, with a short account of a mission success of the Paul and Silas combo, despite the unfriendly circumstances (Acts 16:27–34). Luke's presentation of Paul as a missionary who, in all kinds of situations, is capable of making some converts must be taken as a theological generalization, where the particular case is presented as the model that should be followed.

This aspect of Paul's mission to the Gentiles is further developed in the narrative regarding the mission in Thessalonica (Acts 17:1–9), where the opposition of some Jewish members against Paul is placed in the context of Gentile society. Although Paul's opponents are Jews of the city, they use a "power of propaganda" to make the crowd willing to act against Paul in a legal way (the trial), in accordance with the city law (Acts 17:6). In order to expose that the accusation of the Jews and the crowd is fake (the political aspect of the accusation), Luke, at the beginning of the narrative, describes Paul's teaching to the Jews in Thessalonica (Acts 17:2–3).[640] Here, Paul's teaching is concentrated on Jesus the Messiah, who suffered and was resurrected. The contrast between Paul's teaching and the accusation against him (Acts 17:6–7) exposes the uncompromised

---

[639] Paul's mission activities in places where a large Jewish community was absent may indicate Luke's conscious narrative strategy that serves to underline his main interest in recording the events regarding the Gentiles as the target of Paul's activities (despite his modus operandi).

[640] After presenting anti-Jewish sentiments as the reason for problems with proclaiming the kerygma in Philippi, now Luke proceeds with the Jews' antagonistic attitude toward Paul's mission activities as another obstacle in his mission, which hereafter will be a common pattern of description of Jewish evaluations of Paul's missions.

enmity toward Paul's activities, where an unjust attitude is used as the way to achieve a desirable effect (Acts 17:10).

Despite the final result (Paul had to leave Thessalonica), Luke indicates Paul's mission successes in the city, where some Jews, some Gentiles, and some influential women were attracted by his teaching (Acts 17:4). The mention of the last group is of crucial importance, as it indicates a basic difference between the mission to the Jews, where women seem to be omitted, and the mission to the Gentiles, where conversions of women are highlighted. This pattern is also used in the narrative regarding Paul's mission in Berea (Acts 17:10–15), where in the conversion of Jews, only men seem to be the focus, but when it came to Gentiles, women and men are confirmed to have converted (Acts 17:11–12). The narrative of this mission exposes a method of proclaiming God's Word, which includes the study of the scripture in order to confirm the correctness of Paul's teaching (looks like an academic approach).[641] Indirectly, it shows that Paul's argument for teaching that Jesus is the resurrected Messiah was based on the interpretation of scripture in a way that attested that Jesus is the fulfillment of God's promises to the nation. This narrative exposes another pattern in Paul's mission, which concerns the group of some Jews who consequently "persecuted" Paul, not only in their own place but also in different cities (Acts 17:13–14), in order to disable him from proclaiming the kerygma. This pattern was already exposed in Acts 14:19–20, where the opponents stoned Paul, and now, it is repeated with an emphasis on the danger of their actions, as they came to Berea inciting and unsettling the crowd (Acts 17:14), which indicates the same pattern, like in Thessalonica. Indications that Paul was "escorted" by Berea's brothers to Athens seems to affirm that his situation in Macedonia was on a very dangerous level, and it regarded the possible accusation of stirring up social moods in the city for religious reasons. From a social point of view, this negative reason gave Paul's mission a new opportunity to proclaim the kerygma to

---

641 Paul's use of scripture as the authority attesting to his claims strongly supports the statement that his mission was initially addressed to Jews.

the Gentiles in a way that finally would bring considerable progress of the mission in strictly Gentile environments.

The first account does not confirm this thesis because Paul's mission attempt in Athens hardly can be counted as a success.[642] In the cradle of Greek religion and philosophy, he achieved no more than some degree of attention from the side of the city's authority and citizens, which did not make a significant increase in the number of converts (Acts 17:33). It is obvious that Luke includes this narrative (Acts 17:16–34) not to expose Paul's failure in this city but to complement the exposition of religious obstacles that deeply affected the mission results of Christian missionaries who had been initiated in the narrative of Acts 14:15–18. Paul's anger with the polytheistic religious system of the Athenians (Acts 17:16) exposes his deep conviction regarding the rightness of a monotheistic religion, as well as provoking him to undertake the constructive polemic with polytheistic religious system of Athenians (Acts 17:16–18). Paul's polemic approach toward the polytheism of the Athenians is presented in the majority of his speech, where using the contrast between "God is not like" and "God is like," he exposes the weak points of the Athenians' religious system and, at the same time, shows the superiority of the monotheistic concept of God (Acts 17:23–29).

Lucan Paul, in his speech, heads for the conclusion that faith in the one and only God is necessary for those who are following multiple gods because, in the end, all men will be judged by the only God through the chosen one, who has been resurrected from

[642] The unsuccessful mission attempt at Athens shows that Paul's kerygma was rejected, on occasion, not only by Jews but also by Gentiles, which directly contradicts the thesis that Paul suffered failure in his mission to the Jews but reached considerable success in his mission to the Gentiles. This suggestion is made by Bale. A. J. Bale, *Genre and Narrative Coherence in the Acts of the Apostles*, 145–153. The narrative of Acts shows many successful efforts of Paul, as well as many failures in his work among Jews and Gentiles. However, Luke is especially interested in Paul's achievements with Gentiles, probably because of the addressee of his work.

the dead (Acts 17:30–31).[643] In this way, without departing from a monotheistic concept of God, Lucan Paul introduces Jesus (Acts 17:18. 31) as the "right hand" of God, whose rights to judge humans are attested by his Resurrection, which occurred according to God's will. The idea of being judged by a man who was resurrected from the dead was unacceptable by all standards of Greek philosophy, and for this reason, Paul's kerygma was ignored (Acts 17:32). Luke chose this way to expose another reason why proclaiming the kerygma was challenging. Paul crossed the line of rationality, as it was understood by Greeks, when he attempted to implant, in a culture that was focused on logical and empirical arguments, the concepts that had been developed for hundreds of years within Judaism. Although Paul achieved no success, he did make considerable progress in developing the way of proclaiming the kerygma to Gentiles, which considered recognition of the fact that a consolidated society with a developed culture and ancient religion is a place where success in spreading a new religious concept hardly can be expected.[644] Not only were some Jewish customs (e.g., circumcision) unacceptable to Greeks, but it was also impossible for them to comprehend some religious ideas. Lucan Paul smashed the wall of Gentile polytheism with his head, and the results, according to Luke's narrative, seem to show that while the wall remained almost unscathed, the impact did not stop Paul's efforts.[645]

Not all Gentiles in the world were like the Athenians, as the narrative concerning Paul's mission in Corinth (Acts 18:1–17) proves. The city of Corinth was a relatively young city with the status of a colony, where everyone had come from somewhere else, each

---

[643] Lucan Paul struggles with introducing the idea of monotheism as superior to polytheistic systems. However, introducing a judge who resurrected from the dead, in the opinion of Athenians, goes beyond logic.

[644] C. J. Callan, *The Acts of the Apostles* (Columbia, 2021—reprint of New York 1919 edition), 135.

[645] According to the narrative of Acts, the failure at Athens did not discourage Paul, and Luke presents his next attempt in Corinth as a success, though it did leave a bitter taste in his mouth.

bringing with himself his own culture, religion, and values, hoping to find prosperity. At the beginning of his stay in Corinth, Lucan Paul was active within the Jewish community, and his mission work was restricted to teaching in the synagogue during the Sabbath, which was mostly due to the manual work he had to do to make a living. This is the first time that Luke addresses the economical aspect of the mission journey, describing Paul's self-financing achieved by his labor.[646] The situation changed when his coworkers finally reached Corinth and were able to provide the necessary financial support for Paul so that he could devote himself entirely to the mission among the Jews. Rather ambivalent results of this mission (Acts 18:5-6) forced Paul to undertake mission activity among the Gentiles (Acts 18:6), which is a pattern known from the narrative of the first mission journey. Luke's narrative suggests that Paul was suppressed by the local Jewish community, who probably refused to provide opportunities to teach in the synagogue. In this situation, Paul used the house of a Gentile (Titus Justus) to continue proclaiming the kerygma (Acts 18:7). It is the first indication in Acts when Paul (probably expelled from the local synagogue) uses the hospitality of the Gentiles to provide teaching not only for Gentiles but probably also for Jews, as Acts 18:8 seems to suggest.[647] In this way, Luke highlights another small step Paul made in the direction leading to his deeper involvement, not only in the mission to the Gentiles but also in providing mission activities for strictly Gentile environments (the house of Justus).

Although Luke wrote little about the long (Acts 18:11) and very successful mission in Corinth (Acts 18:10), he exposed two of the most important issues that characterized this mission. The first issue concerns Paul's suffering during this mission, which is indirectly indicated by the contents of his revelation, where Jesus encouraged

---

[646] In Luke's narrative, Acts 18:3 serves also as the preparatory information that will attest to Paul's claim presented in the speech at Miletus (Acts 19:33–35).

[647] Mention of Crispus and Gentiles (Acts 18:8) indicates that some Jews and some Gentiles accepted Paul's kerygma, which makes the matter of acceptance or rejection difficult to attribute to only one of these groups.

Paul to continue the mission (Acts 18:9). Jesus's exhortation includes two of Paul's negative attitudes (fear and to be silent), which may suggest the kind of doubts Paul had about the meaning of this mission. Luke strongly suggests that continuity of the mission in Corinth is a direct result of the revelation (Acts 18:9–11).

The second issue regards the reason for ending the mission in the city, which in Luke's narrative is presented as due to the well-organized opposition to Paul, leading to his trial before the local authorities (Gallio), based on an accusation regarding religious issues but presented as a political and legal matter (Acts 18:3). It would have ended with Paul's first trial before the Roman authorities if Gallio had not refused to judge within Jewish religious issue.[648] The incident was not the direct reason for Paul's return to Syrian Antioch, which indicates that the correct exercise of Roman law by Roman officials, to some extent, protected Paul from the uncompromised opposition of some Jews. This is the second exposition that the Gentiles' environment (after the house of Justus) serves the purpose of helping Paul's mission activities.

Summing up: although Paul follows his modus operandi (mission to Jews first), the Holy Spirit and Jesus himself were leading him to a deeper involvement in the mission among the Gentiles. The strongest stimulation came from the harsh and permanent opposition of some Jews, which slowly but consequently made Paul unable to achieve considerable success among Diaspora Jews.

2.4. The Missions' Fruits

The narrative regarding Paul's third mission journey mostly concentrates on his activities in Ephesus, which became the main headquarters during his mission in Asia Minor. Although addressed to Gentiles, Luke presents it in the context of a developing Christian community structure, where Paul's contribution is clearly shown.

[648] In this way, Luke indicates those who will be more extensively elaborated in the narrative regarding Paul's imprisonment (Acts 23:23–26:32).

Regarding Paul's mission activities in the city, Luke's narrative shows the considerable impact of Paul's teaching on the local society. The first sign of this impact is the fact that Paul has some imitators who, in the name of Jesus proclaimed by Paul, would like to perform miracles (Acts 19:11–17).[649] It indirectly indicates that, at least within Jewish society, the miracles that Paul performed were well known and probably earned him some respect, provoking some Jews of higher ranks to attempt to use Paul's "fame" for personal gain, which was certainly not in accordance with the Lord's will.[650] The unsuccessful attempt of the seven sons of the high priest exposed to the citizens of Ephesus that Paul as the only true witness to Jesus and—most probably to some extent—stimulated the process of their conversions (Acts 19:17–18). Luke particularly exposes Paul's contribution in decreasing the "magic business," which seems to be highly developed in Ephesus, judging by the scale of the negative consequences that were caused by Paul's activities (Acts 18:19).[651] The negative consequences of Paul's activities in Ephesus are further developed in the narrative concerning the unrest caused by Demetrius (Acts 19:23–40).[652] The narrative shows that Paul's mission had considerable influence on the local cult of Artemis, at least on the economic level for craftsmen producing artifacts related to this cult (Acts 19:26–27). Although shaped as a religious accusation (Acts 19:27), the opposition against Paul had an economic reason, as the speech of the town clerk directly indicates (Acts 19:37–40); it exposes a considerable change in the

[649] Concerning the miracles, Luke precisely indicates that the source of miracles is God, and the performer of miracles is Paul (Acts 19:11), which in the context of Acts 14:8–11 may be interpreted as the author's necessary specification because of the extraordinary way of performing miracles, where even part of Paul's garment causes healing and exorcism (Acts 19:12). This background serves to expose even more the spectacular miracle of the resurrection of the young boy in Troas (Acts 20:7–12). This miracle has placed Paul among the biggest prophets of Judaism, and it is the strongest possible authorization of him by God.

[650] Possible similarity to Acts 7:18–24 can be drawn. God's gift can be received from God for realization of God's purpose, but it cannot be taken away.

[651] C. J. Callan, *The Acts of the Apostles*, 143–145.

[652] Averky (Taushev), *The Acts of the Apostles*, 88–90.

balance of Ephesus's social structure and indirectly suggests massive conversions.[653]

Another layer of the narrative regarding the third mission journey concerns Paul's contribution to the development of the local structure of Christian communities. It starts with Paul's mission among the disciples of John the Baptist (Acts 19:1–7), which must be counted as extraordinary by any means, not only due to the fact that it is the only account in Acts that mentions the existence of the John the Baptist movement, several years after the beheading of John, but also because of the very peculiar information that the group contained "about twelve men," which may hint at the messianic inclination of the group. In this context, Paul's teaching addressed to this group was not just another proclaiming of the kerygma; it could have been a successful attempt to convince the group that Jesus, not John, is the Messiah, which was a supposition attested by Paul's question about the kind of baptism they had received. Paul's argument about John's mission (Acts 19:4) and their baptism in the Holy Spirit (Acts 19:6) may indicate the conversion of the members of the John the Baptist movement. If so, Luke would present Paul as a man who contributed to uniting close-but-still-separated messianic groups with the growing-in-strength Christian movement.

Regarding Paul's mission to the Jews in Ephesus, Luke's narrative follows the pattern already known from previous accounts (e.g., mission in Corinth), where he acted according to his modus operandi (mission to Jews first), which brought semi-rejection of his kerygma that forced him to separate from the synagogue and continue in the school of Tyrannus (Gentile environment).[654] This time, however, Luke added minor but very important information regarding the fact that Paul separated from the synagogue, along with his disciples

---

653 Economic reasons shaped as a religious accusation is a pattern used in Luke's narrative regarding Paul's imprisonment in Philippi (Acts 16:19–21).
The pattern of just execution of the local law by the local authorities, as an element important in mission activities, was also used in the narrative regarding the mission in Corinth (Acts 18:14–15).

654 The pattern is similar to that presented in Acts 17:7–8.

(Acts 19:9).[655] It is possible that this information indicates the moment that Jewish disciples of Jesus, attracted by Paul, departed from the local synagogue, which may be an indirect suggestion of the direction in which the Christian communities were developing. In this way, Luke would show another of Paul's contributions in developing the Christian movement, which here means gradual separation from the synagogue (in the case of Jewish Christians).

Another aspect of Paul's activities during the third mission journey concerns supervision of the communities he established (Acts 20:1–6), which here directly relates to the communities dwelling in Macedonia and Achaia. Luke wrote little about this visit and in a very schematic manner, which indicates a possible casualty in the mission activities, known to the reader from previous narratives. On the way to Macedonia and Achaia, Paul stopped in communities for didactic purposes (Acts 20:2), and in Greece, he stayed for three months, after which he planned to return to Syria. Luke wrote nothing about Paul's activities in the region but Acts 19:21 suggests two purposes of Paul's visit. The first one concerns his visiting the communities before he returns to Jerusalem (Acts 19:21) and then to Syria (Acts 20:3), without any reasons given, although Luke most probably was aware of the purpose of Paul's trip.[656] The second purpose of this visit concerns his plan to visit Rome (probably during his next mission journey), which strongly suggests that the visit to the regions of Macedonia and Achaia was a kind of necessary preparation.[657] Another casualty presented in the narrative regards the Jewish opposition toward Paul,

---

[655] Separation of Jesus's disciples from the synagogue in Corinth is not mentioned (Acts 17:7–8).

[656] The Corinthian correspondence puts more light on this visit, which included the financial assistance of the churches in the region for the community in Jerusalem. However, for some reason, Luke decided to stay silent. It is possible that the reason for his approach was caused by his narrative purpose regarding the third mission journey, where the exposition of great achievement in Paul's mission activities seems to be the main theme.

[657] Not only the Corinthian correspondence, which exposes another reason for Paul's visit to the Corinth, but also the contents of Paul's speech to the elders of the Ephesian communities, where Paul directly exposes his conviction about his

which drastically changed his plans (Acts 20:3), forcing him and many of his coworkers in these regions to use the land road through Macedonia (Acts 20:3–4). Naming some of Paul's coworkers from many different places serves to expose the considerably developed structure of Christian communities in these regions, and it indirectly exposes the fruits of Paul's mission activities.

Most crucial for Paul's presentation, however, is the speech that Lucan Paul gives in Miletus to the elders of the Ephesian community (Acts 20:18–35), where Luke presents the most elaborated and coherent characteristic of Paul as the witness to the resurrected Messiah. The basic statement for Lucan Paul's self-understanding is δουλεύων τῷ κυρίῳ (*I served the Lord*; *I was subjected to the Lord*), which exposes Paul's understating of his relationship with Jesus (Acts 20:19). This relationship is described as the subjection of himself to the Lord with all humility, which in daily routines was a time of struggling with Jewish (but not only) opposition (Acts 20:19), which should be taken as the conclusion of the narratives regarding the relationship between Paul and the Jews, rather than as Paul's accusation against Jews.[658] Despite the harsh reality of Paul's mission service, he was bearing witness to both Jews and Gentiles (that means to the whole world) in order that they might receive repentance from God by accepting Jesus as the Messiah (Acts 20:21). This is a very general characteristic of Paul's theological teaching, which, in a very simplified manner, can be exposed as salvation by faith in Jesus, which shows the necessity of faith in Jesus in order to find peace with God.

Concerning this task, Lucan Paul did nothing that could be considered as neglect of his duty (Acts 20:20). Regarding the social aspects of his relationship with his converts, Lucan Paul accents his disinterest in material benefits on one hand and his financial self-support on the other hand (Acts 20:34). Paul's practice of the social obligation of giving assistance to the poor, based on Jesus's teaching,

---

imprisonment in Jerusalem (Acts 20:22–24), seems to contradict the plan to visit Rome (Acts 19:21).

[658] The first self-characteristic: Paul is the servant of Jesus, who, like his Lord, has been rejected by his countrymen.

is hardly attested to in the narrative of Acts (with the exception of offering financial support for the Jerusalem community, as Acts 11:28–30 shows it).[659]

Another aspect of Paul's characteristics presented by Luke concerns his attitude toward communities that he established (Acts 20:26–32). Luke already wrote many times that Paul revisited the communities he himself had established, and during that time, he taught and exhorted them, but here is the first time when, in very general terms, the content of his teaching is directly presented. It starts with the ceding of authority and responsibility for communities to the elders, who should be the keepers of the teachings regarding God's plan of salvation (Acts 21:27). On them lies the duty to cultivate themselves and the communities subordinated to them, which means to preserve and to proclaim the truth of the faith (Acts 28). The cultivation of the community concerns the protection of the believers from the opponents of Christianity, who will act in many different ways to destroy them (Acts 20:29). The cultivation of themselves regards firmly and uncompromisingly proclaiming the true Christian teaching, which must always head for the greater good of the community and never should be concentrated on private ambitions (Acts 20:30).[660] Lucan Paul knows well that it is possible only if they subordinate themselves to God by following his message about grace (Acts 20:32–33).

Lucan Paul is insecure about his fate in Jerusalem (Acts 20:22–24), which the Holy Spirit compels him to visit; it is always something that means trouble for Paul, here named as hardship and imprisonment (Acts 20:23).[661] Paul probably did not know about the things that

[659] This attitude of Paul is attested in his letters (2 Cor. 8:1–9:15).

[660] Both problems are rarely found in the narrative of Acts, but they are issues present in Paul's letters. That indicates that Luke knows (probably from Paul) more then he decided to write down, and for this reason, this particular speech takes on the function of a very general instruction addressed to all elders of the Christian communities.

[661] The information about the main rule of the Holy Spirit in Paul's visit to Jerusalem may explain a difference between the narrative of Acts regarding Paul's wish to visit Rome (Acts 19:21) and the narrative of this speech (also the difference

would happen in Jerusalem, but Lucan Paul knew it perfectly, and for this reason, Luke exposes Paul's willingness to put his own life in danger in order to fulfill the mission for which Jesus chose him (Acts 20:24).[662]

The Lucan Paul's speech to the elders, although still in a schematic and general way, presents the most elaborated characteristic of Paul's mission attitude toward the Christian communities, where his own example is a standard that his successors have to fulfill, in the same way that Paul was fulfilling the order of his Lord. Lucan Paul does not make a difference between himself and his successors in matters of divine assistance, obligations, or responsibility, which makes him nothing less than an example for the elders of the Ephesian community (particularly) and all superiors of all communities (generally). In this way, Luke makes his point in describing the characteristics of Paul as a missionary; Paul, as a servant of Jesus, is a very sufficient example of responsible and unconditional subordination to the task for which he was appointed, but he is not a kind of idol for his successors.

Summing up: the narrative regarding Paul's mission journeys presents him as an example of sufficient mission work in three aspects of his activities. First, Paul is an example of how to mission to the Jews, which was his modus operandi. However ambivalent the results of this mission were not reasons to accuse him of neglecting his duty. Second, Paul is an example of how to mission to the Gentiles, which due to God's will became his biggest success, although not all attempts brought the expected results. Third, Paul is an example of a responsible missionary taking care of the established communities, leading them to possess the capability to exist and progress on their own, without the assistance of the apostles.

---

between Acts 20:22 and Acts 20:3). The narrative of the second mission journey exposed that Paul's plans and the plans of the Holy Spirit are not the same (Acts 16:6–10). Indirectly, the narrative suggests that Paul himself had not wished to go to Jerusalem, but he obeyed the will of his guide.

662 Definitely this part of the speech serves as preparation for the narrative regarding Paul's imprisonment.

3. Paul, the Prisoner

The last part in Luke's presentation of Paul concerns his imprisonment (Acts 21:1–28:31), and the narrative, as in the two previous parts, is something more than just a recording of historical accounts. After the presentation of Saul's growing to the status of a missionary and then after the presentation of Paul as a missionary, now Luke's narrative turns to the presentation of Paul in a time of custody, which, more than the previous two parts, exposes many personal aspects of the apostle to the Gentiles.

3.1. Paul Arrested in Jerusalem (Acts 21:1–22, 29)

Part of the speech to the elders of the Ephesian community (Acts 19:22–24) has made the initial preparation for the narrative regarding Paul's imprisonment, which is further progressed in the narrative regarding Paul's visit to Caesarea (Acts 21:8–14). In Caesarea, the prophet Agabus, under the Holy Spirit's inspiration, prophesies Paul's imprisonment in Jerusalem, which is, for Lucan Paul, the second opportunity to expose his readiness to suffer or even offer his life for Jesus (Acts 21:13). Luke, in the narrative, clearly exposes Paul's awareness about the potential danger of visiting Jerusalem, but despite his past attitude, when he many times ran away from this kind of situation, he is now strongly determined to take a risk.[663] In a somewhat dramatic narrative, Luke indicates that Paul right now has grown up to be not only a successful missionary but also a witness to the resurrected Messiah, and he is ready to testify not only by his words but also by his blood. It does not necessarily mean that Lucan Paul is willing to face martyrdom, which is attested by the

[663] Although not directly, Luke combined two reasons in Paul's decision to visit Jerusalem, where the first regards an almost totally omitted part of the narrative of Acts, the collection for saints in Jerusalem, and the second concerns Luke's narrative strategy, according to which Paul must not only end his mission activities in the place where everything started (Jerusalem) but also fulfill the last gap in his ministry; namely, to proclaim the kerygma to the most influential persons of society.

following narrative, where he will many times fight for his life. In this context, this narrative rather exposes the Lucan Paul's determination to proclaim the kerygma to the inhabitants of Jerusalem.[664] Luke left this aspect of Paul's mission career at the end of his narrative; although in a general manner, he informed readers about Paul's visits to Jerusalem and even the mission attempt three years after his conversion.

The narrative starts with a clarification of two kinds in Paul's relationships, where the first concerns the Christian community in Jerusalem (Acts 21:17–26). Two aspects of this relationship are indicated. Although Paul was accepted by the apostles and the members of the community, who even admired his mission's success (Acts 21:17–19), the controversies regarding Paul still remained and were spreading among some possibly influential members of the community, whose opinion (Acts 21:20–22) James had to take into consideration in the context of Paul's presence in the city.[665] Paul's cooperation with James shows his elasticity in relationships on the level of public image, where the observance of Jewish traditions is equal with orthodoxy of the religion.[666] On the level of the narrative, after Luke clarified the relationship between Paul and the community—excluding the community from responsibility for Paul's imprisonment on one hand, and presenting Paul's cooperative attitude on the other—he progresses with the presentation of Paul's relationship with the inhabitants of Jerusalem.

---

[664] For the very first time, the narrative exposes that Paul proclaimed the kerygma in the Temple, to the Sanhedrin, to the Roman officials, and to the king of Jews. Probably, Luke consciously makes these activities as an apogee of his mission to the Jews and the last stand for Jews in Palestine.

[665] Saul's activities as a persecutor, as well as Paul's stand against the "brothers from Jerusalem," which led to the Jerusalem Council, probably never were forgiven or forgotten. Also, the negative evaluation of Paul's activities and teachings among Diaspora Jews, which were spread by his opponents visiting Jerusalem, permanently kept suspicions toward him at a considerably high level.

[666] Indirectly, Lucan James indicates that the controversies regard Paul's relationship with Gentiles, which were generalized as the simple statement that he does not observe the Mosaic Law (Acts 21:23–25).

Paul was seized in the Temple based on the accusation of Jews from Asia Minor regarding his attitude in the past, and in the present (Acts 21:28), it attests to strong and consolidated anti-Paul opposition among Diaspora Jews, which Luke mentioned many times in his narrative regarding the mission journeys.[667] The narrative regarding the seizing of Paul exposes the purpose (to kill Paul—Acts 21:31, 36; 22:22) of the Jews' action, as well as the initial recognition of Paul's case by Roman soldiers (the leader of the rebellions—Acts 21:38).[668] Both elements serve to create a background for Paul's speech (Acts 21:1–21), which is the main aim of the narrative. Taking into consideration the context in which the speech is given, Paul's speech should be taken as highly provocative, which is a supposition attested to by the final reaction of the crowd at the end of the speech (Acts 22:22–23).

Instead of a skillfully shaped apologetic speech that could convince the crowd of his innocence of the allegation presented by Diaspora Jews, Paul delivered to the crowd a straightforward account of his conversion and the mission to the Gentiles (Acts 22:6–21), which was preceded by his biographical introduction (Acts 22:1–5). The account regarding his conversion, with some slight changes, is mostly a repetition of Acts 9:1–19, but the entirely new event that regards Jesus's revelation to Paul in the Jerusalem Temple shows the divine origin of the order for the mission to the Gentiles, with simultaneous omission of the mission to the Jews in Jerusalem (Acts 18–20).[669] This last part of the speech exposes its purpose, which is not strictly apologetic; rather, it indirectly exposes Paul as the

---

667 Averky (Taushev), *The Acts of the Apostles*, 98–100.

668 The layout of the relationship of Paul and the Roman soldiers serves in Luke's narrative to present some biographical information regarding Paul (Acts 21:39) in a complementary way. In this way, the very schematic presentation of Saul/Paul that Luke has done already will be supplemented by new information, which allows the Lucan picture of Paul to obtain considerable depth.

669 Jesus's message to Paul is clear, and it concerns two aspects of his mission, where the first is the rejection of Paul's mission to the Jews in Jerusalem (particular) and Diaspora Jews (general), and the second regards his mission to Gentiles, which will end with success. Although both statements show a considerable level

example (from a persecutor into a convert) that his listeners should follow, which makes the speech a kerygmatic attempt with a clearly emphasized aspect of Paul's witness to the Lord.

Unlike the narrative regarding Paul's mission among Diaspora Jews, Lucan Paul does not provide the speech that presents the kerygma, with which Paul would approach Jews of Jerusalem, although it is the only opportunity in Acts to do that. Instead, he tries to convince the Jews of Jerusalem that his mission to the Gentiles was a result of his zealous service to God, though this attempt was ultimately rejected by the crowd. In this way, Luke presents Paul's witness as rejected by the inhabitants of Jerusalem.[670]

Another aspect exposed by the narrative concerns the initial recognition of Paul's case by Roman soldiers, where, according to the first evaluation, Paul was suspected to be the Egyptian leader of rebellions (Acts 22:38), and according to a second evaluation, Paul was suspected to be dishonest to the soldiers (Acts 22:24).[671] In relation to the Roman soldiers, Luke presents Paul as a very enigmatic person who should be interrogated in a casual way, but his Roman citizenship prevented him from that (Acts 22:25–29).

Complementary and new information regarding Paul's life concerns his education in the Mosaic Law under the tutelage of the famous Rabbi Gamaliel (Acts 22:9), which makes him a very well-educated Jew, competent in matters concerning scripture. Other

---

of generalization, they correspond well to Luke's narrative approach to present Paul.

670 Like the Sanhedrin (and Saul) rejected the Jesus messianic movement several years earlier, now Jews in the Temple reject Paul's claim concerning God's will toward Gentiles. Saul, who rejected the new messianic movement that claimed the resurrected Messiah, now, as Paul, is rejected by Jews because of his conviction that God also calls Gentiles. It makes the Lucan perspective on Paul's rejection by Jerusalem Jews to be caused by his mission to the Gentiles, rather than on the contents of his kerygma itself.

671 Concerning the time of Paul's visit to Jerusalem, it is not surprising that Roman soldiers were highly suspicious about anything that disturbed social peace in the city, which, in their eyes, made every subject of disturbance a potential leader of a rebellion.

information exposes the cooperation between Saul and the Sanhedrin in his actions against the Way, which goes much farther than the simple recognition or supporting of the persecution, as it suggests a kind of inspiration and coordination that made Saul one of the many "useful tools" of the Temple's authority (Acts 22:5). Concerning Saul's election, Lucan Ananias says that Saul was elected by God himself to meet and believe in Jesus as the resurrected Messiah and then to be Jesus's witness to all people (Acts 22:14–15). This information shows that Saul's conversion has nothing in common with his intentional, conscious, and controlled process of changing his convictions, but all of it is due to God's providence and pure grace. In this way, Luke directly exposes his conviction regarding God's ultimate plan for Saul, which was slowly but consequently realized, step by step, in many different ways, until it brought about the expected results. The last complementary information found in this narrative concerns Saul/Paul's Roman citizenship, which he gained from his parents (Acts 22:25–29). This introductory indicator serves in Luke's narrative as the preparation for the following account regarding Paul's trial before the Roman authority.

Summing up: in the narrative regarding Paul's captivity, Luke presents him as a witness to the Lord, elected by God to give testimony to the inhabitants of Jerusalem, who refused it based on Paul's controversial statement that his mission to the Gentiles was the realization of an order given to him directly by Jesus in the Jerusalem Temple. Acts 22:17–21 exposes Lucan Paul's conviction regarding his vocation and the way it was realized.

3.2. The Trial before the Sanhedrin (Acts 22:30–23:35)

After Luke exposed Paul as the witness who was rejected by the inhabitants of Jerusalem who gathered before the Temple, he proceeds with the narrative, presenting the rejection of Paul by the Temple authorities. Although Acts 23:3 suggests that Paul is on trial before the Sanhedrin, the narrative exposes the rather authoritative and automatic condemnation of Paul (Acts 23:2).[672] Paul's speech starts with casual greetings that show his consciousness of the meaning of permanent and faithful service to God, which makes him a brother to the members of the Sanhedrin. This statement shows that Lucan Paul does not recognize service to the Lord (Jesus) as something different from service to the only God. However, the Sanhedrin thought overwise, and the visible sign of that was the order to strike Paul on the face. Paul's impulsive reaction to this public disgrace makes the situation even worse for him, despite his strange-sounding apology. Lucan Paul immediately recognized the danger of the situation, and because of that, in order to save his life, he exposes the controversial topic that will divide his opponents.[673] The controversial topic regarding the resurrection of the dead, presented here in an academic manner, rather than as a part of his kerygma, proves to be very effective, as it divided the Sanhedrin into two antagonistic groups that focused on arguments, thus leaving Paul's case unsolved (Acts 23:10).[674]

Luke's narrative seems to suggest that only Paul's smart move saved him from the Sanhedrin's condemnation, but the trial itself exposes Paul's rejection by the Temple authority. Mention of Jesus's revelation, which contains the high evaluation of Paul's testimony to him in Jerusalem on the one hand, and exposition of the Lord's will

---

[672] Luke, from very beginning of the narrative regarding the trial, presents the negative determination of the Sanhedrin toward Paul, which is something more than just the narrative background; rather, it also indicates that the Temple authorities shared the opinions of common Jews. Less attested to by the narrative is a supposition that the Sanhedrin still remembered Saul's treachery.

[673] In this way, Luke marks the point from which Lucan Paul starts to fight for his life in a very literal sense.

[674] Indirectly, Luke's narrative suggests that the topic of the resurrection of the dead was a vivid and controversial issue of such degree that it divided the Sanhedrin, and even though the purpose of the meeting was different, as the beginning of the narrative suggests, an opinion of the Sanhedrin's members about the "Paul problem" was shared by all. Luke possibly points to the basis of Paul's teaching (resurrection) as the "concept" that can divide not only the Sanhedrin (particularly) but also Judaism itself (generally).

that similar testimony must be given in Rome on the other hand, indicates the aim of Luke's narrative, and it introduces accounts that in the end will lead to the realization of Jesus's plan (Acts 23:11).[675]

Luke's narrative exposes that although Paul is not in control of the situation, his Lord is still in control of it, and all that is happening to him is another step in fulfilling the plan. The narrative regarding conspiring to exterminate Paul shows that Paul's case put the Jews on a level of despair that became hostility, which made them willing to risk even open combat against Roman soldiers (Acts 23:12–15).[676] It also exposes that the Lord's protection of Paul, in reality, can be done, mediated through the son of Paul's sister, which is very interesting information if one considers Luke's silence regarding the disciple's involvement in protecting or helping Paul. The circumstances forced the commander Lysias to send the prisoner to Caesarea, not only for Paul's safety but also in order to avoid a potential revolt in Jerusalem (Acts 23:23–24). The letter he sent with the prisoner (Acts 23:25–30), in Luke's narrative, is the very first evaluation of Paul's case by Roman authorities. Lysias recognized Paul as a Roman citizen whose life was threatened by Jews and who he saved (Acts 23:27).[677] According to his primary investigation, Paul is innocent of all crimes against Roman law, and the Jews' accusation against him regards issues of Jewish religion, which in this case (Roman citizen accused of a crime against the Mosaic Law) should be judged before

[675] In Acts 19:21, Luke exposes Paul's plan to undertake mission activities in Rome, but now, it is the will of the Lord that will make the mission in Rome possible, although in a different manner.

[676] The mention of the radical determination to assassinate Paul allows us to suppose that the narrative regarding Paul's trial before the Sanhedrin was described by Luke in a manner removing its real roughness but also suggesting the connection between the trial and the conspiracy.

[677] The help from the relatives must be taken as the sign of small but existing support for Paul, and the action of Lysias should be interpreted as the real threat of an uprising in Jerusalem, if the Jewish assassins were willing to attack the Roman soldiers.

Festus (Acts 23:28–30).[678] In this way, Lucan Lysias made the basic statement that exposes the main thesis of Luke's narrative regarding Paul's trials.

Summing up: Paul's captivity in the Temple, the trial before the Sanhedrin, and the conspiracy to kill him were aspects of the most dangerous time for Paul; he was not in control of the situation, and he had to face the uncompromised hostility of his opponents. Luke's narrative suggests that the matter of his surviving is connected to the Lord's protection so that Paul can fulfill the Lord's plan (Acts 23:11).

3.3. The Trials before Roman Governors

Paul's evaluation by Lysias, where the religious aspect of the problem is exposed, forced Lucan Tertullus to present his accusation against Paul in a strictly political manner in order that the accusation could be considered by Felix (Acts 24:5–8). Tertullus's more-demagogic-than-essential speech, which contained accusations without proof, did not make it difficult for Paul to defend himself. However, part of the accusation served Lucan Paul to give testimony regarding his religious convictions and belonging to the Way, called a sect by Jews (Acts 24:10–21). In fact, it is the very first exposition of Lucan Paul's juridical capability, and it presents him as a very convincing and comfortably speaking person, who, with surprising ease, points to the essential weakness of the accusations (lack of proof—Acts 24:11–13) and the inadequacy of his accusers, as they were Jews from Asia and not members of the Sanhedrin (Acts 24:19). He also shows the incapability of the Sanhedrin to sentence Paul during his trial before them (Acts 24:20).[679] During this trial, Lucan Paul

[678] Again, the statement regarding Paul's innocence in Lysias's letter determined the main line of Luke's narrative regarding Paul's trials before the Roman officials.

[679] The fact that the accuser is the Sanhedrin proves the statement that although Paul managed to escape from being sentenced by the Sanhedrin in Jerusalem and assassinated by the fanatic group cooperating with them, the Sanhedrin still makes great efforts to lay their hands on Paul.

is surely in control of the situation, and he won the juridical battle, but it does not change his fate, due to the unjust intentions of the corrupt Roman governor (Acts 24:22. 26). However, the two-year imprisonment in Caesarea and Festus's unjust judgment have brought Paul an opportunity to proclaim the kerygma to the governor and his wife, both of whom already possess a great deal of knowledge about Judaism (Acts 24:24–25).[680] It makes Paul an example of a witness to Jesus, even during times of persecution and imprisonment.

Luke's narrative regarding Paul's second trial, which occurred before the new and inexperienced governor Festus, concentrates mostly on Paul's stance against the unwise and unjust suggestions of the governor, leading to very severe consequences for Paul. Lucan Paul again exposes his innocence regarding Mosaic Law, the Temple, and Roman law (Acts 25:8) but this time without presenting any arguments, which gives his statement the weight of a concluding remark about his innocence and will be confirmed twice by the governor Felix before King Herod Agrippa II (Acts 25:18. 25). Lucan Paul and Lucan Felix differ in their evaluation of the governor's conduct, where the second sees it as almost a perfect example of a proper and professional act, but the first sees it as an unjustified attempt to make favor with the Jews at the expense of himself.[681] This attitude of Felix forced Paul to seek a trial before Caesar in order to save his own life (Acts 25:11).

The narratives regarding Paul's trials before the Roman governors show that Paul, who despite a lack of control over his fate, somehow is capable of finding a solution, even in the most hopeless of circumstances. He is able to defend himself against the well-prepared

---

[680] Both the period of custody and the trial gave Paul an opportunity to meet people he otherwise could not have met. According to Luke's perspective on Paul, Paul used this time to make a missionary effort, in a way similar to that during his short imprisonment in Philippi but not as effective.

[681] Indirectly, the narrative exposes again the Sanhedrin's determination to sentence Paul, which proves the initial interpretation of the narrative concerning the trial before the Sanhedrin in Jerusalem (the Sanhedrin axiomatically, from the very beginning, decides to condemn Paul).

Jewish accusation presented by a professional accuser, and when the governor acts wrongly against Paul, he does not hesitate to use his rights as a Roman citizen in order to save his life (Acts 23:11).

The last narrative regarding Paul's imprisonment in Caesarea regards his speech before King Agrippa II and the elites of the city (Acts 26:1–23), which, from a juridical point of view, was not necessary, but it is of crucial importance for the presentation of Luke's perspective on Paul. Finally, Lucan Paul delivers the speech to the king (according to Acts 9:15), which only at the beginning seems to be an apologetic speech (Acts 26:2–3); in fact, it very soon becomes clear that it is a skillfully crafted mission attempt to gain Agrippa's recognition of his kerygma.[682] After a short biographical introduction (Acts 26:4–5), he directly proceeds with exposition of the issue that caused his imprisonment, which refers to his faith in the resurrected Jesus of Nazareth (Acts 26:6–9).[683] The rhetorical question (Acts 26:8) opens a space for exposing himself as an example of a person who did not believe in the resurrected Messiah and, because of that, fought against the new movement (Acts 26:9–11) until he himself had an experience of the resurrected Jesus (Acts 26:12–18) that made him the Lord's servant.[684] This experience is a reason for his testimony to the resurrected Messiah, whom Paul recognized as the realization of the promises contained in scripture, according to the universal character of the prophecies (Acts 26:22–23). The dramatic attempt to convince King Agrippa II gives a testament to Paul's zeal as a witness (Acts 26:25–29). Paul's last stand, although it does not make the king a Christian, does make the Lucan Agrippa recognize Paul's innocence in matters regarding the Mosaic Law (Acts 26:31), which

---

682 L. R. Farley, *The Acts of the Apostles. Spreading the Word* (Chesterton: Ancient Faith Publishing, 2012), 298–312.

683 The topic of the fulfillment of God's promise corresponds to part of Paul's speech at Pisidian Antioch (Acts 13:22–23).

684 The narrative regarding Paul's conversion in general terms agrees with that presented in Acts 22:12–21, and even here, Jesus's mission order for Paul is shaped in a more comprehensive way, with additional explanation of the purpose for Paul's election (Acts 26:18).

is the last and strongest confirmation of the ungrounded character of the accusation against Paul.[685]

Summing up: the narrative regarding Paul's imprisonment serves Luke to expose the fulfillment of Jesus's plan (Acts 9:15), when, finally, Paul was able to give testimony to the inhabitants of Jerusalem and the most important people of the region, including the king, Herod Agrippa II. Simultaneously, the exposition of two layouts (the Jewish context of Paul's imprisonment and the Roman context of the imprisonment) amplifies the insecurity of Paul's mission activities in the region of Judea, where the Jews' hostility toward Paul, as well as the Roman governors' neglect of the right exercise of their duties, forced Paul to struggle for his life.

4. The Voyage to Rome (Acts 27:1–28:16)

Paul's speech before King Agrippa II is the apogee of the narrative regarding Paul's imprisonment, mostly due to his dramatic attempt to convince the king, which gives the account extreme emotional intensity and fulfills Jesus's order regarding Paul's service (Acts 9:15). After such an intense narrative, the account regarding Paul's voyage to Rome, despite its natural dramaturgy, seems to be just a kind of literary landscape that serves to expose some aspects of Luke's perspective on Paul during the voyage. In the narrative, Lucan Paul seems to be the only passenger aware of the danger of continuing the voyage (Acts 27:10), but his voice was ignored. He seems to also be the only one who makes a considerable and successful effort to keep the hope of the voyagers alive (Acts 27:21–26:37). Lucan Paul also has an extremely good relationship with the centurion, Julius, who commended the Augustan Cohort. He allowed Paul to visit friends in Sidon (Acts 27:3); then, after ignoring Paul's advice

[685] Luke presents the king as a man fully understanding Paul's argument but without the will to accept it. On the other hand, Luke presents Paul as a preacher, who, to the last moment, believes in a successful end.

regarding discontinuing the voyage (Acts 27:11), he follows Paul's advice regarding the sailors (Acts 27:31–32), and after the shipwreck, in order to save Paul's life, he neglects casual procedures regarding prisoners in such a situation (Acts 27:43). This layout exposes Paul's common sense about the real state of things and his skills in interpersonal relationships; both come from his religious convictions.

Another layout regarding Paul during the voyage to Rome concerns events that are related to two miracles that occurred on the island of Malta (Acts 28:1–10). The first miracle concerns Paul, who was bitten by a snake; surprisingly, it did not lead to death, which made the inhabitants change their evaluation of Paul from murderer to god. Both of these evaluations were wrong, but both of them caused Luke to reminisce about the two biggest problem of Paul's life, which have been exposed in the narrative of Acts—the first regards his past as a persecutor (Acts 22:4), and the second shows the problem connected to performing miracles before the Gentiles (Acts 14:8–13).[686] The second miracle regards Paul's healing the father of Publius, the chief official of the island, which is the event that also launched Paul's healing activities among the inhabitants of the island (Acts 28:7–10).[687] This layout shows Paul's relationship with the inhabitants of the island, which develops from suspicion to glorification to practical contribution to the local society.[688]

Summing up: the narrative regarding Paul's voyage to Rome, although it contains records of his miracles and his contributions in surviving a storm, does not inform readers about Paul's teaching

---

686 It is probably just a historical account but including it in the narrative only for historical accuracy seems to be an irrelevant reason, if one considers Luke's skills in using some events in a way that serve to expose his theological or biographical purposes.

687 The chief official of the island gave assistance to the Augustan Cohort and prisoners under their guard, which created for Lucan Paul an opportunity to perform miracles in a way similar to Jesus (Mark 5:23; 7:32; 8:25) and Ananias (Acts 9:12, 17).

688 Luke's narrative suggests that Paul was not allowed to teach or spread the kerygma, but he testified by his healing activities.

activities or conversions, which makes the account have a descriptive and informative character, rather than a narrative with a determined theological or biographical purpose. Paul remains the main hero of the narrative, though the narrative itself seems to be more important than the hero.

5. Paul in Rome (Acts 28:11–31)

Luke treats the narrative regarding Paul's stay in Rome in a very schematic and fragmentary way, which strongly suggests that Luke intended it as a kind of introductory narrative that serves to create the basic background for a more extensive and coherent narrative that possibly was at least planned by him. Luke informs us that Paul stayed in Rome for two years, during which he spent time in house prison, teaching all people (universal aspect) who came to him about Jesus the Messiah and the kingdom of God (Acts 28:28–31). Both aspects of Lucan Paul's teaching were somewhat controversial, considering the circumstances, and probably for this reason, the author underlines that Paul did it with "boldness."[689] It is probably the most direct and final of Luke's expositions of Paul's courage in proclaiming the kerygma.

The majority of this short narrative is dedicated to the topic of Paul's relationship with the Jews of Rome (Acts 28:17–27), where the first part contains his assurance that the appeal to Caesar has nothing in common with his attempt to accuse the nation before the Romans (Acts 28:19).[690] Lucan Paul presents himself as a victim who has been accused by his countrymen of committing crimes against the nation and tradition and who is handed over to the Romans,

[689] Similarly, the boldness of Peter and John before the Sanhedrin (Acts 4:13). Proclaiming Jesus of Nazareth (Jew) as the Messiah (in the political sense) could be interpreted as opposition to Caesar. In the same way, the teaching about the kingdom of God could be treated as opposition to the Roman Empire.

[690] Luke's narrative hardly mentions the Christian of Rome. P. Van't Riet, *Luke, the Jew. Introduction to the Jewish Character of the Gospel of Luke ant the Acts of the Apostles* (Zwolle: Folianti, 2009), 158.

found innocent, and, due to the hostile opposition of the Jews in Jerusalem, is forced to appeal to Caesar. Paul, without specification, exposes his conviction that he shares the same hope as the people of Israel (including the Jews in Rome), and for him, it is the reason for his imprisonment. This kind of exposition amplifies Paul's unfair treatment by the Jews in Jerusalem, which both attests his appeal and creates the basis for a positive relationship with Jews in Rome. However, Jews in Rome are more suspicious about the new sect to which Paul belongs, as the evaluation of the sect was usually very negative (Acts 28:22). It naturally creates space for Paul's proclaiming of the kerygma to Jews in Rome, which, as in many cases before, brought ambivalent results, as some Jews accepted the kerygma, and some rejected it (Acts 28:24–27). This forced Paul to continue his mission among the Gentiles of Rome (Acts 28:25–28) with the strong conviction that they would accept it.[691]

In the narrative regarding Paul's imprisonment in Rome, Luke presents Paul as a man ready to start a new mission, despite the fact that he is a prisoner awaiting trial. He made, according to his modus operandi, initial contact with the Jews in Rome, which led to mission activities among them that brought some positive results; however, Luke amplifies the rejection of Paul's mission to the Jews, which, according to Luke's pattern, directly contributed to Paul's mission among the Gentiles in Rome.

Summing up: the narrative regarding Paul in Rome has an introductory rather than conclusive character, with the imprisonment of Paul initiating a meeting that leads to mission activities among Jews, and then, as the result of rejection, it is extended to Gentiles.[692]

---

[691] Acts 28:28 strongly suggests that Luke probably planned to write another part that most likely would have concerned his mission among the Gentiles of Rome.

[692] The thesis regarding the introductory character of Acts' ending may be attested to by the definite discontinuity of the introduced narrative concerning Paul's criticism toward Jews and the very short and laconic summary of his two-year period in Rome. A conclusive character of the narrative would be possible if Luke's purpose for Acts was to bring Paul to Rome, as Acts 19:21 may suggest,

Luke, in general terms, exposes Paul's active attitude, which is focused on the mission, rather than on the trial. Laconic information about mission activities during his two-year stay in house prison, and especially the controversial thesis in Paul's teaching (Acts 28:28), naturally awakens expectations for more details regarding this period.

---

but Luke's basic line of his presentation of Paul is exposed in Acts 9:15–16, where Paul is sent by Jesus to different groups of people but not to places.

CONCLUSION

As we have indicated in the introduction to this study, we started to work on the book with two strong convictions: the supposition that Luke has his own coherent and unique perspective on Paul, which greatly influenced his presentation of the apostle to the Gentiles in the Acts of the Apostles, and the final effect of Luke's presentation of Paul, which, according to our assumption, should result in some kind of a statue or portrait of Paul. At the end of this study, we have concluded that our first conviction is correct, but our second conviction is not. In other words, we believe Luke had his own perspective on Paul, which he exposed in Acts, but the aim of this exposition did not concern the creation of a kind of idol (statue or portrait) that could be worshipped by followers. Luke's presentation of Paul in Acts does not work toward making him appear to be the greatest apostle; rather, it exposes Paul's great deeds, which did not come from his greatness but from God's grace.

In the study "The Witnesses to the Resurrected Messiah," we argued that Luke presented Peter and Paul as the representative figures for two communities, where Peter is the hero of the narrative regarding the spreading of the kerygma in the regions of Judea and Samaria, and Paul represents all those who were involved in spreading the kerygma among Diaspora Jews and Gentiles.[693] Almost the majority of credit went to these two apostles, but neither of them

[693] J. Kucicki, "The Witnesses to the Resurrected Messiah. Luke's Presentation of the Main Theological Theme of the Acts of the Apostles," *The Biblical Annals* (Sept. 4, 2019): 671–696.

was working alone. Also, each of them (meaning each of the groups) contributed greatly in helping to develop the proclaiming of the kerygma that resulted in complementary cooperation between them, rather than separated and unrelated mission activities. However, because this study concerns Luke's perspective on Paul, we focused particularly on Paul and, more precisely, on the exposition of the characteristics that make Luke's presentation of Paul unique.

The first characteristic of Luke's perspective on Paul concerns placing him in the narrative of Acts. Although Paul is the hero of more than half of Acts (Acts 7:58–8:3; Acts 9; Acts 13–28), Luke connects him to other, more important figures in his narrative, like Peter, James, and Barnabas. In regard to teaching and conviction, Luke relates Paul to Peter, especially in the case of the incorporation of Gentiles among Jewish Christians (Acts 10–11; Acts 15). Concerning the relationship between Paul and the Jerusalem community, Luke relates the apostle to the Gentiles with James. In the process of transferring Paul from a neophyte witness into a successful missionary, Luke almost exclusively relates Paul to Barnabas. Although without a doubt, Paul's case is extraordinary, it is very closely connected to the fate of the whole messianic movement, which indicates that Luke has no intention of presenting Paul in a separate manner as a kind of lone wolf. Paul is another piece of the puzzle that creates the colorful portrait of the early Christian communities. Church tradition created commonly accepted general statements, which presents Peter as the apostle to the Jews and Paul as the apostles to the Gentiles, by blending the Lucan tradition with Paul's tradition in order to establish the two pillars on which church history is built.

Despite the fact that Luke's theology is significantly influenced by Paul's theology, these two traditions are independent and were created for different purposes. Paul's tradition, in large part, is determined by the problems and needs of the communities, where Paul's teaching exclusively serves as a way to overcome temporary crises. However, in the case of the Lucan tradition, Peter and Paul are not independent heroes, despite the fact that they are the center of the Lucan narrative; rather, they are representatives of two stages in the development of the messianic movement, where many other people were also involved. Lucan Peter is a man who contributed much to the work of Paul, starting with the shaping of the basic kerygma of the messianic movement (Acts 2:22–24, 32–33), the establishment of the necessary structure of communities (Acts 1:15–22; Acts 6:1–4), the leading of communities through confrontation with the Sanhedrim (Acts 4, 8–12, 19–20), and, most importantly, the opening of the doors for the incorporation of Gentiles within Judeo-Christian dominated communities (Acts 10:44–11:8; Acts 15:7–11). Peter's contribution to establishing the kerygma and the incorporation of Gentiles are two aspects that especially helped Paul in his proclaiming of the resurrected Messiah (Acts 27:22–23) and the way of salvation for Gentiles that could only be achieved directly by the faith (Acts 15:1–2; Acts 16:4). In Luke's narrative, there is no antagonism between the activities of Peter and the activities of Paul; on the contrary, Paul's mission seems to be a development of the works incited by Peter.[694]

The second characteristic of Luke's perspective on Paul concerns his election by the resurrected Jesus (Acts 9:15–16). Paul speaks about himself as a δοῦλος Ἰησοῦ χριστοῦ (*servant of Jesus Christ*), while the Lucan Jesus speaks about him as a σκεῦος (*vessel*) chosen for a determined purpose.[695] For Paul (Saul) the persecutor, it was unthinkable to accept the idea of the resurrected Messiah, but the revelation of the resurrected Jesus makes him almost instantly recognize Jesus as his own Lord. Luke gives Paul no space for the deliberation or revision of his conviction, and his subordination and his baptism are presented as straightforward events, with no room for opposition. This exposition shows that Lucan Paul did not choose Jesus, but he was chosen by Jesus. Paul could not oppose this election (Acts 27:19), which, according to Luke's narrative, led him to give witness to the resurrected Messiah (Acts 9:20. 22), during which, from the very beginning until the end of the narrative presented in

694 R. I. Pervo, *The Making of Paul. Constructions of the Apostle in the Early Christianity* (Minneapolis: Fortress Press, 2010), 8–12.

695 The meaning of this term is presented in Acts 22:12–16 and Acts 26:14–18.

Acts, he was under the Lord's protection and guidance (Acts 16:6–10; Acts 18:9–10; Acts 22:18; Acts 23:11).

The third characteristic of Luke's perspective on Paul concerns the progressive presentation of his growth in service to the Lord. Luke portrays Paul as a man in a constant process of transformation. Paul's conversion was just the beginning of his long journey, but it was not the final stage in his life, despite the fact that, without a doubt, it was the most crucial part of it. Luke writes little about the three-year period of Paul's witnessing to his new Lord that ends with information regarding his very first testing, during his time of being a hunted man. Luke presents Paul as persona non grata, both among Jerusalem's followers of Jesus (directly) and his former comrades involved in the struggle for pure Judaism (indirectly), which was the main reason that forced him to return to his hometown, where, for a considerably long time, he stayed hidden to the world. By chance, he was "reactivated" by Barnabas, and he terminated his apprenticeship with him in Syrian Antioch, which is the period presented by Luke as the "real break" for Paul in his process of developing into a sufficiently prepared missionary. In the narrative regarding Paul's three mission journeys and the so-called Jerusalem Council, Paul appears as a very active missionary who, despite various obstacles and with varying luck, continues fruitful mission activities addressed to Diaspora Jews (the first mission), Gentiles (the second mission), and to Gentile and Christian communities (third mission), as a determined witness standing for the truth of the Gospel (the Jerusalem Council).

The fourth characteristic of Luke's perspective on Paul concerns his flexibility in his way of proclaiming the kerygma. Luke, at the very beginning of Paul's proclaiming activities, exposes the contents of the kerygma spread by him among the Jews in Damascus, which regards two aspects of Jesus's dignity: first, that Jesus is the Son of God, and second, that Jesus is the Messiah (Acts 9:20. 22). The contents of the kerygma will be detailed more specifically during Paul's mission activities, but the core of the kerygma stays unchanged. The flexibility of Paul's proclaiming of the kerygma concerns exclusively the adaptation of the form in which it was presented to different kind of hearers. Luke presents the neophyte Paul's teaching as bold and uncompromised, which was why it hardly brought positive effects in Damascus and Jerusalem; on the contrary, it brought problems for Paul and those associated with him. The results of his proclaiming activities changed radically when Paul cooperated with Barnabas in Syrian Antioch, as the narrative of Acts shows (Acts 11:19–30; Acts 13:1–14:28).

During the speech at Pisidian Antioch, Lucan Paul acts as the rabbi in his exposition of Jesus as the fulfillment of God's promise (Acts 13:16–41). In speeches at Lystra and at Areopagus (Acts 13:15–17; Acts 17:22–31), Luke shows Paul as a wise teacher who, considering the ignorance of the hearers, includes the necessary introductory teaching (the monotheistic concept of God) before he proceeds with the kerygma. During the speech to the elders of the Ephesian community at Millet, Lucan Paul seems to be the father, the founder of a community that must continue on its own, and because of that, it needs to be directed by the last advice of its founder. When the narrative of Acts turns to the account of Paul's imprisonment, Paul became the fearless witness of Jesus to the inhabitants of Jerusalem, and despite the fact that he must defend his own life, he consequently exposes Jesus as the resurrected Messiah to the authorities of the Temple, as well as to the Roman procurators and finally to the last king of the Jews. To each of the groups, Paul speaks the same kerygma, though it is shaped differently, depending on circumstances.

The fifth characteristic of Luke's perspective on Paul concerns his modus operandi during mission journeys in particular and his relation to Jews in general. Proclaiming Paul to be the apostle to the Gentiles has consequences in the interpretation of Luke's account regarding Paul's relationship with Jews. There are two common mistakes, where the first concerns a social level, and it relates to the conviction that Paul, as the apostle to the Gentiles, put the main focus of the mission to non-Jews, and the second regards a theological level, insisting that Paul's teaching was against Judaism. Neither of the convictions is supported by Luke's account in Acts. On the contrary, from the very first account of Saul/Paul's mission attempts until the last account of Paul's activities in Rome, Luke consciously and permanently exposes Paul's modus operandi, which can be characterized as Jews first, which was also a characteristic of Jesus of Nazareth. Even in places where the local community of Jews was not large enough to possess a synagogue, such as the group in Philippi (Acts 16:3), Paul makes efforts to spread the mission to Jewish women of the city. There is not an account regarding mission activities where Paul neglects his mission to Jews in favor of a direct mission to Gentiles.

Also, Luke's narrative does not contain cases where Paul's teaching is exposed as antagonistic to Judaism, although it is exposed as not accepted by Judaism, due to its rejection of Jesus as the fulfillment of God's promises. Luke, in a general way, exposes Paul as the apostle of Jesus who was not accepted (in a very general sense) by the most influential people of Jewish society and the majority of Diaspora Jews, but at the same time, he was the only Jew who, with considerable success, transferred to the Hellenistic world the strict Jewish monotheistic concept of God in a sufficiently attractive way that made some Gentiles come to accept his new interpretation of Judaism's traditions. The last statements regard the next two important characteristics of Paul's presentation in Acts.

The sixth characteristic of Luke's perspective on Paul concerns the rejection or at least serious suspicion that Paul and his teaching faced. After his conversion, Paul became a traitor not only to his friends, who were all involved in the persecution of the messianic movement, but also to Jerusalem's religious establishment, as well as for Jews of Damascus, who are indicated by Luke as the very first group that concluded that Paul must die (Acts 9:23). The Diaspora Jews who gathered in one of Jerusalem's synagogues, who possibly could have been his former friends (Acts 9:29), as well as the inhabitants of Jerusalem who opposed Paul's teaching (Acts 22:22), came to the same conclusion. About the rejection of Paul by the Sanhedrin, we are informed by Luke's narrative regarding Paul's interrogation before the Sanhedrin that the high priest refused to recognize Paul's claim about his pious Jewishness (Acts 23:1–2). Acts also informs us about

King Herod Agrippa II's rejection of Paul's teaching (Acts 26:28). All these examples show that after Paul's conversion, he was not accepted by Palestinian Judaism, which makes his mission attempts doomed to failure from the start, which Luke indirectly shows by excluding direct references to Paul's establishment of communities in Jerusalem and Judea from his narrative.

Information about Paul's establishing of new communities is included in the narrative regarding Paul's mission activities among Jews of the Diaspora, as well as among Gentiles. The mission among the Jews, which, according to Luke's narrative, was prioritized by Paul, was marked partially by the acceptance and partially by the rejection of his kerygma. The reason for the rejection of Paul's kerygma was that his teaching was about Jesus the resurrected Messiah, which, in the opinion of his opponents, undermined the value and importance of the Mosaic Law in the daily lives of Jews. Concerning Paul's mission among Gentiles, there are several reasons for the rejection of Paul and his kerygma. The first relates to the Gentiles' prejudices against Jews, their religion, and their customs (Acts 16:20–21); the second regards the considerable changes in the socioeconomic situations of places where Paul's kerygma was accepted (Acts 19:17–19. 25–27); and the third concerns the merit of Paul's kerygma, which did not correspond with the local philosophical and religious systems (Acts 17:32).

The rejection of Paul is a theme not restricted to his relationship with Jews; it also appears in the relationship between Paul and the messianic movement's members. The narrative of Acts honesty exposes the initial prejudice against Paul showed by the Christian community in Jerusalem (Acts 9:26). Luke also exposes the opposition of some Christians from Jerusalem toward Paul's teaching, which was a direct reason for a serious crisis (Acts 15:1–2) that had consequences for Paul, even several years later (Acts 21:20–21). All this shows that from Luke's perspective, Paul's activities were controversial for people, but it was not so for God.

The last statement is a good introduction to probably the most important characteristic of Luke's perspective on Paul, which concerns

Paul as God's vessel, used to transmit Judaism's concept of salvation into the Hellenistic world. Luke's narrative makes perfectly clear that Paul's election by Jesus had a particular and determined aim, which would be achieved by using Paul as a sufficient "tool" (Acts 9:15–16). On the other hand, Lucan Paul is perfectly conscious of the purpose for his election (Acts 20:19–21; 22:18–21). Paul, the Diaspora Jew, who made his stand to be more Jewish than Palestinian Jew (Acts 22:3–5), by the will of God changed sides and became one of those whom he had persecuted, which naturally made him seen as a traitor in the eyes of the opponents of the Way. Paul became an unwelcome person in Jerusalem, which is a negative aspect that determined the way he would be used by God. His Diaspora background (Jews living in the Hellenistic world) and his study of scripture in Jerusalem (learning of Palestinian Judaism) made him sufficiently prepared for mission work among Diaspora Jews. Concerning this purpose, Paul was met with considerable success as well as considerable opposition. However, this aspect, although clearly indicated in Acts, is not the main purpose of Luke's narrative regarding Paul's mission journeys and his imprisonment. Luke subtly exposes Paul as the man who gradually transmits the strictly Jewish concept of God and salvation into the philosophy and religion of the Hellenistic world. The event in Lystra (Acts 14:8–18) exposes Paul's way of approaching Gentiles, where the most important thing was to introduce the concept of the one and only God to a society accustomed to polytheistic religions.

In the same way, Paul approached the urban society of Athens, where the majority of his speech concerned exposition of the one and only God, as necessary preparation before the concept of judgment by the resurrected Savior could be approached as a topic. Although in both cases Paul did not succeed, Luke clearly shows that the kerygma about Jesus as the resurrected Messiah could not be separated from Judaic monotheism, which is of critical importance for justifying Paul's teaching. Probably because of that, Luke indicates that Paul's mission successes almost always were connected with his initial activities in Jewish synagogues, which probably, to some extent, naturally prepared the ground for Paul's kerygma. According to Luke's narrative, the version of Judaism that Paul presented was more attractive and easier for the Gentiles to accept than the "classical Judaism" spread by the synagogues around the Mediterranean world. The universal character of Paul's teaching was headed for including itself into the Hellenistic world, rather than attempting to include this world into Judaism, which was a reversal of the common mission approach of the synagogue. Luke presents Paul as the man who made this reversal possible.

Another of Paul's characteristics that Luke presented concerned the effect of his mission attempts. It was not simply reduced to the number of conversions and established communities; most of all, it concerned his kerygma challenging the Hellenistic world (Acts 17:23). Luke's narrative concerning Paul's achievement during the mission in Ephesus (Acts 19:11–20) exposes the considerable changes in society that Paul's kerygma initiated. Despite the fact that Paul's controversial teaching and activities brought great discomfort for him, it also made a deep impact on the society that reacted by accepting or rejecting it because in both cases, the kerygma was considered. Luke's account about Ephesus underlines the departure of Gentiles from the polytheistic religious system and their acceptance of the monotheistic concept of God that directly led them to faith in Jesus (Acts 19:17). That procedure consequently led to economic and religious changes in local society (Acts 19:25–27). The narrative regarding Ephesus is Luke's final exposition of Paul's achievements in the Hellenistic world, and unlike the narrative of the first and second mission journey, he exposes the great impact of Paul's mission (even Paul's letters suggest such an impact). In the Gospel, Luke exposes that the cross of Jesus changed the relationship between God and humankind in a universal way (salvation), and in Acts, he exposes that Paul's mission activities changed this relationship in an individual way (conversion).

In Acts, Lucan Paul is hardly at ease; from the very first exposition till the last moment, he seems to be constantly struggling.[696] This is

---

[696] Concerning the exposition of Paul's suffering in the narrative of Acts and in Paul's letters, cf. T. R. Schreiner, *Paul, Apostle of God's Glory in Christ*, 84–100.

the most exposed characteristic of Paul that Luke presented. From the beginning, the narrative of Acts shows him in the context of his opposition to a new messianic sect, which is presented as an issue of crucial importance for him (Acts 8:1; 26:9). The event of Paul's conversion, at least in the version presented during the speech in the Temple, exposes Paul's struggle with new and unexpected changes (Acts 22:16). The same concerns his activities in Damascus, where, for very first time (but not the last), he had to struggle for his life (Acts 9:24), as well as his first visit to Jerusalem after the conversion, where he had to struggle for the acceptance of the twelve and the local community (Acts 9:26). The period commonly called the "unknown years of Paul," which covers several years between his departure from Jerusalem and his reactivation in Syrian Antioch (Acts 9:30; 11:25–26), about which we know nothing, probably was a time of at least strong inner and psychological struggle. The narrative concerning the mission journey is another opportunity for Luke to expose Paul's constant struggle, which was caused, among many others, by opposition to his kerygma (Acts 18:6), prejudice toward Jews (Acts 16:21), economic interests of his opponents (Acts 19:18), jealousy for his success (Acts 17:5), danger of death (Acts 14:19), unproved accusations (Acts 18:14–15), an idolatrous and polytheistic religious world (Acts 14:11–12; 17:16), running from place to place (Acts 14:5-6), and Christian controversy (Acts 15:2).

However, the most difficult period of Paul's life must be recognized as the time of his two-year imprisonment, during which he had to face false accusations from the Jews (Acts 21:27–29), escape from the wrath of the crowd (Acts 22:22), experience rejection from the Sanhedrin (Acts 23:2), prevent his assassination (Acts 22:23), suffer unjust treatment by the Roman officials (Acts 24:22, 26; 25:9) who forced him to appeal for trial before Caesar (Acts 25:11), be rejected by King Herod Agrippa II (Acts 26:28, 32), suffer danger on the sea (Acts 27:20), and uncertainty about the reaction of Roman Jews (Acts 28:17). All these are part of the realization of Jesus's words regarding suffering, which Paul would have to taste in his time of service to his Lord (Acts 9:16). The constant struggle is probably the most accurate description of Paul's service to Jesus as his witness, but in order to balance this exposition, Luke also includes the positive effects of this struggle (Acts 20:18–24; 26:20–22).

The last Lucan perspective on Paul concerns his imprisonment, which, despite the unfavorable circumstances, became an opportunity for the boldest proclaiming of Jesus as the resurrected Messiah to the Jews of Jerusalem and even to the last king of the Jews, Herod Agrippa II. In this way, Luke shows that Jesus's orders concerning Paul (Acts 1:8; 9:15–16; 22:18–21; 23:11) were fulfilled not only during Paul's active life but also during his imprisonment.

Luke used all presented characteristics to create his own perspective on Paul, based on his knowledge, experiences, and understanding. However, despite the fact that Luke's presentation of Paul in Acts is sufficiently comprehensive, it does not mean that it created one precise design or exposed the portrait or the statue of Paul with a determined message, which the reader should recognize and accept. Luke does not determine the reader's understanding of Paul with the simple statement "Paul is …"; rather, he exposes Paul's many deeds, which speak more about Paul's fulfillment of the task for which he was elected than about Paul himself. Luke's aim in his presentation of Paul does not concern directly the indication that Paul is an apostle, witness, or missionary; rather, it concerns the way in which Paul executed all the tasks for which he was called. Luke's interest lies not in Paul himself but rather in his life, which the author of Acts evaluated strongly in the context of God's election for an already determined aim.

In the story of Luke, the most important concern is not the main hero (Paul) but the way he was used by his Lord in order to expose the exclusively divine guidance of Paul. The most probable message in the narrative that Luke wants to pass to the reader regarding Paul is in regard to God's providence, which guides those who subordinate themselves to the Lord. That means Luke's exposition of Paul in Acts serves as a kind of definition by example for the term *the witness to the resurrected Messiah.* Concerning this aspect, Luke's presentation of Paul in Acts may be possibly evaluated as completed and finished because the author provides a sufficient number of examples that show to the reader how a witness to the Lord should exercise his election. However, concerning the presentation of Paul itself, the exposition Luke provided in Acts must be recognized as unfinished because although Luke wrote the story several years after Paul's death, he ended the presentation of Paul at the most intriguing moment of Paul's life without leaving any clue regarding a reason for it.[697]

[697] For a proposition concerning the reason, cf. P. W. Walaskay, *And so we came to Rome*, 18–22.

APPENDIXES

APPENDIX 1.
SAUL'S CONVERSION[698]

In Acts, Luke three times, in different contexts, returns to the event at Damascus (Acts 9:1–19; 22:3–21; 26:12–19), where each account contributes some new aspect regarding the event.[699] The event, in a direct or an indirect way, is also mention in primary sources, that are the letters recognized as Paul's writings (Gal. 1:15–17, 22–24; Phil. 3:6–7), as well as in writings in which Paul's authorship is discussed (Eph. 3:1–3; 1 Tim. 1:12–16). The narratives of the event in Acts contain some literary and theological disagreements that should not be taken as the reason for doubting the historical credibility of the event; rather, it exposes that the interpretation of the event goes through some changes, according to the context in which the accounts are given.[700] The historicity of the event is not the most problematic issue; rather, interpretation of the event is a subject of different opinions that sufficiently change the presentation of Paul. Namely, was the event "the conversion of Saul" or "the appointment

[698] In this appendix, we utilized partly (184–190) modified results of analyses presented in our studies that were published only in a Japanese periodical: J. Kucicki, "Saul of Tarsus, the Man Who became the Apostol Paul," *Nanzan Shingaka* 34 (2010): 143–192.

[699] Despite some differences between these testimonies (cf. Acts 9:7 and Acts 22:9), the historicity of the event itself cannot be doubted, as well as the fact that the event radically changed Saul's life; cf. H. Conzelmann, *Acts of the Apostles*, 72–73.

[700] The arguments concerning the apologetic nature of Acts or the literary and theological form of the testimonies of Acts 9:1–19 are not sufficiently convincing.

of Saul to a special mission"? Since the publishing of Stendahl's study, the issue has become the crucial point in the interpretation of Saul/Paul's life.[701] Because the question is critical for presentation of Luke's perspective on Paul, we will show our analyses of both possible interpretations.

A. Appointment of Saul to a special mission.

According to this thesis, the event at Damascus was not the conversion of Saul; on the contrary, it was his appointment to a particular mission. Stendahl thinks that Saul's experience at Damascus did not result in his change of religion (from Judaism to Christianity), but it caused his new perspective (understanding) of Mosaic Law in aspects regarding a relationship with Gentiles. That means that Saul, in a religious sense, remained a Jew, and as the zealous Jew, he was appointed for the mission to Gentiles, where the main purpose was proclamation of the one God to those who were not Jews. The thesis that Saul, in a religious sense, remained a Jew is sufficiently supported by the number of testimonies found in the New Testament.[702] The statement that Saul remained in Judaism is also self-evident, as Christianity, as a new religion, had not yet separated from Judaism; it was part of Judaism, called sometimes the "sect" or the "Way." Without doubt is also the last statement—that Saul became a missionary to Gentiles. However, in our opinion, each of these statements contains a great portion of generalization (socioreligious perspective), which causes overlooking of personal context of the event (personal consciousness). Saul/Paul remained a Jew (in socioreligious terms), even after the event at Damascus (there is no testimony in the New Testament where such a statement is explicitly exposed), but the change concerns that fact that before the event, he was an opponent of all Jews who

---

[701] K. Stendahl, *Paul among Jews and Gentiles* (Philadelphia: Fortress Press, 1976).

[702] Some of the most important testimonies: Acts 21:17–26; 22:17; 24:14; Romans 11:1.

believed in Christ; after the event, he became, according to Acts 24:14, a member of a Jewish sect called *Christian.*

Saul, after the event at Damascus, became a Jew who believed in Jesus as the resurrected Messiah (Acts 11:26; 26:28), and for this reason, he was identified with the group later called *Judeo-Christian.* Among Jews, at least Palestinian Jews, a rift between those who believed in Jesus and those who did not accept Jesus as the Messiah (Acts 8:1–3; 21:13; 26:9) had begun. However, the coexistence of Judeo-Christian and Judaism continued (even in spite of the persecutions and growing controversies); namely, Jewish Christians kept observing many Jewish habits and gathered together in the Temple (Acts 21:26) and synagogues for praying (Acts 26:11), and some Jews were attracted by the teaching of Jesus's followers. It can be assumed that final separation of the Judeo-Christian from Judaism was not only a matter of faith in Jesus as the Messiah, the persecutions, and the increasing number of Gentiles among Judeo-Christians but also the destruction of the Jerusalem Temple, which played a very important role in connecting the new sect with mainstream Judaism.[703]

After the destruction of the Temple, the remaining link between the new sect and Orthodox Judaism was just the scripture, but Judeo-Christians, searching for their own self-identity, interpreted it in a new way that was not acceptable to mainstream Judaism, which consequently led to enmity and excluding the sect from Judaism. This factor, together with a constantly increasing number of Gentiles among Judeo-Christians, were the most crucial points that slowly separated Judeo-Christians from Judaism, which in the end led to establishing the separate religion called Christianity.

At the time of Saul's conversion, Christianity did not yet exist as an organized religion, but there were already Jews and Gentiles who believed in Jesus as the resurrected Messiah. Saul, as a Jew, Pharisee, and persecutor of Jesus's believers, at Damascus experienced a vision

---

[703] P. Prigent, Upadek Jerozolimy [*La fin de Jerusalem*] (Warsaw: Cyklady, 2003), 79–80; M. Rosik, *Judaizm u poczatkow ery chrzescijanskiej* [*Judaism in the Early Christian Era*] (Wrocław: TUM, 200), 198–201.

that radically changed his views and consequently his life. The experience of the risen Jesus did not replace Saul's Judaic background (upbringing, education, culture, religious regulations, and standards of conduct), but it radically contributed to his reinterpretation of an already possessed cultural and religious background. Saul still continued to pray in the synagogues and the Temple, to read the scripture and other Judaic literature, to interpret the Mosaic Law, and to observe the religious customs (Acts 21:23–26), but after his conversion, all this was intended for a new purpose—to proclaim Jesus as the resurrected Messiah. For Saul, the fact of Jesus's Resurrection became the axiomatic principle for his reinterpretation of the Jewish scriptures, as well as recognition of Jesus's Resurrection as the fulfillment of the Mosaic Law (Rom. 10:4). At the socioreligious level of Palestinian Jews, Saul, as the believer of Jesus, was not accepted by most of his own countrymen and was no longer counted as a trustworthy and faithful Jew (Acts 21:21). In the eyes of Jews, Saul was a traitor and a blasphemer (Acts 9:22–23, 29; 21:28), and this evaluation never has changed.

In this context, the thesis that the event at Damascus was a call for a special mission among Gentiles meets several difficulties. The first account regarding the event at Damascus (Acts 9:1–9) does not contain the direct missionary order addressed to Saul. The statement concerning designation of Saul for a mission to Gentiles is a part of dialogue between Jesus and Ananias, and it functions as an argument that has to convince Ananias to undertake an action required by Jesus (Acts 9:13–16). According to a second account regarding the event at Damascus (Acts 22:3–21), Saul received a direct mission order to the Gentiles during his praying in the Jerusalem Temple but not during the event itself (Acts 22:17–21). The third account of the event at Damascus includes the missionary mandate (Acts 26:17), but it refers to the mission among the Jews and Gentiles and not only to a mission among Gentiles. In our opinion, all three accounts of the event at Damascus indicate that the main purpose of the event was not directly connected to the special mission to the Gentiles given to Saul by his new Lord. Saul's mission among Gentiles, inspired by Barnabas (Acts 11:25–26), was a result of a new situation in which Saul found himself after his conversion, as well as a result of the mission needs caused by the development of Jesus's messianic movement.

In our opinion, Acts 9:15 is an introductory indicator that has a retrospective and apologetic character, and it exposes the Lucan narrative strategy, where the topic of the following narration is previously mentioned. The analysis of Acts relating to the relationship between Saul and his opponents (Acts 9:20–23, 29), as well as between Paul and the disciples of Jesus (Acts 9:26–27, 30), after his conversion proves that Saul's mission in Jerusalem (Judea) was controversial and problematic, which naturally makes the mission to the Gentiles the only option left.

B. The conversion of Saul

The scholars accepting the thesis that the event at Damascus should be interpreted as the call to a special mission among Gentiles but not as Saul's conversion argue that Saul has not changed his religion, and, as a zealous Jew, he spreads the idea of the one God among Gentiles. The main problem of this thesis concerns understanding of the term *conversion.*[704] Stendhal and his supporters take the socioreligious and confessional meaning of the term, assuming that the conversion requires a change of religion or confession. The event at Damascus should not be interpreted in these categories; rather, the semantic meaning of the term should be fully exposed. Indeed, the socioreligious understanding of the term *conversion* may require discontinuity (putting an end to the practice of one religion and embracing the practices of another). In Saul's case, however, there is no discontinuity of practicing Judaism (abandonment of Judaism);

[704] We left without comment the fact that Saul/Paul mainly proclaimed the kerygma about Jesus, the resurrected Messiah, and the teaching regarding the monotheistic concept of God was just a necessary preparation before he presented the kerygma (Acts 14:15–17; 17:22–31).

rather, there is a reinterpretation of Judaism caused by acceptance of Jesus of Nazareth as the resurrected Messiah, which means that Jesus is a fulfillment of promises given by God to Israel by the Law and the scriptures.[705]

The event at Damascus did not change Saul's religion, but it definitely changed his faith.[706] Saul's faith in Jesus as the resurrected Messiah was a reason for his rejection as a faithful Jew and his formal accusation of derogation of the faith (Acts 18:13; 21:21, 28; 24:5–6). Saul, who always saw himself as a Jew (in the religious and social sense), evaluated the rejection of Jesus as the Messiah by many of his countrymen as an error. However, his belief in the realization of the God's promise for Israel allowed him to interpret this error as being part of God's plan of salvation (Rom. 11).[707] The entire eleventh chapter of the letter to the Romans reveals that, for Saul, acceptance of Jesus as the resurrected Messiah was not an act of abandonment of Jewish religious identity; he realized it as a fulfillment of the Jewish religion, which brought a chance for salvation to Gentiles, and in the future, it would also bring it to all Jews (Rom. 11:25–26).[708] Saul himself did not think that because of his faith in Jesus, he no longer was a Jew (in the socioreligious sense); on the contrary, there were Jews who thought that because of his conviction, he should no longer be considered as an Orthodox Jew.

In the case of Saul and the first generation of Jewish-Christians, the faith in Jesus as the resurrected Messiah did not mean changing of religion because Christianity as an independent religion was in an

[705] "Christ is the end of the law so that there may be righteousness for everyone who believes" (Rom. 10:4).

[706] Saul, who before the event was a persecutor of Jesus's believers, was baptized after his conversion in the name of Jesus, and he believed and preached that Jesus is the resurrected Messiah (Acts 9:18; 22:16).

[707] "I ask then: Did God reject his people? By no means! I am an Israelite myself, a descendant of Abraham, from the tribe of Benjamin" (Rom. 11:1).

[708] Saul proclaimed Jesus as the Messiah and the fulfillment of the messianic hope of Judaism.

embryonic stage.[709] For this reason, interpreting the event at Damascus as a conversion in the socioreligious sense seems unjustified. The event at Damascus should be interpreted as a Saul's conversion but understood according to the Greek meaning of the term μετάνοια (a *change of mind*).[710] Before the event at Damascus, Saul was faithfully serving God—a zealous Pharisee convinced of the necessity of confronting the new Jewish sect, which was declaring a controversial and crucified teacher, Jesus of Nazareth, as the resurrected Messiah. His conviction was accompanied by strong feelings of hatred and a desire for destruction of the sect, which took the shape of severe persecution of the Way. The event at Damascus, in its consequences, changed Saul the persecutor into Saul the believer, which is hardly due to his own action, as Luke gives all credits to Jesus. His belief in Jesus as the resurrected Messiah changed his thinking, convictions, attitude, understanding, and interpretation of Judaism, as well as his system of values. However, he did not change religions. In Saul's case, that was μετάνοια in its full meaning. The event at Damascus is therefore a conversion of Saul from a Jew who does not believe in Jesus as the Messiah into a Jew who does believe in Jesus as the resurrected Messiah. Saul remained a Jew (in the socioreligious sense) but a Jew belonging to "a remnant chosen by grace," who recognized the Messiah in Jesus (Rom. 11:5).[711] In our opinion, Luke

---

[709] In our opinion, this statement does not mean that Christianity is a Judaic religion. It means that the Christian religion initially developed within Judaism (the period of Judeo-Christianity).

[710] The term μετάνοια is not used in the narrative regarding the event at Damascus (the conversion of Saul). In Acts, it appears five times. The term appears in relation to the conversion of Israel (Acts 5:31; 13:24; 19:4), in relation to Gentiles (Acts 11:18), and in relation to both Israel and Gentiles (Acts 20:21; 26:20). In all cases, the term appears in the context of believing in Jesus as the Messiah.

[711] It is extremely important to accurately identify the group of Jews with whom Paul ranked himself. In many studies, it is stressed that Paul did not change religion (he remained a Jew), but rather he changed from one "sect" to another within Judaism (he became a Christian-Jew); cf. M. Borg and J. D. Crossan, *The First Paul* (New York: Harper On, 2009), 19–27. However, in his letters, Paul ranked himself among the remnant of Israel (Rom. 11:5), whose obligation was to Jesus as the resurrected Messiah in order that the all Jews would believe in him

did not intend the narrative of the event at Damascus to be interpreted in socioreligious terms but in accordance with the Greek meaning of the term μετάνοια.

(Rom. 11:11–12). For this reason, concerning Saul/Paul, the name *Judeo-Christian* is a more accurate description of the group of the first generation of Jesus's believers to whom he belongs. However, considering that Paul preached salvation in name of Jesus also to Gentiles without necessity of circumcision, it seems to be hardly accurate to identify Saul/Paul only with group called "Jewish-Christian."

APPENDIX 2.
SAUL AT DAMASCUS[712]

In Galatians 1:15–18, Paul informs that immediately (εὐθέως) after the event at Damascus, he left for Arabia, and then, after a unspecified period, he (πάλιν) returned to Damascus. The last verse (v. 18) exposes that after three years in Damascus, Saul returned to Jerusalem (Ἔπειτα μετὰ ἔτη τρία ἀνῆλθον εἰς Ἱεροσόλυμα). This information determines a period of Saul's stay in Damascus during AD 34–37, if the year of his conversion was AD 34. More problematic than determining the time spam Saul spent in Damascus is an issue concerning sequences and dates of Saul's activities during his stay at the city. Certain is that Saul left Damascus for Arabia as the same year he came to Damascus (AD 34), but it is impossible to determine the date of his return to Damascus, due to lack of information regarding this issue.[713] There are scholars who think that Saul spent three entire years in Arabia, as Galatians 1:15–18 mentions.[714] This opinion must be rejected because of information provided by Acts 9:23, where

[712] In this appendix, we utilized partly (117–124), in modified way, the results of analyses presented in our studies that were published only in a Japanese periodical: J. Kucicki, "Persona Non Grata? Saul Between Damascus and Antioch," *Academia* 5 (2013): 115–134.

[713] cf. F. F. Bruce, *The Epistle to Galatians* (Grand Rapids: Eerdmans, 2002), 97; E. D. Burton, *The Epistle to the Galatians* (Edinburg: T&T Clark, 1921), 58–59; R. N. Longnecker, *Galatians* (Mexico City, Thomas Nelson, 1990), 37.

[714] J. Eadie, *A Commentary on the Greek Text of Paul's Letter to the Galatians*, (Birmingham, Solid Ground Christian Book, 2005), 50; F. J. Matera, *Galatians* (Collegeville, Sacra Pagina, 2007), 65–66.

Luke directly indicates that Saul, before returning to Jerusalem, spent considerable time (Luke's narrative suggests three years) in Damascus. Some scholars assume that the three years Luke indicates should be counted from Saul's return from Arabia to Damascus.[715] We are of the opinion that Saul's visit to Arabia was not significantly long enough to make a relevant difference in counting the three years from his conversion or from his return to Damascus. We assume this based on the fact that Saul's stay in Arabia is overlooked in Acts 9:20–25, as well as that Galatians 1:17 provides information regarding the visit to Arabia in very general manner, without additional information concerning duration, place, or purpose.[716]

Another problem referring to Saul's visit to Arabia is a place of dueling, since in Greek writings, the name Ἀραβίαν is used to describe the entire region of the Sinai Peninsula, with the exception of Judea and Phoenicia.[717] Although it cannot be verified, it at least should be taken as a proposition of some scholars, assuming that Saul, at that time, visited Mount Sinai (Gal. 4:25).[718] More relevant seems to be the interpretation of Galatians 1:17 as referring to the territory of the Nabatean kingdom, which had not yet expanded to the territory of Damascus. Those scholars who accept a mission purpose of Saul's visit to Arabia point to Petra, the capital of the kingdom, as the place where Saul stayed. However, those scholars who interpret Saul's visit to Arabia as private visit suggest places situated near Damascus. The laconic character of Galatians 1:17 and Luke's overlooking this information permits us to say nothing certain about the place.[719]

---

715 J. Eadie, *A Commentary on the Greek Text*, 49.

716 Campbell strongly opts for Saul's mission in the Nabatean region. D. A. Campbell, *Paul. An Apostle's Journey* (Grand Rapids, Eerdmans 2018), 25–29.

717 E. D. Burton, *The Epistle to Galatians*, 57.

718 R. N. Longenecker, *Galatians*, 34.

719 The fact that Galatians 1:17–18 provides only laconic information concerning Saul's visit to Arabia, and any precise information regarding Saul's stay at Damascus may be explained by the character and purpose of Paul's testimony, which was apologetic in nature. Since the text takes an apologetic character, only single information—proving that the origin of the Gospel of Paul comes from

The last issue regarding Saul's visit to Arabia concerns the purpose of visiting Arabia. Based on the fact that information regarding Saul's visit to Arabia (Gal. 1:17) is placed after a statement regarding Paul's identity as the apostle of the Gentiles, the majority of scholars accept the thesis that the purpose of the Saul's visit to Arabia was the mission activities.[720] The statement regarding Paul's identity as the apostle of nations (Gal. 1:15–17) exposes, in a very general manner, Paul's self-identity, presented in context of a purpose for his conversion but not necessarily in the context of his mission activities, as his apology regards the issue of his independence from the twelve.[721]

Another argument that supported the mission purpose of Saul's visit to Arabia is information shown in 2 Corinthians 11:32–33, which often is linked to the information from Galatians 1:17, and consequently creates the thesis that Saul's activities in Arabia were a direct reason for his persecution in the city (Acts 9:23–25).[722]

Jesus and not from any human authorities—is included in his writing, without being broadly elaborated. The main focus of Paul's apology concerns a short account of Saul's life from the time of his conversion, and it does not include the account of his mission activities. Fortunately, the narrative concerning Saul's stay and activities at Damascus are provided in Luke's narratives (Acts 9:1–25; 22:2–21; 26:12–19), which, however, does not include information concerning Saul's visit to Arabia, and for this reason, it makes Galatians 1:17–18 the only valuable source.

[720] W. Rakocy, *Paweł Apostoł* [Paul the Apostle], 52–53.

[721] Lucan narrative (Acts 9:10–19) exposes that the mission purpose of Saul's conversion was revealed by the Lord to Ananias but not yet to Saul himself. The second Lucan narrative (Acts 22:3–21), given by Paul to the Jews in the Temple, exposes that specification of Saul's mission (mission to Gentiles) occurred not in Damascus but in Jerusalem (three years later) during the Saul's vision of the Lord in the Temple (Acts 22:18–21). The account proves that during a period at Damascus, Saul's mission activities had a rather general character (all people) for that particular mission to Gentiles. The similar meaning takes the third account of the event (Acts 26:12–19), which underlines the general character of Saul's mission activities. Although in Acts 26:17–18, Gentiles are mentioned together with Jews, in a quotation from Jeremiah 1:5–9 and Isaiah 42:7,16, the account still takes the general character.

[722] J. Murphy-O'Connor, *Paul. A Critical Life*, 81–85; W. Rakocy, *Paweł Apostoł*, 51–54.

However, 2 Corinthians 11:32–33 does not mention the governor or King Aretas as the initiator of Saul's persecution; rather, it indicates a time when the action against Saul was undertaken by Jews from Damascus (Acts 9:23–25).[723] The simple reason for the governor's action could be disturbances among the citizens of Damascus, caused by Saul's activities not being accepted by Jews in the city, rather than his mission activities in Arabia, three years earlier.[724]

Very often, it is assumed that Saul/Paul as the missionary of the Gentiles must, after his conversion, immediately proclaim the Gospel to Gentiles (and it regards also the visit in Arabia).[725] Although it is attested by Acts 9:20 that Saul immediately, after his conversion, started to share his personal experience and proclaim Jesus as Son of God to Jews living in the city, there is no proof in the New Testament that he did the same in Arabia.[726]

---

[723] It happened, most probably, in AD 37–39, when King Aretas (king of the Nabadean kingdom) ruled Damascus for a short time. M. J. Harris, *The Second Epistle to the Corinthians* (Grand Rapids: Eerdmans, 2005), 820–823.

[724] It is highly probable that the action of the city's authority against Saul was undertaken on the direct request of some Jews from Damascus. This supposition may be attested by Acts 9:23–25. If the opposition against Saul was not caused by Jews, the accounts of Acts 9:13–35 and 2 Corinthians 11:32–33 disagreed.

[725] Many theories concerning Saul's activities in Damascus are influenced more by a general picture of Paul as the apostle to Gentiles than by the information provided by available sources. This approach leads to a semi-axiomatic statement that from the very beginning, Saul (after his conversion) was a missionary to Gentiles, which makes no difference between Saul and Paul. We are of the opinion that it takes Saul (zealous neophyte) a considerably long time to become Paul (the apostle to Gentiles). The event at Damascus was only an initiatory (however, the most important) event in the process of Saul's transformation, but it did not change Saul into Paul from day to day. Before the transformation would be completed, Saul had too many things to learn, where one of crucial importance was proclaiming the kerygma first to Jews (Acts 9:20, 29; 13:5) and, at the same time, also to the Gentiles.

[726] We would like to present a reason for our skepticism of the theory of Saul's mission activities in Arabia. First, Paul, with exception of Galatians 1:17–18, never directly said anything about this mission in his other letters. Second, Paul's modus operandi, not only at the beginning but also during his mission journeys, was to proclaim the kerygma to Jews in the synagogue by interpreting the scripture in a

Saul was in his mid-twenties when he went to Damascus.[727] During his years in Jerusalem, he was accurately educated in the Mosaic Law by well-known teacher Gamaliel (Acts 22:3). He was the young member of the Pharisees (Phil. 3:5), where he earned the reputation of being a zealous Jew (Acts 26:9; Gal. 1:22; Phil. 3:4–5). Most probably, his activities as the persecutor of the new messianic sect earned him the trust of religious authorities in Jerusalem (Acts 9:1–2; 22:4–5; Gal. 26:10–12), which possibly could have been a promising start for the career of this young person with an already shaped mind and deep convictions regarding religious identity (Acts 26:9).[728]

The event at Damascus is mentioned both in the primary sources (Gal. 1:15–17, 22–24) and three times in the secondary sources (Acts 9:1–19; 22:3–21; 26:12–19). These two sources are complementary (despite some differences), as the testimony of Galatians provides information concerning the chronology of Saul's life in Damascus (with little narrative regarding Saul's social situation after his conversion). Luke, in three different accounts (Acts 9:1–19; 22:3–21; 26:12–19), provides information concerning Saul's socioreligious activities after his conversion.

The narrative of Acts 9:1–19 indicates that before Saul entered

---

way that attested the statement that Jesus is the Messiah. It should be recognized as likely possible that Saul's mission activities were addressed to Jews living in Arabia; even more doubtful is Saul's mission to the Gentiles of Arabia. Third, Saul never again visited Arabia, and there is no mention of his mission activities again in this region, which suggests that Arabia was a single occurrence related to Saul's life, rather than to his mission activities. Fourth, Galatians 1:17–18 highlights Saul's activity after his conversion as his private action, in order to prove one of the main theses of Galatians, which is Paul's independence from the twelve. However, concerning the following accounts of Acts 9:26–31 and Galatians 1:18–24, it is unlikely that Saul immediately, after his conversion, was fully independent in his mission activities.

727 Concerning the chronology, we accept that Saul was born around AD 8 (during AD 6–12) and the event at Damascus happened around AD 34 (AD 33–35).

728 Due to his age, it is rather unlikely that Saul, during his activities as the persecutor in Jerusalem, was a member of the Sanhedrin. For a different opinion, cf. J. Murphy-O'Connor, *Paul. A Critical Life*, 65–70.

Damascus to continue his persecution activities, he was defeated by Jesus (Acts 9:3–6). It affected the manner in which he entered Damascus—he was no longer the young and powerful man on his quest (Acts 9:2); he was led by his companions as the blind and weak young man who needed assistance (Acts 9:7–9).

According to the Luke's account, Saul received the assistance from the community of Jesus's believers (represented by one of the members, named Ananias), after direct intervention of Jesus. He was the main initiator of the relationship between Saul and the community (Acts 9:10), as an argument between Jesus and Ananias (Acts 9:10–16) exposed Ananias's kind of resistance, caused by his extensive knowledge of Saul's activities in Jerusalem and even his purpose for coming to Damascus, as well as his lack of information regarding Saul's actual situation.[729] Jesus's explanation concerning a future purpose of Saul's conversion (Acts 9:15–16) made Ananias more flexible as Jesus's tool in the process of Saul's transformation (Acts 9:17–18). This account, shaped in a highly theologized manner (the revelation and divine intervention), indicates the problem of accepting Saul (at least initially) among Jesus's believers in Damascus.[730]

Saul's stay in Damascus is presented extensively in Acts 9:19–25, where the main focus concentrates on his mission activities among Jews in this city (Acts 9:20, 22–24).[731] Verse 20 and verses 22–24 refer

---

729 The second testimony (Acts 22:3–21) appears in Paul's speech to the Jews, given in the Jerusalem Temple, during the time of his arrest. In general terms, the testimony gives the same information about the event at Damascus (Acts 22:6–11) and his encounter with Ananias (Acts 22:12–16), but it is not free from some differences in details, compared to Acts 9:3–19. The third testimony (Acts 26:12–19) gives simple information regarding the event at Damascus, where the main concern regards the revelation of Jesus in the Jerusalem Temple.

730 According to Luke's account (Acts 9:9, 19) the process of Saul's integration within the community of Jesus's followers in Damascus took no longer than three days, and during those days, Ananias was convinced by Jesus; then Ananias was healed and convinced Saul in order to baptize him, which should be taken as the end of the event of Saul's conversion.

731 Contrary to Galatians 1:17–18, Lucan narrative does not mention Saul's visit to Arabia.

to Saul's same mission activities.[732] According to Luke's narrative, after his conversion, Saul spent some time with the community in Damascus (v. 19b) before he started his mission activities among the Jews in Damascus, proclaiming, in synagogues, Jesus as the Son of God (v. 21).[733] His activities greatly confused the local Jewish community (vv. 21–22), which resulted with in their plot against Saul, which forced him to escape from the city (vv. 23–25).[734] The last information gives an impression that Saul's first mission activities in Damascus hardly can be counted as a success.[735]

Concerning the relationship between Saul and Jesus's believers in Damascus, the accounts of Galatians 1:15–17, 22–24 and Acts 26:12–19 do not provide information. Two other accounts from Acts (Acts 9:1–25; 22:3–21) contain information regarding this issue. Acts 22:3–21 concerns Ananias, who acts as a messenger of God's will to Saul (Acts 22:12–15), and in the end, he probably baptized Saul (Acts 22:16). There is the only information regarding the relationship between Saul and the Damascus community, which is provided in Acts 22:3–21. The basic account that provides the majority of information about this relationship is Acts 9:1–25. First, Acts 9:10–16 presents Ananias as a person who represents the community at Damascus, who was the first to contact Saul,

---

[732] Some theories claim that v. 20 refers to Saul's mission activities in Damascus before his visit to Arabia, but vv. 22–24 refer to his activities in Damascus after visiting Arabia. F. F. Bruce, *The Book of the Acts*, 190.

[733] Luke shows that the action was Saul's private initiative.

[734] The term *disciples* in Acts 9:25 indicates Jesus's followers in Damascus, rather than the Saul's disciples (new Jewish converts). E. J. Schnabel, *Acts. Exegetical Commentary on the New Testament*, 455. The Acts of the Apostles describes the period of Saul's stay at Damascus as "after many days had gone by" (Acts 9:23 NIV), which is a rather undefined description. It can, however, be determined more precisely if the information of Galatians 1:19 (three years) is considered.

[735] Regarding other accounts: Acts 22:3–21 does not mention Saul's mission activities at Damascus; and Acts 26:12–19 indicates Damascus as a place of his activities, but it does not provide details. Additionally, Acts 26:12–19 informs us that Saul proclaimed the Gospel also in Jerusalem and in all of Judea, information that seems in opposition to Galatians 1:22, where Paul says that he was not known to Jesus's followers in Judea.

due to Jesus's revelation that he had received (Acts 9:11–17); this directly shows that it was not his initiative.[736] The second item of information provided by Acts 9:17–19 indicates that Saul's temporary blindness was cured during Ananias's visit, and he also baptized Saul immediately after healing him (v. 18). The third item of information (Acts 9:20) regards the fact that after baptism, Saul spent a short time within the community of Jesus's followers, which most probably refers to the house of Ananias. The fourth item of information (vv. 20–22) concerns Saul's activities in the city, paying little attention to the issue of Saul's relationship with members of the community, which results in the fact that almost nothing certain can be said about the three-year relationship between Saul and the people who were hosting him.[737] The fifth item of information (Acts 9:23–25) regards Saul, who, due to his mission activities, found himself in conflict with the Jews, and at the time of his distress, he received assistance from the Damascus believers, who made possible his escape from the city. This last information is actually the only cooperation between Saul and the community mentioned in Luke's narrative.[738] The fact that the cooperation between Saul and the community is mentioned only at the beginning (Acts 9:20) and at the end of the account

---

[736] The argument between Ananias and Jesus suggests that Ananias, during the revelation, for the very first time heard about Saul's conversion (vv. 13–14), and only Jesus's words convinced him to trust the information concerning the Saul's conversion (v. 17).

[737] According to Acts 9:1–28; 22:12, 16, Ananias is the only member of the Damascus community who is mentioned by name. The reason for that may be his important role in Saul's transformation process after the conversion. There is no direct mention regarding cooperation concerning the mission activities in the city between Saul and members of the Damascus community, which suggests the individual character of Saul's activities in the city.

[738] There is a lack of information regarding the subject of Saul's decision. The narrative suggests that it was Saul's decision. There is also no information concerning the consequences for the Damascus community regarding the Saul's disturbing activities among Jews in the city. Again, the narrative suggests that Saul's activities caused no trouble at all for the community (v. 34).

(Acts 9:25) opens the possibility of two different conclusions: occasional cooperation of both sides (Saul's independence from the community) or constant cooperation between them (Saul's cooperation with the community).

APPENDIX 3.
SAUL IN JERUSALEM (ACTS 9:26–30)[739]

Concerning the chronology of Saul's first visit to Jerusalem after his conversion, if Saul's conversion occurred in AD 34, and three years passed before Saul was forced to leave, and he headed for Jerusalem, the date of his visit to Jerusalem could be around AD 37.[740] Although the date is not entirely certain, it gives a basis for recreating Saul/Paul's chronology. Concerning the Saul's visit to Jerusalem, the first problem concerns the length of Saul's stay in the city, as valuable sources give different impressions regarding the time span.[741] The primary source of Galatians 1:18–19 informs us that Saul stayed in Peter's house for only fifteen days, which gives the impression that Saul's stay in Jerusalem was short; this statement has much in common with Paul's main thesis—that he has not learned the

---

[739] In this appendix, we utilized partly (124–128), in a modified way, the results of analyses presented in our studies that were published only in a Japanese periodical: J. Kucicki, "Persona Non Grata? Saul between Damascus and Antioch," *Academia* 5 (2013): 115–134.

[740] The date of Saul's visit to Jerusalem after his conversion depends on the date of Saul's conversion. However, the second date is also determined with a considerable percentage of probability, due to its dependence on the date of Jesus's crucifixion.

[741] Scholars who recreate Paul's chronology point to autumn AD 37 as the time of Saul's visit to Jerusalem, but they usually do not specify the length of the visit. J. Murphy-O'Connor, *Paul*, 90–95; W. Rakocy, *Paweł Apostoł*, 62–63.

Gospel from the apostles (Peter and Jacob).[742] Unfortunately, the Lucan account of Saul's visit to Jerusalem (Acts 9:26–30) gives the impression that the visit was longer than two weeks. The impression is cause by the range of events Luke mentioned; he first shows Saul's problem as accepted by the community and the apostles (Acts 9:26), and then he indicates that it was possibly due to the assistance that Barnabas gave Saul (Acts 9:27). When the problem with relationship between the Jerusalem community and Saul was solved to some extent, Saul started to proclaim the kerygma in the city (Acts 9:28), which, in the end, finally provoked some Diaspora Jews, who took severe action against him (Acts 9:29). As presented by Luke, Saul's stay in Jerusalem, with little doubt, requires a time span of longer than two weeks.

The sources (Acts 9:26–30; 22:17–21; 26:20; Gal. 1:18–22) attest that after escaping from Damascus, Saul went directly to Jerusalem.[743] Although the sources differ, each of them contributed some new information, which allows us to recreate, to some extent, a coherent picture of Saul's stay in Jerusalem. Luke's testimony from Acts 9:26–30 begins the account by pointing directly to the difficulties Saul met in joining the apostles and the community (v. 26). The main obstacles to accepting Saul was that the community was suspicious, which Luke describes as, "They were all afraid of him, not believing that he really was a disciple" (Acts 9:26 NIV). The information shows that for a three-year stay in Damascus, Saul probably established himself as a trustworthy convert for the community in Damascus, but none of this was known to the apostles in Jerusalem, at least not to the level that allowed them to recognize and accept Saul as a trustworthy convert. Indirectly, the information also indicates that the community

---

[742] Saul could have met Jacob during his stay at Peter's house, or he could have done it on another occasion.

[743] The fact that Saul went directly to Jerusalem exposes that he had a rather limited possibility concerning the place to escape, since it was rather unlikely that he was unaware of the problems waiting for him in Jerusalem, relating to his relationship with Jesus's disciples, as well as with Jewish authorities; cf. F. F. Bruce, *The Book of the Acts*, 193.

in Damascus did not support Saul by sending a recommendation to Jerusalem, neither during Saul's stay in Damascus nor during his escape from the city.

For a significant period, Saul made constant effort to contact the disciples in Jerusalem but with little if any success.[744] Finally, his attempts brought a positive result; then Barnabas crossed the line by assisting Saul in the initial process of integration with community, which is the attitude that raised a question regarding Barnabas's motivation. Did he do it because his character (Acts 4:36–37) or, as some scholars suggest, because before Barnabas met Saul in Jerusalem, he was acquainted with him?[745] The second supposition must be taken as hypothetical, as there is no evidence in the New Testament to support it. It leaves us with the only possibility—that Barnabas's attitude was influenced by his character—which is supported by the fact that his name was changed from Joseph to Barnabas, which means "son of encouragement" (Acts 4:36 NIV), as well as that he consequently became Saul's first mentor, preparing him to fulfill the task given to him by the Lord.[746] It makes Barnabas not only the first one who gave Saul assistance but also the first one who recognized Saul's potential. This supposition may be supported later by Barnabas's attitude in Antioch, where he accepted Saul as his valuable and capable coworker for activities within the mixed community (Acts 11:25–26).[747]

---

[744] The term ἐπείραζεν (*he tried*—indicative imperfect active) indicates constant action without achieving the aim.

[745] F. F. Bruce, *The Acts of the Apostles*, 243.

[746] The real name of Barnabas was Joseph, the Diaspora Jew from Cyprus, from the tribe of Levi (Acts 4:36). According to Colossians 4:10, he was a cousin of the evangelist Mark. He sold his possessions in Cyprus and brought the entire payment to the apostles (Acts 4:37). He earned sufficient esteem within the community, which entrusted him with the mission of the Jerusalem church at Antioch (Acts 11:22–24; 13:1). He earned the opinion that "He was a good man, full of the Holy Spirit and faith" (Acts 11:24 NIV). P. C. Bosak, *Postacie Biblii II* [The People of the Bible II] (Pelplin: Bernardinum, 2001), 110–115.

[747] Concerning Luke's narrative strategy, the information in Acts 9:27–28 can take the function of connecting two agents, persons who, in following narration, will

Luke's narration presents Barnabas as Saul's mediator with the apostles (Acts 9:27), who, judging from the result, accurately presents to the still-very-suspicious community the controversial issue in a way that finally earned their trust (Acts 9:28).[748] Acts 9:28 indicates that Saul was allowed to join and stay with community, but also that as a member of the community, he was free to undertake the mission activities in the city.[749] Regarding these mission activities, Luke's narrative provides some interesting information—the first item concerns Saul's manner of spreading the kerygma: "παρρησιαζόμενος ἐν τῷ ὀνόματι τοῦ κυρίου [speaking boldly in the name of the Lord]" (Acts 9:28 NIV). It shows that Saul, in an uncompromised way, without hesitation or fear, proclaims the kerygma to those who possibly could know him for his activities as a persecutor. The information that Saul was speaking in a bold manner may correlate with the information of Acts 9:20–22, where Saul's mission activities in Damascus are presented in a fashion that suggests an uncompromised attitude.[750] Both accounts underline the neophyte's zeal as the reason for Saul's actions. Saul's mission activities in Jerusalem was carried "in the name of the Lord" (Acts 9:28 NIV), which is the expression that may indicate some degree of

became the main heroes of the narrative (Acts 11:22–30; 13:1–14:28). Worthy of notice is the fact that Luke, in Acts 9:26–30, uses no other names.

[748] The account of Acts 9:26–30 differs from Paul's own account in Galatians 1:18–24, and for this reason, some scholars insist that Acts 9:26–30 and Galatians 1:18–24 should not be assimilated; cf. H. Conzelmann, *Acts of the Apostles*, 75.

[749] L. T. Johnson, *The Acts of the Apostles*, 172.

[750] Concerning the mission activities at Damascus: "speaking boldly in the name of Jesus" (Acts 9:27 NIV). Concerning the mission activities in Jerusalem: he was "speaking boldly in the name of the Lord" (Acts 9:8 NIV). Although the two phrases are not identical, the similarities between them are striking. Because of that, it seems to be attested to draw a conclusion concerning the topic of Saul's teaching in Jerusalem, where the topic of Saul's teaching is not directly mentioned by Luke, based on the topic of Saul's teaching at Damascus, which is determined by Luke as "Jesus is the Son of God" (Acts 9:20 NIV) and "Jesus is the Messiah" (Acts 9:22 NIV).

authority.[751] In Luke's narrative regarding Saul's visit to Jerusalem, there is no sign suggesting that Saul received such authority from the apostles, which indicates that this information is in accordance with Paul's statement presented in Galatians 1:12–13.[752] That means that Luke refers here to the revelation of Jesus to Saul on the road to Damascus, connecting it with Saul's designation for the mission to the Gentiles, even if, according to Acts 9:1–19, such an order was not given directly to Saul by Jesus.[753]

The second item of information in the narrative regarding Saul's activities in Jerusalem concerns those to whom he addressed the kerygma. The narrative informs: "He [Saul] talked and debated with the Hellenistic Jews" (Acts 9:29 NIV), where the term *the Hellenistic Jews* refers to Greek-speaking Jews, who, in Jerusalem, were gathering in the synagogue mentioned in Acts 6:9.[754] This synagogue may be the same as is included in the Theodotus Inscription, which attested to an existence of the Hellenistic Jews' synagogue in Jerusalem before the Jewish-Roman wars.[755] In this case, Luke, indirectly but consciously,

---

[751] F. F. Bruce, *The Acts of the Apostles*, 243–244; E. J. Schnabel, *Acts. Exegetical Commentary on the New Testament*, 163.

[752] Similar to presentation of Saul's activities of at Damascus, his activities in Jerusalem also had an individual character, where the cooperation work is not mentioned. Acts 9:28–29 does not allow, in our opinion, for drawing a conclusion that Saul joined the apostles in their mission work in Jerusalem, although Acts 9:28 strongly suggests it; rather, he was allowed to do his own mission, which is the supposition attested by Acts 9:29 and testimony of Galatians 1:22. For a different opinion, cf. E. J. Schnabel, *Acts. Exegetical Commentary on the New Testament*, 457.

[753] The narrative of Acts 9:27–30 may support the account of Galatians 1:12–20 concerning independence of the Gospel proclaimed by Paul from the authority of the apostles, as no information regarding the apostles' influence on Saul's kerygma is provided.

[754] Some scholars doubt the existence of the synagogue in Jerusalem in the first century AD; cf. H. H. Keen, "Early Christianity in the Galilee: Reassessing the Evidence from the Gospels," in *The Galilee in Late Antiquity*, ed. L. I. Levine (New York: Jewish Theological Seminary of America, 1992), 3–32.

[755] The stony tablet (75/41 cm) was discovered in 1913 by R. Weill, on the southeast hill of Old Jerusalem. It contains an inscription in Greek, which mentions the name of Theodotus, the son of the archisynagogos, who built the synagogue in

links the information from Acts 9:29 with the narrative regarding the martyrdom of Stephen (Acts 6:8–9), during which Luke, for the very first time, introduces the person of Saul (Acts 7:58; 8:1). Lucan Saul, after his conversion, during his first visit to Jerusalem, proclaimed the kerygma to the Hellenistic Jews in the place (the Synagogue of Freedmen) where his own activities as a persecutor had started.[756] Lucan narration concerning the persecution of Jesus's believers in Jerusalem and Judea, in which Lucan Saul played a critical part, makes a circle, which starts with Saul's opposition to Stephen's mission activities among the Hellenistic Jews (Acts 6:8–8:1), and ends with Saul's mission activities addressed to the same group in the same place (Acts 9:29–30).[757]

The third item of information concerns Saul's mission's modus operandi and the effects of his activities. The modus operandi in Jerusalem (Acts 9:29) was similar to that used in Damascus (Acts 9:20). Saul used to enter the synagogue where he would κηρύσσω (*proclaim*) (at Damascus), λαλέω (*speak*, *talk*) and συζητέω (*argue*, *discuss*) (in Jerusalem). The place of Saul's teaching shows that the main target of Saul's activities was Hellenistic Jews, those with whom Saul most probably associated before his conversion.[758] This modus operandi, which here means "first, mission to Jews," became Saul's standard mission attitude that did not change until the end of his mission activities (Acts 17:2).

Another similarity between Saul's mission in Jerusalem and in Damascus are the results (consequences) of his activities. Luke's narrative, in both cases, does mention directly no mission successes,

---

Jerusalem for the Jews from the Diaspora. R. Bauckhan, *The Book of Acts in Its First-Century Setting. Palestinian Setting*, vol. 4 (Grand Rapids: Eerdmans, 1995), 192–200, 204–206.

[756] It is highly possible that in Jerusalem, Saul was associated with the Synagogue of Freedmen, since he was a Jew from Tarsus in Cilicia, who also spoke Greek.

[757] Lucan narration exposes the possibly high influence of this literary and theological concept that determined his interpretation of the sources.

[758] It is worthy to underline that Luke distinguished between Saul's activities at Damascus, where he taught that "Jesus is the Son of God" (Acts 9:20 NIV) and his mission in Jerusalem, where he was arguing with the Hellenistic Jews.

either in Damascus or in Jerusalem. Also, in both cases, Luke directly proceeds with information regarding the opposition and hostile attitude toward Saul undertaken by Jews in both cities, who decided to ἀναιρέω (*take up, do away with, kill*) him. In this way, Luke makes the strong suggestion that in terms of results (earning converts), Saul's activities brought unspectacular success. To the contrary, it brought him the opposition of strongly determined enemies, taking an action that would lead to his death. Most probably, Saul's mission activities and the kerygma he proclaimed offended them and was recognized as dangerous for Judaism, which was the same reason that made Saul, before his conversion, a strongly determined persecutor of the Way. If it was so, Saul's mission activities in Jerusalem, to some extent, could possibly have affected the entire community of Jesus's followers.

Saul found himself in a serious problem with the Jews in Damascus and also with the Jews in Jerusalem, and he was not capable of solving it himself. For this reason, in both cases, the disciples of these cities provided him assistance to run away (Acts 9:24–25, 30). In the case of Damascus, the disciples' assistance concerns helping him to go over the city's walls without indicating a safe place. In case of Jerusalem, however, the disciples not only assisted him to escape from the city but also determined the place (Tarsus) where he should seek safety. Saul's presence in Jerusalem (particularly) and in the region (generally) caused, in general terms, many problems for the believers of Jesus, and this statement concerns both periods of Saul's presence in Jerusalem (the time before his conversion, as well as the time after his conversion), although the kind of problems and results of problems undoubtedly differ.[759] This statement seems

[759] Lucan narration regarding Saul's visit to Jerusalem has a very general character (kind of summary), and it exposes some similarities with the narration concerning the Damascus period. For these reasons, some scholars think that Luke created a narration regarding the visit to Jerusalem based on information concerning Saul's stay at Damascus, due to the lack of historical sources concerning Saul's visit to Jerusalem; cf. F. F. Bruce, *The Book of the Acts*, 194–195; M. Zerwick and M. Grosvenor, *A Grammatical Analysis of the Greek New Testament*, 443–444.

to be attested by Acts 9:31, where Luke presents a fine conclusion of the narrative concerning Saul's persecution of believers in Judea and Samaria (Acts 5:17–9:31), connecting (possibly) a peaceful life of Jesus's believers in Judea, Galilee, and Samaria after Saul's return to Tarsus.

Saul's visit to Jerusalem is attested also by two other accounts found in Acts; the first one is a part of Paul's speech to Jews in the Temple (Acts 22:17–21), and the second is a part of Paul's speech before King Agrippa (Acts 26:20). The second text (Acts 26:20) confirms Saul's activities among the citizens of Damascus and Jerusalem and, in this way, gives credibility to the narrative of Acts 9:19–30. Acts 26:20, however, also includes information regarding Saul's activities in the region of Judea, which cannot be found in Acts 9:19–20.[760] The first text (Acts 22:17–21) confirms the narrative of Acts 9:19–30 regarding Saul's visit to Jerusalem (v. 17) and rejection of his proclaiming by Jews of the city (vv. 18–20). This information, however, is placed in a different context (the revelation in Jerusalem Temple) and is used for apologetic purposes (v. 18).[761]

There are differences between the accounts of Acts regarding Saul's visit to Jerusalem, which can be, to some extent, explained by different contexts, purposes, and audience. The same applies to the only primary source (Gal. 1:17–20) that regards Saul's visit to Jerusalem. Paul's testimony mentioned nothing about his troubles in Damascus, directly showing the purpose of his visit to Jerusalem, which was in regard to his wish to meet Cephas.[762] Concerning the visit itself, Paul underlines that his stay in Peter's place was no longer than fifteen

---

[760] Although this information seems to be contrary to Galatians 1:22, there is a grammatical reason for taking the phrases as a scribe's correction that does not come from Luke (phrases ἐν Δαμασκῷ πρῶτόν and τε καὶ Ἱεροσολύμοις are in dative case, but πᾶσάν τε τὴν χώραν τῆς Ἰουδαίας are in accusative case); cf. L. T. Johnson, *The Acts of the Apostles*, 437; B. Witherington III, *The Acts of the Apostles*, 746. The problem will be discussed below.

[761] In general terms, the narrative of Acts 22:17–21 omits a large amount of information included in the narrative of Acts 9:19–30.

[762] Although the information is not included in the narrative of Acts 9:19–30, it does make it contrary to Gal 1:17–18.

days. Mentioning the short staying in Jerusalem and exposing only an encounter with James instead of the whole twelve disciples, serves Paul's apologetic purpose heading to prove his independence from the apostles and the church in Jerusalem (vv. 18–19). The information concerning Saul's period of staying in Jerusalem is not necessarily opposite the account of Acts 9:26–30, which suggests a longer period of Saul's staying in Jerusalem, because the information (Gal. 1:18) refers only to his stay with Peter, but it does not automatically refer to the entire period of Paul's visit to Jerusalem.

Galatians 1:17–20 also omits information concerning Saul's meeting with Barnabas (who was not an apostle) and his assistance during the difficulty in contacting the disciples (Acts 9:19–30), but Galatians 1:17–20 does not undermine Luke's accounts, as Paul's focus regards his relationship only with apostles. Problematic may be the absence in Galatians 1:17–20 of information regarding Saul's mission activities in Jerusalem (Acts 9:29) and in Judea (Acts 26:20), which are of crucial importance for Lucan narrative purposes but does not serve Paul's purpose well in Galatians 1:17–18. Most probably, the main reason for omitting all the information in Galatians 1:17–20 concerning Saul's mission activities is the main topic of Paul's speech (his relationship with the apostles) and its purpose (Paul's mission mandate does not depend on the apostles). For this reason, Galatians 1:21 also presents Saul's leaving for Cilicia as his own decision and free action (without presenting a reason), although Acts 9:28–30 presents Saul's leaving for Cilicia as the disciples' decision.

Despite the differences between accounts concerning the problem of Saul's mission activities in Judea (Acts 26:20; Gal. 1:17–22), there are two reasons that should prevent us from harshly judging that these testimonies are opposite each other. The first reason is of a grammatical nature, and the second is the Lucan narrative mentioning Saul's mission activities only in Acts 26:20, but he omitted it in accounts of Acts 9:17–30; 22:17–21.[763] Even if in Acts 26:20, the

[763] It must be considered as hardly possible that Acts 26:20 refers to the same event as the narrative of Acts 15:3–4. Some stops made on the way to Jerusalem by the

information is Lucan, the reason for including the region of Judea in Paul's speech was probably caused by the fact that the speech is addressed to King Agrippa.

Due to different purposes of the accounts (Saul's presentation in Acts 9:17–30; and Paul's apology in Galatians 1:17–22) concerning Saul's stay in Jerusalem, both testimonies put attention to different aspects of the event, which naturally makes some information unnecessary or useless for the narrative purpose.

Antioch community and connecting with it, in the reports about the first mission journey, do not mean mission activities in these regions.

APPENDIX 4.
SEVERAL YEARS IN TARSUS[764]

According to the narrative of Acts, after a rather short stay in Jerusalem, Paul has to run away from the city; passing Caesarea, he returns to his hometown of Tarsus, where he lives until the beginning of his work with Barnabas in Antioch. Taking into consideration the ambivalence of chronology regarding Saul's conversion, with considerable probability, Saul left Damascus around AD 37, heading for Jerusalem, where, due to his controversial mission activities among the Diaspora Jews, he spent no longer than a few weeks before he was sent back to Tarsus by the disciples of the Jerusalem community in order to save his life. This year is the beginning of Paul's life sometimes called the "unknown years of Saul," due to the fact that no information regarding this period is provided by Luke in the Acts. The end of the period is connected with the beginning of Saul's mission cooperation with Barnabas in Syrian Antioch, which may be determined by information provided in Acts 11:25–30; 12:25, as well as by nonbiblical historical information concerning King Herod Agrippa I and Imperator Claudius. King Herod Agrippa I ruled the kingdom of Judea from AD 41 to 44, due to the generosity of his close friend Claudius, who also began his reign in AD 41. Luke's narrative regarding the financial support for the Jerusalem community (Acts 11:27–28) cared for by Barnabas and Saul includes information that

[764] In this appendix, we utilized partly (128–131), in a modified way, the results of analyses presented in our studies that were published only in a Japanese periodical: J. Kucicki, "Persona Non Grata? Saul between Damascus and Antioch," 115–134.

the event took place when Claudius was the imperator, which could not happen before AD 41. Other useful information provided by Luke concerns the accomplishment of Barnabas and Saul's support for Jerusalem, which happened after the sudden death of King Agrippa I, and their road back to Antioch (Acts 12:25), which points to the years AD 43–44 as the first year of Saul's cooperation with Barnabas at Syrian Antioch.[765] Lucan narration strongly suggests that Barnabas and Saul did not stay in Jerusalem for long, and the purpose of their visiting Jerusalem could differ or expand from that shown by Luke in Acts 11:30. Luke also indicates that before the short visit in Jerusalem, Barnabas and Saul worked together in Antioch for one year (Acts 11:26), which, with a certain portion of caution, allows us to indicate the year AD 43 as the most probable end of the "unknown years of Saul".

The information that Saul, after he left Jerusalem, returned to Tarsus in Cilicia is provided by two sources—the secondary one in Acts 9:30 and the primary one in Galatians 1:21, where the Lucan account contains more detailed information than Paul's account. Luke indicates the disciples from Jerusalem as the agents who sent Saul through Caesarea to his hometown, Tarsus, in Cilicia, which also shows details concerning the road (Jerusalem, Caesarea, Tarsus) and in an indirect manner, the way of traveling (by ship).[766] Contrary to the information provided by Luke, Paul, in the account of Galatians 1:21, excluded involvement of the disciples from Jerusalem in his leaving Jerusalem for Tarsus, giving the impression that this decision was exclusively his own.[767] Paul also indicates a different road (Syria, Cilicia, and probably finally Tarsus) that suggests that Saul traveled to his hometown using a land road, and during this trip he possibly was involved in kind of mission activities in each of place he was

765 F. F. Bruce, *The Book of the Acts*, 243.

766 The city of Caesarea was the harbor for Jerusalem (Judea) and Seleucia Pieria was the harbor for Tarsus (Cilicia), which suggests that Saul was sent back to Tarsus by ship, much safer and faster travel for him, considering the circumstances; cf. F. F. Bruce, *The Epistle to the Galatians*, 102–103.

767 It is understandable, if the character and purpose of Galatians 1:21 is considered.

passing through, as Galatians 1:22 seems to suggest. Although these observations could be useful for establishing the beginning of what is usually called the "unknown years of Saul," unfortunately, in the New Testament there are no accounts concerning this stage of Saul's life, the span of which can reach seven years.[768] For this reason, a possible reconstruction of this period always remains dependent on a particular perspective of Paul, accepted by each of the scholars. Most probably, those scholars who think of Paul as the apostle of the Gentiles, from the very beginning of his action as a fresh convert, following the Paul's account in Galatians 1:13–24, indirectly doubt the existence of such a period as the "unknown years,"[769] arguing that Saul's period in Tarsus was actually a time of his mission activities in various places.[770]

On the other hand, those scholars who see Paul's life as a paradigm of the life of Saul and the life of Paul, following Luke's account in Acts, think that at this stage of his life, he was hardly involved in mission activities,[771] and in the best case, his activities could be restricted to the regions of Syria and Cilicia, or it did not bring the considerable results that could be important for the presentation of Paul.[772] Concerning the chronology of Paul's life, we usually prefer the account of Acts, despite the fact that in many cases, it has more in common with narrative creativity than with historical accuracy. Nevertheless, in the case of "unknown years," sending Saul to Tarsus by ship (Acts 9:30) and keeping him for years in silence

---

[768] The exception is information from 2 Corinthians 12:2, considering Paul's revelation, which he had fourteen years before he wrote the letter. Considering the date of writing of 2 Corinthians, it is possible that the mentioned revelation could have occurred during the "unknown years of Paul" (AD 40–44); cf. W. Rakocy, *Paweł Apostoł*, 76.

[769] J. Knox, *Chapters in a Life of Paul* (New York: Abingdon-Cokesbury Press, 1950), 74–85; G. Lüdemann, *Paul, Apostle to the Gentiles. Studies in Chronology* (Philadelphia: Fortress Press, 1984), 262–263.

[770] R. E. Osborne, "St. Paul's Silent Years," *JBL* 84 (1965): 59–65.

[771] O. Bauernfeind, *Kommentar und Studien zur Apostelgeschichte* (Tübingen: Mohr Siebeck, 1980), 136.

[772] W. Rakocy, *Paweł Apostoł*, 74.

(Acts 11:25) exposes Luke's approach to recording in Acts events that concern Saul, which are closely related to his perspective on Paul. The argument regarding Luke's lack of knowledge about the period should be recognized as hardly probably; more probable is Luke's evaluation of the period as not significantly important enough for his narrative, which prefers exposition of the picture of Paul before the picture of Saul. The reason for preferring Luke's account before the primary account is that Galatians 1:11–24 is a part of Paul's apologetic speech, heading for attesting his independence and any influence of the Jerusalem community on his kerygma, which makes his testimony concentrated on a particular aim that causes its subjectivity. Even if it is possible that, from the beginning, Tarsus was not a goal of Saul's journey, and before he finally reached his hometown, he visited many places where he occasionally proclaimed the kerygma, it is better not to think about these activities in the category of strategic mission activities, which could take considerable time.[773] Considering a silence in the New Testament regarding Paul's activities in these regions in a later period, it is possible to suppose that even if the mission in these regions took place, it did not bring spectacular success, or Luke, for some reason, consciously omitted it.

Another problem created by Paul's account (Gal. 1:22–23) concerns information that he, until the time of writing the letter to the Galatians, was unknown to communities in Judea.[774] This

---

[773] Saul's return to his hometown was simply forced by circumstances and was undertaken to save his life.

[774] Participle present passive ἀγνοούμενος (*I remained unknown*) indicates a continuance of the state; cf. E. W. Burton, *A Critical and Exegetical Commentary on the Epistle to the Galatians* (Edinburgh: T&T Clark, 1921), 62–64. Since establishing a precise date of writing the letter is highly problematic (according to the South Galatia hypothesis, the earliest year could be AD 47, and according to the North Galatia hypothesis, the latest year could be AD 56), as well as determining the addressers (the South Galatia hypothesis or the North Galatia hypothesis), interpretation of the information from Galatians 1:21–22 will differ, depending on the accepted theory. For the purpose of this study, we accept that the letter to Galatians was written after the event recorded in Galatians 2:1–10 and Acts 15. For more information concerning the letter to Galatians, cf. G.H.

information, coming from a primary source, created some problems, due to the fact that, according to the account in Acts, Saul/Paul visited Jerusalem twice already (Acts 9:26–31; 15:4–12), and his mission cooperation with Barnabas was noticed by believers in Jerusalem and Judea (Gal. 2:3–4). Due to the former context (his visit in Syria and Cilicia) and also to the apologetic character of the letter, the purpose of the section (Gal. 1:11–24) is to indicate that Paul was not dependent in any way on the apostles from Jerusalem.[775] The differences between the two accounts raise the suspicion of some scholars, pointing to the fact that Acts 26:20 and Galatians 1:22 give information concerning the same issue, but they seem to oppose each other.[776] The differences in these two accounts have considerable power only if they are analyzed in the context of their literary meaning, but considering the purpose of each writing and the function of each account's disagreement of details, do not dismiss the general agreement about the places where Saul was heading.

Concerning the account of Acts 26:20, it is important to notice that from a literary approach, Acts 26:20 seems to oppose not only Galatians 1:22 but also to two of Luke's other accounts (Acts 9:26–30; 22:17–21), which do not contain information concerning the mission activities of Saul in the territory of Judea (with the exception of Jerusalem). According to Luke's account, during Paul's interrogation before King Agrippa II, Paul confessed: "First to those in Damascus, then to those in Jerusalem and in all Judea, and then to the Gentiles, I preached that they should repent and turn to God and demonstrate their repentance by their deeds" (Acts 26:20 NIV). The sentence itself is a general outline of Paul's mission activities, containing information attested by the narrative of Acts (mission activities at Damascus, in Jerusalem, and to the Gentiles) and other the New Testament writings. The only information that cannot be attested by

---

Hansen, "Letter to the Galatians," in *Dictionary of Paul and His Letters*, eds. G. F. Hawthorne and R. P. Martin (Leicester: InterVarsity Press, 1993), 323–334.

[775] E. W. Burton, *The Epistle to the Galatians*, 63.

[776] cf. J. Eadie, *A Commentary on the Greek Text of Paul's Letter to the Galatians*, 54–55.

other testimonies in the New Testament regards the statement "and in all Judean" (Acts 26:20 NIV).[777] This fact gives a reason for doubting the historical value of the information, which raises the question of including such information in Lucan Paul's speech. Based on the conclusions concerning the shortness of the narrative regarding Saul's stay in Jerusalem, Luke did not have enough information about this period of Paul's life and, due to circumstances, was forced to create a generalized account, which, even without historical details, would agree with other testimonies found in the New Testament.[778]

The same probably could be said about the account regarding Paul's interrogation before King Agrippa II, during which, beyond a doubt, Luke's was not present, and he did not have access to any kind of record.[779] Although there is no reason to doubt the historical value of the information included in Acts 21:19–26:32, Luke's creative contribution should be considered, at least in the passages that contain Paul's speeches (Acts 22:1–21; 23:1, 6; 24:10–21; 26:2–32). The two most extensive speeches (Acts 22:1–21; 26:2–32) contain information referring to the same events of Paul's life, but they put attention on the different details, which are caused by different functions of the speeches in the narrative regarding Paul's imprisonment. During the speech given to the Jews in the Jerusalem Temple (Acts 22:1–21), Paul mentions the revelation he received in the Temple (Acts 22:17–21), which is an account that is not found in other writings. Similarly, in Acts 26:2–32, Paul, speaking before King Agrippa II, mentioned his mission activities in the region of Judea, which also does not

---

[777] Also, Acts 26:20 does not mention Saul's mission activities in Arabia and the region of Syria and Cilicia.

[778] There is similarity between narrations concerning Saul's activities at Damascus and his activities in Jerusalem.

[779] From Acts 21:27, Luke, in his narration, changed first-person plural (we) to third-person singular (he), which exposes that from this point of the narrative, Luke is not an eyewitness to Paul's activities, until the narrative regarding Paul's voyage to Rome (Acts 27:1) because always, when Luke assisted Paul (Acts 16:10–21:18; 27:1–28:15), he used first-person plural (we) in the narrative. Luke was not with Paul from the moment of his arrest (Acts 21:27) until the beginning of voyage to Rome (Acts 27:1); cf. F. F. Bruce, *The Book of the Acts*, 444.

appear in other accounts. For this reason, this kind of extraordinary information should be explained in the perspective of its function in the narrative in which it is placed, as one pattern Luke used for writing the Acts concerns exposition of certain information, only if it suits the particular narrative and contributes to it with detailed specifications.

In the case of Acts 26:20, the most probable function of the phrase "and in all Judea" (Acts 26:20 NIV) is to indicate the public character and scope of Saul's activities as a part of the messianic movement to which he belongs. This explanation may be attested by an idiomatic expression used in verse 26: οὐ γάρ ἐστιν ἐν γωνίᾳ πεπραγμένον τοῦτο ("because it was not done in a corner") (Acts 26:26 NIV), which in Greek literature is used to stress the public character of an event.[780]

---

[780] B. Witherington III, *The Acts of the Apostles*, 479–450. According to Luke's narration, King Agrippa II knows that the name of the group Paul's belongs to is called Christians (Acts 26:28). "Then Felix, who was well acquainted with the Way" (Acts 24:22 NIV), and Festus knows almost nothing about Jewish religion (Acts 25:19).

APPENDIX 5.
MISSION IN ANTIOCH[781]

In Acts 11:26, Luke directly informs the reader that Saul, together with Barnabas, was involved in mission activities in Antioch for one year. Probably during this period, Saul and Barnabas traveled to Jerusalem with financial support for the community (Acts 11:30; 12:25), and the end of their mission is connected, in Lucan narrative, with the death of King Herod Agrippa I (Acts 12:20–25). After returning to Antioch, Saul and Barnabas went to their mission journey in Cyprus, but the time span between their return from Jerusalem and the beginning of the mission journey cannot be determined due to lack of information.[782] The beginning of Saul's activities in Antioch can be the year AD 44, if King Herod died at the end of year, but if the king died in the middle of AD 44, the beginning of his mission in Antioch could be the first half of AD 43. The second possibility seems more likely.

Concerning this stage of Saul's life, there is no other account outside of Luke's Acts (Acts 11:19–30; 12:25; 13:1–3).[783] The short

---

[781] In this appendix, we utilized partly (131–133), in a modified way, the results of analyses presented in our studies that were published only in a Japanese periodic: J. Kucicki, "Persona Non Grata? Saul between Damascus and Antioch," 115–134.

[782] It is impossible to determine the length of time that passed from their return to Antioch from Jerusalem and the start of their mission journey.

[783] The fact that Saul's mission in Syrian Antioch is not mentioned in Paul's letters, sometimes serves as the argument for doubting the historicity of the Acts. However, considering the fact that in the letter to the Galatians, Paul straggles to proof his independence (concerning his mission mandate and the kerygma

account of Acts 11:19–30 is placed after the narrative regarding Peter's encounter at Cornelius's house (Acts 10:1–11:18), which is the very first account in Acts that concerns the problem of incorporation, among the Jewish Christians, those believers in Jesus who came from the Gentiles. Before Luke gives the account regarding the community in Antioch, he exposes a detailed and precise background of various groups of believers, dueling outside Judea, presenting first a sociohistorical reason for spreading the Gospel outside Jerusalem (Acts 11:19), with an indication of places and a group of addressers.[784] Next, he informs about those who, as a first, proclaimed the kerygma to Gentiles inhabiting Antioch (Acts 11:20),[785] with amplified exposition of their success, which had forced the Jerusalem community to delegate Barnabas to Antioch as the official in order to evaluate the situation in the community that consisted of Jews and Gentiles (Acts 11:22–23).[786]

The positive evaluation of the community and the prospect of greater achievement in the city forced Barnabas to undertake the trip to Tarsus to find Saul and bring him to Antioch for cooperation in spreading the kerygma (Acts 11:25–26). It is most possible, although not shown directly, that Barnabas was convinced of Saul's usefulness

proclaimed by him) from Barnabas, the official delegate of the Jerusalem church working in Syrian Antioch (Acts 11:22), as well as his independence from the twelfth disciples in Jerusalem (Acts 11:23–24), the mentioning of events included in the Acts would work against his claim present in the letter to Galatians. In our opinion, the omission of Saul's activities in Syrian Antioch in the letter to Galatians has a strong and logical explanation, and it does not confirm the unhistorical character of Acts.

784 The city of Antioch is mentioned, but the mission activities in this city seem to be limited only to Jews.

785 All mentioned persons were Diaspora Jews (Cyprus and Cyrene) and none of them was a Jew from Jerusalem or Judea.

786 Concerning this task, Luke informs us, "he [Barnabas] was glad and encouraged them all to remain true to the Lord with all their hearts" (Acts 11:23 NIV). Barnabas was Jew from the Diaspora in Cyprus (Acts 4:36), and those who started to proclaim the Gospel to Gentiles in Antioch also came from Cyprus. The information in verse 24 gives a reason for the statement presented in verse 23, which indicates Barnabas's positive attitude toward the mission to the Gentiles.

for a mission in Antioch, and for that reason, he brought him to the city. The supposition may be attested by the way Luke used four verbs: ἐξῆλθεν (*left for*), ἀναζητῆσαι (*to look for*), εὑρὼν (*he found him*), ἤγαγεν (*he brought him*).[787] The account directly shows Barnabas as the agent who acts freely and authoritatively and Saul as an object of his action. The one-year cooperation with Saul in Antioch (Acts 12:26) proved Barnabas's expectations regarding Saul—the number of new followers of Jesus increased to a considerably large community, possessing their own specific identity, which allowed Gentiles to recognize a distinction between Jews and Christian Jews (Acts 11:26).[788] In the narrative concerning the so-called the first mission journey, Luke informs us that Saul, after the year he spent in Antioch, was counted among others as a prophet and teacher, which amplifies his considerable development during his cooperation with Barnabas (Acts 13:1–3). Luke presents Saul as a man who, for one year, proved himself as a pupil of Barnabas and earned the trust of the community, not only in matters concerning financial assistance to brothers in Jerusalem (Acts 11:30; 12:25) but also in matters concerning a mission of the Antioch community to Diaspora Jews living on Cyprus (Acts 13:3–4). According to Luke's narration, the period of Saul's cooperation with Barnabas in Antioch was a real break for him, in terms of success in proclaiming the kerygma (effects) and his preparation for future mission work (skills). Luke's narrative of Acts 11:19–30 strongly suggests that in Antioch, under Barnabas's supervision, Saul ended his apprenticeship.

[787] There are two important items of information: the first concerns Barnabas as the only member of the Jerusalem community who gave him assistance (Acts 9:27), and second regards the fact that Barnabas was the Diaspora Jew, and Saul was also.

[788] Luke presents Saul's cooperation with Barnabas in Antioch as the very first positively evaluated success of Saul's mission activity, which does not end the troubles for Paul. Notice that the information regarding the fact that in Antioch, for the very first time, Jesus's followers were called Christians, meaning that they were the "different kind of Jews," as distinguished from "normal Jews). The factor that determined the distinction could be the association of Jesus's followers with the Gentiles of the city.

APPENDIX 6.
THE MISSION ON CYPRUS[789]

Luke's account regarding the first mission journey is rather short and schematic, with little information of a geographical, sociological, or cultural nature. Despite the fact that the reader of his writing could not know well the eastern part of the Roman Empire, he provides only names of places visited by Barnabas and Saul, without coherent presentation of the place, which robs his narrative of necessary background that, in some cases, is of crucial importance for full comprehension of the accounts. We will provide more detailed and necessary information regarding the places Barnabas and Saul visited, with hope that it contributes to a more realistic reading of the Luke's account.

1. Antioch in Syria

Our knowledge concerning the city of Antioch comes from ancient writers like Strabo, Evagrius, Procpius, Libanius, Emperor Julian, John Chrysostom, and John Malalas.[790] The ancient sources,

---

[789] In this appendix, we utilized partly (138–18–149), in a modified way, the results of analyses presented in our studies that were published only in a Japanese periodical: J. Kucicki, "Places and People in Luke's Narrative of the Mission Journey of Saul. Socio-narrative interpretation of Acts 13–14," *Nanzan Shingaka* 36 (2013): 135–162.

[790] J. McRay, "Antioch on the Orontes," in *Dictionary of Paul and his Letters*, eds. G. F. Hawthorne and R. P. Martin (Leicester: InterVarsity Press, 1993), 23–25.

however, contain only short information referring to the city, with the exception of *Chronogaphia* by Ioannis Malalae, written in the sixth century AD.[791] The extensive work of Malalae (eighteen volumes) mostly focus on Syrian Antioch, but it is actually a mix of myths, biblical narrations, and historical fact.[792] Because Antioch (today called Antakya) is still an inhabited city, archaeological excavations are very limited, which creates a problem in confirming the ancient sources known to us.

The city of Antioch was established by Seleucus I Nicator in 301 BC and was named after his father, Antiochus from Orestis.[793] Because the city lies on the crossroads between south (Egypt) and north (Syria) and east (Near East) and west (Rome), its strategic location predestined it to become the capital of the Seleucid kingdom (312–63 BC).[794] The city lies between the River Orontes (on the east) and Mount Silpius (on the west), and it is connected by the River Orontes to the sea and its own harbor, Selecia Pereia.[795] In Strabo's *Rerum Geographicarum*, the city was called Tetrapolis due to the fact that the city inside the wall was divided into four parts, according to the classic model of Hellenistic cities.[796] The city was protected by a wall build by Seleucus I (311–281 BC) and then enlarged during the time of Antioch Epiphanes (175–164 BC).[797]

Since 63 BC, Syrian Antioch was part of the Roman Empire,

---

791 F. Millar, *The Roman Near East 31 BC–AD 337* (Cambridge: Harvard University Press, 1993), 259.

792 G. Downey, in his history of Antioch, extensively used the work of Malalae; cf. G. Downey, *A History of Antioch in Syria from Seleucus to the Arab Conquest* (Princeton: Princeton University Press, 1961).

793 G. E. Fant and M. G. Reddish, *A Guide to Biblical Sites in Greece and Turkey* (Oxford: Oxford University Press, 2003), 143.

794 Tacitus, in his *Historiae* (105), says that Antioch was "*Syrieae ... caput*"; cf. Tacitus, *Historiae* II. xxviii.

795 Today, the river is called Asi; cf. G. E. Fant and M. G. Reddish, *A Guide_to Biblical Sites*, 143.

796 P. Dreyfus, *Święty Paweł. Reporter na tropach Apostoła* [*Saint Paul. Un grand reporter sur les traces de l'Apôtre*] (Inowrocław: Święty Paweł, 1990), 118.

797 J. McRay, *Antioch on the Orontes*, 24.

with the status of a free city.[798] The city was the place of residence for Roman governors of Syria, and the empire's military forces on the east stayed in Raphaneae (which lay near Antioch).[799] Josephus called the city "the metropolis of Syria," and he ranked it as the third largest city in the Roman Empire.[800] Although without significant political meaning, the city was a center of economy and Hellenistic culture in the region.[801] Archaeological excavation proves the existence of places like a circus, an aqueduct, a bathhouse, a theater, the Pantheon, and *Kaisareion*, which served as a place for the cult of Rome.[802] From the times of Caesar Claudius (AD 41–54), the Olympic games of Antioch took place every five years.[803] From north to the southern part of the city ran the colonnaded street (almost ten meters wide) with 3,200 granite columns (mostly), which naturally created the east and the west parts of the city.[804] Schools, libraries, and temples of Antioch are often compared to those in Rome or Alexandria. The city was not only a mixing place for many cultures and religions, but it was also the place where the west met the east, which naturally made Antioch a cosmopolitan city in every way. In the middle of first century, Antioch had a large Jewish Diaspora (around fifty thousand)

---

798 The freedom of the city was first confirmed by Pompey and then also by Julius Caesar in 47 BC.

799 P. Trebilco, "Syria," in *The Book of Acts in Its First Century Setting*, vol. 2, eds. D. W. J. Gill and C. Gempf (Carlisle: Eerdmans, 1994), 236.

800 Antioch was the third largest city in the Roman Empire (after Rome and Alexandria); cf. Josephus, Jewish War III, ii, 4. In the first century AD, the population of the city was about half a million people; cf. P. Dreyfus, *Święty Paweł*, 117. Today, the city is called Antakya, and it is in the Hatay province of southern Turkey; cf. G. E. Fant and M. G. Reddish, *A Guide to Biblical Sites*, 143.

801 P. Dreyfus, *Święty Paweł*, 117.

802 These facilities were successively developed by Marcius Rex, Pompey, and Julius Caesar; cf. J. McRay, *Antioch on the Orontes*, 24. Later, the construction activities were continued by August Caesar (27 BC–AD 14) and Tiberius (AD 14–37).

803 G. E. Fant and M. G. Reddish, *A Guide to Biblical Sites*, 143.

804 Herod the Great is mentioned by Josephus as the author of the construction (*BJ* 1.425).

with four synagogues, the religious activities of which also attracted some Greeks (Josephus, *BJ* 7, 43–45; *AJ* 12,199).

In the New Testament, Antioch is presented as a city where the kerygma was successfully proclaimed not only to Diaspora Jews but also to Gentiles (Acts 11:19–30). According to Luke, those believers of Jesus who fled from Jerusalem spread the kerygma only among the Jews living in Cyprus, Phoenicia, and in the city of Antioch (Acts 11:19).[805] This information is followed by the mention of Diaspora Jews (from Cyprus and Cyrene) as those who first approached Gentiles in Antioch. Luke indicates the way (εὐαγγελιζόμενοι τὸν κύριον Ἰησοῦν) in which the Diaspora Jews approached the Gentiles (Acts 11:20). In this way, Luke suggests to the reader that initially the Jerusalem community had no intention of approaching Gentiles.[806] In Antioch, for the first time, the messianic Jews (Christian community) were distinguished from Jews (Acts 11:25).[807] Those who coined the name most probably were not Jesus's believers or Jews but rather the Gentiles living in the city, who did not accept the kerygma, but they were able to recognize the difference between Jewish religious teaching and the teaching of those who believed in Jesus. It is also possible that another difference was a custom of Jesus's believers to associate not only with Jews but also with Gentiles, which was behavior not accepted by Jews due to the Mosaic Law.

The city was the place where, according to Luke's narrative, Saul's proclaiming of the kerygma finally brought positive results (Acts 13:1), and probably because of that, the city, until his imprisonment, stayed the place to which he always went back (Acts 14:26; 15:22, 30, 35; 18:21–22). Again, Luke directly indicates that Barnabas was

---

[805] Indirectly, Luke's account exposes a higher degree of religious tolerance in those cities (Acts 11:19). Concerning the situation of Diaspora Jews in Antioch, cf. I. Levinskaya, *The Book of Acts in Its First-Century Setting. Diaspora Setting*, 127–136.

[806] Concerning the problem of the texts' diversity (Greeks/Hellenists), cf. J. A. Fitzmyer, *The Acts of The Apostles*, 476.

[807] F. F. Bruce, *The Book of the Acts*, 227–228; J. A. Fitzmyer, *The Acts of The Apostles*, 477–478.

Saul's most important mentor at the beginning of his relationship with the city (Acts 11:25–26).[808] As Barnabas's coworker (Acts 11:26, 30; 12:24), Saul earned the name of prophet and teacher (Acts 13:1), which most probably decided his involvement in the mission expedition started by the Antioch community (Acts 13:1–3).[809]

---

[808] Although Luke mentioned Saul as one of the teachers and prophets in the Antioch community, the narrative attests his teaching contribution (Acts 11:26) but stays silent about his prophetic activities (Acts 13:9–11); cf. B. Witherington III, *The Acts of the Apostles*, 391. The fact that names of Barnabas and Saul are listed in Acts 13;1 among three other names (Simeon called Niger, Lucius of Cyrene, Manaen) may suggest that they were not the only possible candidates for the mission in Cyprus.

[809] The reason Luke gives for the mission in Cyprus has a pneumatology character, and it is in accordance with his theological perspective presented in Acts, where the Holy Spirit's inspiration serves as the "engine" of mission progress. However, it is possible that the reason for the mission in Cyprus had more "earthly" roots, which is related to Barnabas's background. Barnabas, the Jew from Cyprus, was sent by the Jerusalem community (Acts 11:22) to Antioch as an official, whose task was to evaluate the situation within the local community. His evaluation was positive, and it led to his personal involvement in mission activities in the city (Acts 11:23–24), which included cooperation with Saul that caused his successfully proclaiming the kerygma at Antioch (Acts 11:25–26). Probably, his visit to Jerusalem, by way of giving assistance to the poor in Jerusalem, gives a rapport concerning the situation at Antioch (Acts 11:30). On the way back to Antioch, he took Mark, his cousin (Acts 12:25), who would participate on the mission in Cyprus (Acts 13:5) and who left the combo of Barnabas and Saul; then the mission journey ended in Cyprus and was extended to the territory of Pamphylia (Acts 13:13). The reason for Mark's decision stays subject to speculation, but his decision later was because of arguing between Barnabas and Paul, which in the end caused a split of the combo of Barnabas and Paul (Acts 15:37-40). The fact that after the split, the combo of Barnabas and Mark headed for Cyprus (Acts 15:39) seems to attest that the primary aim of mission activities of the Antioch community, in territory dependent on the Jerusalem community (Cyprus), was restricted only to this island. The narrative concerning the mission in Cyprus is limited to few laconic items of information: teaching at the synagogues of Salamis (Acts 13:5); the trip through the island, which included the mission activities (Acts 13:6); and one more elaborated episode at Paphos (Acts 13:6–12). Lack of any information regarding a relationship between the mission combo and the local communities is puzzling in the context of Acts 11:20.

2. Seleucia

Seleucia Pereia was located thirty-two kilometers from Antioch in Orontes (the northern coast of Syria).[810] The city was established by Seleucus I Nicator in the fourth century BC as a seaport for Antioch. Seleucia always stayed in the shadow of Antioch, despite its importance as a commercial city. In the Hellenistic period, the city was under the dominion of Seleucids (300–246 BC; 219–146 BC; 138–63 BC), with few exceptions, when it fell under the dominion of Ptolemy (246–219 BC; 146–138 BC). In the Roman Empire period (60 BC), by the will of Pompey, Antioch was proclaimed a free city. In the New Testament, the name of the city appears only once, in Acts 13:8, as the harbor from which the mission journey of Barnabas, Mark, and Saul began.[811] Naturally, we can suppose with considerable certainty that when Paul traveled by sea, headed for Antioch, he always visited the port of Seleucia. Nothing can be said about mission activities in the city, which most probably were undertaken by members of the Antioch community but not necessarily by Barnabas and Saul themselves.

3. Cyprus

Cyprus is an island located in the eastern part of the Mediterranean Sea, seventy kilometers from the west coast of Syria and ninety-five kilometers from the southern coast of Turkey. The island is 225 kilometers long and 100 kilometers wide (with a total area of 9,251 kilometers). The name of the island most probably comes from the Greek word κύπρος (copper).[812] The island was famed for

---

810 P. Dreyfus, *Święty Paweł*, 137.

811 The city is mentioned in 1 Macc. 11:8.

812 According to other theories, the etymology of the name derives from the Greek word *κυπάρισσος* (henna plant) or from the Sumarian words *zubar* (copper) or *kubar* (bronze). F. H. Fisher, *Cyprus: Our New Colony and What We Know About It* (Whitefish: Kessinger Publishing, 2010), 13–14. In the Old Testament, the island

copper mines, which were the source of its wealth.[813] The historical account of the island starts with the first international relation in the Middle Bronze Age (2000 BC). It is supposed that until 1000 BC, the island was independent, but since the tenth century BC, it became dependent on many different rulers of the region, starting with Phoenicians.[814] Since the eighth century BC, the island was ruled by Assyria (708–545 BC), Persia (545–333 BC), Alexander the Great of Greece, and afterward by Ptolemaic Egypt, and since 58 BC by Rome.[815] Cyprus was a senatorial province since AD 22.[816] During the Roman domination, Pathos was the capital city and also a place of residency for the governor of Cyprus.[817] Cyprus in Roman Empire times, due to its location, served as a natural stop for those who traveled across the northeastern part of the sea, and it was also recognized as a border of the western world. With harbors Salamis (on the eastern part of the island) and Pathos (on the western side), Cyprus makes it possible to combine sea travel with land travel.[818] The Jewish community on the island was present since the Ptolemy

---

is called *Eliša* (Gen. 10:4; 1 Chron. 1:7; Ezek. 27:7) after the Mesopotamian name *Alašiya* (the Mari text).

[813] Archaeological excavations in Egypt, Mesopotamia, and Asia Minor show that many products made of copper were made in Cyprus; cf. D. A. Dorsey, "Cyprus," in *Encyklopedia Biblijna* [*The Harpers Collins Bible Dictionary*], ed. P. J. Achtemeier (Warsaw: Vocatio, 2004), 175.

[814] The information concerning a full independence of Cyprus until the tenth century BC can be doubted, if we consider that the correspondence between the king of Alašya and Pharaoh Akhenaten (around 1440 BC) contains information about tribute to Egypt; cf. P. Gaber, "Cyprus," in *Eerdmans Dictionary of the Bible*, ed. D. N. Freedman (Grand Rapids / Cambridge Eerdmans, 2000), 303–305.

[815] Egypt, for a short time, dominated Cyprus during the period between the Assyrian and Persian domination in the region, as well as during the Roman Empire's domination; cf. D. W. J. Gill and C. Gempf, *The Book of Acts in Its First-Century Setting. Graeco-Roman Setting*, 280–281.

[816] H. Conzelmann, *Acts of the Apostles*, 99.

[817] Acts attests that Sergius Paulus was the governor of Cyprus at the time that the Antiochian community mission was undertaken (AD 46–48); cf. J.A. Fitzmyer, *The Acts of The Apostles*, 501–502.

[818] This way was used by the mission team (Acts 13:4–6).

period (1 Macc. 15:23; 2 Macc. 12:2). In the New Testament, the island is mentioned several times but only in the Acts of the Apostles (Acts 4:36; 11:19–20; 13:4; 15:39; 21:3, 16; 27:4).[819] Paul visited the island only once (Acts 13:4–13), when together with Barnabas (who came from Cyprus) and Mark; they visited the island during their mission journey. At that time, Cyprus was the senatorial province of the Roman Empire, ruled by the proconsul (τῷ ἀνθυπάτῳ Σεργίῳ Παύλῳ) Sergius Paulus (AD 46–48).

3.1. Salamis. Salamis was a major harbor on the east coast of Cyprus, founded after the Trojan War by Teucer, son of Telamon.[820] Until the Persian period, there were many city-kingdoms on Cyprus; Salamis was the one of them. It was mentioned even in Assyrian inscriptions. During the Persian domination, Evagoras (410–374 BC), the king of Salamis, led other kingdoms of Cyprus to fight for independence, and afterward, he became the first king of the united island.[821] Since the Hellenistic time, the island and the city were under the rule of a Ptolemaic governor (since 311 BC). Even after Paphos became the capital of the island, Salamis remained an important city-harbor, which was favored by the Roman emperors (Trajan and Hadrian). Also, during the Roman Empire period, the city was of great importance until the earthquake in 15 BC, which destroyed the city. The city was rebuilt by Emperor Augustus and renamed *Sebaste Augusta.*[822]

In the New Testament, the city is mentioned only once (Acts 13:5). In time, when Barnabas, Saul, and Mark visited Salamis, the city was a Greek city, and this status remained unchanged since Ptolemaic times. As a harbor, the city was a commercial center with

[819] Concerning Barnabas and Jews from Cyprus, cf. Acts 4:36; 11:19–20; 15:39; 21:16. Concerning Barnabas, Mark and Saul, cf. Acts 13:3–14.

[820] M. R. Fairchild, "Salamis," in *Eerdmans Dictionary of the Bible*, ed. D. N. Freedman (Cambridge: Eerdmans, 2000), 1152–1153.

[821] Cyprus was again conquered by Persians during the rule of King Artaxerxes III (425–338 BC).

[822] D. W. J. Gill and C. Gempf, *The Book of Acts*, 280–281.

mixed nationalities, cultures, and religions. The Jewish Diaspora community was present in the city since the Hellenistic period (Josephus, *AJ* 13.10.4).[823] We can suppose there was a quite large Jewish community in the city because Luke used, in Acts 13:5, the plural ἐν ταῖς συναγωγαῖς, strongly suggesting that in the city there was more than one synagogue.[824] That indirectly indicates that period of the mission activities had considerable length (probably more than a few weeks); the information that John was helping Barnabas and Saul may indicate that his assistance was necessary to manage their activities.[825]

According to the local tradition of Christian church, Barnabas was martyred in the city of Salamis (AD 61).[826]

3.2. Paphos. Paphos is a harbor city in the southwest part of Cyprus. The place was inhabited since the second millennium BC. The founder of the city, according to tradition, was the Arcadian Agapenor or Cinyras. In the twelfth century BC, the temple of Aphrodite was built in that place. In ancient times, the city was famous for its devotion to the goddess of love and beauty, who, according to myth, was born at the seaside of Petra dou Romiou near Old Paphos.[827] The significant importance of the city is related to the Hellenistic period, when Ptolemy ruled the island. There are two different locations of the city: the Old Paphos (now called Koukulia) was built on an eminence about twenty-one kilometers from the sea, and it was destroyed by an earthquake in the fourth century BC. After the disaster, the city was rebuilt about fifteen kilometers north

---

[823] F. F. Bruce, *The Acts of the Apostles*, 295.

[824] Luke underlines that the modus operandi during the mission at Salamis included exclusively proclaiming the kerygma to Jews (Acts 13:5).

[825] Acts 13:1–3 does not include the name of Mark among those of Barnabas and Saul, which suggests that he was not officially appointed to this mission but rather was co-opted by Barnabas.

[826] M. R. Fairchild, *Salamis*, 1152. The date of Barnabas's martyrdom is not known, but Walker thinks that it took place around AD 75; cf. P. Walker, *In the Steps of Paul* (Grand Rapids: Zondervan, 2008), 60.

[827] D. W. J. Gill and C. Gempf, *The Book of Acts*, 280.

of the old location as a harbor city, and it was named Neo Paphos. Since the second century and during the Roman Empire, Paphos was a capital of Cyprus and place of residence for the governor.

In the New Testament, the name of the city is mentioned only twice (Acts 13:6, 13) in the context of the mission activities of Barnabas, Mark, and Saul (Acts 13:4–12). Luke's account confirms that Paphos was a place of residence for the governor of the island (Acts 13:7). Surprisingly, Luke's account concerning the mission at Paphos is limited to the meeting of a Jewish prophet Elymas and a (probable) conversion of proconsul Sergius Paulus (13:6–8). There is absence of other information concerning teaching in synagogues or meeting Jews, which must be counted as strange, if we consider that this mission was addressed to Diaspora Jews. It is rather impossible that the activities of the mission team were so limited, and for this reason, it can be supposed that Barnabas and Saul met the prophet Elymas in a synagogue, and it was Elymas who introduced the case of the missionaries to the proconsul before he called them.[828] It can be also supposed that Sergius Paulus met Barnabas and Saul several times before he became believer because of things he saw and the teaching he heard (13:12). Luke's very schematic account puts everything to one meeting, for some reason, making the mission at Paphos and in Cyprus as short as possible.[829] However, in Luke's account concerning the mission at Paphos, in a very tactful way, indicates a very important change in Saul's life. In Acts 13:9, he indicates that Saul was also called Paul, and after this point in his narrative, he hardly uses the name Saul.[830] We are skeptical about the thesis that

---

[828] The mission in Cyprus was primarily addressed to Jews (Acts 13:4; 15:39); an unlikely possibility is that Barnabas and Saul went to meet the governor.

[829] A reason for that Lucan approach was not a lack of information but his consciously chosen omission, in order to expose little connection between Saul/Paul and the community in Cyprus.

[830] Conzelmann thinks that the term ὁ καὶ Παῦλος indicates Saul's possessing the name of Paul from his birth and not from the meeting of the governor. He argues that Luke used the event on Pathos as an opportunity to activate an already possessed name, in order to underline a new stage of Paul's presentation. H. Conzelmann, *Acts of the Apostles*, 100.

the change of his name from Saul to Paul has something in common with Saul/Paul's obtaining Roman citizenship from the hands of Sergius Paulus, because according to Acts 22:28, he possessed it from the birth because his parents possessed it.[831] It is rather possible that from the mission on Cyprus, Saul's mission activities were connected to the western world with Roman influences (not only administration) more intense than in the Syrian province. For this reason, using a Roman name (Paulus) seems to be more convenient for the Jewish missionary.[832] However, from a literary perspective, the change of the name may also serve to indicate Luke's conscious division of Paul's life for the life of Saul and the life of Paul, where the demarcation line is the end of the mission on Cyprus.

In our opinion, Paphos was a last stage of the mission that had been planned by the Antioch community. Barnabas, Saul, and Mark proclaimed the kerygma from Salamis (east coast of the island) to Paphos (west coast of the island); that is a literary parable indicating evangelization of the whole island. The results of their mission are summarily shown in the narrative regarding the possible conversion of the proconsul, which took place in the capital city of Cyprus. This information allowed us to count the mission as a real success. We suppose that after ending the mission on Cyprus, the mission team was expected to return to Antioch. However, Proconsul Sergius Paulus, who had extended property in the region of Pisidian, possibly asked the mission team to proclaim the Gospel also in that region and especially in the city of Pisidian Antioch, which hosted a large community of Jews (Josephus, *AJ* 12.147–153).[833] If the supposition is correct, the decision for mission activities in this region was made

---

[831] Fitzmyer thinks that Saul had two names, where the name Paulus was a Roman *cognomen*. J. A. Fitzmyer, *The Acts of the Apostles*, 502–503.

[832] L. T. Johnson, *The Acts of the Apostles*, 223.

[833] The connection between the governor of Cyprus, Sergius Paulus, and the region of Pisidia is assumed, based on an inscription found by W. Ramsay near Pisidian Antioch, which most probably contains the name of his family relatives; cf. W. M. Ramsay, *Bearing of Recent Discovery on the Trustworthiness of the New Testament* (London: Hodder and Stoughton, 1920), 150–172.

not by the Antioch community but by Paul, who, as Luke indicates in Acts 13:13, became a leader of the mission team during activities in Asia Minor. These suppositions explain two confusing problems. First, it gives an explanation of Mark's leaving and its consequences (Acts 13:13; 15:36–40), and second, it explains why the main speech is given by Paul and is placed by Luke in Pisidian Antioch (Acts 13:14–49). If the suppositions are correct, it is possible to conclude that Paul's first mission journey de facto started from Paphos, not from Syrian Antioch.

APPENDIX 7.
THE SPEECH AT PISIDIAN ANTIOCH (ACTS 13:16–41, 46–47)

The speech is placed in a positive context; the rulers of the synagogue asked the new visitors, Paul and Barnabas, to give a speech to the community gathered for prayers (v. 15). Paul's speech begins with a casual address (v. 16b), exposing Jews living in the Diaspora as the Israelites but also including the God-fearers (Gentiles who were attracted by the Jewish religion but were not yet proselytes).[834] In the first part of the speech (narratio), Paul provides a short account of God's powerful works in the history of the chosen nation (vv. 17–22), which begins with the saving works in the land of Egypt (v. 17), followed by an account of God's patience during the time in the desert (v. 18), and granting the land of Canaan to the Israelites (v. 19).[835]

---

[834] The God-fearers who appear in verse 16 and verse 26 are not a part of Israel. In verse 43, Paul speaks about Gentiles who converted to Judaism. L. T. Johnson, *The Acts of the Apostles*, 230.

[835] The text of Acts 13:16–47 contains several textual problems that highly affect its interpretation. Concerning this problem, cf. B. Metzger, *A Textual Commentary*, 357–367. Lucan Paul's perspective on the history of Israel, until the chosen nation enters the promised land, concentrates exclusively on the positive aspects of the history of the Israelites in order to glorify the greatness of God's deeds. J. A. Fitzmyer, *The Acts of the Apostles*, 510–511. Due to this approach, the name and role of Moses are totally omitted, which shapes his Jewish history presentation in an extraordinary manner, where many details, in general, differ from Stephen's version of Jewish history in his speech (Acts 7:2–60). B. Witherington III, *The Acts of the Apostles*, 409.

In this land, God prepared the nation by giving them first the judges (v. 20), then the prophet (Samuel), and at last King Saul, before the Davidic dynasty was established (vv. 21–22).[836] This very schematic presentation of hundreds of years of the nation's history does not concentrate on a particular period of history or on exceptionally eminent persons, but it hardly mentions the most important stages of developing the twelve tribes into the one nation, which resulted in establishing the Davidic dynasty. The main aim of the account is the presentation of King David as the chosen servant of God, who received special promise and was established to fulfill God's will.[837] The function of the account (Acts 13:17–22) is to stress God's power and his grace, amplifying the statement that everything in the history of the nation is connected with the will of God.

In the next part of the narratio (vv. 23–25), Paul goes directly to the account concerning Jesus, who is presented here as the fulfillment of the promise given to David, omitting almost one thousand years of Jewish history (v. 23).[838] There is no mention of what kind of promise is fulfilled, but it is rather clear, at least to the Jews, that it refers to the Savior from the house of David.[839] In order to expose Jesus as the Savior, Paul adds an apologetic explanation, in which John the Baptist

---

[836] Luke's narrative concerning Saul's reign agrees with the testimony of Josephus *Ant.* 6.378 (forty years) but differs from the testimony of 1 Samuel 13:1 (two years) and Josephus *Ant.* 10, 143 (twenty years). Concerning the election of David, Paul uses the term ἐγείρω (*to raise up*) that is also used in verse 30, where it refers to Jesus's Resurrection. Probably in this way, Luke indicates a deliberate typology: David–Jesus. L. T. Johnson, *The Acts of the Apostles*, 232. This typology seems to be attested by verse 23, where Jesus is presented directly as a descendent of David.

[837] Verse 22, concerning David as the chosen one, contains three texts from the Old Testament: Psalm 89:21 (LXX Ps. 88:21); 1 Samuel 13:14; Isaiah 44:28.

[838] J. A. Fitzmyer, *The Acts of the Apostles*, 513.

[839] Second Samuel 7:12, 16 are the main texts referring to the descendant of David as the Savior of Israel, but other texts speak of "future David" (Jer. 30:9; Hosea 3:5; Ezek. 37:24–25). The textual problem of Acts 13:23 is that we accept Metzger's explanation that the reading "God has brought to Israel salvation" is the error, and it should be read as "God has brought to Israel a Savior, Jesus." B. M. Metzger, *A Textual Commentary*, 359.

is presented as the man preceding Jesus in order to prepare the way for the Savior (vv. 24–25).[840]

The next part of the speech in the narrative is propositio (v. 26), which exposes Paul and Barnabas as the witnesses who have been chosen to proclaim Jesus the Savior (v. 26).[841] In order to emphasize that Paul and Barnabas share the same religious expectation, Paul uses the new title *brothers*, referring to Jews and God-fearers.[842] Paul claims that he and his coworker are legitimate witnesses, proclaiming the true teaching about Jesus as the Savior, and proof of this claim is the extensively provided in next part of the speech, called probatio (v. 27–37).[843] The proof of the statement starts with a negative argument pointing at those who, while supposedly have become Jesus's witnesses, have not recognized him as the Savior (v. 27).[844] This accusation concerns inhabitants of Jerusalem and the authorities of the Temple,[845] who, by their ignorance, unconsciously fulfilled the prophecy concerning the rejection of God's servant.[846] In order to

---

[840] It is possible that among people who considered John the Baptist as the Messiah were some Jews from Antioch (cf. Acts 18:23–19:7). The account concerning John the Baptist serves to indicate that the preparation of the messianic age has ended, and John was the one who actually accomplished this stage of God's salvation plan by pointing to Jesus as the Messiah. H. Conzelmann, *Acts of the Apostles*, 104. The quotation of John's words comes from Luke 3:16 and John 1:20, 27. John's mission (repentance) is also attested by Josephus (*Ant.* 18.116–119).

[841] The proclaiming of Jesus as the Savior to Jews and God-fearers of Gentiles indirectly amplified the universal nature of the message.

[842] J. Munck, *The Acts of the Apostles* (Garden City: Anchor Bible, 1967), 123.

[843] For Bauckham, Acts 13:26–31 is the one of the major kerygma summaries. R. Bauckham, "Kerygmatic Summary in the Speeches of Acts," in *History Literature and Society in the Book of Acts*, ed. B. Witherington III (Cambridge: Eerdmans, 2007) 213.

[844] H. Conzelmann, *Acts of the Apostles*, 105.

[845] Luke, in the account concerning the Sanhedrin, Pilate, and Herod, uses the term *rulers* to include both the religious and political character of the rulers (Luke 22:64–23:25).

[846] There is not quotation of a particular text, but texts that probably are similar to Isaiah 52:13–53:12 seem to be considered, which is a statement that may be supported by following verses. Mention that the passage reads as a prayer during a prayer meeting indicates the suggestion that it is well known to Jesus, hearing the

emphasize innocence of Jesus on one hand and the authorities' guilt on the other hand, Paul amplifies that, without reason, the authorities condemned Jesus to the death and insisted that Pilate act according to their decision (v. 28).[847] The condemnation of Jesus, his death on the cross, and his burial were the way in which the prophecy concerning the fate of God's servant was fulfilled (v. 29).[848] That makes the people of Jerusalem and the Temple authorities as agents that fulfilled the prophecy, but it does not free them from responsibility for their actions (v. 29). This statement in Paul's speech serves as proof that the people in Jerusalem acted wrongly. This is the way in which Lucan Paul discredited the authorities of the Jerusalem Temple as credible witnesses chosen by God to proclaim his salvation for Israel.[849] The agents of Jesus's destruction were the authorities of the Temple, but the agent of his glorification was God himself by the act of resurrecting Jesus from the dead (v. 30).[850]

Paul sees the act of God also as a part of his divine plan of salvation that must be proclaimed to the nation by those who have not rejected Jesus as Savior.[851] The risen Jesus appeared to the disciples

---

Paul's speech. Keener is of the opinion that verse 27 is ironic, running throughout the *Corpus Lucanorum*, where those who rejected Jesus somehow contributed to fulfill the scripture's prophecy. C. S. Keener, *Acts. An Exegetical Commentary*, vol. 2, 2067.

[847] This Lucan Paul's presentation of those who rejected Jesus serves to justify ignorance that led them to ill-willing and unjust action; cf. Luke 23:4; 15–14–15; 22–23. 25; Acts 3:14.

[848] Most probably in order to avoid the negative image of the cross, naturally seen as the tool of severe punishment, Lucan Paul uses the term *tree* or *wood* instead. C. A. J. Pillai, *Apostolic Interpretation of History: A Commentary on Acts 13:16–41* (Hicksville: Exposition, 1980), 40. The narrative regarding Jesus's burial amplifies the reality of his death, and it serves to prepare the base for a narrative concerning Jesus's Resurrection that is presented in the next verse (Acts 13:30). H. Conzelmann, *Acts of the Apostles*, 105.

[849] Acts 13:32 attests this interpretation and, together with verse 26, creates the frame that exposes the kerygma proclaimed by Paul.

[850] R. F. O'Toole, "Christ's Resurrection in Acts 13:13–52," *Bib* 60 (1979): 361–372.

[851] This short kerygma exposes three crucial statements regarding God as the agent of the event: the reality of Jesus's death, the reality of Jesus's Resurrection,

in order that they would prepare to give witness to the world that Jesus was resurrected by God (v. 32).[852] Indication of Jesus's activities after his Resurrection, emphasizing the reality of his Resurrection, points to the twelve as eye-witnesses to the events; they now take responsibility for proclaiming the kerygma about the resurrected Messiah.

Despite the fact that the speech does not make a direct connection between the mandate of the twelve and the mandate of Paul and Barnabas, it is understandable, based on the argument presented in verses 27–29, that not the authorities of the Temple but Paul and Barnabas proclaim the kerygma to the Jews (v. 32) concerning the salvation of Israel, which was promised to their ancestors and now has been brought to its fulfillment (v. 33).[853]

The kerygma concerns the realization of God's promise (v. 26), which was done by Jesus (v. 23) and more precisely by God through the Jesus, resurrected by God (v. 33b); this serves in Luke's narrative as proof of the statement presented in verses 32–33a. Further argument of the statement is based on the three quotations from the scripture (Ps 2:7; Isa. 55:3; 16:10) and concerning the Resurrection of the chosen one.[854] Lucan Paul shows his extraordinary rhetorical skills, connecting the quotation from the scripture that refers to King David and interprets (vv. 36–37) it in a way that shows that they can't refer to David, but they must refer to his descendant, who is Jesus of Nazareth.[855]

Lucan Paul's messianic interpretation of the scripture, where King David is a *type* (the one to whom God gave the promise), exposes Jesus as an *antitype* (the one whose Resurrection is the fulfillment of

---

and it is justified by evidence (v. 31) as well as by the scripture's interpretation (vv. 33b-41). J. A. Fitzmyer, *The Acts of the Apostles*, 515.

[852] Third-person plural pronoun excludes Paul and Barnabas from the group of apostles who saw the resurrected Jesus.

[853] The use of the first-person plural shows that Paul and Barnabas include themselves and all Jews in Antioch among the descendants of the ancestors.

[854] All quotations in this section come from LXX, and in some cases the text differs from the Hebrew manuscripts.

[855] L. T. Johnson, *The Acts of the Apostles*, 234–235.

God's promise given to David). The last part of the speech (peroratio) repeats again the direct address "brethren" (v. 38), pointing to Jews as the addressers of the most important statements in the kerygma proclaimed by Paul. It concerns Jesus, who is a descendant of King David, who was rejected by the Jerusalem authorities, who died on the cross, who was resurrected by God, who fulfilled God's promise, who is the only one by whom humanity can be justified.[856]

The consequence of justification by the faith in Jesus is forgiveness of sins, which was not possible to obtain by the deeds of the Mosaic Law. In this way, Lucan Paul comes to the conclusion that what was impossible for the Jews to obtain by the Law now has been granted freely to all those who believes in Jesus as the Savior of Israel (vv. 38–39).[857] This statement is following by the threat (vv. 40–41), containing a quotation from the LXX version of the book of Habakkuk (Hab. 1:5), which is intended to prevent the Jews from neglecting Paul's message, lest they meet the same consequences that befell the people in the time of Habakkuk (Hab. 5–11).[858] However, this warning does not prevent Jews from opposing Paul, mostly

---

[856] Luke knows Paul's teaching regarding justification by faith. Luke usually refers to the faith in context of the miracles (Luke 5:20; 7:9; 8:25; 17:6; 18:42), but here, he presents, typical of Paul's kerygma, connecting the faith with the forgiveness of sins. The theme of justification by faith is characteristic of Paul (Rom. 3:22; 10:4, 11), and it concerns Jesus as the expiation offering for the sins of humankind (Rom. 3:24–25). C. S. Keener, *Acts. An Exegetical Commentary*, vol. 2, 2074–2075.

[857] The phrase πᾶς ὁ πιστεύων (*everyone who believes*) refers here to Jews and Gentiles, as Acts 2:44; 10:43 confirmed it. L. T. Johnson, *The Acts of the Apostles*, 236; J. J. Kilgallen, "Acts 13:38–39: Culmination of Paul's Speech in Pisidia," *Bib* 69 (1988): 480–506.

[858] T. Novick, "Eschatological Ignorance and the Haftarah on Acts 3:27," *NovT* 54 (2012): 174. In this way, Lucan Paul tries to prevent the Antioch audiences from rejecting the Messiah. J. A. Fitzmyer, *The Acts of the Apostles*, 519. This warring connects the main part of the speech (Acts 13:16–41) with an additional part (Acts 13:46–47), which shows that some of the Jews rejected Paul's words. This fact was Paul's reason for his decision to turn the mission to the Gentiles. Similar worrying can be found, especially in the twelve minor prophets, where the consequences of possibly spurning the prophets' words are severe.

not on account of his teaching but out of jealousy on the part of some Jews, who could not accept the wide interest in the kerygma proclaimed by Paul (Acts 13:45).[859] This part of narrative contains some very interesting information; the first refers to the fact that some Jews accepted Paul's teaching (vv. 42-43), but others rejected it, partly based on envy toward Paul's success among non-Jews. The second concerns Paul's conviction that the kerygma should be proclaimed first to the Jews. The third indicates a causal connection between rejection of God's words (Paul's kerygma about Jesus) and a kind of self-condemnation, which reveals Luke's conviction about salvation only in the name of Jesus (Acts 4:12). The fourth shows that the rejection was a direct reason for spreading the kerygma also to the Gentiles dueling in the city (Acts 13:46). The fifth indicates that this "extension" is seen by Lucan Paul as God's will, which is attested by the words of the prophet (Acts 13:47).[860]

---

[859] The concluding remarks (Acts 13:46–47) actually do not directly relate to the content of the speech (Acts 13:16–41).

[860] Acts 13:47 contains a quotation from Isaiah 49:6 (LXX). The conjunction ἐπειδὴ (*since/because*) indicates the causal relation between the rejection of Paul's message by the Jews and Paul's decision regarding the mission to the Gentiles. L. T. Johnson, *The Acts of the Apostles*, 241.

APPENDIX 8.
MISSION IN PISIDIA, PAMPHYLIA, AND LYCAONIA

1. Perga in Pamphylia

Perga was an ancient city in Pamphylia, situated about fifteen kilometers north of the harbor city of Attalia at the junction of two small streams (Sarisu and Aksu Cayi). Since 25 BC, the city and the province Pamphylia were a part of the Roman Empire. Before that, the city was under the control of Persians from 546 BC until the Hellenistic period (333 BC). In the Hellenistic times, the city was under the dominion of Seleucids, and from that period till the Byzantine times, Perga was a metropolis of Pamphylia.[861] The best known citizen of the city was the mathematician Apollonius (262–190 BC). The local cult that made the city famous was cult of Artemis (Diana), the ancient goddess of the hunt, and the great temple for her glory. In the Acts of Apostles, the city is mentioned only twice, the first time in Acts 13:14, as one of the cities that Barnabas and Saul passed by on the road to the Pisidia region during their first mission journey. It happened at this place that Mark left Paul and Barnabas, returning to Jerusalem. Absence of information concerning the mission activities in the city (at this stage of the journey) indirectly

[861] W. C. Brice, "Perga," in *Encyclopedia Britannica*, vol. 17, *Encyclopedia Britannica* (Chicago, 1971), 605.

indicates that the aim of the mission team was the city of Antioch in Panphilia (Acts 13:14). For the second time, the city is mentioned in Acts 14:25 as the place where Barnabas and Saul proclaimed the kerygma on their return to Antioch in Syria. This time, the mission activities (λαλήσαντες—active aorist participle) are mentioned (Acts 14:24) but without specific information concerning targets, method, and results of the activities.

2. Antioch (in Pisidia)

Pisidia was a region of southern Asia Minor located to the north of Pamphylia and to the west of Cilicia.[862] A large part of Pisidia was incorporated into the Roman province of Galatia in the year 25 BC. In the third century BC, Seleucus I Nicanor founded the city of Antioch (Pisidian Antioch), which was located south of the main Roman road *Via Sebaste* (from the Meander Valley to the Cilician Gates) on the slopes of the Sultan Daglari range (about 1,100 meters above sea level).[863] This Greek-speaking city was inhabited by many different populations, which made the city a melting pot of many cultures and religions. From 189 BC until 11 BC, Pisidian Antioch was a free city, but after this period, Emperor Augustus declared it a colony, with the proper title *Pisidarum Colonia Caesarea Antiochia.* During that time, the city was an important civil and military center of the southern part of the Roman province of Galatia, which was connected to the long and strong process of Romanization of the city.[864] At the end of the first century BC, Publius Sulpicius Qurinius rebuilt the

---

[862] W. C. Brice, "Pisidia," in *Encyclopedia Britannica*, vol. 17, 1110. Although geographically the city belongs to the region of Phrygia, in the first century AD, Antioch administratively belonged to the province of Galatia. The city was incorporated into Pisidia at the end of the third century AD, during the reign of Diocletian (AD 295); cf. B. Witherington III, *The Acts of the Apostles*, 404–405.

[863] W. C. Brice, "Antioch in Pisidia," in *Encyclopedia Britannica,* vol. 2, 75.

[864] F. F. Bruce, *The Book of the Acts*, 251.

city in Roman fashion.[865] In the New Testament, the city is mentioned in Acts 13:14; 14:19, 21; and 2 Timothy 3:11. Judging from the length of the account (forty verses), the activities of Barnabas and Paul at Antioch is the main point of Luke's account in the narration regarding the first mission journey.[866] Despite the fact that when Barnabas and Paul came to Antioch, the city[867] was under strong Romanization activities, the population still consisted of many different groups, among which the Jewish community was the one with significant social power (Acts 15:50).[868] The existence of a large Jewish Diaspora with their own synagogue (Acts 13:15) is testified by an inscription found in Antioch.[869] Luke indicates the synagogue as a place of mission activities, which shows that Barnabas and Paul, in their mission activities, followed the modus operandi of approaching Jews first (Acts 12:14–15).

According to Luke's narrative, the first contact was a success, which earned interest from the Jews (v. 42), as well as from some Gentiles who were gathering for the next Sabbath (v. 44). Surprisingly, this time, Barnabas and Paul were offended by Jews in front of Gentiles (v. 45), which was an incident that, in the end, caused Paul's public declaration of beginning the mission to Gentiles in the city but without abandoning the mission to the Jews (v. 46). This strategy earned many believers among Gentiles, but it caused some Jews to plot against Paul and Barnabas (vv. 48–50). Luke's

---

[865] In Acts 13:14, Luke uses the term *Pisidian Antioch* in order to accurately determine to which Antioch city (from many cities bearing the same name) he is referring.

[866] Compared to the laconic narrative regarding the mission in Cyprus (Acts 13:5–14–12), the account concerning the mission at Antioch is much longer, but more than half of the narrative contains Lucan Paul's speech, which is an example of the kerygma proclaimed by Paul to Diaspora Jews.

[867] Between Perge and Pisidian Antioch, there is a distance of about 160 kilometers.

[868] Pisidian Antioch was among the few cities in the Roman Empire where women's involvement in political affairs was acceptable (Acts 15:50). J. White, *Evidence & Paul's Journeys* (Hilliard: Parsagard Press, 2001), 12.

[869] The use of term οἱ ἀρχισυνάγωγοι (*the synagogue rules*) in Acts 13:15 is historically correct. J. White, *Evidence*, 11.

narrative concerning the mission in Pisidia presents Paul as the fully developed witnesses who is about to cross the Rubicon, regarding to the mission to the Gentiles. Paul not only becomes the head of the mission team (Acts 13:13), but he also gives his first (recorded by Luke in the Acts) official speech that contains his kerygma (Acts 13:16–41).[870] During the speech, he makes a statement concerning his mission to the Gentiles, and he indicates a socioreligious reason for his decision (Acts 13:46–47, 51). Luke, in his narrative regarding Paul, chose the city of Pisidian Antioch, where, for very first time, he presents his own perspective on Paul in the context of Paul's mission to Diaspora Jews.[871]

3. Iconium

Ancient Iconium (today known as Konya in the central Anatolia region of Turkey) was a city of the Phrygian kingdom, established in the eighth century BC. The city was located on the plateau of Lycaonia and was bordered on the west by the Pisidian Mountains.

---

[870] The speech of Lucan Saul (Paul), which must be considered as the literary narrative reconstruction, rather than as the precisely recorded original speech of Saul, focuses on one topic that regards "God's will," which is indispensable as related to "God's choice." The speech starts directly with the statement that God chose the ancestors of the Israelites (Acts 13:17), and it is followed by a short and schematic historical account of Israel until the time of King David (Acts 13:20, 21, 22). The next part of the speech suddenly jumps directly to the time of Jesus (Acts 13:23, 28–31) and John the Baptizer (Acts 13:24–25). The finale aim of the speech is to present himself and Barnabas as servants chosen by God to proclaim Jesus of Nazareth as the fulfillment of God's promise (Acts 13:26–27, 32–33). The kerygma proclaimed by Paul concerns Jesus as the Savior (v. 23), chosen by God but refused by the Israelites (vv. 27–29), who died and was resurrected by God (v. 30) and by whom a forgiveness of sins is given to those who believe (vv. 38–39).

[871] Because Luke learned about this mission journey of Paul and Barnabas from sources, it is highly possible that the narrative of Acts 13:13–52 is Luke's narrative construct (particularly the speech at the synagogue), which strongly reflects his theological thoughts and his perspective on Paul, which heads for the exposition of the modus operandi used by the apostle during the first mission to the Diaspora Jews.

The region of Anatolia had been inhabited since 3000 BC, and it was controlled by Hittites (c. 1500 BC) and the Sea People (c. 1200 BC). At the beginning of the seventh century, it was overtaken and successively controlled by Cimmerians, Persians, and Greeks. The Greek historian Xenophon of Athena (430–354 BC) describes Iconium as the last city of Phrygia. During the Hellenistic time, the city was ruled by the kings of Pergamon, and after the death of the last king, Attalus III (133 BC), the city became part of the Roman Empire.[872] During this period the name of city was changed to *Claudioconium*, during reign of Emperor Claudius (AD 41–53), and after to *Colonia Aelia Hadriana*, during the reign of Emperor Hadrian (AD 117–138). Iconium, although ethnically Phrygian, was described by ancient writers (Cicero, Strabo) as the city of Lyconium, according to its geographic boundaries.[873] In 25 BC, the city was included in the Roman province of Galatia.

The city is mentioned in the New Testament in Acts 13:51; 14:1, 19. 21; and 2 Timothy 3:11. There is not much information concerning a Jewish community living in the city, but according to Luke's account (Acts 14:1–6), there was a Jewish community with a synagogue in Iconium (Acts 14:1).[874] Paul and Barnabas, after walking a distance of 190 kilometers from Antioch to Iconium, came to the city and stayed for a rather long time, despite some unpleasant circumstances (vv. 2–3). The mission's modus operandi was similar to the one used in

---

[872] Phrygian language was still used in this city event at the end of the third century BC, despite the fact that the region and the city was strongly influenced by Greek language and culture; cf. W. C. Brice, "Konya," in *Encyclopedia Britannica*, vol. 13, 451.

[873] Luke's information in Acts 14:6, "συνιδόντες κατέφυγον εἰς τὰς πόλεις τῆς Λυκαονίας Λύστραν καὶ Δέρβην καὶ τὴν περίχωρον," is correct if we look at it not in geographical categories but in ethnic or political categories, which were preferred and in use during the earlier period of the Roman Empire, when the Lycaonia region only partly was administrated by Rome; cf. J. White, *Evidence*, 13–14.

[874] Some scholars discuss a hypothesis regarding a relationship between the biblical flood story and the etymology of the city's name; cf. I. Levinskaya, *The Book of Acts*, 150–152.

Pisidian Antioch—they attended the synagogue and proclaimed to the Jews that Jesus is the fulfillment of God's promises (v. 1). Their activity had two consequences: the first one (positive) was that many Jews and non-Jews came to the faith in Jesus (v. 1), and the second one (negative) was that their activities caused a split within society of the city (vv. 2, 4). Consequently, opposition from those who did not accept the kerygma forced Paul and Barnabas to leave this place and flee to another city (vv. 5–6).

This rather short account of the lengthy activities of the mission team shows Luke's schematic approach to his diary of the first mission journey (v. 1). Despite this fact, however, it indicates some details in exposing Luke's theological concept in the narrative of Acts.[875] The account regarding mission in Iconium is a place where the teaching of Paul and Barnabas, for the very first time, is testified (μαρτυροῦντι) by signs and wonders done by Jesus through the hands of Paul and Barnabas (Acts 14:3). Because non particular sign is mentioned, the information can be taken as Luke's general summary, which amplified the fact that miracles and wonders were attesting Paul and Barnabas's proclaiming of the kerygma (Acts 14:4).[876]

4. Lycaonian

Lycaonian is a region of Asia Minor that borders with Cappadocia on the east, Cilicia on the south, Galatia on the north, and Phrygia/ Pisidia on the west. In Persian times, the region was largely independent, but in Hellenistic times, it become a part of the Seleucid kingdom. During the early Roman period (after 187 BC), the region was given to the king of Phrygia (Eumenes II). In 160

---

[875] The short account concerning the mission activities in Lystra, Iconium, and Antioch on the road back to Syrian Antioch (Acts 14:21–23) seems to be a summary of the entire first mission journey and especially of the part concerning activities in the regions of Pisidia and Panphilia.

[876] Probably no Jews are here in Luke's focus.

BC, the region was added to Galatia, but in 129 BC, the eastern part of the region was incorporated into Cappadocia, and in 64 BC, northern Lycaonian became a part of Galatia.[877] In AD 37, the part of Lycaonian where the city of Lystra and Derby were located was incorporated into the Roman Empire as a part of the Galatia province.[878]

In the New Testament, the region is mentioned only in Acts 14:6 as the place where Paul and Barnabas ran from the region of Phrygia. According to some ancient writers, Iconium was a city in Lycaonian, so Luke's account is sometimes taken as incorrect.[879] Other ancient writers, however, called Iconium a city in Phrygia.[880] The Christians' accounts from the third century refer to Iconium as a city in Phrygia.[881] Also, inscriptions from the second century AD show that Iconium inhabitants spoke the Phrygian language.[882] Because Iconium was located on the border between the regions of Phrygia and Lycaonia, it was connected differently by ancient writers to one of those two regions.

5. Lystra

Lystra was a town located thirty kilometers south of Iconium.[883] It was established in 26 BC as a colony (*Julia Felix*) by Caesar

---

[877] The region suffered several administrative changes during the Roman period.

[878] J. White, *Evidence*, 12–13.

[879] Iconium is called a Lycaonian city by Cicero (first century BC) in *Epistulae ad Familiares*, 15.4.2.

[880] Iconium was called a city in the Phrygia region by Xenophon (430–354 BC) in *Anabasis* 1.2.19.

[881] Cyprian, in his epistles (75.7), called Iconium a place in Phrygia, on the occasion of mentioning the local church council (AD 323).

[882] F. F. Bruce, *The Acts of the Apostles*, 319.

[883] There is discussion among scholars whether Iconium was the city on the road called Via Sebaste; cf. F. F. Bruce, *The Acts of the Apostles*, 320; H. Conzelmann, *Acts of the Apostles*, 107.

Augustus in order to control the region.[884] Administratively, Lystra was part of the Galatian province. Although the town was built in Roman fashion, it remained insignificant as a market town, where the local language and customs did not disappear under the pressure of Romanization. Concerning Luke's account regarding the local cult, there are archaeological and literary evidences that the Zeus cult was known and practiced in Lystra.[885]

The name of the city is mentioned in the New Testament in Acts 14:6, 8, 21; 16:1–2, and 2 Timothy 3:11, exclusively in the context of Paul's mission activities in the city. The account from Acts 14 considers the mission activity of Paul and Barnabas in the city, the final result of which was establishing the community of Jesus's followers. Surprisingly, this fact is not directly indicted by Luke (indirectly, it is mentioned in verse 20), but it may be deduced based on the direct account from Acts 16:1–5. In Paul's primary source (2 Tim. 3:11), the name of the city is mentioned together with names of other cities that Paul visited during his first mission journey, and there he suffered persecution.[886]

Luke's account regarding the mission in Lystra differs radically from other narrative concerning the mission journey. The first difference is that there is no information on establishing the community in the city as a result of Paul and Barnabas's activity.[887]

---

[884] The most probable location of Lystra is known to the public due to the discovery of J. R. Sitlington Sterrett in the late nineteenth century (1885). The excavation of this archeological site is still unfinished, so the consensus regarding this place is that the city was not of significant importance in the time Paul visited it; cf. G. E. Fant and M. G. Reddish, *A Guide to Biblical Sites*, 240–241.

[885] cf. H. Conzelmann, *Acts of the Apostles*, 110; J. A. Fitzmyer, *The Acts of the Apostles*, 530–532; J. White, *Evidence*, 14.

[886] The narrative context of the exhortation concerns suffering as an internal part of a Christian's life at that time. Although the account of Acts 16:1–5 is similar to the account of 2 Timothy 3:11, the context in which the accounts are placed differs.

[887] The existence of a community of Jesus's believers in the city at the time of Paul's stoning is confirmed by Acts 14:20 (directly) and also by Acts 16:1–2 in an indirect way. Luke informs about the existence of the community, but he said nothing about the origin of the community, which causes a question if the community was established by Paul or someone else. Thanks to the fact that Paul

Second, there isn't any narrative regarding the mission activities in this city, only laconic information that the kerygma was proclaimed in Derbe and Lystra.[888] Third, there is no account concerning the modus operandi or place of Paul and Barnaba's activity.[889] Fourth, there is no information to indicate the length of the activity in the city.[890] Without casual introduction or background, Luke's narration

---

visited the community during his next mission journey, it is possible to say at least that that the community in Lystra was active (Acts 16:2) and most probably established a strong emotional relationship with Paul, which is the information that strongly suggests the community was established by Paul (Acts 14:20).

[888] Although Luke does not,write directly about Paul and Barnabas's mission activities in Lystra, he attested to an existence of the disciples (Acts 14:20), possible offspring of Paul and Barnabas, which indirectly attests to the mission activities in the city.

Luke also informs that Jews from Antioch (160 kilometers from Lystra) and Iconium were the initiators of the opposition and plot against the missionaries in the city. The reason for their action could be the growing influence of the missionaries among local community (Jews), about which Luke wrote not even a word. Suspicious, however, is the fact that the Jews from Antioch were aware of Paul's mission among Gentiles. Most probably the account is an abbreviated narrative of a more complex and extensive event.

[889] The fact that Luke does not mention the Jewish community possessing a synagogue in Lystra, as well as excluding Jews of Lystra from other Jews who were acting against Paul (Acts 14:19), suggests that even if a Jewish community existed in the city, that was not of considerable size and social influence. Mentioning Timothy's mother (Acts 16:1) supports the supposition that some Jews were present in this city. Bruce presents a different opinion; cf. F. F. Bruce, *The Book of the Apostles*, 278.

[890] Luke's narration gives impression that Paul and Barnabas were active in the city for a short period; although the narrative regarding the miracle is placed almost instantly after the missionaries arrive at the city, the miracle hardly occurred on the same day, and between the event of the miracle and the stoning of Paul, Luke's narrative suggests a considerable time span. Additionally, it must be considered impossible that that very next day after his stoning, Paul was ready to leave Lystra and went to Derbe. Based on these considerations, we suppose that Paul and Barnabas's stay in Lystra is of considerable time, and it even may extend to a few months.

It is most probable that Luke's narrative regarding the first mission journey shows a sign of haste to end it, rather than showing the real state of things concerning Paul and Barnabas's mission activities in the city.

regarding Lystra starts directly with the event of a miracle, which in the Lucan narrative is the perfect opportunity to place Paul's first speech addressed strictly to the Gentiles, who barely had been exposed to Jewish monotheism. Based on Acts 14:11, 19, it can be supposed, with considerable probability, that there were no Jews among the Gentile crowd who attempted to divine Barnabas and Paul. Also, an interpretation of Paul's miracle and its consequences have a strictly Hellenistic setting (Acts 14:11–13).

Paul's speech consists of two parts: the first one is explanatory and contains a declaration that Paul and Barnabas are only human, as subject to suffering as everyone else (Acts 14:14–15). The second part of the speech contains a proclamation of God, the Creator, who can be recognized by everyone through his creation of the existing world (Acts 14:15–17). In both parts, the arguments Paul used were not appropriate for Jewish context, and for this reason, it is striking that Paul refers to the expression εὐαγγελιζόμενοι ὑμᾶς (*bringing you good news*), not to Jesus but to God.[891] Luke indicates also that the reason for the stoning of Paul was not directly related to the event of a miracle or even the refusal to accept the offering but only was the plot of Jews who came from other cities (Acts 14:19).[892]

6. Derbe

Almost nothing certain is known about the origin and history of the city.[893] Derbe was probably located around twenty-four kilometers northeast of the city of Laranda and southeast of Iconium, under the slope of the volcano Karadag (2,288 meters). There are no remains of the city, and the name of the city is known to history due to Luke's

---

[891] B. Witherington III, *The Act of the Apostles*, 426.

[892] There are no reasons for direct connection of the miracle with the stoning of Paul. The Gentiles of Lystra, who wanted to deify Paul and Barnabas, did not want to stone them. Between these two events (the miracle and the stoning) was not only a considerable time span but also time for the Jews' propaganda against Paul among local Gentiles; cf. D. G. Peterson, *The Acts of the Apostles*, 411–412.

[893] The city has been destroyed during the Diocletian persecution (AD 303–313).

account in Acts 14:6; 16:1 and some coins and inscriptions.[894] Strabo, in his geographical work, wrote that in the first century BC, the city of Derbe belonged to the local ruler Antipater Derbetes, until Amyntas, the king of Galatia, overtook it. It is most probable that in 25 BC, the city was a part of the Roman province of Galatia.[895]

The name of the city is mentioned four times in the New Testament (Acts 14:6, 20; 16:1; 20:4).[896] Except for information on the mission activity in the city (Acts 14:6–7) and its effect (Acts 14:21), no other details or descriptions are provided. Due to that, nothing can be said about the length of the mission and its methods, nor about the characteristics of the community that were established. Based on Acts 16:1–5 and Acts 20:4, it is possible to suppose that Paul and Barnabas's presence in Derbe (and Lystra) was sufficiently long enough to create the community, which soon was capable of giving some kind of delegates from the community who were accurately prepared to help Paul in his work in the region of Macedonia (Acts 16:1; 20:3–5). This supposition can be supported by the laconic summary in Acts 14:21 that directly refers to the results of the mission but not directly to the mission itself.[897]

The Lucan narrative concerning the mission in Derbe raised a question concerning Luke's knowledge of the mission, especially if we consider that Luke associated with Paul for a short time

---

[894] W. Ramsay, *The Cities of St. Paul: Their Influence on His Life and Thought, The Cities of Eastern Asia Minor* (London: Hodder and Stoughton, 1907), 385–404. The chronological artifacts found in the city, like coins (with the name *Claudioderbe*) and inscriptions (tombstone with the name of Derbe), comes from a period later than Paul's mission activities in this region.

[895] G. E. Fant, M.G. Reddish, *A Guide to Biblical Sites*, 174–176.

[896] The cities of Derbe and Lystra are mentioned in Acts 14:6 and Acts 16:1, where the first mention (Acts 14:6–7) is placed in the context of the mission activities of Barnabas and Paul during the first mission journey, and the second mention (Acts 16:1) is placed in the context of the beginning of Paul's second mission journey, when he revisited the community established during his first mission journey. Luke mentions Gaius from the Derbe community and Timothy from the province of Asia (Acts 20:4), despite the fact that according to Acts 16:1, Timothy comes from Lystra.

[897] cf. D. G. Peterson, *The Acts of the Apostles*, 412–414.

(Acts 16:11), as well as associating with the delegates of the Derbe community (Acts 20:5). It seems logical to suppose that Luke knew much more than he wrote down. However, this supposition raises another question regarding the reason for Luke's approach. In this case and probably many others, Luke did not feel the pressure of obligation to give a detailed account of each stage of the first mission journey, but he was fully aware of giving a historically accurate account in the way best suited for the narrative concept that served to expose his historical and theological perspective on the messianic movement.[898] The beginning of the Gospel contains Luke's honest statement, exposing his following the other authors who made attempts to write the accounts regarding Jesus's movement (probably Mark and Matthew), and he also is about to write on the same subject after his solid preparation (παρηκολουθηκότι ἄνωθεν πᾶσιν ἀκριβῶς), which enabled him to present, in a systematic way (Luke 1:3), early Christian tradition, which here means not only the narrative concerning Jesus (the Gospel) but also the early period after Jesus (the Acts of the Apostles).[899]

Luke, however, did not claim that he would write a precise story or full account of Jesus's life and early history of the first Christian communities. Rather, as the beginning of verse 1 (ἐπειδήπερ πολλοὶ ἐπεχείρησαν ἀνατάξασθαι διήγησιν) and verse 3 (ἔδοξε κἀμοὶ παρηκολουθηκότι ἄνωθεν πᾶσιν ἀκριβῶς καθεξῆς σοι γράψαι) suggest, Luke, for some reason, was not fully satisfied with the existing material (possibly socio-theological issues), or at least he valued the material as concentrating only on the past, neglecting the present that was raised from this past. Luke wrote his own account in a systematic manner, which is superior to previous ones in terms of a carefully created structure, chronology of presentation, and continuity of the narration that goes behind the event of Jesus. What is true about the Gospel of

[898] I. H. Marshall, *The Gospel of Luke* (Grand Rapids: Eerdmans, 1978), 40–41.

[899] Concerning differences in exegetical interpretation of Luke 1:1–3, cf. J. A. Fitzmyer, *The Gospel According to Luke*, 290–301.

Luke is also true about the Act of the Apostles. Luke's approach to narrating the mission journeys of Paul is very schematic and takes a very general character (cf. one speech of Paul for each of the mission journeys), where the most important socio-theological teaching is always placed in the speeches. The account of each of mission journey has its precisely determined (by Luke) theological aim and focus, where the narrative part of the account takes additional character.

APPENDIX 9. THE CONFLICT BETWEEN PAUL AND BARNABAS (ACTS 15:36–40)

1. Narrative Concerning the Conflict

The narrative concerning the second mission journey starts with the expression μετὰ δέ τινας ἡμέρας (*some time later*) (Acts 15:36 NIV), which, despite indicating the considerable time span between the previous narrative and the new narrative, serves as the demarcation line in Luke's narration, beginning a new section of the Acts of the Apostles.[900] In the first section of Acts (Acts 1:1–15:35), Luke, in a general manner, gives a short but coherent theological and historical account of the first generation of Jesus's followers, pointing to several events that shaped the messianic movement in way that enabled its developing into the future Christian Church, despite the fact that the movement still existed within Judaism and was strongly connected to it by the fact that the majority of the believers were Jews.

In the second chapter of his work, Luke changes his approach from the general to the particular by giving almost exclusive attention to Paul's career (Acts 15:36–28:31). Although the majority of those who were mentioned in the first part of the narration were still active in the second part, Luke refers to them only as they relate to the

[900] F. F. Bruce, *The Acts of the Apostles*, 349; J. A. Fitzmyer, *The Acts of the Apostles*, 570; B. Witherington III, *The Acts of the Apostles*, 471.

account of Paul's activity, which makes Acts 15:36–28:31 to be the de facto "Acts of Paul."

The narrative concerning the conflict between Paul and Barnabas starts with Paul addressing Barnabas with plans for a new mission journey (Acts 15:36), which was probably planned as the second visit to the place where they were working during their first mission journey.[901] Paul is the initiator of the new mission, which indicates that, according to Luke's narrative, it was not an initiative launched by the Antioch community, which makes it strictly Paul's private undertaking. It makes verse 36 expose Paul as the independent agent, who, however, does not depart from the Antioch community, since the new planning mission was supposed to cover the places that were evangelized during the mission of the Antioch community, without the desire to extend it to a new territory.[902]

Paul's initiative shows his sense of responsibility for community he established, which is more appreciate if we consider the events at Lystra (Acts 14:19–20). Barnabas was pleased by Paul's proposal, which exposes his sharing the same idea with Paul without any dissonance about the mission activities. Barnabas's idea of establishing the same mission team (Paul, Barnabas, Mark) to revisit the same places seems to be perfectly understandable.[903] Surprisingly, Paul was opposed

---

[901] D. G. Peterson, *The Acts of the Apostles*, 446–447.

[902] Paul and Barnabas still act as the members of the Antioch church (Acts 18:18–22), despite the fact that Luke changed his approach from generally (the Antioch community) to particular (Paul exclusively).

[903] In the narrative of Acts 15:17, Mark again is presented in Antioch, but the reason for his stay in the city is not clear, and it can be explained by several possibilities. Mark came to Antioch just because Barnabas invited him for another journey. The narrative of Acts 15:35 excluded Mark from the Paul-Barnabas team, which makes this possibility hardly probable. Mark worked with Barnabas in Antioch during the period between the first and the second journey. The narrative of Acts does not confirm this supposition (Acts 15:35), and if Mark were working together with Barnabas, Paul could hardly work with Barnabas, and the split would have taken place before the narrative in Acts 15:36–41.
Luke uses the verb συμπαραμένω (*to take along with*) also in Acts 12:25 in reference to bringing Mark from Jerusalem to Antioch, and in Acts 15:37, he uses it in reference to Barnabas's wish.

(Acts 15:38),[904] due to his negative evaluation of Mark's actions at Perga, which led him to count Mark as not really suitable for mission work.[905] Lucan Paul's very critical judgment of Mark was the result of two accusations: the first, τὸν ἀποστάντα ἀπ' αὐτῶν ἀπὸ Παμφυλίας (*because he had deserted them in Pamphylia*) (Acts 15:38 NIV), shows Paul and Barnabas's disapproval for Mark's decision. Despite the fact that both of them critically evaluated Mark's actions, they took different approaches to the consequences of Mark's decision—Paul did not forgive and forget the incident, but Barnabas did.

The second accusation concerns the fact that Mark did not work with Barnabas and Paul during the mission in Pisidia and Pamphylia (καὶ μὴ συνελθόντα αὐτοῖς εἰς τὸ ἔργον (*and had not continued with them in the work*) (Acts 15:38 NIV), which, according to Luke's narrative, was the most crucial part of the first mission journey. Mark had not experienced the hardship and suffering in Lystra that Barnabas and Paul experienced because of proclaiming the kerygma, and the lack of this experience made him unsuitable for mission work in Paul's eyes, not only on Cyprus but also in Pisidia and Pamphylia.[906] Paul's disagreement met Barnabas's opposition, which led to a severe argument between Barnabas and Paul, resulting in the split between them (Acts 15:39). It seems that Barnabas was strongly irritated by Paul's opposition and arguments, which could have been caused not only by his disagreement with Paul's evaluation of Mark but also by Paul's stubbornness in excluding the possibility of a second chance.[907]

---

904 Luke uses two expressions—Παῦλος δὲ ἠξίου (…) μὴ συμπαραλαμβάνειν—which strongly shows deliberate action, rather than emotional and impulsive behavior.

905 Paul did not take the problem of Mark that occurred during the first mission as a one-time incident but as a sign of overall unsuitability for mission work; that is Paul's severe evaluation to which Barnabas could not agree.

906 F. F. Bruce, *The Acts of the Apostles*, 349. Despite the temporary disagreement that put an end to the mission cooperation of Barnabas and Paul as the mission duo, according to other canonical writings, Mark later again cooperated with Paul (Col. 4:10; 2 Tim. 4:11).

907 D. Peterson thinks that Barnabas's attitude—he was ready to give Mark a second chance—shows Barnabas's character (Acts 4:36–37). A few years earlier,

Paul, who was indebted to Barnabas due to his assistance in developing Saul into Paul, now become his opponent, which involved Barnabas, despite his calm and gentle nature, in an unexpected and very emotional conflict with the man he had trusted, as the very first disciples in Jerusalem, and later invited him for mission work in Antioch.[908] Barnabas was not ready to abandon Mark, which caused the split of the team of Barnabas and Paul into the two teams.[909] Barnabas, together with Mark, undertook a mission journey on Cyprus, but Luke's narrative became no longer interested in the fate of this team (Acts 15:39).[910]

Paul found a new coworker, Silas, and after his mission was blessed by the Antioch community, he chose the northern way and went directly to Pisidia and Pamphylia, probably because Barnabas and Mark chose the southern way and went to Cyprus (Acts 15:40).[911] Instead of one mission team, two mission teams started their mission journeys by going by on different roads but seeking to visit the communities established during the first mission journey of the Antioch community.

Barnabas was the only member of Jerusalem community who offered Saul assistance and gave him a chance. The fact that Paul, who had received a second chance from Barnabas, now was not disposed to give favor to his nephew, which should have been very irritating for him, explains his harsh disagreement with Paul and, consequently, the split between them. D. G. Peterson, *The Acts of the Apostles*, 447.

908 The main point is that Mark was a cousin of Barnabas. J. F. Fitzmyer, *The Acts of the Apostles*, 571.

909 F. F. Bruce, *The Acts of the Apostles*, 349–350. The fact that Mark later became a useful coworker seems, that time, to have proved Barnabas right about Mark's mission capabilities.

910 Nothing can be found in narrative of the Acts in regard to Barnabas and Mark's second mission journey in Cyprus; this does not doubt, however, the historicity of the mission.

911 Luke's narrative strongly suggests that, most probably, Barnabas and Mark never entered the Pisidia and Pamphylia regions, and that Paul never again worked in Cyprus.

2. After the Conflict. The conflict caused a split between the missionaries and friends, Paul and Barnabas, who had worked and fought together for the truth of the Gospel for about seven years. Although the splendor of the past experience was not forgotten, now it was lost. Barnabas and Mark disappeared from Luke's narrative, and for this reason, their achievements remain unknown. In Luke's narrative, their disappearance (especially Barnabas) works in favor of progressing the presentation of Luke's perspective on Paul, who, according to Lucan Jesus's words, consequently progressed on his way to become the apostle of the Gentiles (Acts 9:15–16) and, according to Luke's narrative strategy in Acts, became, together with Peter, the most important and greatest witness to the resurrected Messiah.

Although Barnabas does not reappear in the Acts, his name is mentioned five times in Paul's letters (Gal. 1:2, 9; 2:11–13; 1 Cor. 9:6; Col. 4:10), most commonly in a retrospective or explanatory context, which helps little to establish the account of a possible relationship between Paul and Barnabas after the conflict.[912] Fortunately, there is one passage that can be of some service in this: "ἢ μόνος ἐγὼ καὶ Βαρναβᾶς οὐκ ἔχομεν ἐξουσίαν μὴ ἐργάζεσθαι; [Or is it only I and Barnabas who lack the right to not work for a living?]" (1 Cor. 9:6 NIV). This phrase may suggest that Barnabas was working in Corinth. Some scholars interpret 1 Corinthians 9:6 retrospectively, saying that the phrase refers to the first mission journey when Paul and Barnabas decided to work for their livings and not to be a burden for the communities.[913] However, this explanation has two weaknesses: first, there is no mention in Acts 13:1–14 about Paul and Barnabas working for their livings; and second, there is no reason why Paul would mention Barnabas's name to the Corinthians, as Barnabas was not known to them personally. The argument that Paul mentioned his name because Barnabas and his life were known to the Corinthians

[912] cf. R. Baukham, "Barnabas in Galatians," *JSNT* 2 (1979): 61–70.

[913] A. Robertson and A. Plumer, *First Epistles of St. Paul to the Corinthians* (New York: Scribner, 1929), 183; A. C. Thiselton, *The First Epistle to the Corinthians* (Grand Rapids, Eerdmans, 2000), 682–683.

would raise the question of how the Corinthians first came to know Barnabas. The most satisfactory solution would be that Barnabas was working in Corinth, but it is only a highly hypothetical possibility because Paul does not mention Barnabas as his coworker in any of his letters. Supposition that Barnabas was working alone in Corinth is greatly reduced by the absence of his name among other witnesses working independently in Corinth (1 Cor. 1:10–17).[914]

If Barnabas was personally known to the Corinth community, that could have been possible only due to his occasional visits to the city. The mention of Barnabas in 1 Corinthians 9:6, however, has greater significance because it indicates that at the time of writing the letter to the Corinthians, there was no ill will in the relationship between Barnabas and Paul. It allows us to say, with considerable probability, that the conflict mentioned in Acts 15:36–40 was not a definite break in the relationship but only a temporary difference of opinion, strongly influenced by their own opinions. If this was the case, the reason for including this slightly confusing account in the narrative of Acts remains problematic. In fact, the account has its function in the narrative regarding Luke's perspective on Paul, and for this reason, Luke only mentions the conflict and its results, without providing information concerning the real content of the argument between Paul and Barnabas. He merely mentions arguing as an objective fact, without going into the details. It exposes Luke's aim of including the account that does not concern the conflict itself, but it indicates the time and reason for Paul's separation from his mentor, Barnabas.

---

914 The New Testament Pseudepigrapha writing called *Periodi Barnabae* (written by Alexander, a monk of the monastery of St. Barnabas near Salamis, in the sixth century AD) preserves a tradition, according to which Barnabas, after the mission with Mark in Cyprus, later continued the mission on this island until his death.

BIBLIOGRAPHY

1. Primary sources

1.1. The Bible Texts

Aland, B., et al., eds. *The Greek New Testament*, Stuttgart: Deutsche Bibelgesellschaft, 1994.

Brenton, L. C. L., ed. *The Septuagint with Apocrypha: Greek and English*, Peabody, Hendrickson Publisher, 2005.

Elliger, K., and W. Rudolph, eds. *Biblia Hebraica Stuttgartensia*. Stuttgart: Deutsche Bibelgesellschaft, 1997.

Nestle, E., and K. Aland, eds. *Novum Testamentum Graece*. Stuttgart: Deutsche Bibelgesellschaft, 1993.

Pismo Święte Starego i Nowego Testamentu: W przekładzie z języków oryginalnych. Poznań: Pallottinum, 2000.

Popowski, R., and M. Wojciechowski, eds. *Grecko-polski Nowy Testament: Wydanie interlinearne z kodami gramatycznymi*. Warsaw: Vocatio, 1993.

Rahlfs, A., ed. *Septuaginta: Id est Vetus Testamentum graece iuxta LXX interpretes*, Stuttgart: Deutsche Bibelgesellschaft, 1979.

1.2. Hellenistic and Early Christian Writings

Flavius, Josephus. *Jewish Antiquities*, vol. 9, LCL. London: Harvard University Press, 1965.

Flavius, Josephus. *De bello Iudaico*, vol. 2, LCL. London: Harvard University Press, 1967.

Philo. *De cherubim*, vol. 2, LCL. London: Harvard University Press, 1968.

Philo. *De opificio mundi*, vol. 1, LCL. London: Harvard University Press, 1971.

Philo. *Life of Moses*, vol. 5, LCL. London: Harvard University Press, 1966.

Plato. *Gorgias*, vol. 5, LCL. London: Harvard University Press, 1952.

Plato. *Apologia*, vol. 1, LCL. London: Harvard University Press, 1953.

Seneca. *Epistulae Morales*, vol. 1, LCL. London: Harvard University Press, 1953.

Tacitus, *Historiae* II, xxviii, LCL. London: Harvard University Press, 1972.

2. Commentaries

Bauernfeind, O. *Kommentar und Studien zur Apostelgeschichte*. Tübingen: Mohr Siebeck, 1980.

Barret, C. K. *The Acts of the Apostles*, vol. 1. Edinburg: T&T Clark, 1994.

Barrett, C. K. *A Critical and Exegetical Commentary on the Acts of the Apostles*. Edinburgh: Bloomsbury T&T Clark, 1998.

Bruce, F. F. *The Acts of the Apostles: Greek Text with Introduction and Commentary*. Leicester: Eerdmans, 1990.

Bruce, F. F. *The Book of the Acts*. Grand Rapids: Eerdmans, 1988.

Bruce, F. F. *The Epistle to Galatians*. Grand Rapids: Eerdmans, 2002.

Burton, E. D. *The Epistle to the Galatians*. Edinburgh: T &T Clark, 1921.

Collins, R. F. *First Corinthians*, Collegeville: The Liturgical Press, 1999.

Conzelmann, H. *Acts of the Apostles*. Philadelphia: Fortress Press, 1987.

Dunn, J. D. G. *The Acts of the Apostles*. Nottingham: Eerdmans, 2016.

Eadie, J. *A Commentary on the Greek Text of Paul's Letter to the Galatians*. Birmingham: Solid Ground Christian Book, 2005.

Fernando, A. *Acts*, NIVAC. Grand Rapids: Zondervan, 1998.

Fitzmyer, J. A. *The Acts of the Apostles*. New Haven–London: Yale University Press, 1998.

Fitzmyer, J. A. *The Gospel According to Luke*. New York: Doubleday & Company, 1981.

Haenchen, E. *The Acts of the Apostles*. Philadelphia: Westminster John Knox Press, 1971.

Harrington, D. J. *The Acts of the Apostles*. Collegeville: The Liturgical Press, 1992.

Harris, M. J. *The Second Epistle to the Corinthians*. Grand Rapids: Eerdmans, 2005.

Holladay, C. R. *Acts. A Commentary*. Louisville, Kentucky: Westminster John Knox Press, 2016.

Johnson, L. T. *The Acts of the Apostles*. Collegeville: The Liturgical Press, 1992.

Keener, C. S. *Acts: An Exegetical Commentary*, vol. 1. Grand Rapids: Baker Academic, 2012.

Keener, C. S. *Acts: An Exegetical Commentary*, vol. 2. Grand Rapids: Baker Academic, 2013.

Keener, C. S. *Acts: An Exegetical Commentary*, vol. 3. Grand Rapids: Baker Academic, 2014.

Keener, C. S. *Acts: An Exegetical Commentary*, vol. 4. Grand Rapids: Baker Academic, 2015.

Kurz, W. S. *Acts of the Apostles*. Grand Rapids: Baker Academic, 2013.

Le Cornu, H., and J. Shulam. *A Commentary on the Jewish Roots of Acts*, vol. 1–2. Jerusalem: Academon, 2003.

Lightfoot, J. B. *The Acts of the Apostles*. Downers Grove: IVP Academic, 2014.

Longenecker, R. N. *Galatians*. Mexico City: Thomas Nelson, 1990.

Longenecker, R. N. "Acts." In *The Expositor's Bible Commentary. Luke-Acts*, edited by T. Longman III and D. E. Garland, 663–1102. Grand Rapids: Zondervan, 2007.

Marshall, I. H. *The Acts of the Apostles*. Grand Rapids: Eerdmans, 1980.

Marshall, I. H. *The Gospel of Luke*. Grand Rapids: Eerdmans, 1978.

Matera, F. J. *Galatians*. Collegeville: Sacra Pagina, 2007.

Martin, F. M., ed. *Ancient Christian Commentary on Scripture: New Testament*, vol. 5: Acts. Downers Grove: IVP Academic, 2006.

Metzger, B. M. *A Textual Commentary on the Greek New Testament*. Stuttgart: Deutsche Bibelgesellschaft, 2002.

Munck, J. *The Acts of the Apostles*. Garden City: Doubleday, 1967.

Neil, W. *The Acts of the Apostles*. London: Oliphants, 1973.

Peterson, D. G. *The Acts of the Apostles*. Grand Rapids: Eerdmans, 2009.

Robertson, A., and A. Plumer. *First Epistles of St. Paul to the Corinthians*. New York: Scribner, 1929.

Schnabel, E. J. *Exegetical Commentary on the New Testament*. Grand Rapids: Zondervan, 2012.

Talbert, C. H. *Reading Acts: A Literary and Theological Commentary on the Acts of the Apostles*. Macon: Smyth & Helwys Publishing, 2005.

Thiselton, A. C. *The First Epistle to the Corinthians*. Grand Rapids: Eerdmans, 2000.

Witherington III, B. *Conflict & Community in Corinth. A Socio-Rhetorical Commentary on 1 and 2 Corinthians.* Grand Rapids–Cambridge: Eerdmans, 1995.

Witherington III, B. *The Acts of the Apostles: A Socio-Rhetorical Commentary.* Grand Rapids–Cambridge: Eerdmans, 1998.

3. Monographs and articles

A

Aune, D. E. "Ephesus." In *Dictionary of the Bible*, edited by D. N. Freedman, 413-415. Grand Rapids–Cambridge: Eerdmans, 2000.

Ascough, R. S. "Berea." In *Dictionary of the Bible,* edited by D. N. Freedman, 167–168. Grand Rapids: Eerdmans, 2000.

Ascough, R. S. "Thessalonica." In *Dictionary of the Bible,* edited by D. N. Freedman, 1300–1301. Grand Rapids: Eerdmans, 2000.

Ashton, J. *The Religion of Paul the Apostle.* London: Yale University Press, 2000.

Averky (Taushev), *The Acts of the Apostles*, Jordanville–New York: Holy Trinity Seminary Press, 2020.

B

Boccaccini, G. "The Tree Paths to Salvation of Paul the Jew." In *Paul the Jew. Rereading the Apostle as the Figure of the Second Temple Judaism*, edited by G. Boccaccini and C. S. Segovia. Minneapolis: Fortress Press, 2016.

Bale, A. J. *Genre and Narrative Coherence in the Acts of the Apostles.* London: T&T Clark, 2015.

Barton, S. C. "Paul as Missionary and Pastor," In *The Cambridge Companion to St. Paul*, edited by J. G. Dunn. Cambridge: Cambridge University Press, 2004.

Bauckham, R. "Barnabas in Galatians," *JSNT* 2 (1979): 61–70.

Bauckham, R. "Kerygmatic Summary in the Speeches of Acts." In *History Literature, and Society in the Book of Acts*, edited by B. Witherington III, 185–217. Cambridge: Cambridge University Press, 2007.

Beyer, H. W. "ἐπίσκοπος." In *TDNT*, vol. 2, 608–622. Grand Rapids: Eerdmans, 1973.

Bird, M. F. *An Anomalous Jew.* Grand Rapids: Eerdmans, 2016.

Borg, M. and J. D. Crossan. *The First Paul*. New York: Harper One, 2009.

Bosak, P. C. *Postacie Biblii II* [The People of the Bible II]. Pelpin: Bernardinum, 2001.

Brice, W. C. *Encyclopedia Britannica*, vol. 2. s.v. "Antioch in Pisidia." Chicago, 1971.

Brice, W. C. *Encyclopedia Britannica*, vol. 13. s.v. "Konya." Chicago, 1971.

Brice, W. C. *Encyclopedia Britannica*, vol. 17. s.v. "Perga." Chicago, 1971.

Brice, W. C. *Encyclopedia Britannica*, vol. 17. s.v. "Pisidia." Chicago, 1971.

Brooks, S. S. "Saul and Saul's Family." In *Dictionary of the Old Testament. Historical Books*, edited by B. T. Arnold & H. G. M. Williamson, 880–884. Downers Grove/Leicester: InterVarsity Press, 2005.

Bruce, F. F. *Paul. Apostle of the Heart Set Free.* Grand Rapids: Eerdmans, 1977.

Bruce, F. F. "The Significance of the Speeches for Interpreting Acts." *SwJT* 33 (1990): 2–28.

C

Callan, Ch. J. *The Acts of the Apostles.* Columbia, 2021 (reprint of New York 1919 edition).

Campbell, D. A. *Paul. An Apostle's Journey.* Grand Rapids: Michigan, 2018.

Capes, D. B., R. Reeves, and E. R. Richards. *Rediscovering Paul. An Introduction to His World, Letters, and Theology.* Downers Grove: InterVarsity Press, 2017.

Cassidy, R. J. *Society and Politics in the Acts of the Apostles.* New York: Orbis, 1987.

Crossan, J. D., and J. L. Reed. *In Search of Paul.* New York: Harper San Francisco, 2004.

Crowe B. D. *The Hope of Israel. The Resurrection of Christ in the Acts of the Apostles.* Grand Rapids: Baker Academic, 2020.

D

Dibelius, M. *Studies in the Acts of the Apostles.* London: SCM Press, 1956.

Dodd, C. H. *Apostolic Preaching and Its Developments.* New York: Harper & Brothers Publisher, 1944.

Donaldson, T. L. *Paul and the Gentiles: Remapping the Apostle's Convictional World.* Minneapolis: Fortress Press, 1997.

Dorsey, D. A. "Cyprus." In *Encyklopedia Biblijna* [*The Harpers Collins Bible Dictionary*], edited by P. J. Achtemeier, 175. Warsaw: Vocatio, 2004.

Downey, G. *A History of Antioch in Syria from Seleucus to the Arab Conquest.* Princeton: Princeton University Press, 1961.

Downing, F. G. "Ethical Pagan Theism and the Speeches in Acts." *NTS* 27 (1981): 544–563.

Dreyfus, P. *Święty Paweł. Reporter na tropach Apostoła* [*Saint Paul. Un grand reporter sur les traces de l'Apôtre*]. Inowrocław: Święty Paweł, 1990.

Drimbe, A. *The Church of Antioch and the Eucharistic Traditions (ca. 35–130 CE)*. Tübingen: Mohr Siebeck, 2020.

Dunn, J. D. G. *The New Perspective on Paul*. Grand Rapids/ Cambridge: Eerdmans, 2005.

E

Ehrensperger, K. *Paul at the Crossroads of Culture*. London: Bloomsbury T&T Clark, 2013.

Erric, R. A., and G. M. Lamsa. *Aramaic Light on the Acts of the Apostles*, Smyrna, Georgia: The Noohra Foundation, 2007.

Eright, N. T. *Paul. A Biography*. New York: Harper-Collins Publishers, 2018.

F

Fairchild, M. R. "Salamis." In *Eerdmans Dictionary of the Bible*, edited by D. N. Freedman, 1152–1153. Cambridge: Eerdmans, 2000.

Fant, G. E., and M. D. Reddish. *A Guide to Biblical Sites in Greece and Turkey*. Oxford: Oxford University Press, 2003.

Farley L. R. *The Acts of the Apostles. Spreading the Word*. Chesterton: Ancient Faith Publishing, 2012.

Fisher, F. H. *Cyprus: Our New Colony and What We Know about It*. Whitefish: Kessinger Publishing, 2010.

Fitzmyer, J. A. "κύριος." In *EDNT*, vol. 2, 328–331.

G

Gaber, P. "Cyprus." In *Eerdmans Dictionary of the Bible*, edited by D. N. Freedman, 303–305. Grand Rapids/Cambridge: Eerdmans, 2000.

Garroway, J. D. "'Apostolic Irresistibility' and the Interrupted Speeches in Acts." *CBQ* 74 (2012): 738–752.

Gill, D. W. J. Achaia. In *The Books of Acts in Its First-Century Setting. Greaco-Roman Setting*, vol. 2, edited by D. W. J. Gill and C. Gempf, Carlisle: The Paternoster Press, 1994.

Green, J. B. *Luke as Narrative Theologian.* Tübingen: Mohr Siebeck, 2020.

Greenway, R. S. "Success in the City: Paul's Urban Mission Strategy (Acts 14, 1–28)." In *Mission in the Acts. Ancient Narratives in Cotemporary Context*, edited by R. L. Gallagher and P. Hertig, 183–195. New York: Orbis Books, 2004.

H

Haacker, K. "Paul's Life." In *The Cambridge Companion to St. Paul*, edited by J. G. Dunn. Cambridge: Cambridge University Press, 2004.

Hanges, J. C. *Paul, Founder of Churches*. Tubingen: Mohr Siebeck, 2012.

Hansen, G. H. "Letter to the Galatians." In *Dictionary of Paul and his Letters*, edited by G. F. Hawthorne and R. P. Martin, 323–334. Leicester: InterVarsity Press, 1993.

Harrill, J. A. *Paul the Apostle. His Life and Legacy in Their Roman Context*. Cambridge: Cambridge University Press, 2012.

Hertig, P. *Mission in the Acts. Ancient Narratives in Cotemporary Context.* New York: Orbis Books, 2004.

Hickling, C. J. A. "The Portrait of Paul in Acts 26." In *Les Actes des Apôtres: Traditions, redaction, théologie*, edited by J. Kremer, 499–503. Leuven: Leuven University Press, 1979.

Horsley, G. H. "Speeches and Dialogue in Acts." *NTS* 32 (1986): 609–614.

Horsley, R. A. "Paul's Shift in Economic "Location" in the Locations of the Roman Imperial Economy." In *Paul and Economics*, edited by T. R. Blanton IV and R. Pickett, 112–117. Minneapolis: Fortress Press, 2017.

J

Jervell, J. *The Theology of the Acts of the Apostles*. Cambridge: Cambridge University Press, 1996.

Jewett, R. *Chronology of Paul Life*. Philadelphia: Fortress Press, 1979.

K

Keen, H. "Early Christianity in the Galilee: Reassessing the Evidence from the Gospels." In *The Galilee in Late Antiquity*, edited by L. I. Levine, 3–32. New York: Jewish Theological Seminary of America, 1992.

Kilgallen, J. "Acts 13, 38–39: Culmination of Paul's Speech in Pisidia." *Bib* 69 (1988): 480–506.

Kim, S. *The Origin of Paul's Gospel.* Grand Rapids: Eerdmans, Grand Rapids, 1981.

Knox, J. *Chapters in a Life of Paul*. New York: Abingdon-Cokesbury, 1950.

Kucicki, J. "Saul of Tarsus, the Man Who became the Apostle Paul." *Nanzan Shingaku* 34 (2010): 143–192.

Kucicki, J. "Persona Non Grata? Saul Between Damascus and Antioch," *Academia [Nanzan]* 5 (2013): 115–134.

Kucicki, J. "The Witnesses to the Resurrected Messiah. Luke's Presentation of the Main Theological Theme of the Acts of the Apostles." *The Biblical Annals* (Sept. 4, 2019): 671–696.

Kurichianil, J. "The Speeches in the Acts and The Old Testament." *Indian Theological Studies* 17 (Feb. 1980): 181–186.

Kyrychenko, A. *The Roman Army and the Expansion of the Gospel. The Role of the Centurion in Luke-Acts.* De Gruyter: Berlin/Boston, 2014.

L

Lizorkin-Eyzenberg, E. *The Jewish Apostle Paul.* Middletown: Independently Published 2021.

Long, W. R. "The Trial of Paul in the Book of Acts: History, Literary, and Theological Considerations." PhD diss., Brown University, 1982.

Lüdemann, G. *Paul, Apostle to the Gentiles. Studies in Chronology.* Philadelphia: Fortress Press, 1984.

M

Malherbe, A. J. "Not in a Corner: Early Christian Apologetic in Acts 26, 26." In *Paul and the Popular Philosophers*, edited by A. J. Malherbe, 147–163. Minneapolis: Fortress Press, 1989.

Marguerat, D. *The First Christian Historian: Writing the 'Acts of the Apostles'.* Cambridge: Cambridge University Press, 2002.

Martinson, P. V. "The Ending Is Prelude: Discontinuities Lead to Continuities." In *Mission in the Acts. Ancient Narratives in Cotemporary Context*, edited by R. L. Gallagher and P. Hertig, 313–323. New York: Orbis Books, 2004.

Matera, F. J. "The Responsibility for the Death of Jesus according to the Acts of the Apostles." *JSNT* 39 (1990): 77–93.

McRay, J. M. "Antioch on the Orontes." In *Dictionary of Paul and His Letters*, edited by G. F. Hawthorne and R.P. Martin, 23–25. Leicester: InterVarsity Press, 1993.

McRay, J. M. "Corinth." In *Dictionary of New Testament Background*, edited by A. Craig, A. Eavens, and S. E. Porter, 227–231. Downers Grove/Leicester: InterVarsity Press, 2000.

Medančić, R. T. "*Cognitio extra ordinem* u rimskom pravu [*Cognitio extra ordinem* in Roman Law]." *Pravnik* 40 (Jan. 2006): 79–109.

Meeks, W. A. *The First Urban Christians.* New Haven: Yale University Press, 2003.

Millar, F. *The Roman Near East 31 BC–AD 337.* Cambridge: Harvard University Press, 1993.

Mils, G. B., and G. Trompf. "Luke and Antiphon: The Theology of Acts 27–28 in the Light of Pagan Beliefs about Divine Retribution, Pollution, Shipwreck." *HTR* 69 (1976): 259–267.

Moore, E. C. *Claiming Places.* Tübingen: Mohr Siebeck, 2020.

Murphy-O'Connor, J. *Paul: A Critical Life*. Oxford: Oxford University Press, 1996.

N

Neyrey, J. "Acts 17, Epicureans, and Theodicy." In *Greeks, Romans, and Christians*, edited by D. Balch. Minneapolis: Fortress Press, 1990.

Nobbs, A. "Cyprus." In *The Book of Acts in Its First-Century Setting. Volume 2. Graeco-Roman Setting*, edited by D. W. J. Gill and C. Gempf, 280–289. Grand Rapids: The Paternoster Press, 1994.

Novick, T. "Eschatological Ignorance and the Haftarah on Acts 3, 27." *NovT* 54 (2012): 168–175.

O

Oliver, I. W. "The "Historical Paul" and the Paul of Acts. Which is more Jewish?" In *Paul the Jew: Rereading the Apostles as a Figure of Second Temple Judaism*, edited by G. Boccaccini and C. A. Segovia, 54-57. Minneapolis: Fortress Press, 2016.

O'Neill, J. C. "The Connection Between Baptism and the Gift of the Spirit in Acts." *JSNT* 63 (1996): 87–103.

O'Toole, R. F. "What Role Does Jesus' Saying in Acts 20, 35 Play in Paul's Address to the Ephesian Elders?" *Bib* 75 (1994): 329–349.

O'Toole, R. F. "Christ's Resurrection in Acts 13, 13–52." *Bib* 60 (1979): 361–372.

O'Toole, R. F. *Acts 26: The Christological Climax of Paul's Defense*. AB 78. Rome: Pontifical Biblical Institute, 1978.

Osborne, R. E. "St. Paul's Silent Years." *JBL* 84 (1965): 59–65.

P

Padilla, O. *The Acts of the Apostles. Interpretation, History and Theology*. Downers Grove: IVP Academic, 2016.

Padilla, O. *The Speeches of Outsiders in Acts. Poetics, Theology, and Historiography*. Cambridge: Cambridge University Press, 2008.

Pervo, R. I. *Dating Acts: Between the Evangelists and the Apologists*. Santa Rosa: Polebridge, 2006.

Pervo, R. I. *The Making of Paul. Constructions of the Apostle in the Early Christianity*. Minneapolis: Fortress Press, 2010.

Picirilli, R. E. *Paul the Apostle. Missionary, Martyr, Theologian*. Chicago: Moody Publishers, 2017.

Pillai, C. A. J. *Apostolic Interpretation of History: A Commentary on Acts 13:16–41*. Hicksville: Exposition, 1980.

Pollock, J. *The Apostle. A Life of Paul.* Colorado Springs: David Cook, 1985.

Praeder, S. M. "Acts 27, 1–28, 16: Sea Voyages in Ancient Literature and the Theology of Luke-Acts." *CBQ* 46 (1984): 683–706.

Prigent, P. *Upadek Jerozolimy [La fin de Jerusalem].* Warsaw: Cyklady, 2003.

R

Ramsay, R. M. *Bearing of Recent Discovery on the Trustworthiness of the New Testament.* London: Hodder and Stoughton, 1920.

Ramsay, W. *The Cities of St. Paul: Their Influence on His Life and Thought, The Cities of Eastern Asia Minor.* London: Hodder and Stoughton, 1907.

Rakocy, W. *Pawel Apostol* [*The Apostle Paul*]. Czestochowa: Edycja Świętego Pawła, 2003.

Rankov, B. "Military Force." In *The Cambridge History of Greek and Roman Warfare*, vol. 2, edited by P. Sabin, H. van Wees, and M. Whitby, 30–75. Cambridge: Cambridge University Press, 2007.

Robinson, V. K. "By Land and by Sea: The We-Passages and Ancient Literature and the Voyages." In *Perspective on Luke-Acts*, edited by C. H. Talbert, 215–242. Danville: Association of Baptist Professors of Religion, 1978.

Rosenblatt, M. E. "Recurring Narration as a Lukan Literary Convention in Acts: Paul's Jerusalem Speech in Acts 22:1–22." In *New Views on Luke and Acts,* edited by E. Richard, 94–105. Collegeville: Liturgical Press, 1990.

Rosik, M. *Judaizm u poczatkow ery chrzescijanskiej [Judaism in the Early Christian Era].* Wrocław: TUM, 2008.

Rothschild, C. K. "Pisidian Antioch in Acts 13: The Denouement of the South Galatian Hypothesis." *NovT* 54 (2012): 334–353.

S

Sanders, E. P. *Paul and Palestinian Judaism.* Minneapolis: Fortress Press, 1977.

Sanders, E. P. *Paul. The Apostle's Life, Letters, and Thought.* Minneapolis: Fortress Press, 2015.

Sanders, J. T. "Who Is a Jew and Who Is a Gentile in the Book of Acts." *NTS* 37 (1991): 434–455.

Schmidt, J. "ἐκκλησία" In *TDNT,* vol. 3. 1995. 504–505.

Schreiner, T. R. *Paul, Apostle of God's Glory in Christ. Paulin Theology.* Downers Grove: IVP Academic, 2020.

Schreiner T. R. *Acts and Paul's Letters.* Grand Rapids: Baker Academic, 2019.

Schwartz, D. R. *Reading the First Century.* Tübingen: Mohr Siebeck, 2013.

Soards, M. L. *The Speech in Acts. Their Content, Context, and Concerns.* Louisville: Westminster/Knox, 1994.

Soards, M. L. "The Speech in Acts in Relation to Other Pertinent Ancient Literature." *ETL* 70 (Jan. 1994): 65–90.

Stendahl, K. *Paul among Jews and Gentiles.* Philadelphia: Fortress Press, 1976.

Strange, W. A. *The Problem of the Text of Acts.* Cambridge: Cambridge University Press, 2005.

Strelan, R. *Studies in the Acts of the Apostles.* Eugene: Pickwick Publisher, 2020.

T

Tabor, J. D. *Paul and Jesus. How the Apostle Transformed Christianity.* New York: Simon & Schuster Paperbacks, 2012.

Talbert, C. H. *Reading Acts: A Literary and Theological Commentary on the Acts of the Apostles.* Macon: Smyth & Helwys Publishing, 2005.

Trebilco, P. "Syria." In *The Book of Acts in Its First-Century Setting*, vol. 2, edited by D. W. J. Gill and C. Gempf, 236. Grand Rapids: Eerdmans, 1994.

V

Van't Riet, P. *Luke, the Jew. Introduction to the Jewish Character of the Gospel of Luke ant the Acts of the Apostles.* Zwolle: Folianti, 2009.

Van Ryn, A. *Acts of the Apostles. The Unfinished Work of Christ.* Palala Press, 2018.

Veltman, F. "The Defense Speeches of Paul in Acts." In *Perspectives on Luke-Acts*, edited by C. H. Talbert, 243–256. Edinburgh: T. & T. Clark, 1978.

W

Walaskay, P. W. *And So We Came to Rome: The Political Perspective of St. Luke*. Cambridge: Cambridge University Press, 1983.

Walker, P. *In the Steps of Paul*. Grand Rapids: Zondervan, 2008.

Walton, S. *Leadership and Lifestyle: The Portrait of Paul in the Miletus Speech and 1 Thessalonians*. Cambridge: Cambridge University Press, 2000.

Watson, D. F. "Paul's Speech to the Ephesian Elders (Acts 20, 17–38): Epideictic Rhetoric of Farewell." In *Persuasive Artistry: Studies in Honor of George A. Kennedy*, edited by D. Watson, 184–208. Sheffield: Sheffield Academic Press, 1991.

Williams, M. H. *The Jews among the Greeks & Romans. A Diasporan Sourcebook.* London: Johns Hopkins University Press, 1998.

Wilson, S. G. *The Gentiles and the Gentile Mission in Luke-Acts*. Cambridge: Cambridge University Press, 1973.

Wiseman, J. *The Land of Ancient Corinth: Studies in Mediterranean Archeology, Volume 50*. Göteberg, 1978.

Winter, B. W. "Official Proceedings and the Forensic Speeches in Acts 25–26." In *The Book of Acts in Its First-Century Setting*, vol. 1, edited by B. W. Winter and A. D. Clarke, 305–336. Grand Rapids: Eerdmans, 1993.

Witherington III, B. *The Paul Quest. The Renewed Search for the Jew of Tarsus*. Leicester: InterVarsity Press, 1998.

Wright, N. T. "Paul and Missional Hermeneutics." In *The Apostle Paul and the Christian Life*, edited by S. McKnight and J. B. Modica, 179–192. Grand Rapids: Baker Academic, 2016.

Wright, N. T. *Paul. A Biography*. New York: Harper-Collins Publishers, 2018.

Z

Zetterholm, M. *Approaches to Paul. A Student's Guide to Recent Scholarship*. Minneapolis: Fortress Press, 2009.

3.1. Additional articles and monographs

Barnes, G. P. "The Art of Finishing Well: Paul as Servant Leader, Acts 18, 1–29 and 20, 17–38." In *Mission in the Acts. Ancient Narratives in Cotemporary Context*, edited by R. L. Gallagher and P. Hertig. New York: Orbis Books, 2004.

Barrett, C. K. "Light on the Holy Spirit from Simon Magus (Acts 8, 4–25)." In *Les Actes des Apôtres: traditions, rédaction, théologie*, edited by J. Kremer, 281–295. Leuven: Leuven University Press, 1979.

Barrett, C. K. "Paul's Address to the Ephesian Elders." In *God's Christ and His People*, edited by J. Jervell and W. A. Meeks, 107–121. Oslo: Universitetsforlaget, 1977.

Bowker, J. W. "Speeches in Acts: A Study in Proem and Yelammedenu Form." *NTS* 14 (19671968): 96–111.

Brawley, L. R. "The Spirit, the Power, and the Commonwealth in Acts." *BibTh* 37 (1999): 268–75.

Brinks, C. L. "'Great– is Artemis of Ephesians': Acts 19, 23–41 in Light of Goddess Worship in Ephesus." *CBQ* 71 (2009): 776–794.

Brooks, J. A. "Felix." In *Dictionary of the Bible*, edited by D. N. Freedman, 459–460. Grand Rapids/Cambridge: Eerdmans, 2000.

Bruce, F. F. *The Speeches in Acts.* London: Tyndale Press, 1944.

Bruce, F. F. "The Significance of the Speeches for Interpreting Acts." *SwJT* 33 (1990): 2–28.

Cadbury, H. J. "The Speeches in Acts." In *The Acts of the Apostles. Additional Notes to the Commentary*, part 1, vol. 5 of *The Beginnings of Christianity*, edited by F. J. F. Jackson and K. Lake, 402–427. London: Macmillan, 1933.

Cadbury, H. J. *The Book of Acts in History.* London: A&C Black, 1955.

Combrink, H. J. *Structural Analysis of Acts 6:8–8:3.* Cape Town: Dutch Reformed Church Publishers, 1979.

Conzelmann, H. "The Address of Paul on the Areopagus." In *Studies in Luke-Acts: Essays in Honor of Paul Schubert*, edited by L. E. Keck and J. L. Martyn, 217–230. Nashville: Abingdon, 1966.

Davies, P. "The End of Acts." *ExT* 94 (1983): 89–127.

Dibelius, M. "The Speeches in Acts and Ancient Historiography." In *Studies in the Acts of the Apostles*, edited by H. Greewen, 138–185. New York: Charles Scribner's Sons, 1956.

Downing, F. G. "Ethical Pagan Theism and the Speeches in Acts." *NTS* 27 (1981): 544–563.

Duncan, G. S. "Paul's Ministry in Asia." *NTS* 3 (1957): 211–218.

Gaventa, B. R. *The Acts of the Apostles*. Nashville: Abingdon Press, 2003.

Gorman, M. J. *Apostle of the Crucified Lord. A Theological Introduction to Paul and His Letters.* Grand Rapids: Eerdmans, 2017.

Goulder, M. D. *Type and History in Acts*. London: SPCK Publishing, 1964.

Gray, P. "Athenian Curiosity (Acts 17, 21)." *NovT* 47 (2005): 109–116.

Green, J. B. "Internal Repetition in Luke-Acts: Contemporary Narratology and Lukan Historiography." In *In History, Literature, and Society in the Book of Acts*, edited by B. Witherington III, 283–299. Cambridge: Cambridge University Press, 1996.

Greenway, R. S. "Success in the City: Paul's Urban Mission Strategy (Acts 14, 1–28)." In *Mission in the Acts. Ancient Narratives in Cotemporary Context*, edited by R. L. Gallagher and P. Hertig, 183–195. New York: Orbis Books, 2004.

Hertig, P. *Mission in the Acts. Ancient Narratives in Contemporary Context.* New York: Orbis Books, 2004.

Horsley, R. A. "Paul's Shift in Economic "Location" n the Locations of the Roman Imperial Economy." In *Paul and Economics*, edited by T. R. Blanton IV and R. Pickett, 112–117. Minneapolis: Fortress Press, 2017.

Jervell, J. *The Theology of the Acts of the Apostles*. Cambridge: Cambridge University Press, 1996.

Kloppenborg, J. S. "Paul's Collection for Jerusalem and the Financial Practices in Greek Cities." In *Paul and Economics*, edited by T. R. Blanton IV and R. Pickett. Minneapolis: Fortress Press, 2017.

Lease, G. "The Caesarea Mithraeum: A Preliminary Announcement." *BA* 38 (1975): 2–10.

Linthicum, R. C. "The Apostle Paul's Acts of Power." In *Mission in the Acts. Ancient Narratives in Contemporary Context*, edited by R. L. Gallagher and P. Hertig, 297–312. New York: Orbis Books, 2004.

Longenecker, R. J. "Acts." In *The Expositor's Bible Commentary*, edited by T. Longman and D. E. Garland, 665–1102. Grand Rapids: Zondervan, 2007.

Losie, L. A. "Paul's Speech on the Areopagus. A Model of Cross-cultural Evangelism." In *Mission in the Acts. Ancient Narratives in Cotemporary Context*, edited by R. L. Gallagher and P. Hertig, 221–238. New York: Orbis Books, 2004.

Maddox, R. *The Purpose of Luke-Acts.* Edinburgh: T&T Clark, 1982.

Martinson, P. V. "The Ending Is Prelude: Discontinuities Lead to Continuities." In *Mission in the Acts. Ancient Narratives in Cotemporary Context*, edited by R. L. Gallagher and P. Hertig, 313–323. New York: Orbis Books, 2004.

Matera, F. J. "The Responsibility for the Death of Jesus According to the Acts of the Apostles." *JSNT* 39 (1990): 77–93.

Medančić, R. T. "*Cognitio extra ordinem* u rimskom pravu [*Cognitio extra ordinem* in Roman Law]." *Pravnik* 40 (Jan. 2006): 79–109.

Neyrey, J. "The Forensic Defense Speech and Paul's Trial Speeches in Acts 22–26: Form and Function." In *Luke-Acts: New Perspectives from the Society of Biblical Literature Seminar*, edited by C. H. Talbert, 210–224. New York: Crossroad, 1984.

Nielsen, A. E. "The Purpose of the Lucan Writings with Particular Reference to Eschatology." In *Luke-Acts: Scandinavian Perspectives*, edited by P. Luomanen, 76–93. Göttingen: Vandenhoeck & Ruprecht, 1991.

Pettis, S. J. "The Fourth Pentecost: Paul and the Power of the Holy Spirit." In *Mission in the Acts. Ancient Narratives in Contemporary Context*, edited by R. L. Gallagher and P. Hertig, 248–256. New York: Orbis Books, 2004.

Porter, S. E. *Paul in Acts.* Peabody, MA: Hendrickson, 2001.

Redford, S. B. "The Contextualization and Translation of Christianity." In *Mission in the Acts. Ancient Narratives in Cotemporary Context*, edited by R. L. Gallagher and P. Hertig, 283–296. New York: Orbis Books, 2004.

Reimer, A. M. *Miracle and Magic: A Study in the Acts of the Apostles and the Life of Apollonius of Tyana.* London: T&T Clark, 2002.

Reisenfeld, H. "The Text of Acts X, 36." In *Text and Interpretation*, edited by E. Best and R. M. Wilson, 191–194. Cambridge: Cambridge University Press, 1979.

Rothschild, C. K. "Pisidian Antioch in Acts 13: The Denouement of the South Galatian Hypothesis." *NovT* 54 (2012): 334–353.

Schubert, P. "The Final Cycle of Speeches in the Book of Acts." *JBL* 87 (1968): 1–16.

Schubert, P. "The Place of the Areopagus Speech in the Composition of Acts." In *Transitions in Biblical Scholarship*, edited by J. C. Rylaarsdam, 235–261. Chicago: University of Chicago Press, 1968.

Schwartz, D. R. "The Futility of Reading Moses (Acts 15:21)." *Bib* 67 (1986): 276–281.

Schweitzer, E. "Concerning the Speeches in Acts." In *Studies in Luke-Acts: Essays in Honor of Paul Schubert*, edited by L. E. Keck and J. L. Martyz, 208–216. London: Abingdon Press, 1968.

Seifrid, M. A. "Jesus and the Law in Acts." *JSNT* 30 (1987): 39–57.

Sherwin-White, A. N. *Roman Society and Roman Law in the New Testament*. Oxford: Clarendon Press, 1963.

Simon, M. *St. Stephen and the Hellenists in the Primitive Church.* New York: Longmans Green, 1958.

Spencer, F. S. *Acts.* Sheffield: Sheffield Academic Press, 1997.

Spencer, F. S. "Acts and Modern Literary Approaches." In *Ancient Literary Setting*, vol. 1 of *The Book of Acts in Its First-Century Setting*, edited by B. W. Winter and A. D. Clarke, 381–414. Grand Rapids: Eerdmans, 1993.

Stoops, R. F. "Riot and Assembly: The Social Context of Acts 19, 23–41." *JBL* 108 (1989): 73–91.

Strong, D. K. "The Jerusalem Council: Some Implications for Contextualization." In *Mission in the Acts. Ancient Narratives in Contemporary Context*, edited by R. L. Gallagher and P. Hertig, 196–208. New York: Orbis Books, 2004.

Strauss, M. L. *The Davidic Messiah in Luke-Acts: The Promise and its Fulfilment in Lukan Christology.* Sheffield: Sheffield Academic Press, 1995.

Tajra, H. W. *The Trial of St. Paul. A Juridical Exegesis of the Second Half of the Acts of the Apostles.* Tübingen: Mohr/Siebeck, 1989.

Tannehill, R. *The Narrative Unity of Luke-Acts: A Literary Interpretation*, vol. 1–2. Minneapolis: Fortress Press, 1986.

Turner, M. *Power from on High: The Spirit in Israel's Restoration and Witness in Luke-Acts.* Sheffield: Sheffield Academic Press, 1996.

Van de Sandt, H. "An Explanation of Acts 15, 6–21 in the Light of Deuteronomy 4, 29–35 (LXX)." *JSNT* 46 (1992): 73–97.

Winter, B. W. "Rehabilitating Gallio and His Judgement in Acts 18, 14–15." *TynBul* 57 (2006): 291–308.

4. Dictionaries, concordances, introductions

Balz, H., and Schneider, G. *Exegetical Dictionary of the New Testament*, vol. 1–3. Grand Rapids: Eerdmans, 1994–2000.

Brown, R. E. *An Introduction to the New Testament.* New York/ London: Doubleday, 1997.

Evans, C. A. and S. E. Porter, eds. *Dictionary of the New Testament Background.* Downers Grove/Leicester: InterVarsity Press, 2000.

Freedman, D. N. *Dictionary of the Bible*. Grand Rapids/Cambridge: Eerdmans, 2000.

Hatch, E., and Redpath, H. A. *A Concordance to the Septuagint.* Grand Rapids: Baker Academic, 1998.

Hawthorne, G. F., R. P. Martin, and D. G. Reid, eds. *Dictionary of Paul and His Letters.* Downers Grove/Leicester: InterVarsity Press, 1994.

Holladay, C. R. *A Critical Introduction to the New Testament.* Nashville: Abingdon Press, 2005.

Kittel, G., ed. *Theological Dictionary of the New Testament*, vol. 1–9. Grand Rapids: Eerdmans, 1995.

Kennedy, G. A. *New Testament Interpretation through Rhetorical Criticism.* Chapel Hill: University of North Carolina Press, 1984.

Kümmel, W. G. *Introduction to the New Testament.* London: SCM Press, 1979.

Moulton, W. F. and A. S. Geden. *A Concordance to the Greek Testament.* Edinburgh: T&T Clark, 1978.

Puskas, C. B. *An Introduction to the New Testament*. Peabody, MA: Hendrickson, 1989.

Rengstorf, K. H. *A Complete Concordance to Flavius Josephus,* vol. 1–4. Leiden, Netherlands: E. J. Brill, 1973–1983.

Van der Toorn, K., B. Becking, and P. W. van der Horst, eds. *Dictionary of Deities and Demons in The Bible*. Leiden, Netherlands/New York/Köln, Germany: E. J. Brill, 1995.

Wigram, G. V. *The Englishman's Greek Concordance of the New Testament*. Peabody, MA: Hendrickson, 2002.

Wigram, G. V. *The Englishman's Hebrew Concordance of the Old Testament*. Peabody, MA: Hendrickson, 2001.

5. General references

Bauckham, R. "Palestinian Setting." In *The Book of Acts in Its First-Century Setting*, vol. 4. Grand Rapids: Eerdmans, 1995.

Foakes Jackson, F. J., and K. Lake, eds. "Additional Notes to the Commentary." In *The Beginnings of Christianity, Part One: The Acts of the Apostles: V5*. London: Macmillan, 1933.

Gill, D. W. J., and C. Gempf, eds. "Graeco-Roman Setting." In *The Book of Acts in Its First-Century Setting*, vol. 2. Grand Rapids: Eerdmans, 1994.

Levinskaya, I. "Diaspora Setting." *The Book of Acts in Its First-Century Setting*, vol. 5. Grand Rapids: Eerdmans, 1996.

Rapske, B. *Paul in Roman Custody*. In *The Book of Acts in Its First-Century Setting*, vol. 3. Grand Rapids: Eerdmans, 1994.

Winter, B. W., and A. D. Clarke, eds. "Literary Setting." In *The Book of Acts in Its First-Century Setting*, vol. 1. Grand Rapids: Eerdmans, 1993.

6. Other reference tools

Achtemeier, J., ed. *Harper's Bible Dictionary*. San Francisco: Harper & Row, 1985.

Balz, H. and G. Schneider, eds. *Exegetisches Wörterbuch zum Neuen Testament*, vol. 1–3. Stuttgart: Kohlhammer, 1980–1983.

Blass, F., and A. Debrunner. *A Greek Grammar of the New Testament and Other Early Christian Literature*. Chicago/London: The University of Chicago Press, 1961.

Brown, S., S. Driver, and C. Briggs. *The Brown-Driver-Briggs Hebrew and English Lexicon*. Massachusetts: Hendrickson, 2005.

Crim, K. ed. *Interpreter's Dictionary of Bible*. Nashville: Abingdon, 1976.

Ehrman, B. D. *After the New Testament: A Reader in Early Christianity*. Oxford: Oxford University Press, 1999.

Hawthorne, G. F., R. P. Martin, and D. G. Reid, eds. *Dictionary of Paul and His Letters*. Leicester: InterVarsity Press, 1993.

Jurewicz, O. *Słownik Grecko-Polski*. Warsaw: Vocatio, 2001.

Liddell, H. G., and R. Scott. *A Greek-English Lexicon of the New Testament*. Oxford: Oxford Clarendon Press, 1996.

Lust, J., E. Eynikel, and K. Hauspie. *A Greek-English Lexicon of the Septuaginta*. Stuttgart: Deutsche Bibelgesellschaft, 1992.

Metzger, B. M. *The Text of the New Testament*. Oxford: Oxford University Press, 1979.

Moore, B. R. *Doublets in the New Testament*. Dallas: Summer Institute of Linguistics, 1993.

Moulton, J. H. *A Grammar of New Testament Greek*, vol. 1–4. Edinburgh: T&T Clark, 1963.

Popowski, R. *Grecko-polski Nowy Testament: Wydanie interlinearne z kodami gramatycznymi*. Warsaw: Vocatio, 1993.

Popowski, R. *Wielki słownik grecko-polski Nowego Testamentu.* Warsaw: Vocatio, 1995.

Rubinkiewicz, R., ed. *Wstęp do Nowego Testamentu.* Poznań: Pallottinum, 1996.

Szlaga, J., ed. *Wstęp ogólny do Pisma Świętego.* Poznań/Warsaw: Pallottinum, 1986.

Thayer, J. H. *Thayer's Greek-English Lexicon of the New Testament.* Massachusetts: Hendrickson, 2005.

Turner, N. "Syntax." In *A Grammar of New Testament Greek,* vol. 3, edited by J. H. Moulton. Edinburgh: T&T Clark, 1963.

Zerwick, M., and M. Grosvenor. *A Grammatical Analysis of the Greek New Testament.* Rome: Pontifical Biblical Institute, 1996.

INDEX

1. Index of Biblical Passages

1.1. The Old Testament

1.2. New Testament

1.3. Josephus Flavius's Writings

2. Index of Authors

3. Index of Topics

Printed in the United States
by Baker & Taylor Publisher Services